T0207270

Lecture Notes
in Business Information Processing 481

Series Editors

Wil van der Aalst ⓘ, *RWTH Aachen University, Aachen, Germany*
Sudha Ram ⓘ, *University of Arizona, Tucson, AZ, USA*
Michael Rosemann ⓘ, *Queensland University of Technology, Brisbane, QLD, Australia*
Clemens Szyperski, *Microsoft Research, Redmond, WA, USA*
Giancarlo Guizzardi ⓘ, *University of Twente, Enschede, The Netherlands*

LNBIP reports state-of-the-art results in areas related to business information systems and industrial application software development – timely, at a high level, and in both printed and electronic form.

The type of material published includes

- Proceedings (published in time for the respective event)
- Postproceedings (consisting of thoroughly revised and/or extended final papers)
- Other edited monographs (such as, for example, project reports or invited volumes)
- Tutorials (coherently integrated collections of lectures given at advanced courses, seminars, schools, etc.)
- Award-winning or exceptional theses

LNBIP is abstracted/indexed in DBLP, EI and Scopus. LNBIP volumes are also submitted for the inclusion in ISI Proceedings.

Yiliu Tu · Maomao Chi

Editors

E-Business

Digital Empowerment for an Intelligent Future

22nd Wuhan International Conference, WHICEB 2023
Wuhan, China, May 26–28, 2023
Proceedings, Part II

 Springer

Editors
Yiliu Tu ⓘ
University of Calgary
Calgary, AB, Canada

Maomao Chi ⓘ
China University of Geosciences
Wuhan, China

ISSN 1865-1348   ISSN 1865-1356 (electronic)
Lecture Notes in Business Information Processing
ISBN 978-3-031-32301-0   ISBN 978-3-031-32302-7 (eBook)
https://doi.org/10.1007/978-3-031-32302-7

This Springer imprint is published by the registered company Springer Nature Switzerland AG
The registered company address is: Gewerbestrasse 11, 6330 Cham, Switzerland

Preface

The annual Wuhan International Conference on E-Business (WHICEB) is an AIS affiliated conference. The 22nd Wuhan International Conference on E-Business (WHICEB 2023) was held at Wuhan from May 26 to 28, 2023. WHICEB promotes intellectual research and facilitates academic and corporate networking in e-business and related fields. The intent is to encourage academic research and business development through exchanging ideas about e-business, global and corporate financial issues, and the necessity for continuous innovation. The conference aims at presenting innovative research findings, solutions and approaches to make the Internet a productive and efficient vehicle for global commerce. Whether running an e-business or transforming a business into an e-business, we constantly encounter challenges ranging from technological to behavioral issues, from marketing to data analysis issues, and from effectiveness to security issues. In recent years all over the world initiatives have been started for the next step of development, i.e., Industry 4.0 or the fourth industrial revolution. After consumer-oriented mass production we focus nowadays on personalized products and services, which demands cyber physical systems, cloud computing and big data. There are integration issues for management of technology, management of supply chains, management of human resources and management of knowledge and intelligence that are being resolved in an e-business environment. Organizations, regardless of their locations and sizes, should consider having a strategic decentralized planning effort that includes e-business as a pillar for sustainable competitive advantage.

The proceedings of the 22nd WHICEB document the breadth and depth of research from different aspects of business and from different disciplines that have major implications for e-business. There are fifteen tracks in the proceedings and the proceedings will be listed in the appropriate indexes. The selected best papers from the proceedings will be recommended to international academic journals including but not limited to the following: Electronic Commerce Research and Applications, Electronic Commerce Research, and International Journal of Networking and Virtual Organizations (Compendex).

The research papers in the proceedings went through a double-blind peer review process. Papers were accepted based upon a clear research methodology and contributions to the knowledge of e-business including but not limited to case study, experiment, simulation or survey. The efforts made by our track chairs in reviewing submissions are really appreciated, for they ensured the quality of the proceedings. On behalf of the conference organization, I thank them for their professional diligence. They are: Xiaobo (Bob) Xu, Weiyong Zhang and Fei Ma, *Digital Empowerment and Social Impact*; Yaobin Lu, Ling Zhao and Jiang Wu, *Artificial Intelligence & IoT (AIoT) Enabled Business Innovation*; Guoyin Jiang, Xiaodong Feng and Wenping Liu, *Computing and Complexity in Digital Platforms*; Dongxiao Gu, Jia Li, Ying Yang, Zhixiong Zhang, Fenghong Liu, Yiming Zhao, Shuping Zhao and Xiaoyu Wang, *Data Analytics and Data Governance in Behavioral and Social Science Studies*; Cong Cao, Xiuyan Shao, Jun Yan and Wen-Lung Shiau, *Digital Economy*; Zhongyun (Phil) Zhou, Yongqiang Sun and Xiao-Ling Jin, *Digital Enablement and Digital Governance*; Yi Wang, Yuan Sun, Si Shi and Jindi Fu, *Digital Technologies and New Ways of Working*; Xiaoling Li, Lu Wang and Qing Huang, *E-business Strategy & Digital Marketing*; Shaobo Wei, Xiayu Chen, Jinmei Yin and Hua Liu, *Emerging Technologies and Social Commerce*; Nannan Xi, Hongxiu Li, Juan Chen and Juho Hamari, *Engaging Technologies*; Zhaohua Deng, Tailai Wu and Jia Li, *Healthcare Service and IT Management*; Haichao Zheng, Yuxiang Zhao, Bin Zhu, Bo Xu and Kai Li, *Human-Machine/Robot Interaction in the Era of AI*; Hefu Liu, Zhao Cai and Meng Chen, *Information Systems and Operations Management*; Zhao Du, Fang Wang, Shan Wang and Ruoxin Zhou, *Information Technology in Education*; Chunmei Gan, Yong Liu and Ming Yi, *User Behavior in Information Systems*.

This year, the proceedings consists of two volumes. The papers which are included in the proceedings have gone through at least three double-blind reviews by the members of the Editorial Board of the Proceedings. We would like to thank all of them for their invaluable contribution, support and efforts.

Yiliu Tu
Maomao Chi

Organization

Conference Hosts

The Center for International Cooperation in E-Business, China University of
  Geosciences, Wuhan, China
School of Economics and Management, China University of Geosciences, Wuhan,
  China
Baden-Wuerttemberg Cooperative State University Heidenheim, Heidenheim,
  Germany
College of Business, Alfred University, Alfred, New York, USA

Organizers

The Center for International Cooperation in E-Business, China University of
  Geosciences, Wuhan, China
School of Economics and Management, China University of Geosciences, Wuhan,
  China

Conference Co-chairs

Jing Zhao   China University of Geosciences, China
Juergen Seitz   Baden-Wuerttemberg Cooperative State
                              University Heidenheim, Germany
Doug Vogel   Harbin Institute of Technology, China

Conference Honorary Chair

Wilfred V. Huang (Deceased)   Alfred University, USA

Publication Chairs and Proceedings Editors

Yiliu (Paul) Tu   University of Calgary, Canada
Maomao Chi   China University of Geosciences, China

Program Committee

Chairs

Weiguo (Patrick) Fan	University of Iowa, USA
Zhen Zhu	China University of Geosciences, China

Members

Yukun Bao	Huazhong University of Science & Technology, China
Zhao Cai	University of Nottingham Ningbo China, China
Cong Cao	Zhejiang University of Technology, China
Meng Chen	Soochow University, China
Xiayu Chen	Hefei University of Technology, China
Xusen Cheng	Renmin University of China, China
Maomao Chi	China University of Geosciences, China
Zhaohua Deng	Huazhong University of Science & Technology, China
John Qi Dong	University of Dublin, Ireland
Rong Du	Xidian University, China
Qiang Gong	Zhongnan University of Economics and Law, China
Dongxiao Gu	Hefei University of Technology, China
Tailai Wu	Huazhong University of Science and Technology, China
Juho Hamari	Tampere University, Finland
Zhongyi Hu	Wuhan University, China
Yi Jiang	China University of Geosciences, China
Yuanchun Jiang	Hefei University of Technology, China
Xiaoling Jin	Shanghai University, China
Hongxiu Li	Tampere University, Finland
Jia Li	East China University of Science and Technology, China
Mengxiang Li	Hong Kong Baptist University, China
Xiaoling Li	Chongqing University, China
Hefu Liu	University of Science and Technology of China, China
Yaobin Lu	Huazhong University of Science & Technology, China
Jian Mou	Pusan National University, Korea
Rohit Nishant	University of Laval, Canada

Xiaoliang Shen	Wuhan University, China
Si Shi	Southwestern University of Finance and Economics, China
Yongqiang Sun	Wuhan University, China
Yuan Sun	Zhejiang Gongshang University, China
Yiliu (Paul) Tu	University of Calgary, Canada
Kanliang Wang	Renmin University, China
Shan Wang	University of Saskatchewan, Canada
Lu Wang	Zhongnan University of Economics and Law, China
Yi Wang	Southwestern University of Finance and Economics, China
J. Christopher Westland	University of Illinois at Chicago, USA
Qiang Wei	Tsinghua University, China
Shaobo Wei	University of Science and Technology of China, China
Hong Wu	Huazhong University of Science & Technology, China
Jiang Wu	Wuhan University, China
Tailai Wu	Huazhong University of Science & Technology, China
Nannan Xi	Tampere University, Finland
Huosong Xia	Wuhan Textile University, China
Jinghua Xiao	Sun Yat-sen University, China
Wenlong Xiao	Zhejiang University of Technology, China
Xiaobo (Bob) Xu	Xi'an Jiaotong-Liverpool University, China
Jun Yan	University of Wollongong, Australia
Xiangbin Yan	University of Science and Technology Beijing, China
Junjie Zhou	Shantou University, China
Zhongyun Zhou	Tongji University, China
Ling Zhao	Huazhong University of Science & Technology, China
Weiyong Zhang	Old Dominion University, USA

Session Chairs

Kanliang Wang	Renmin University, China
Jinghua Xiao	Sun Yat-sen University, China
Rong Du	Xidian University, China
Yi Jiang	China University of Geosciences, China

Organization Committee

Chair

Shuwang Yang   China University of Geosciences, China

Members

Yao Zhang   China University of Geosciences, China
Fei Wang   China University of Geosciences, China
Jing Wang   China University of Geosciences, China
Xiaochuan Wang   China University of Geosciences, China
Luxi Lin   China University of Geosciences, China
Qian Zhao   China University of Geosciences, China
Rui Guo   China University of Geosciences, China
Jianzhong Xiao   China University of Geosciences, China
Guangmin Wang   China University of Geosciences, China
Jundong Hou   China University of Geosciences, China
Sheng Cheng   China University of Geosciences, China

Secretary General

Yao Zhang   China University of Geosciences, China

International Advisory Board

Chairs

Joey George   Iowa State University, USA
Robert Kauffman   Copenhagen Business School, Denmark
J. Christopher Westland   University of Illinois at Chicago, USA

Pacific Asian

Patrick Chau   University of Hong Kong, China
Guoqing Chen   Tsinghua University, China
Wei Kwok Kee   City University of Hong Kong, China
Ting-Peng Liang   National Sun Yat-sen University, Taiwan
Feicheng Ma   Wuhan University, China

Jiye Mao	Renmin University, China
Michael D. Myers	University of Auckland, New Zealand
Bernard Tan	National University of Singapore, Singapore
Kanliang Wang	Renmin University, China
Nilmini Wickramasinghe	Swinburne University of Technology, Australia
Kang Xie	Sun Yat-sen University, China
Qiang Ye	Harbin Institute of Technology, China
J. Leon Zhao	City University of Hong Kong, China

North American

Bob Carasik	Wells Fargo Bank, USA
Weiguo Fan	Virginia Tech, USA
Joey George	Iowa State University, USA
Zhangxi Lin	Texas Tech University, USA
Ning Nan	University of British Columbia, Canada
Paul A. Pavlou	Temple University, USA
Arun Rai	Georgia State University, USA
Richard Watson	University of Georgia, USA
Christopher Yang	Drexel University, USA
Han Zhang	Georgia Institute of Technology, USA
Zhongju Zhang	Arizona State University, USA

European

David Avison	ESSEC, France
Niels Bjorn-Andersen	Copenhagen Business School, Denmark
Marco De Marco	Università Cattolica, Italy
Reima Suomi	Turku School of Economics, Finland
Yao-Hua Tan	Vrije University Amsterdam, The Netherlands
Hans-Dieter Zimmermann	Eastern Switzerland University of Applied Sciences, Switzerland

Editorial Board of the Proceedings

Editors

| Yiliu (Paul) Tu | University of Calgary, Canada |
| Maomao Chi | China University of Geosciences, China |

Digital Empowerment and Social Impact

Xiaobo (Bob) Xu	Xi'an Jiaotong-Liverpool University, China
Weiyong Zhang	Old Dominion University, USA
Fei Ma	Chang'an University, China

Artificial Intelligence and IoT (AIoT) Enabled Business Innovation

Yaobin Lu	Huazhong University of Science & Technology, China
Ling Zhao	Huazhong University of Science & Technology, China
Jiang Wu	Wuhan University

Computing and Complexity in Digital Platforms

Guoyin Jiang	University of Electronic Science and Technology of China, China
Xiaodong Feng	Sun Yat-sen University, China
Wenping Liu	Hubei University of Economics, China

Data Analytics and Data Governance in Behavioral and Social Science Studies

Dongxiao Gu	Hefei University of Technology, China
Jia Li	East China University of Science and Technology, China
Ying Yang	Hefei University of Technology, China
Zhixiong Zhang	China Academy of Sciences, China
Fenghong Liu	China Academy of Sciences, China
Yiming Zhao	Wuhan University, China
Shuping Zhao	Hefei University of Technology, China
Xiaoyu Wang	First Affiliated Hospital of Anhui University of Chinese Medicine, China

Digital Economy

Cong Cao	Zhejiang University of Technology, China
Xiuyan Shao	Southeast University, China
Jun Yan	University of Wollongong, Australia
Wen-Lung Shiau	Zhejiang University of Technology, China

Digital Enablement and Digital Governance

Zhongyun (Phil) Zhou	Tongji University, China
Yongqiang Sun	Wuhan University, China
Xiao-Ling Jin	Shanghai University, China

Digital Technologies and New Ways of Working

Yi Wang	Southwestern University of Finance and Economics, China
Yuan Sun	Zhejiang Gongshang University, China
Si Shi	Southwestern University of Finance and Economics, China
Jindi Fu	Hangzhou Dianzi University, China

E-Business Strategy and Digital Marketing

Xiaoling Li	Chongqing University, China
Lu Wang	Zhongnan University of Economics and Law, China
Qing Huang	Chongqing Technology and Business University, China

Emerging Technologies and Social Commerce

Shaobo Wei	Hefei University of Technology, China
Xiayu Chen	Hefei University of Technology, China
Jinmei Yin	Nanjing University of Aeronautics and Astronautics, China
Hua Liu	Anhui University, China

Engaging Technologies

Nannan Xi	Tampere University, Finland
Hongxiu Li	Tampere University, Finland
Juan Chen	Anhui University of Finance and Economics, China
Juho Hamari	Tampere University, Finland

Healthcare Service and IT Management

Zhaohua Deng	Huazhong University of Sci. & Tech., China
Tailai Wu	Huazhong University of Sci. & Tech., China
Jia Li	East China University of Science and Technology, China

Human-Machine/Robot Interaction in the Era of AI

Haichao Zheng	Southwestern University of Finance and Economics, China
Yuxiang Zhao	Nanjing University of Science and Technology, China
Bin Zhu	Oregon State University, USA
Bo Xu	Fudan University, China
Kai Li	Nankai University, China

Information Systems and Operations Management

Hefu Liu	University of Science and Technology of China, China
Zhao Cai	University of Nottingham Ningbo China, China
Meng Chen	Soochow University, China

Information Technology in Education

Zhao Du	Beijing Sport University, China
Fang Wang	Wilfrid Laurier University, Canada
Shan Wang	University of Saskatchewan, Canada
Ruoxin Zhou	University of International Business and Economics, China

User Behavior in Information Systems

Chunmei Gan	Sun Yat-sen University, China
Yong Liu	Aalto University, Finland
Ming Yi	Central China Normal University, China

Best Paper Award and Journal Publication Committee

Chairs

Yiliu (Paul) Tu	University of Calgary, Canada
Maomao Chi	China University of Geosciences, China

Members

Alain Chong	University of Nottingham Ningbo China, China
Chris Yang	Drexel University, USA
J. Christopher Westland	University of Illinois at Chicago, USA
Doug Vogel	Harbin Institute of Technology, China
Patrick Chau	University of Nottingham Ningbo China, China
Jun Wei	University of West Florida, USA
John Qi Dong	University of Groningen, The Netherlands
Weiguo (Patrick) Fan	University of Iowa, USA
Wen-Lung Shiau	Zhejiang University of Technology, China

Sponsors

Association for Information Systems (AIS)
China Association for Information Systems (CNAIS)
China Information Economics Society
University of Calgary, Canada
Swinburne University of Technology, Australia
University of North Dakota, USA
New Jersey Institute of Technology, USA
University of Turku, Finland
Harbin Institute of Technology, China
Huazhong University of Science & Technology, China
Wuhan University, China
Wuhan University of Technology, China
Zhongnan University of Economics and Law, China
Huazhong Normal University, China
Wuhan Textile University, China
Digital Economy Research Centre, UNNC-SUS Tech, China

Sponsoring Journals

Electronic Commerce Research (SSCI index)
Electronic Commerce Research and Applications (SSCI index)
Electronic Markets-The International Journal on Networked Business (SSCI index)
Internet Research (SSCI index)
Journal of Organizational and End User Computing (SCI & SSCI index)
Journal of Information & Knowledge Management (Compendex & Scopus index)
International Journal of Networking and Virtual Organizations (Compendex & Scopus index)
Journal of Systems and Information Technology (Compendex & Scopus index)

Contents – Part II

Contents – Part I

The Impact of Digital Finance on the Operating Performance of Commercial Banks: Promotion or Inhibition?

Mengxue Dai and Huaihu Cao[(⊠)]

School of Information, Central University of Finance and Economics, Beijing 102206, China
linyacufe@163.com

Abstract. The vigorous development of digital finance has lent fresh impetus to the traditional financial market, and has also had an influence on the business situation. This article uses crawler technology to construct digital finance indicators, and based on the financial data of 42 listed commercial banks from 2011 to 2021, uses the SYS-GMM model to study the impact effect, transmission mechanisms and heterogeneity of digital finance on the operating performance from two dimensions of profitability and risk level. The results show that: First, in terms of linear relationship, digital finance reduces the profitability and increases the risk level of commercial banks; Second, as regards nonlinear relationship, there is a U-shaped relationship between digital finance and the profitability of commercial banks, and an inverted U-shaped relationship with the risk level of commercial banks; Third, digital finance inhibits the operating performance by deteriorating the deposit structure, loan structure and increasing the proportion of non-interest income. Fourth, compared with national commercial banks, the inhibitory influence on the profitability of regional banks is more pronounced, but its impact on risk level is not significantly different.

Keywords: Digital Finance · Commercial Bank · Operating Performance

1 Introduction

The process of deep interaction between digital finance and commercial banks is full of competition and cooperation. On the one hand, with the help of emerging technologies, the operational capacity of banks has been significantly improved. On the other hand, digital finance has also launched fierce competition with commercial banks in traditional financial business.

There are two main points of view on this topic in academia: The first view is that it will improve the performance, and the second view is that it will inhibit the performance. In the first view, by analyzing the problem from the perspective of commercial bank risk-taking, the data results show that digital finance will reduce the systemic financial risk [1]. At the same time, when the asset size is larger, the impact will be more obvious [2]. Then it is found that it will reduce the credit risk of enterprises by improving the Total Factor Productivity and reducing the degree of Asymmetric Information [3]. In the second view, digital finance intensifies bank risk-taking by raising management costs [4]. And it is found that it has impacted the capital side and debt side [5], and will restrain their operating performance [6]. To sum up, this impact has both promotion and inhibition effects, and it has not yet reached a consensus conclusion on this issue [7]. However, through the combing of the literature, we can find that the current research still has shortcomings in the following aspects: The existing research focus more on the profitability side, but ignores the risk side, and does not start with the three major businesses of commercial banks. In addition, since digital finance is still in the process of sustainable development, its impact on the operating performance should change in the dynamic process. However, the academia has not paid attention to the dynamic changes of this impact.

In view of this, this article examines the effect of digital finance on the operating performance from the perspectives of profitability and risk level, deeply analyzes the impact transmission mechanism from three aspects of deposit business, loan business and intermediate business, and analyzes the dynamic changes of the impact.

2 Theoretical Analysis and Hypotheses

2.1 Linear and Nonlinear Impacts of Digital Finance on the Operating Performance

Digital finance will promote technological progress and improve business performance through technology spillover effect [8]. Through the optimization of the risk management model, digital finance reduces the default risk faced by banks [9]. More importantly, commercial banks optimize the service process through the enhancement of digital finance, improve operational process through technological innovation [10].

Digital finance has competitive spillover effect on the market covered by traditional banks by virtue of its advantages [11]. In terms of deposit business, digital financial transactions are more flexible and convenient, and its deposit interest yields are higher [12]. Therefore, digital finance diverts the deposit business of traditional commercial banks, the dependence of commercial banks on financial products and inter-bank liabilities has significantly increased [13], which also increases the cost of liabilities and risk of banks [14]. This situation forces commercial banks to develop intermediate business, support deposit and loan business with non-interest income. At the same time, commercial banks will be forced to explore the long tail customers with high default risks by lowering the qualification approval threshold [15], which leads to the increase of risk preference of commercial banks [16].

At present, digital finance in China is not yet fully developed, it will affect the stability of the banking system to a certain extent [17]. However, after the underlying technology is mature and can be widely applied, competitive spillover effect will gradually weaken until it is replaced by technology spillover effect.

The hypotheses are as follows:

H1: Digital finance inhibits the operating performance of commercial banks.
H1A: The development of digital finance reduces ROA.
H1B: The development of digital finance improves the NPL ratio.

H2: There is a nonlinear relationship between digital finance and the operating performance.

H2A: There is a U-shaped relationship between digital finance and ROA.

H2B: There is an inverted U-shaped relationship between digital finance and the NPL ratio.

2.2 Heterogeneity of the Impact of Digital Finance on the Operating Performance

Due to the differences in asset size, employee education level and technical foundation, banks have different abilities to resist this impact.

State-owned and joint-stock commercial banks account for a relatively large proportion of intermediate business, while urban and rural commercial banks specialize in traditional credit business [18]. National banks have larger assets and stronger ability than regional banks to resist risks. In addition, state-owned and joint-stock commercial banks have strong strength, sufficient internal talent reserves and good technical support, so they are less affected by the impact on deposit business, loan business and intermediate business. Urban and rural commercial banks, due to their long-term roots in counties, have higher customer acquisition costs, and a large proportion of long tail customers. Coupled with the small size of the bank, the lack of internal talents in the bank, poor technical conditions, and weak ability to resist the impact, the inhibitory effect on them will be even stronger.

The hypothesis is as follows:

H3: The impact of digital finance on the operating performance is different between national and regional commercial banks.

3 Research Design

3.1 Variable Setting and Description

Explanatory Variables. There are two explanatory variables in this paper. The first one is the development level of digital finance A (BDFIN), which will be used to test the benchmark model of the impact. The second is the development level of digital finance B (DIGIFIN), which will be used to test the robustness of the impact.

The Development Level of Digital Finance A. This variable is synthesized through Baidu news crawler and Principal Component Analysis. The specific steps are as follows: Firstly, a total of 24 keywords are selected from the four perspectives of Financial Security, Payment and Settlement, Channel Technology and Resource Allocation, the original thesaurus is shown in Table 1, then crawl Baidu news search results through "city + keyword", and count the search volume of 24 keywords corresponding to each city every year. Secondly, through Principal Component Analysis, the search volume of 24 keywords in each city is reduced to synthesize this indicator. The cumulative variance contribution rate of the digital finance development level A synthesized by Principal Component Analysis is 72.38%, indicating that this indicator has a high explanation rate for the overall search volume.

Table 1. Original thesaurus of digital finance.

Financial Security	Payment and Settlement	Channel Technology	Resource Allocation
Investment Decision Support	NFC Payment	Cloud Computing	Internet Finance
Intelligent Customer Service	Open Bank	Big Data	Intelligent Data Analysis
Robo-Advisor	Mobile Payment	Machine Learning	Smart Contract
Biometrics	Third-Party Payment	AI	Mobile Internet
ASR	DC	Deep Learning	NUCC
Credit Investigation	Authentication	Blockchain	Crowdfunding

The Development Level of Digital Finance B. This variable is obtained by secondary calculation of the provincial and municipal indices in the Digital Financial Inclusion Index of Peking University [19]. The specific calculation method is as follows: The digital finance development level of regional commercial banks is measured by the index of the cities where the banks' headquarters are located in that year. The development level of national banks is calculated as follows:

$$DIGIFIN_{i,t} = \sum_{p=1}^{34} \frac{B_{i,p,t} F_{p,t}}{\sum\limits_{p=1}^{34} B_{i,p,t}} \qquad (1)$$

where $DIGIFIN_{i,t}$ represents the development level of digital finance faced by bank i in the year t, $t = 2011, 2012, \cdots, 2021$; $B_{i,p,t}$ represents the number of bank outlets in the province p in the year t of bank i; $F_{p,t}$ represents the index of the province p in the year t; $\sum_{p=1}^{34} B_{i,p,t}$ represents the sum of the number of bank outlets in all provinces of the country in the year t of bank i.

Predicted Variables. This paper analyzes the commercial banks' operating performance from the two perspectives of profitability and risk level. Profitability is measured by ROA, and risk level is measured by the NPL ratio.

Controlled Variables. Banks' operating performance is not only affected by banks' micro factors, but also by the macroeconomic factors. Therefore, this paper selects four bank micro indicators of equity-to-asset ratio (HA), total asset level (LNASSET), capital adequacy ratio (CAR), and net interest margin (NIM), as well as two macroeconomic indicators of economic level (LNGDP) and inflation rate (CPI).

Mediators. The mediation effect is analyzed from three perspectives: deposit business, loan business and intermediate business. The deposit business is measured by the deposit-liability ratio (DS). The loan business is measured by the loan-to-asset ratio (LA). The intermediate business is measured by the proportion of non-interest income (NI).

3.2 Model Setting

Linear Relationship. The models are as follows:

$$ROA_{i,t} = \alpha_0 ROA_{i,t-1} + \alpha_1 BDFIN_{i,t} + \sum_{k=2}^{5} \alpha_k Control_{k,i,t}$$
$$+ \alpha_6 LNGDP_t + \alpha_7 CPI_t + \mu_i + \varepsilon_{i,t} \tag{2}$$

$$NPL_{i,t} = \beta_0 NPL_{i,t-1} + \beta_1 BDFIN_{i,t} + \sum_{k=2}^{5} \beta_k Control_{k,i,t}$$
$$+ \beta_6 LNGDP_t + \beta_7 CPI_t + \mu_i + \varepsilon_{i,t} \tag{3}$$

where $ROA_{i,t}$ means the ROA of the bank i in the year t; $NPL_{i,t}$ means the NPL ratio of the bank i in the year t; $BDFIN_{i,t}$ means the development level of digital finance faced by bank i in the year t; $Control_{k,i,t}$ means the controlled variables related to the micro characteristics of commercial banks; $LNGDP_t$ means the economic level of the year t; CPI_t means the inflation rate of the year t; μ_i means the characteristics of each bank that do not change over time; $\varepsilon_{i,t}$ means the stochastic disturbance term.

Nonlinear Relationship. The models are as follows:

$$ROA_{i,t} = \varsigma_0 ROA_{i,t-1} + \varsigma_1 BDFIN_{i,t} + \varsigma_2 BDFIN2_{i,t} + \sum_{k=3}^{6} \varsigma_k Control_{k,i,t}$$
$$+ \varsigma_7 LNGDP_t + \varsigma_8 CPI_t + \mu_i + \varepsilon_{i,t} \tag{4}$$

$$NPL_{i,t} = \xi_0 NPL_{i,t-1} + \xi_1 BDFIN_{i,t} + \xi_2 BDFIN2_{i,t} + \sum_{k=3}^{6} \xi_k Control_{k,i,t}$$
$$+ \xi_7 LNGDP_t + \xi_8 CPI_t + \mu_i + \varepsilon_{i,t} \tag{5}$$

where $BDFIN2_{i,t}$ means the quadratic term of $BDFIN_{i,t}$.

Mediation Effect Models. The models are as follows:

$$MED_{\lambda,i,t} = \chi_1 BDFIN_{i,t} + \sum_{k=2}^{5} \chi_k Control_{k,i,t} + \chi_6 LNGDP_t$$
$$+ \chi_7 CPI_t + \mu_i + \varepsilon_{i,t} \tag{6}$$

$$ROA_{i,t} = \delta_0 ROA_{i,t-1} + \theta MED_{\lambda,i,t} + \delta_1 BDFIN_{i,t} + \sum_{k=2}^{5} \delta_k Control_{k,i,t} \tag{7}$$
$$+ \delta_6 LNGDP_t + \delta_7 CPI_t + \mu_i + \varepsilon_{i,t}$$

$$NPL_{i,t} = \eta_0 NPL_{i,t-1} + \varphi MED_{\lambda,i,t} + \eta_1 BDFIN_{i,t} + \sum_{k=2}^{5} \eta_k Control_{k,i,t} \tag{8}$$
$$+ \eta_6 LNGDP_t + \eta_7 CPI_t + \mu_i + \varepsilon_{i,t}$$

4   Empirical Results

4.1   Linear Relationship: The Impact of Digital Finance on Bank Performance

Columns (1) and (2) of Table 2 report the impact on commercial bank operating performance in a linear relationship.

    The test results of the impact from the perspective of linear relationship show that digital finance will inhibit the profitability and increase the risk level, that is, it will inhibit the operating performance of commercial banks.

Table 2. The impact on the operating performance of banks.

Variables	(1) ROA	(2) NPL	(3) ROA	(4) NPL
L.ROA	0.854*** (0.187)		0.810*** (0.196)	
L.NPL		0.735*** (0.103)		0.725*** (0.113)
BDFIN	−0.066** (0.031)	0.210*** (0.057)	−0.320** (0.150)	0.826* (0.423)
BDFIN2			0.001* (0.001)	−0.003** (0.001)
Controlled Variables	Yes	Yes	Yes	Yes
Bank FE	Yes	Yes	Yes	Yes
AR(2)	1.248	−1.610	0.503	−1.343
AR(2)-P	0.212	0.107	0.615	0.179
Hansen	15.292	25.401	16.393	18.851
Hansen-P	0.359	0.330	0.229	0.128

***p < 0.01, **p < 0.05, *p < 0.1, the same below.

4.2 Nonlinear Relationship: The Impact of Digital Finance on Bank Performance

Columns (3) and (4) of Table 2 report the impact on bank performance in a nonlinear relationship. The result of column (3) shows that there is a U-shaped relationship between digital finance and the profitability of commercial banks. The result of column (4) shows that there is an inverted U-shaped relationship between digital finance and the NPL ratio. The impacts on the profitability and risk level at different stages of development is different, making it change from restraining profits and improving risk level to promoting profits and reducing risk level.

4.3 Heterogeneity Analysis

Due to the differences in profit, service, size and other micro-levels, they respond differently to this influence.

To examine the different impacts, this paper divides ROA and NPL into two groups according to whether the bank belongs to the national commercial banks. It can be preliminarily found that compared with the NPL ratio, the difference of ROA between the two groups is more obvious.

Next, the Independent Samples t-test is carried out on the two groups of ROA and NPL ratio. According to the test results, it can be found that only ROA has significant differences among different types of banks.

Based on the conclusions obtained from the above analysis, this paper conducts group regression on ROA of national and regional commercial banks. The group regression results are shown in Table 3 below. It shows that the inhibitory effect on regional banks is more significant. This conclusion is also consistent with the previous theoretical analysis.

Table 3. Heterogeneity analysis of ROA.

Variables	National ROA	Regional ROA
L.ROA	0.593** (0.215)	0.472 (0.338)
BDFIN	−0.025 (0.038)	−0.161** (0.060)
Controlled Variables	Yes	Yes
Bank FE	Yes	Yes
AR(2)	0.313	1.066
AR(2)-P	0.755	0.286
Hansen	12.604	2.571
Hansen-P	0.399	0.922

4.4 Mediation Effect Analysis

In order to test whether the three businesses of commercial banks are the inter-mediate transmission mechanism of the impact, this paper focuses on the deposit-liability ratio (DS), loan-to-asset ratio (LA) and non-interest income ratio (NI). The three variables are analyzed by establishing mediating effect models. The mediation effect analysis process consists of two steps: Step 1, as shown in Table 4 below, reports the impact on the three intermediate variables. Step 2, as shown in Table 5 below, reports the impact of the three intermediate variables together with the digital finance on the operating performance.

Column (1) in Table 4 shows the influence on the deposit-liability ratio, indicating that digital finance will reduce the deposit-liability ratio and deteriorate the deposit structure. Column (2) shows the influence on the loan-to-asset ratio, indicating that digital finance will reduce the loan-to-asset ratio and deteriorate the loan structure. Column (3) shows the influence on the proportion of non-interest income, indicating that it will increase the proportion of non-interest income, and digital finance has promoted the development of intermediate business, which is also a manifestation of the influence on the deposit business and loan business, forcing banks to develop intermediate business.

Table 4. Mediation effect step 1.

Variables	(1) DS	(2) LA	(3) NI
L.DS	−0.860** (0.331)		
L.LA		0.765*** (0.131)	
L.NI			0.961*** (0.073)
BDFIN	−0.280* (0.161)	−0.018* (0.010)	0.078* (0.041)
Controlled Variables	Yes	Yes	Yes
Bank FE	Yes	Yes	Yes
Number of ID	34	34	34
AR(2)	−0.930	−0.55	−1.211
AR(2)-P	0.352	0.585	0.226
Hansen	5.431	24.684	11.783
Hansen-P	0.711	0.645	0.161

The result of column (1) in Table 5 shows that the deposit-liability ratio has no significant impact on ROA. The result of column (2) shows that the higher the deposit-to-liability ratio, the lower the NPL ratio will be. Therefore, it can be concluded that the deposit-liability ratio plays a partial mediating effect in the impact on the NPL ratio.

The result of column (3) in Table 5 shows that the higher the loan-to-asset ratio is, the stronger the profitability will be. The result of column (4) shows that the higher the loan-to-asset ratio, the lower the NPL ratio will be. Therefore, it can be concluded that the loan-to-asset ratio plays a partial mediating effect on the impact on ROA, and a complete mediating effect on the impact on the NPL ratio.

The result of column (5) in Table 5 shows that the higher the proportion of non-interest income, the weaker the profitability will be. The coefficient of the proportion of non-interest income in column (6) is not significant, it has no significant impact on the NPL ratio. Therefore, it can be concluded that the proportion of non-interest income plays a fully mediating role in the impact on the profitability.

Table 5. Mediation effect step 2.

Variables	(1) ROA	(2) NPL	(3) ROA	(4) NPL	(5) ROA	(6) NPL
L.ROA	1.029*** (0.228)		0.709*** (0.196)		0.740*** (0.187)	
L.NPL		0.395*** (0.088)		0.299 (0.365)		0.722*** (0.092)
DS	0.066 (0.123)	−0.055* (0.030)				
LA			0.025*** (0.006)	−0.101* (0.051)		
NI					−0.312** (0.128)	0.156 (0.301)
BDFIN	−0.067* (0.035)	0.189** (0.072)	−0.133*** (0.048)	0.083 (0.232)	−0.010 (0.038)	0.167** (0.073)
Controlled Variables	Yes	Yes	Yes	Yes	Yes	Yes
Bank FE	Yes	Yes	Yes	Yes	Yes	Yes
Number of ID	30	31	30	34	30	34
AR(2)	−0.531	−0.936	0.718	−0.576	0.678	−1.513
AR(2)-P	0.595	0.349	0.473	0.565	0.498	0.130
Hansen	16.254	17.072	11.103	7.302	20.854	23.321
Hansen-P	0.236	0.381	0.134	0.199	0.184	0.717

4.5 Robust Test

This article verifies the robustness of this impact by replacing the variable of digital finance development level.

Columns (1) and (2) of Table 6 show the impact of the linear relationship. Columns (3) and (4) of Table 6 show the impact of the nonlinear relationship. The model results show that the impact analyzed in this article is robust.

Table 6. Robustness test results.

Variables	(1) ROA	(2) NPL	(3) ROA	(4) NPL
L.ROA	0.775*** (0.146)		0.757*** (0.228)	
L.NPL		0.804*** (0.118)		0.761*** (0.087)
DIGIFIN	−0.038*** (0.010)	0.201*** (0.044)	−0.119** (0.046)	0.375*** (0.084)
DIGIFIN2			0.001* (0.001)	−0.002* (0.001)
Controlled Variables	Yes	Yes	Yes	Yes
Bank FE	Yes	Yes	Yes	Yes
Number of ID	29	33	29	33
AR(2)	−1.041	−0.842	−1.524	−0.528
AR(2)-P	0.298	0.400	0.127	0.598
Hansen	15.102	11.530	21.57	18.29
Hansen-P	0.372	0.117	0.119	0.248

5   Suggestions

Combining the current background of digital finance and the conclusions of this article, the suggestions are proposed from the perspectives of macro policy and micro banking:

First, promote and regulate the development of digital finance, reduce digital financial risk factors through penetrating supervision. Digital financial technology has many advantages, but due to its insufficient development, it has a temporary inhibitory effect on banks. Therefore, policies should continue to promote the development of digital finance and prudently treat the risk factors brought by digital finance, use penetrating supervision to reduce the uncertainty of digital finance development.

Second, we should continue to empower the business development of commercial banks with technological attributes, and strengthen the digital risk management capabilities. Commercial banks should actively innovate financial products and services, and improve their technical foundation by introducing talents and increasing technology investment. In addition, strengthen the risk management of banking business, focusing on the rationality of deposits, loans, non-interest income and other indicators.

Third, in the process of digital finance development, we should focus more on regional commercial banks. Regional commercial banks have small assets, weak technical foundation, which are more prone to generate large risks. Therefore, more attention and support should be paid to small and medium-sized commercial banks.

References

1. Berg, T., Burg, V., Gombović, A., Puri, M.: On the rise of FinTechs: credit scoring using digital footprints. Rev. Financ. Stud. **33**(7), 2845–2897 (2020)
2. Cai, Y.P., Liu, Y.X.: Does fintech affect the liability structure of commercial banks. Manag. Eng. **27**(5), 1007–1199 (2022). (in Chinese)
3. Beck, T., Pamuk, H., Ramrattan, R., Uras, R.B.: Payment instruments, finance and development. J. Dev. Econ. **133**, 162–186 (2018)
4. Stoica, O., Mehdian, S., Sargu, A.: The impact of internet banking on the performance of Romanian banks: DEA and PCA approach. Procedia Econ. Finance **20**, 610–622 (2015)
5. Arnold, I.J.M., van Ewijk, S.E.: Can pure play internet banking survive the credit crisis. J. Bank. Finance **35**(4), 783–793 (2011)
6. Jia, D., Han, H.Z.: Fintech, bank liabilities and competition. J. World Econ. **46**(2), 183–208 (2023). (in Chinese)
7. Zhang, J.C.: Financial technology, commercial bank competition and risk-taking. J. Henan Univ. Eng. (Soc. Sci. Ed.) **36**(4), 34–42 (2021). (in Chinese)
8. Hauswald, R., Marquez, R.: Information technology and financial services competition. Rev. Financ. Stud. **16**(3), 921–948 (2003)
9. Cheng, M.Y., Qu, Y.: Does bank FinTech reduce credit risk? Evidence from China. Pac. Basin Finance J. **63**, 101398.1–101398.24 (2020)
10. Begenau, J., Farboodi, M., Veldkamp, L.: Big data in finance and the growth of large firms. J. Monet. Econ. **97**, 71–87 (2018)
11. Thakor, A.V.: Fintech and banking: what do we know. J. Financ. Intermediation **41**, 100858.1–100858.46 (2020)
12. Chen, Y., Wang, J., Liu, X.Y.: Analysis of marketing strategy of commercial banks under the background of digital finance. FinTech Time **28**(6), 48–54 (2020). (in Chinese)
13. Sun, X.R., Wang, K.S., Wang, F.R.: FinTech, competition and bank credit structure—based on the perspective of small and medium-sized enterprises financing. J. Shanxi Univ. Finance Econ. **42**(6), 59–72 (2020). (in Chinese)
14. Saunders, A., Schumacher, L.: The determinants of bank interest rate margins: an international study. J. Int. Money Financ. **19**(6), 813–832 (2000)
15. Liao, W.L.: Research on the impact of internet finance on risk level of commercial banks. Am. J. Ind. Bus. Manag. **8**(4), 992–1006 (2018)
16. Larrain, B.: Do banks affect the level and composition of industrial volatility. J. Finance **4**(8), 1897–1925 (2006)
17. He, J.F., Zhu, A.Q., Li, J.: Research on the influence of digital finance development on the operation robustness of commercial banks. J. South China Univ. Technol. (Soc. Sci. Ed.) **24**(5), 17–28 (2022). (in Chinese)
18. Wang, R., Yang, S.J.: Research on the impact of digital finance on commercial banks' risk-taking: based on empirical analysis of China's banking industry. J. Shanghai Lixin Univ. Account. Finance **34**(1), 29–43 (2022). (in Chinese)
19. Guo, F., Wang, J.Y., Wang, F., Kong, T., Zhang, X., Cheng, Z.Y.: Measuring China's digital financial inclusion: index compilation and spatial characteristics. China Econ. Q. **19**(4), 1401–1418 (2020). (in Chinese)

How Story Plot Affect the Effect of Short Video Marketing

Yanli Pei[1]([✉]), Jianna Li[1], Shan Wang[2], and Fang Wang[3]

[1] International Business School, Beijing Foreign Studies University, Beijing, China
`peiyanli@bfsu.edu.cn`
[2] Department of Finance and Management Science, University of Saskatchewan, Saskatoon, Canada
[3] Lazaridis School of Business and Economics, Wilfrid Laurier University, Waterloo, Canada

Abstract. More and more enterprises promote their products by publishing short videos on social platforms, but not all short video marketing can achieve the expected results. There are many factors that affect the marketing effect. This study aims to explore how the narration of short video, especially the story plot, impress consumers to realize marketing goals, on the basis of Narrative Transportation Theory. In this study, 402 sample questionnaires were collected and the model was verified by structural equation model. The conclusion shows that the six factors affect advertising attitude and product attitude through narrative transportation. Finally, according to the conclusion, the corresponding suggestions for the creation of short video are provided.

Keywords: Story Plot · Narrative Transportation · Short Video · Story Marketing

1 Introduction

Marketing is one of the important links in enterprise competition. In recent years, with the intensification of market competition, how to carry out effective marketing and improve the efficiency of marketing has become the focus of enterprises. In recent years, story marketing has gradually attracted the attention of academia and enterprises. Storytelling is a very effective tool to convey experience. It can promote the emotional connection between consumers and brands, and even affect consumers' purchase decisions. At the same time, short video has a large number of users, which provides the basis for story marketing. Therefore, it is necessary to explore the story marketing of short video.

At present, most of the relevant studies are based on the brand story and the text materials. Different from previous studies, first of all, this study systematically hackled the relationship between the relevant characteristics of the story plot and narrative transportation. Second, this study is based on the emerging media of Douyin short video. The content on Douyin short video mainly comes from the creation of ordinary users which is different from the brand stories, and short video presents more vivid information to the audience. Third, this study points out that the relationship between plot familiarity and narrative transportation is negative in the context of Douyin short video, which is

Y. Tu and M. Chi (Eds.): WHICEB 2023, LNBIP 481, pp. 12–22, 2023.
https://doi.org/10.1007/978-3-031-32302-7_2

contrary to the conclusion of previous studies in the field of story marketing about story familiarity. Therefore, this study aims to supplement the narrative transportation theory by exploring the relationship between plot characteristics and narrative transportation, and provide some reference for the creators of short video in terms of content creation.

2 Literature Review

2.1 Narrative Transportation Theory

In addition to being quantified as a concept to measure the level of transportation, narrative transportation is also a unique persuasive theoretical mechanism of stories or novels. When the audience is exposed to the story, the audience will stay away from the surrounding real world and enter the world in the story. When they return to the original real world, the audience's beliefs and attitudes will change and become consistent with those in the story.

2.2 Influencing Factors of Narrative Transportation

At present, the academia has carried out extensive research on story marketing based on narrative transportation theory. The current research on the influencing factors of narrative transportation shows that these influencing factors are mainly divided into the factors of the story itself and audience related factors.

In terms of the factors of the story itself, the degree to which individuals are transported into the narrative world depends on the quality of the story. Some scholars also believe that the attractiveness of the text itself, the attractiveness of books, the font definition and the text quality of story will affect the transportation level [1]. Narrative structure is also the key influencing factor of narrative transportation. In addition, the story plot also has a certain impact on narrative transportation. Story plot refers to the narration of a series of coherent events. The vivid plot helps the audience to imagine and immerse themselves in the story, just like their real experience [2], which will enhance the transportation level of they experience. Relevant research shows that the clarity of the story can reflect a good structure, and also prove that the clearer the plot, the higher the narrative transportation level of the audience through empirical research.

In terms of audience related factors, Dal Cin et al. and Laer et al. point out that some people are easier to be transported than others [3, 4]. This is a personal trait. This difference is called transportability, which has nothing to do with the story itself, the situation and other external factors, but depends on their own empathy and psychological simulation ability [3]. An individual's motivation for emotional needs also affects the level of transportation they experience. Individuals with anxiety type attachment personality hope to obtain attention or support by asking or controlling their partners, which is a morbid personality. People with high anxiety type attachment have a higher level of narrative transportation than others. The audience's familiarity with the story will affect its narrative transportation level [2]: the audience's prior knowledge or personal experience will affect its transportation level. If the audience is familiar with the content or theme of the story, it will help them experience a higher level of narrative transportation. In addition, the similarity between the audience and the story characters is also one of the important factors affecting the audience's narrative transportation [5].

From the relevant literature on the factors affecting narrative transportation mentioned above, it can be found that relevant scholars have pointed out some factors that will affect narrative transportation, but no one has systematically explored the relationship between the plot and narrative transportation, so we will make a systematic exploration of the plot.

2.3 Short Video Features

Short video advertising attracts the audience with its short and interesting characteristics, which meets the audience's consumption demand for content in the era of fragmentation [6]. Entertainment motivation is one of the main motivations for users to use Douyin through empirical analysis of Douyin's users. In the research on the original short video advertisement of Douyin, it is pointed out that in the list of Douyin video products, the drama beauty and comedy categories account for a large proportion and can carry out product publicity without trace. Entertainment funny videos mainly meet the entertainment needs of the audiences. In the short video application, the creators will not be subject to strict language norms. Many content creators and characters in the video are of grass-roots origin, and they come from all corners of the world. In the videos they create, the reasonable use of voice and intonation, local dialect, network language and action expression constitute the humorous and funny style in the short video.

In addition, in the short video platform, the content seen by users is recommended according to users' preferences, which is also the difference between short video and traditional video. In the process of watching short videos, the short video platform often recommends similar short videos to the same users. When users often watch the content, they are likely to be disgusted with the video content.

The Douyin has these unique characteristics, which may lead to different impacts on the audience. Therefore, this paper focuses on the story advertisements in Douyin, explores which characteristics of the story plot will affect the advertising effect, and tests the intermediary mechanism, thus supplementing the relevant literature on short video advertising.

3 Hypothesis Development

In this study, we first conducted in-depth interviews with 16 users who have watched Douyin and bought beauty products. The main question of in-depth interviews is "what features of the story plot in short videos are attractive". Through the summary of the interview content, we found these six factors. According to Laer's theoretical model in meta-analysis, it can be divided into two categories from the perspective of storytelling and reception [3] (Fig. 1).

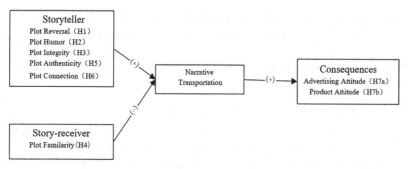

Fig. 1. Theoretical model

3.1 Plot Reversal

Story plot refers to a series of events that develop and change according to the time sequence and causality. There will be many conflicts or contradictions in the development of these events. The characters in the story need to solve these conflicts or contradictions in order to promote the development of the story. Plot reversal refers to the climax or turning point of the story, which represents that the protagonist's emotions or actions have taken surprising turns or reached unexpected levels [7]. When there is a reversal of the plot, the audience will feel unexpected and more attracted. When there are more contradictions and conflicts in the story, there will be more suspense and these suspense will urge the audience to receive and process the content to think about how the story characters will solve the difficulties, so the audience's attention will be more convergent to pay close attention to the development of the plot. At the same time, suspense will keep the audience in a state of hope and fear, which will make the story more dynamic and make the audience at a higher level of arousal. This will also make the audience feel more creative and more enjoy the content, so as to achieve emotional touch. In addition, this reversal of the plot makes the plot more vivid, it helps to promote the audience's imagination of the story.

H1: Plot reversal positively affects narrative transportation.

3.2 Plot Humor

Plot humor refers to the audience's perception of the degree of plot humor [7]. Many humorous and interesting advertisements will leave a deep impression on people. Humorous information helps the audience form a positive attitude towards the product and enhance the persuasive effect of the information [8]. Humor is a monotonous destroyer and it can be used as a tool. The audience will be attracted by the humor of advertising. Humor can bring the audience from the busy and anxious real world to a relaxed and happy world. Therefore, when the plot is humorous, it will make the story more attractive, make the audience's attention more focused, and generate more associations, making the audience happy. Relevant scholars believe that watching humorous advertisements can improve the audience's attention and improve the possibility of audience's understanding. Relevant research also points out that humor can enhance the user's cognition.

In the short video, the humorous plot matches the audience's entertainment purpose, providing good conditions for the audience to enter the story world.

H2: Plot humor positively affects narrative transportation.

3.3 Plot Integrity

Plot integrity refers to the degree to which the story fully and completely presents the whole story content [9]. Information integrity can reduce uncertainty. Compared with uncertain situations, people have a higher preference for certain situations. In addition, processing fluency refers to the degree of difficulty the audience feels in the process of processing information. A full and clear plot will make it easier for the audience to process the information during watching the short video and feel a higher sense of fluency, which helps the audience give positive feedback to the relevant information. In the process of watching the short video, the audience mainly focuses on the development of the story. A complete and sufficient plot can make the audience more fully immersed in the story, compared with no results, stories with positive results can arouse the audience's love to a greater extent and it can bring satisfaction, joy and other positive emotions to the audience, and urge the audience's thinking to follow the development of the plot and imagine the subsequent development of the story [9]. In the study of brand stories using text materials, it is believed that the clearer and fuller the plot, the higher the narrative transportation level of the audience.

H3: Plot integrity positively affects narrative transportation.

3.4 Plot Familiarity

Plot familiarity refers to the prior knowledge or experience of the audience on the story [3]. In relevant studies, it is believe that the more familiar the audience is with the theme of the story, the higher the narrative transportation level of the audience will be [3]. However, as an application with content ecosystem service as the core, ordinary users can participate in the creation of short videos, and it can use its recommendation algorithm to push the content to the target users. In this case, when an interesting video appears on the Douyin, it will attract a large number of users' imitation and creation. Coupled with the push of its recommendation algorithm, it is likely to push videos with similar content to the same group of users. In the research on familiarity in other fields, it is pointed out that familiarity will reduce the persuasive effect, so when the audience is familiar with the content and routines of the story, it will lead to the negative emotion of the audience's boredom with the story. Therefore, in this situation, if the audience is familiar with the story, they may be tired of it and will not be attracted by the story, so the level of transportation in the story is low.

H4: Plot familiarity negatively affects narrative transportation.

3.5 Plot Authenticity

As one of the important elements of a story, authenticity is the key to determine whether a story is a good story. Authenticity is often fiction, not fact. When the audience thinks it is true, it is true. When the audience compares the clues in the advertisement with those in real life and feels that they are similar, they will feel that it is in line with their psychological expectations, and then they will think that it is true. Plot authenticity refers to the possibility that that the audience perceives that the plot is close to life and actually occurs in real life [10]. Relevant empirical studies have proved that the authenticity of stories has an important impact on consumers' cognition [11]. When the plot is true, consumers are more motivated to reduce risks by obtaining personal experience from others' real experience [12]. Similar to Green's research, Laer et al. also believe that the authenticity of the story refers to the possibility of the actual occurrence of the story, and prove that the authenticity of the story has a positive impact on the audience's narrative transportation level through meta-analysis [3]. When the storyteller uses real sentences to express, such as "this is my personal experience", the audience will be more willing to believe. The more authentic the plot is, the more likely the audience is to use cognitive resources to connect the plot with their own memories and deepen their understanding and immersion of the story [13].

H5: Plot authenticity positively affects narrative transportation.

3.6 Plot Connection

Plot connection refers to the degree to which the product is integrated into the story [14]. According to the anchoring and adjustment theory, when people face a situation, they will generate an initial anchor point according to the initial state. When they are stimulated, the anchor point will also change accordingly, thus affecting the final attitude. In story advertisements, products generally appear with the development of the plot, that is, they generally appear in the middle of short video advertisements. Advertisements with low plot connection are easy to be identified by the audience, which is very obvious and abrupt. When this kind of advertisement appears in the short video, it may be the stimulus that causes the audience's anchor point to change. According to the anchoring and adjustment theory, the audience will produce an initial anchor point when they see a storytelling advertisement. And they think that it is a story. When the product and the plot fit well, the audience's initial anchor point will not be adjusted, so it will be easier to accept the advertisement in the story and the product information. On the contrary, if the product and plot fit relatively low, the audience's initial anchor point will change due to the appearance of advertising information, that is, the anchor point will be adjusted from story to advertisement. This kind of advertisements show high intrusiveness and this intrusiveness of advertising will lead to the audience's cognitive, emotional and other aspects of the advertising avoidance response, which will affect the audience's concentration on the whole short video and affect the emotional connection between the audience and the story due to the audience's resistance, so it is likely to make the audience lose interest in the whole short video story and no longer imagine and think about the subsequent plot.

H6: Plot connection positively affects narrative transportation.

3.7 Narrative Transportation and Advertising Effect

When Green proposed narrative transportation, he also proved the persuasive effect of narrative transportation when reading novels [1]. When the audience is exposed to the story and in the state of narrative transportation, they will experience a sense of suspension that is physically far away from the real world, as if they are separated from the real world and enter the story world. At this time, they will not feel the gap between the story world and the real world. When people are in this state, they will inhibit the formation of their own counterargument. In addition, the audience will sympathize with the story characters and feel the world in the same way as the story characters, which will enable the audience to establish a positive emotional connection with the story. When the audience experiences the story world and returns to the real world, they will retain their attitude in the story world. Therefore, narrative transportation will make the audience have the same attitude as in the story [3].

H7: Narrative transportation positively affects advertising effects.
H7a: Narrative transportation positively affects advertising attitude.
H7b: Narrative transportation positively affects product attitude.

4   Methodology

4.1   Treatment Design

In this study, first of all, through literature review and in-depth interviews with 16 users, six variables of story plot are summarized. After that, a questionnaire was designed. Because beauty products are widely popular in short video advertisements, this research is about beauty products. The video material in the questionnaire is short videos with high ratings on Douyin. Finally, 402 valid questionnaires were received.

4.2   Measurement

The scale of this questionnaire is as follows. First of all, about the independent variables, five items were adapted from Lan [13], Chiu [7] and interviews to measure plot authenticity (e.g. "The plot in the short video is true"). Five items were adapted from Chiu [7]and interviews to measure plot reversal (e.g. "In this short video, there is a climax in the story"). Five items were adapted from Russel [14], Fontaine [15] and interviews to measure plot connection (e.g. "Products play an important role in this story"). Five items were adapted from Chiu [7] to measure plot humor (e.g. "The plot is interesting"). Five items were adapted from Laer [3] to measure plot familiarity (e.g. "I am familiar with the content and routine of this short video"). Five items were adapted from Jun [9] and Ryan [16] to measure plot integrity (e.g. "The plot is complete"). For mediating factor, we adapted 13 items from Green [1] to measure narrative transportation (e.g. "When I watch this story, I can easily describe the events in it"). For dependent variables, three items were adapted from Mitchell [17] to measure advertising attitude (e.g. "Overall, I think this type of advertising is very good"). Other three items were adapted from Dawar [18] and Gillespie [19] to measure product attitude (e.g. "I like this product"). Finally, for control variables, three items were adapted from Dal [4] to measure transportability (e.g. "I will immerse myself in the story"). Other three items were adapted from Bhatnagar [20] to measure self character similarity (e.g. "I am very similar to the characters in the story").

5 Data Analysis

5.1 Measurement Model Assessment

Because narrative transportation is a construct with three dimensions, the two-stage method of SmartPLS is used in this study. The reliability and validity are good. Cronbach's alpha is over 0.7 (except for transportability, this control variable's Cronbach's alpha is over 0.6, it's also acceptable), the CR is over 0.6, the AVE is over 0.5, and the values of square root of AVE on the diagonal are larger than the correlation below the diagonal. In addition, the factor loading of every indicator in itself is larger than other's (Relevant tables are omitted here).

5.2 Hypothesis Test Results

PLS results are shown in the table below. The sample of boosttrap is 5000, and all hypothesis have been verified. In addition, the two control variables are also significant (Table 1).

Table 1. Conclusion

Path	Coefficient	p-Value	Conclusion
Narrative Transportation → Product Attitude	0.796	0.000	Support
Narrative Transportation → Advertising Attitude	0.805	0.000	Support
Transportability → Narrative Transportation	0.069	0.031	–
Plot Connection → Narrative Transportation	0.141	0.001	Support
Plot Reversal → Narrative Transportation	0.112	0.003	Support
Plot Humor → Narrative Transportation	0.084	0.030	Support
Plot Familiarity → Narrative Transportation	−0.097	0.001	Support
Plot Authenticity → Narrative Transportation	0.099	0.005	Support
Plot Integrity → Narrative Transportation	0.164	0.000	Support
Self Character Similarity → Narrative Transportation	0.382	0.000	–

(*continued*)

Table 1. (*continued*)

Path	Coefficient	p-Value	Conclusion
Goodness of model fit SRMR = 0.076			
Structural model fit R^2 (product attitude) = 0.634 R^2 (advertising attitude) = 0.648 R^2 (narrative transportation) = 0.826			

6   Conclusion and Discussion

In the past, the research of story marketing took the story as the research object, and did not specifically study the story plot. This study systematically explored story plot and it is based on the emerging short video. Specifically, it explored which features of story plot are important in short video advertisement, and verified the relationship between these features of story plot and narrative transportation, advertising effects. Conclusions are as follows:

We take the story plot as the research object rather than the story as the research object, and point out that plot reversal, plot humor, plot integrity, plot authenticity, and plot connection will positively affect the narrative transportation and indirectly affect the advertising attitude and product attitude, which means that the more prominent these plot characteristics of short video advertisement are, the better the advertising effect will be. However, the plot familiarity will negatively affect the narrative transportation to affect the advertising attitude and product attitude, which shows that when the audience is familiar with the plot, it will have a negative effect, it is contrary to previous research findings in the field of story marketing. In addition, the transportability and self character similarity also have a positive impact on the narrative transportation, which means that these two factors related to individuals will have a positive impact on the advertising effect through the positive impact of narrative transportation.

7   Theoretical Contribution and Practical Significance

7.1   Theoretical Contribution

First of all, in the previous study of story marketing, the story was the research object. This study took the story plot as the research object, systematically explored the relationship between the relevant characteristics of story plot, narrative transportation and advertising effect, and supplemented the relevant literature in the field of narrative transportation. Second, due to the insufficient research on the plot in the past, the scale of the plot is immature, this study supplements the scale of the plot. Third, short video has its unique characteristics. This study uses narrative transportation theory to study short video advertising, and also supplements the relevant literature of short video marketing.

7.2 Practical Significance

In traditional advertising, the traces of advertising are obvious, and the audience is easy to get tired of this kind of advertising with obvious persuasive intention. In order to meet the needs of the audience and better promote the products, advertising needs to be more creative. With the development of short video applications, each short video application has become a high-quality platform for advertising, and short video applications give users more control. In this case, the creativity of advertising has become more important. This study mainly studies the influence of story plot related factors in short video advertising on its advertising effect, which can provide some reference for content creators and short video platform, so as to help related beneficiaries improve the efficiency of advertising. For content creators, they should create short video advertisement with plot reversal, humor, integrity, authenticity and high connection to the product, and try not to imitate others to reduce familiarity. For short video platforms, the frequency of pushing short videos with similar plots to the same users should be reduced at the level of its recommendation algorithm.

8 Research Limitations and Future Prospects

First, the material used in this study is from short video, which contains rich information and many uncontrollable factors. In future research, we can consider using experimental research methods to better control variables. Second, the mechanism of the influence of narrative transportation on subsequent behavior and attitude has not been further explored in this study. In future research, we can further explore the mediating mechanism before narrative transportation and behavior and attitude variables. Third, this study is based on beauty products. In the future, we can consider using other products for research or explore the differences between different categories of products. Finally, this study does not explore the moderating factors, which can be further explored in future research.

Acknowledgement. This research was supported by the Fundamental Research Funds for the Central Universities under Grant 2020JJ026.

References

1. Green, M.C., Brock, T.C.: The role of transportation in the persuasiveness of public narratives. J. Pers. Soc. Psychol. **79**(5), 701 (2000)
2. Green MC (2004) Transportation Into Narrative Worlds: The Role of Prior Knowledge and Perceived Realism: Discourse Processes: Vol 38, No 2. Discourse Processes
3. Laer, T.V., Ruyter, K.D., Visconti, L.M., Wetzels, M.: The Extended Transportation-Imagery Model: A Meta-Analysis of the Antecedents and Consequences of Consumers' Narrative Transportation. Journal of Consumer research **40**(5), 797–817 (2014)
4. Dal Cin, S., Zanna, M.P., Fong, G.T.: Narrative persuasion and overcoming resistance. Resistance persuasion **2**(175–191), 4 (2004)
5. Green MC (2021) Transportation into narrative worlds. Entertainment-education behind the scenes: Case studies for theory:87–101

6. Chen, Y.: Reflection on Short Video Advertising in the New Media Era – Taking Douyin Short Video Platform as an Example. View on Publishing **16**, 68–70 (2019). (In Chinese)
7. Chiu, H.-C., Hsieh, Y.-C., Kuo, Y.-C.: How to align your brand stories with your products. Journal of Retailing Consumer Services **88**(2), 262–275 (2012)
8. Sternthal, B., Craig, C.S.: Humor in advertising. J. Mark. **37**(4), 12–18 (1973)
9. Fan, J., Pan, J.: The Impact of Brand-Plot Information in Story Advertisement on Audience's Dissemination Will. Journal of Marketing Science **2**, 13 (2016). (In Chinese)
10. Green, M.C., Brock, T.C., Kaufman, G.F.: Understanding media enjoyment: The role of transportation into narrative worlds. Commun. Theory **14**(4), 311–327 (2004)
11. Grayson, K., Martinec, R.: Consumer Perceptions of Iconicity and Indexicality and Their Influence on Assessments of Authentic Market Offerings. Journal of Consumer Research **31**(2), 296–312 (2004)
12. Edson EJ Self-Referencing and Persuasion: Narrative Transportation versus Analytical Elaboration. Journal of Consumer Research (4):421–429
13. Xu, L., Zhao, S., Cui, N., Zhang, L.X., Zhao, J.Y.: How story design mode affect consumer brand attitude. Manage. World **36**(10), 76–95 (2020). (In Chinese)
14. Russell, C.A.: Investigating the effectiveness of product placements in television shows: The role of modality and plot connection congruence on brand memory and attitude. Journal of consumer research **29**(3), 306–318 (2002)
15. Fontaine I (2001) Le placement de marques dans les films : apports du cadre théorique de la mémoire implicite et proposition d'une méthodologie. economics papers from university paris dauphine
16. Ryan, M.-L.: Cheap plot tricks, plot holes, and narrative design. Narrative **17**(1), 56–75 (2009)
17. Mitchell, A.A.: The effect of verbal and visual components of advertisements on brand attitudes and attitude toward the advertisement. Journal of consumer research **13**(1), 12–24 (1986)
18. Dawar, N., Lei, J.: Brand crises: The roles of brand familiarity and crisis relevance in determining the impact on brand evaluations. J. Bus. Res. **62**(4), 509–516 (2009)
19. Gillespie, B., Joireman, J., Muehling, D.D.: The moderating effect of ego depletion on viewer brand recognition and brand attitudes following exposure to subtle versus blatant product placements in television programs. The Journal of Advertising **41**(2), 55–65 (2012)
20. Bhatnagar, N., Wan, F.: Is self-character similarity always beneficial? J. Advert. **40**(2), 39–50 (2011)

Exploring the Effect of Intelligent Recommendation Systems on Users' Emotional Attachment: The Moderating Role of Personality Trait

Zesen Zhan, Yuechen Ou, Zhibin Hu, and Hualong Yang[✉]

Guangdong University of Technology, 161 Yinglong Road, Guangzhou 510520, China
hualongyang_gut@sina.com

Abstract. Users' emotional attachment is the key to promoting their loyalty. However, few studies have explored how to improve users' emotional attachment in the context of intelligent recommendation systems. To bridge the research gaps, our research mainly uses attachment theory and uses and gratifications theory as our research basis to explore the effect of intelligent recommendation systems (i.e., accuracy, serendipity, and personalization) on users' emotional attachment. The mediating effect of self-construction (i.e., self-actualization, self-pleasure, and self-expressiveness) and the moderating effect of personality trait are also explored in our research. To examine our theoretical model, we conduct a survey and collect 305 valid questionnaires. The research results show: (1) Accuracy, serendipity, and personalization have positive and significant effect on users' self-actualization, self-pleasure, and self-expressiveness respectively; (2) Self-pleasure and self-expressiveness are positively associated with users' emotional attachment, while self-actualization do not have significant effect on users' emotional attachment; (3) Extraversion has a positive moderating effect on the relationship between personalization and self-expressiveness. However, our research does not find evidence to support the moderating effect of extraversion on the relationship between accuracy and self-actualization as well as the relationship of serendipity and self-pleasure. This study can help developers of intelligent recommendation systems understand users' continuous usage behavior from the perspective of emotional attachment.

Keywords: Intelligent recommendation system · Emotional attachment · Uses and gratifications theory · Extraversion

1 Introduction

In recent years, intelligent recommendation systems have become increasingly popular due to their ability to provide personalized recommendations and enhance user experience. However, the impact of these systems on users' emotional attachment and subsequent loyalty is not yet fully understood. Emotional attachment plays a vital role in promoting user loyalty towards intelligent recommendation systems. However, few

Y. Tu and M. Chi (Eds.): WHICEB 2023, LNBIP 481, pp. 23–34, 2023.
https://doi.org/10.1007/978-3-031-32302-7_3

studies have explored how to improve users' emotional attachment to these systems. A recommendation system provides personalized recommendations to users based on their preferences, which creates a sense of satisfaction for the users. Existing research shows that if users' satisfaction with the entity continues, they will have emotional attachment to the entity [1].

Attachment theory suggests that individuals have a fundamental need for attachment and that their attachment style influences their behavior and relationships [2]. Furthermore, the use and gratifications theory suggests that users actively seek out media that fulfill their needs, including the need for emotional attachment [3]. In the context of intelligent recommendation systems, recommendation systems can directly or indirectly influence users' emotional attachment level, thereby affecting their continued use behavior. The direct impact of a recommendation system refers to providing more personalized and accurate recommendations, thereby enhancing users' emotional attachment to the product or service. The indirect impact refers to the recommendation system increasing users' satisfaction and trust in the entire platform, thereby strengthening users' emotional attachment to the platform. Understanding the impact of recommendation systems on emotional attachment can help us better design and optimize recommendation algorithms. This improves users' satisfaction and emotional attachment to products or services, and then promote users' continued usage and loyalty.

Moreover, personality traits can also play a significant role in the user's emotional attachment and experience with intelligent recommendation systems. Previous studies have shown that extraversion, one of the Big Five personality traits, can influence users' responses to personalized recommendations [4]. Therefore, it is reasonable to assume that extraversion may have a moderating effect on the relationship between intelligent recommendation systems and emotional attachment.

In summary, this study contributes to the understanding of the impact of intelligent recommendation systems on users' emotional attachment and the role of personality traits in this relationship. By exploring the mediating effect of self-construction and the moderating effect of extraversion, this study provides insights for developers of intelligent recommendation systems to improve user loyalty and satisfaction.

2 Literature Review

A recommendation system is an information technology tool based on the web network. It can provide personalized recommendations based on users' historical records, preference orientations, and other information. The most important characteristic of a recommendation system is its ability to "guess" users' preferences and interests by analyzing their behavior, thereby generating personalized recommendations [5]. Personalization and accuracy are key attributes of recommendation algorithms. On the one hand, when users feel that the recommended content is personalized to their needs, they will perceive the recommendations as useful and experience a sense of satisfaction. On the other hand, high-quality recommendations can improve users' experience. The quality of the recommended content depends on the accuracy of the system's recommendations. However, although accuracy metrics can enhance users' perception of the quality of generated recommendations, they can only partially reflect the overall user experience. To address this situation, some researchers have evaluated other features beyond accuracy, such as diversity and novelty, which are expected to be the future development trend of intelligent recommendation systems [6]. Chen et al. found that serendipity positively affects user satisfaction and its contribution is much higher than that of novelty and diversity [7]. Therefore, this paper examines how the three features of recommendation systems - accuracy, personalization, and serendipity - affect user emotional attachment and continued usage behavior.

3 Theoretical Basis and Research Hypotheses

3.1 Attachment Theory

According to attachment theory, emotional attachment refers to individuals' tendencies to form, maintain, and dissolve intimacy with specific others [8]. This concept has been widely explored and lots of scholars have developed its meaning. Among them, Park has provided a conceptual framework to show that individuals are more likely to be attached with products that satisfy their functional (self-realization), experiential (self-gratification), and emotional (self-enrichment) needs [2]. The concepts of self-enrichment, self-realization, and self-gratification have similar connotations to users' self-expressiveness, self-actualization, and self-pleasure, respectively. In the context of the intelligent recommendation system, self-expressiveness means that users show their preferences and personalities by clicking likes and collecting recommended information; Self-actualization means that intelligent recommendation system enables users to obtain their favorite contents more efficiently, so as to satisfy their own expectations; Self-pleasure indicates that intelligent recommendation system recommends information that users are interested in, helping users to obtain the sense of pleasure and enjoyment more easier. Our research uses self-expressiveness, self-actualization and self-pleasure as the mediations to explore the relationship between intelligent recommendation systems and users' emotional attachment.

3.2 Uses and Gratifications Theory

Uses and gratifications theory was first proposed by Katz, which suggests that users produce certain needs and goals based on their own living environment and psychology thoughts, rather than passively and blindly choose and contact entities that meet their needs [9]. Uses and gratifications theory mainly consists of two different parts: seeking and obtaining satisfaction. Seeking satisfaction is identified as the corresponding need to use a particular medium, while obtaining satisfaction is considered as an actual result or obtained satisfaction [3]. Uses and gratifications theory proposes that users choose and consume the media according to their own needs to actively meet their own needs. In the context of intelligent recommendation system, different feature designs of intelligent recommendation systems can affect users' adoption of the technology and subsequently influence their willingness to use it [10]. Intelligent recommendation system can bring users pleasure and encourage users to continue to use intelligent recommendation system. Therefore, uses and gratifications theory is used as the theoretical basis in our research.

3.3   Self-construction Affects Emotional Attachment

Our research mainly explores the self-construction in three aspects: self-actualization, self-pleasure, and self-expressiveness, which is in line with prior research.

Self-actualization Affects Emotional Attachment. Self-actualization is related to the realization of an effective and capable "self". Prior research has indicated that competence is the key for users to satisfying themselves, which further leads to users' emotional attachment [11]. The user's sense of self-actualization efficacy arises from the situation of effectively solving problems and meeting actual needs. The sense of efficacy makes users think they are capable and efficient at solving real problems. When individuals perceive that their abilities are not enough for them to meet their needs of development, they will actively seek reliable entity to help themselves achieve their goals. When a reliable entity helps users to have the ability to complete a take, the users become emotionally attached to it. For users, intelligent recommendation systems can be regarded as a reliable entity. Users expect that using intelligent recommendation systems can help them have the ability to effectively complete tasks and saving time, which means that users hope that they can obtain the targeted information quickly. When users realize that intelligent recommendation systems can help them achieve goals that they could not achieve in the past, users will regard intelligent recommendation systems as the extension of their ability, thereby leading to users' emotional attachment. Based on the discussion above, we propose the following hypothesis:

H1: Self-actualization is positively associated with users' emotional attachment.

Self-pleasure Affects Emotional Attachment. Self-pleasure is related to satisfying individuals' hedonic needs, which involves user's positive sensory experience of products. It is the perception of mental and physical pleasure and enjoyment for users. Intelligent recommendation systems can analyze users' historical browsing history and then provide related contents. This can bring sensory pleasure and relaxing experience to users. When intelligent recommendation systems motivate users to have pleasure and satisfy their hedonic needs for many times, individuals will view intelligent recommendation systems as useful tools to require entertainment, thus resulting in users' emotional attachment. Based on the discussion above, we propose the following hypothesis:

H2: Self-pleasure is positively associated with users' emotional attachment.

Self-expressiveness Affects Emotional Attachment. Self-expressiveness refers to revealing information about "self" to others, which can strengthen the intimacy between people [12]. Users will have a closer emotional bond with the entity that can meet their psychological needs to express themselves. In the context of intelligent recommendation system, users display information that are associated with their self-personality to others by clicking likes and collecting contents. Such behaviors can express who they are. Intelligent recommendation systems accurately recommend information that meets users' preferences, which can be regarded as the symbol of the "self". During this process, intelligent recommendation systems can meet users' psychological needs to express themselves and motivate their continuous usage, thus leading to users' emotional attachment. Based on the discussion above, we propose the following hypothesis:

H3: Self-expressiveness is positively associated with users' emotional attachment.

3.4 Recommendation System Affects Self-construction

Accuracy Affects Self-actualization. Moussawi et al. argue that intelligent systems with high efficiency and adaptability will help users perform daily tasks and achieve personal goals [13]. Intelligent recommendation systems have the advantages of high efficiency, adaptability, goal-oriented behavior, and the ability to handle complex information. Its accuracy can improve users' satisfaction with recommended results, thereby increasing their trust and frequency of use in recommendation systems. When recommendation systems can accurately recommend products or content that users are interested in, users can quickly find the information they need, save time and energy, and have a better user experience. In this way, users can better understand their interests and needs, and are more likely to achieve self-goals and improve self-worth. Based on the above discussion, we propose the following hypothesis:

H4: Accuracy is positively associated with self-actualization.

Serendipity Affects Self-pleasure. Improving the serendipity of recommendation systems is a common way to improve users' satisfaction. Existing research has shown that most serendipity can increase user preferences [14]. Recommendation systems with high serendipity should be related to users' current needs and bring unexpected surprises to users. When using intelligent recommendation systems with high serendipity, users can receive a content which is interesting but difficult for them to find out by themselves. The unexpected and interesting recommendations can bring cognitive stimulation and sensory excitement to users, allowing them to obtain hedonic satisfaction and pleasure. Based on the discussion above, we propose the following hypothesis:

H5: Serendipity is positively associated with self-pleasure.

Personalization Affects Self-expressiveness. Brand or product with personalized design can help users display their core identity and extent their self-awareness [15]. Prior research indicates that providing users with personalized services can affect users' emotional attachment [16]. In the context of intelligent recommendation systems, artificial intelligence can accurately predict a range of intimate personal attributes to recommend information that meet users' preferences and aesthetics. In order to express their personalized tastes, users can actively share these recommended contents with others. During this process, intelligent recommendation systems help users achieve their identity construction and self-expressiveness. Based on the discussion above, we propose the following hypothesis:

H6: Personalization is positively associated with self-expressiveness.

3.5 Moderating Effect of Extraversion

Individual differences play an important role in user's perception of various information systems. Prior research has indicated that integrating the elements that reflect users' personalized characteristics into the intelligent systems can improve users' satisfaction [17]. Among them, extraversion has an impact on user's continued use of recommendation systems, and it has been demonstrated to be positively correlated with addictive tendencies [18]. Extraversion reflects that individuals are easy to get excited, good at expressing and social interaction, Individuals with high extraversion are more eager to show themselves to others for social purposes. In contrary, introverts do not have high level of socialization. They use virtual space to delight themselves and counteract negative emotions such as loneliness. In the context of intelligent recommendation systems, extraversion can affect the relationship between recommendation system characteristics and users' self-construction, which can be reflected in the following aspects. First, our research proposes that individuals with high extraversion prefer to express themselves in the spotlight of the crowds in a way that expresses themselves. They want to present their unique self-image through personalized contents, thus satisfying their needs of self-expressiveness. Second, accurate intelligent recommendation systems provide users with meaningful information, which can achieve users' utilitarian goals Our research proposes that individuals with high extraversion have stronger motivations and clearer goals for task achievement, which is related to their self-confidence and other characters. Therefore, users with high extraversion are more inclined to complete tasks with the help of intelligent recommendation systems, resulting in feelings of being confident to complete goals. Third, our research proposes that introverted users may pay more attention to hedonic feelings than highly extraverted users. They not only have less motivation to complete tasks, but also try to avoid social interactions online. The presence of loneliness prompts them to have some kind of sensory stimulus to divert attention from loneliness. Therefore, they prefer using intelligent recommendation systems to delight themselves and get positive emotions such as happiness. Based on the discussion above, we propose the following hypotheses:

H7a: Extraversion positively modulates the relationship of accuracy and self-actualization.
H7b: Extraversion negatively modulates the relationship of serendipity and self-pleasure.
H7c: Extraversion positively modulates the relationship of personalization and self-expressiveness.

Figure 1 shows the research model in this paper.

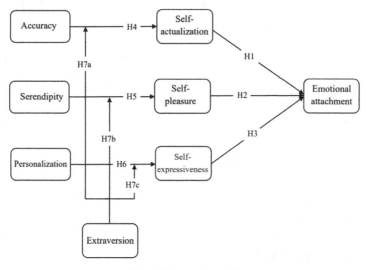

Fig. 1. Research model

4 Empirical Research

4.1 Data Analysis

To examine our theoretical model, we conducted a survey to collect our research data. The measurement items of the constructs in our questionnaire are adapted from prior research based on the context of NetEase CloudMusic. NetEase CloudMusic is a music software that includes music recommendation and sharing, friend recommendation and social networking. It is much popular in China. Users have high stickiness to it. We use a seven-point Likert scale (1 = strongly disagree; 7 = strongly agree) to score and access the measurement items. The measurement items of our questionnaire are concluded in Table 1. We distributed questionnaire through Wenjuanxing Website, which is the largest and the most popular online survey website in China. We collected a total of 330 questionnaires at first and removed 25 invalid questionnaires according to the following rules: (1) respondents who did not pass the attention test; (2) respondents spent less than 52 s filling out the questionnaire. At last, 305 valid questionnaires were collected. Table 1 shows the basic information of respondents in our research.

We also analyze the research data to test its reliability and validity of all measurements. Our research finds that: (1) Cronbach's alpha values for all constructs were higher than 0.5; (2) The value of combined reliability (CR) was greater than 0.7; (3) The value of average variance extracted values (AVE) was greater than 0.5. Hence, our research data has well reliability and validity.

Table 1. Sample characteristics

Variable	Indicator	Frequency	Percentage
Gender	Male	132	43.3
	Female	173	56.7
How often you use NetEase Cloud Music	Every day	114	37.4
	Once every two or three days	98	32.1
	Once a week	37	12.1
	Once a month	8	2.6
	Once a few months	5	1.6
	Seldom	43	14.1
Age	<18	5	1.6
	18–24	278	94.1
	25–30	8	2.6
	>30	5	1.6
Time spent using NetEase Cloud Music	Less than a month	35	11.5
	One month to half a year	17	5.6
	Half a year to a year	15	5.0
	More than a year	238	78.0

4.2 Hypothesis Validation

Empirical Results. In this paper, the method of Bollen-Stine Bootstrap method was used to estimate the Chi-square value of the model. The main fitting index of the model is as follows: $\chi^2/DF = 1.473$, RMSEA $= 0.039$, GFI $= 0.941$, TLI $= 0.978$, and CFI $= 0.980$, which shows that our empirical model fits well. The results of our empirical model are presented in Fig. 2.

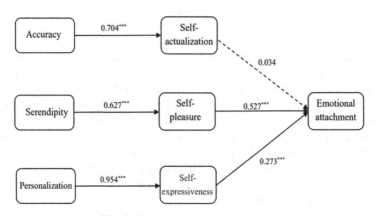

Fig. 2. The results of research model

First, our research proposes that three needs (i.e., self-actualization, self-pleasure, and self-expressiveness) to achieve self-construct are positively associated with users' emotional attachment. The empirical results show that self-pleasure (H2: $\beta = 0.527$, p < 0.001) and self-expressiveness (H3: $\beta = 0.273$, p < 0.001) are positively related to users' emotional attachment. However, our research does not find statistically significance between self-actualization and emotional attachment (H1: $\beta = 0.034$, p = 0.699 > 0.05). Hence, H2 and H3 are supported while H1 is not supported in our research. Second, our research proposes that three characteristics of intelligent recommendation systems (i.e., accuracy, serendipity, and personalization) are respectively related to three needs of self-construction (i.e., self-actualization, self-pleasure, and self-expressiveness). Our research finds that all three characteristics have positive effect on three needs of self-construction (H4: $\beta = 0.704$, p < 0.001; H5: $\beta = 0.627$, p < 0.001; H6: $\beta = 0.954$, p < 0.001). Therefore, H4, H5, and H6 are all supported in our research.

Results of Moderation Effect. Our research also examines the moderation effect of extraversion on the relationship between intelligent recommendation and self-construction. Table 2 shows the results of the mediating effects. The result indicates that extraversion has a positive moderating effect on the relationship between personalization and self-expressiveness (H7c: $\beta = 0.113$, t = 2.556, p = 0.011 < 0.05). But we do not find statistical evidence on the moderation effect of extraversion on the relationship between accuracy and self-actualization (H7a: $\beta = 0.585$, t = 0.944, p = 0.345 > 0.05) as well as the relationship between serendipity and self-pleasure (H7b: $\beta = 0.004$, t = 0.067, p = 0.947 > 0.05). Hence, the results of our research support H7c but do not provide evidence to support H7a and H7b.

Table 2. Results of moderation effect

Variable			Coefficients			
IV	M	DV	β	t	p	Type of mediation
A	E	SA	0.585	0.944	0.345	No
S	E	SP	0.004	0.067	0.947	No
P	E	SE	0.113	2.556	0.011	Partial

5 Discussion and Implications

5.1 Discussion of Results

Based on the use-satisfaction theory and attachment theory, this study explored the effects of intelligent recommendation system on user's emotional attachment as well as the mediating effects of extraversion. Table 3 shows the hypothesis testing results in this paper.

Table 3. Hypothesis testing results

Hypotheses		Support
H1	Self-actualization → Emotional attachment	No
H2	Self-pleasure → Emotional attachment	Yes
H3	Self-expressiveness → Emotional attachment	Yes
H4	Accuracy → Self-actualization	Yes
H5	Serendipity → Self-pleasure	Yes
H6	Personalization → Self-expressiveness	Yes
H7a	Extraversion → Accuracy and Self-actualization	No
H7b	Extraversion ← Serendipity and Self-pleasure	No
H7c	Extroversion → Personalization and Self-expressiveness	Yes

First, self-pleasure and self-expressiveness have positively effect on user's emotional attachment while self-actualization does not have statistically effect on users' emotional attachment. The possible explanations are as follows: our research context is NetEase Cloud Music, which makes it very easy for users to get the results they expect. Getting the desired results too easily may lead to the lack of self-fulfillment of users' sense of efficacy.

Second, three characteristics of intelligent recommendation systems (i.e., accuracy, serendipity, and personalization) have positively effect on users' self-construction (i.e., self-actualization, self-pleasure, and self-expressiveness) respectively. Accurate recommendation enables users to have the sense of self-actualization; Occasional recommendation provides users with psychological satisfaction and personalized recommendation information helps users express themselves better. Therefore, characteristics of intelligent recommendation systems can affect users' self-construction.

Third, extraversion, one of personality traits, positively moderates the relationship between personalization and self-expression. However, extraversion does not significantly moderate the relationship between accuracy and self-actualization and the relationship between serendipity and self-pleasure. The possible explanations are as follows. Extraversion is typically associated with aspects such as sociability and exploration. However, serendipity and self-pleasure involve more psychological processes and emotional experiences. They may not have a strong correlation with extraversion. Therefore, even if extraversion has some impact on the relationship between serendipity and self-pleasure in the context of recommendation systems, its moderating effect may not be significant.

5.2 Theoretical Implications and Practical Implications

This study has several theoretical contributions. Firstly, this study innovatively combines attachment theory with the uses and gratifications theory. This provides insights for future research on user's continued use of intelligent recommendation systems. Secondly, attachment theory is rarely used in the field of intelligent recommendation systems. The issue of user retention requires an integrated exploration from both technological and marketing perspectives. This study discussed from the perspective of intelligent recommendation systems, broadening the application field of attachment theory. Third, this paper explores the moderating effect of extraversion on the relationship between recommender system characteristics and emotional attachment antecedent variables, this helps us better understand the complex relationship between recommendation systems and emotional attachment. The results of this paper also bring two practice implications as follow: First, the conclusion of this study supports enterprises to conduct AI social marketing activities. If enterprises want to use the intelligent recommendation system for social marketing and achieve good results, it is important to make users invest emotions in the intelligent recommendation system, which can be implemented from the three perspectives of self-actualization, self-pleasure and self-expressiveness. Second, for intelligent recommendation system designers, this study depicts the design direction of recommendation systems. When designing a recommendation system, enterprises can adjust it according to the function of the software and the emotional expectations of users, so that users can truly participate in the recommendation system.

6 Conclusion

Although there are many studies on emotional attachment, few academic researchers pay attention to the moderating effect of personality traits on the relationship between intelligent recommendation systems and users' emotional attachment. To bridge the research gaps, our research mainly uses attachment theory and uses and gratifications theory as our research basis to explore the effect of intelligent recommendation systems (i.e., accuracy, serendipity, and personalization) on users' emotional attachment. The mediating effect of self-construction (i.e., self-actualization, self-pleasure, and self-expressiveness) and the moderating effect of personality trait are also explored in our research. To examine our theoretical model, we conduct a survey and collect 305 valid questionnaires. The research results show: (1) Accuracy, serendipity, and personalization have positive and significant effect on users' self-actualization, self-pleasure, and self-expressiveness respectively; (2) Self-pleasure and self-expressiveness are positively associated with users' emotional attachment, while self-actualization do not have significant effect on users' emotional attachment; (3) Extraversion has a positive moderating effect on the relationship between personalization and self-expressiveness. However, our research does not find evidence to support the moderating effect of extraversion on the relationship between accuracy and self-actualization as well as the relationship of serendipity and self-pleasure. This study can help developers of intelligent recommendation systems understand users' continuous usage behavior from the perspective of emotional attachment.

References

1. Ghorbanzadeh, D., Rahehagh, A.: Emotional brand attachment and brand love: the emotional bridges in the process of transition from satisfaction to loyalty. Rajagiri Manag. J. **15**(1), 16–38 (2021)

2. Park, C.W., Macinns, D.J., Prester, J.: Beyond attitudes: attachment and consumer behavior. Soc. Sci. Electron. Publishing **12**(2), 3–36 (2006)
3. Hussain, A., Shabir, G., Taimoor, U.H.: Cognitive needs and use of social media: a comparative study of gratifications sought and gratification obtained. Inf. Discov. Deliv. **48**(2), 79–90 (2020)
4. Meng, K.S., Leung, L.: Factors influencing TikTok engagement behaviors in China: an examination of gratifications sought, narcissism, and the Big Five personality traits. Telecommun. Policy **45**(7), 102172 (2021)
5. Resnick, P., Varian, H.R.: Recommender systems. Commun. ACM **40**(3), 56–58 (1997)
6. Cano, E., Morisio, M.: Hybrid recommender systems: a systematic literature review. Intell. Data Anal. **21**(6), 1487–1524 (2017)
7. Chen, L., Yang, Y., Wang, N., et al.: How serendipity improves user satisfaction with 38 recommendations? A large-scale user evaluation. In: World Wide Web Conference (WWW), pp. 240–250 (2019)
8. Bowlby, J.: The making and breaking of affectional bonds: I. Aetiology and psychopathology in the light of attachment theory. Br. J. Psychiatry **130**(3), 201–210 (1977)
9. Katz, E.: Utilization of mass communication by the individual. In: The Uses of Mass Communications: Current Perspectives on Gratifications Research, pp. 19–32 (1974)
10. Pu, P., Chen, L., Hu, R.: Evaluating recommender systems from the user's perspective: survey of the state of the art. User Model. User-Adap. Interact. **22**(4), 317–355 (2012)
11. Ki, C.W.C., Cuevas, L.M., Chong, S.M., et al.: Influencer marketing: social media influencers as human brands attaching to followers and yielding positive marketing results by fulfilling needs. J. Retail. Consum. Serv. **55**, 102133 (2020)
12. Puntoni, S., Reczek, R.W., Giesler, M., et al.: Consumers and artificial intelligence: an experiential perspective. J. Mark. **85**(1), 131–151 (2021)
13. Moussawi, S., Koufaris, M., Benbunan-Fich, R.: How perceptions of intelligence and anthropomorphism affect adoption of personal intelligent agents. Electron. Markets **31**(2), 343–364 (2021). https://doi.org/10.1007/s12525-020-00411-w
14. Kotkov, D., Konstan, J.A., Zhao, Q., et al.: Investigating serendipity in recommender systems based on real user feedback. In: Proceedings of the 33rd Annual ACM Symposium on Applied Computing, pp. 1341–1350 (2018)
15. Belk, R.W.: Possessions and the extended self. J. Consum. Res. **15**(2), 139–168 (1988)
16. Cao, X., Gong, M., Yu, L., et al.: Exploring the mechanism of social media addiction: an empirical study from WeChat users. Internet Res. **30**(4), 1305–1328 (2020)
17. Nguyen, T.T., Maxwell Harper, F., Terveen, L., et al.: User personality and user satisfaction with recommender systems. Inf. Syst. Front. **20**(6), 1173–1189 (2018). https://doi.org/10.1007/s10796-017-9782-y
18. Blackwell, D., Leaman, C., Tramposch, R., et al.: Extraversion, neuroticism, attachment style and fear of missing out as predictors of social media use and addiction. Personality Individ. Differ. **116**, 69–72 (2017)

Understanding Multi-platform Social VR Consumer Opinions: A Case Study in VRChat Using Topics Modeling of Reviews

Dion Deng$^{(\boxtimes)}$, Mila Bujic, and Juho Hamari

Tampere University, Tampere, Finland
`xiaohang.deng@tuni.fi`

Abstract. Due to the significant advancements in virtual reality (VR) technologies over the years, more research has been done on how these technologies could promote more effective communication in social applications to enhance collaboration and social connectivity. Most studies about social VR conducted experimental tasks in different communication contexts to evaluate communication quality, which has limited relevance to the VR industries and ambiguous generalizability of findings outside of lab settings. This study tries to solve this problem by conducting a case study on one of the most popular commercial social VR applications to understand what factors impact consumers' user experience in social VR applications. We used the Structural Topic Model (STM) based text mining of VRChat's steam reviews to explore topics that users discuss and classified the topics into four clusters, including avatars and behaviors, complaints, hardware and connection, and recommendation. The implications for game developers and future social VR research are discussed.

Keywords: VRChat · Topic Modeling · Steam · Social VR

1 Introduction

Virtual reality (VR) is an immersive, multimodal technology that immerses users in and allows them to interact with environments that are not physically present to them [1, 2]. Social VR refers to the applications that allow users to communicate with one another in virtual spaces using head-mounted displays (HMDs) [3]. People may already communicate remotely via text, voice, or video thanks to the widespread use of social networking programs like Facebook and Zoom. However, compared to face-to-face communication, these forms of communication do not offer an immersive communication environment, which makes users feel less present and deprives them of opportunities for physical and emotional closeness as well as interaction with their surroundings and objects. With VR, an emerging alternative, users can "meet" in a shared, immersive virtual environment and engage with virtual versions of each other, improving communication experiences [4] and consequently, for example, collaborative efforts.

Commercial social VR applications such as VRChat, Rec Room, AltspaceVR, and Facebook Spaces have recently drawn a large user base to engage in social interaction on

© The Author(s), under exclusive license to Springer Nature Switzerland AG 2023
Y. Tu and M. Chi (Eds.): WHICEB 2023, LNBIP 481, pp. 35–46, 2023.
https://doi.org/10.1007/978-3-031-32302-7_4

both flat screens and VR displays [4]. These applications are being used in a variety of fields, including employment, education, counselling, and entertainment [5]. Platforms such as Mozilla Hubs have thus been increasingly used in professional and educational contexts, driving the need for understanding user experiences, and fostering consumer satisfaction and efficient use of the medium.

The rapid evolution of VR technology and social VR applications raise social VR consumers' expectations of their experience in the applications. According to the expectation confirmation theory (ECT), if the actual performance of the applications does not meet users' expectations, users' satisfaction will decrease, which will impact users' intention to continue the use of social VR applications (Bhattacherjee, 2001). To improve user experience and intention to use social VR applications, it is essential to understand users' expectations on social VR and their perceived performance of the applications.

To study users' expectations on social VR and assess user experiences, research is predominantly based on laboratory experiments in different communication contexts [4, 6]. For example, letting participants play roles in collaborative tasks, talking tasks, competitive tasks, etc., and assessing their communication efficiency [3]. In social VR research, experiments are suitable to test theories about user interaction in VR environments in controlled settings with little intervention from reality. However, their limitation for practical implications lies in the severe restriction to the experiment context and commonly a one-time experience, with uncertain generalizability of findings outside of laboratory conditions [7].

One way to fill these limitations is to conduct big data case studies on typical social VR applications. Since social VR is still a relatively new area of study, case studies could be used to give rich data describing phenomena involving communication in VR environments. Research that focuses on describing and understanding particular phenomena as well as constructing a hypothesis or theory utilizing grounded-theory methodologies is particularly well suited to case studies [7].

Most social VR applications as experiential products have many customers who like sharing their reviews online, which helps form social VR communities. To match new trends in social VR, there is a high demand for online review analysis and user profiling [8]. End-user evaluations of existing applications with a wide and diverse consumer base, such as video games, can offer helpful insights that designers can use to advance their applications [9].

To further the understanding of the advantages and pitfalls of social VR features, this study employs a data mining approach on a large dataset of users' reviews to explore: **what factors impact consumers' user experience in social VR applications.**

2   Related Works

2.1   Social VR

Two crucial elements, avatar and nonverbal cues, that influence users' communication patterns in social VR were found by Wei et al. [4] based on their systematic review of social VR. Many studies about social VR have tested these two elements' effects on social VR communication through experiments. For example, Latoschik et. al. (2017) investigated the effect of avatar realism on embodiment and social interactions in VR

[10]. They discovered that the realistic avatars were evaluated as much more human-like when employed as avatars for others and provoked a stronger acceptance in terms of virtual body ownership when compared with abstract avatar representations based on a wooden mannequin. In another experiment, male and female virtual confederates with joyful, angry, and neutral faces approached the real males and females to see if they altered their interpersonal distance in different ways. They found that individuals preferred longer distances with virtual confederates who were furious rather than neutral or cheerful [11].

Some qualitative studies also provided empirical data demonstrating how social VR platforms enable novel occurrences, identity behaviors, and potential design ramifications for future applications. Freeman and Maloney (2020) describe an extensive empirical assessment of the presentation and perception of self in Social Virtual Reality using outcomes of interview research [12]. In Freeman et al.'s (2020) study, they discovered three major themes from 30 interviews that emerged in people's perceptions and experiences with their avatars in various social VR applications, including "A More Challenging Way to Create and Craft Avatars", "Body as the Immediate and Sole interface to Experience Avatars", and "A More Engaging and Embodied Approach to Explore One's Own Identity" [13].

2.2 User Satisfaction on VR

The expectation-confirmation theory (ECT) has been used extensively in studies on consumer behavior. It explains the connection between an object's reuse and the satisfaction of consumer expectations. Bhattacherjee (2001) developed ECT on information systems and discovered that there are discrepancies between an individual's initial expectations about a certain product before purchase or use and their subsequent expectations. According to the expectation-confirmation hypothesis, a crucial factor in defining a user's first user experience (UX) when using technology and in determining how satisfied they are overall is the confirmation of expectations, which in turn affects their continuance intentions.

VR as a developing technology needs to stick users to build a stronger metaverse ecology. In recent years, many studies have applied ECT in the context of VR environments. For example, a study related to VR learning exhibited the participants' intent to continue using VR technology, their satisfaction with intercultural learning made possible by VR technology, and their perception that the technology met their expectations (Shadiev et al., 2020). Bujic and Hamari's (2020) study provides a steppingstone for increasing our understanding of the expectation-confirmation theory in new contexts and some of the demographic aspects of immersive journalism that may have an impact on theory and practice. However, few studies with the context of ECT and VR analyze costumers' reviews of existing VR applications.

Except for expectations, users' perceived satisfaction can be impacted by other factors, such as users' intrinsic motivation, perceived usefulness, and perceived ease of use (Deci et al., 2017; Venkatesh and Davis, 2000). According to Przybylski et al.'s (2009) investigation on the connection between people's motivation and satisfaction in multiuser virtual environments, intrinsic motivation in a virtual environment is positively correlated with feelings of autonomy, competence, and relatedness, which is in accordance with the Self-Determination Theory (SDT). The Technological Acceptance Model (TAM) is also relevant when discussing VR. Perceived usefulness and perceived simplicity of use were proven to be significant predictors of intention to use in earlier studies (Venkatesh and Davis, 2000).

3 Methods

3.1 Data Collection

Steam is one of the biggest digital distribution platforms for PC gaming with more than 8,000 titles accessible and more than 184 million active users. Steam reviews are widely studied to evaluate product quality [14]. The game reviews offer a comprehensive data source that can be used to better comprehend user-reported problems [15].

In this study, we gathered user review data for VRChat from the Steam platform using Steamreviews, an open-source Python web crawling technology. Steamreviews requests appID to get the review data. AppID is a unique number in the URL of each game's steam store webpage. For example, VRChat's store page's URL is "https://store.steamp owered.com/app/438100/VRChat/" and its appID is "438100". Steamreviews allows us to restrict the reviews' language, and this study collected English reviews only because it is difficult to train a topic model with multi-language text data. We collected all 116,480 reviews in English from VRChat's release date, April 5th, 2018, to September 21st, 2022. For each review, Steamreviews can also collect its metadata including the review date, the review sentiment (recommend or not recommend), and the hours the reviewer spends on VRChat before reviewing. The metadata will be used for the topic modeling.

3.2 Text Analysis

To analyze the VRChat review data, we employed Structural Topic Models (STM), which enables researchers to adaptably estimate a topic model that incorporates document-level metadata (Roberts et al., 2019). STM has widely been used to analyze gaming communities such as Steam reviews [9, 16] and Reddit discussions [17]. Compared to the traditional topic modeling method Latent Dirichlet Allocation (LDA), STM enables researchers to identify the key elements of study abroad participants' experiences and connected them to learning context metadata [16].

By fitting the topic model to the data set, it is possible to identify the underlying subjects and their prevalences in each document in the collection. Topic modeling describes document content as a mixture of underlying themes, each of which has a distribution of typical terms. The subjects that emerge and how frequently they appear across the documents can then be examined. The resulting topics can be used to characterize debate topics as well as other aspects, such as writing style. Some collections of themes may be very different from one another, but others may be more similar, expressing variations in the emphasis placed on the same issue [9].

Prior to the analysis, the data were cleaned using a common preprocessing method that involved eliminating stop-words and words that were often used in this text as well as stemming the corpus of text [17].

Using the searchK function included in the STM R package, we selected the number of topics following the model diagnostics (Roberts et al., 2019). First, we conducted a 10-point interval search for topics with the values K = 40, 50,..., and 80. The search was concentrated on K = 50 based on four metrics to estimate the model: held-out likelihood, residuals, semantic coherence, and exclusivity. A more thorough search for potential enhanced values with K = 46 to 54 was then carried out. Finally, the optimal number of topics was set as K = 50.

To make the most significant connections between subjects in a text corpus clear, we employed another R package, Factoextra, to cluster the 50 topics based on their correlations with each other. With the function fviz_nbclust, N = 8 was selected as the optimal cluster number.

4   Results

We first investigated the discovered themes and assigned them descriptive titles and example reviews that prominently referenced the topic [9]. We listed each topic's descriptive titles, the words that were used the most frequently, and the overall proportion ("Pr (%)") that indicated how much of the review material was related to that topic. As the next step, we analyzed the clusters processed by Factoextra to organize the mass topics. One of the clusters was redundant because of over-clustering, including T24 pog, 0.04%; T7 VRChat is good, 0.74%; T10 spam reviews, 0.82%. We removed T10 and moved T24 and T7 to the cluster Recommendation. We also merged three clusters that are both about complaints to VRChat. One cluster contains content that has low relation with VRChat, including T26 make up stories, 1.11%; T2 jokes, 0.96%; T20 folk, 1.31%; T12 recipe, 0.46%; T5 other unrelated topics, 0.28%. Reviews in this cluster will not be analyzed in this paper. Finally, there are a total of four clusters, which will be explained in the following section. Clusters and topics in each cluster are displayed in Fig. 1.

4.1   Avatars and User Behaviors

This cluster includes discussions of avatars (T16 male voice with female avatars, 1.89%; T47 furries and weebs, 0.45%), in-game behaviors that show some players' motivations (T34 entertainment activities, 1.24%; T22 escape from reality, 0.81%; T37 sitting in front of a mirror, 0.95%; T25 full body tracking, 1.66%), negative behaviors (T11 rude behaviors, 2.4%; T45 sexual behaviors on children, 1.71%; T46 annoying kids, 0.56%), and two other topics that are not highly correlated with the cluster (T43 time spending on VRChat, 4.08%; T18 silence protest against VRChat, 3.11%).

Interestingly, for reviews related to avatars, most people share their observations on avatars' inconsistency. Some inconsistencies are caused by non-human avatars such as animals ("This game will turn you gay and into a furry lover."). Some are caused by a perceptual mismatch between voice and appearance, such as a female avatar with a male voice ("Im not sure how to feel about seeing a bunch of anime girls and hearing deep male voices to go with them."). People's opinions on inconsistent avatars are mixed. Some like them because they are fun ("Danced to Kpop and Vocaloid songs with a bunch of Russian dudes in anime girl avatars. 10/10 would rush B again"), and some feel uncomfortable ("Lots of weebs and made me cringe so hard that my own headset killed its self").

Some players' in-game behaviors that are inconsistent with their age, race, etc. cause negative effects on others, such as children players' sexual behaviors ("It's just wrong seeing 10 years old children roaming freely everywhere and witnessing cussing and indecent content and behavior").

4.2 Complaints

This cluster includes players' negative feedback on VRChat (T44 disappointed, 1.28%; T29 abuse developers, 1.26%; T3 editing reviews, 0.89%; T40 bad; T4 VRChat is shooting itself, 1.2%), the reasons why they complain (0.81%; T1 VRChat's Cease & Desist letters, 1.13%; T27 spyware, 1.06%; T50 VRChat was fun, 0.88%), suggestions to new players (T19 stay away from VRChat, 0.99%), and complaints on Easy anti-cheat (EAC) (T8 developers ignore the community, 2.87%; T48 complains on EAC, 3.24%; T49 revise reviews because of EAC, 2.14%; T39 play other social VR games, 1.96%; T15 bad update, 2.33%; T21 developers ignore the players, 3.42%, T30 feedbacks on EAC, 2.11%; T32 EAC destroys mods for deaf people, 4.06%; T36 why shouldn't apply EAC, 2.66%, T35 VRChat releases EAC).

Most of reviews in this cluster are aimed at explaining their complaints to the developers, including problems caused by EAC, Cease & Desist letters, spyware, etc. There are also a few reviews that suggest consumers should not engage with VRChat because of the ramifications of toxic user behavior. For example, one review said ("Stay away from this horse sh** game unless you want your mental health to decline and to meet 1 or 2 decent people in a sea of backstabbing pricks").

The sentiment of reviews about EAC is overwhelmingly negative. On July 26, 2022, VRChat implemented its EAC into VRChat, which blocked all modified clients and broke plenty of mods. After that, a large number of reviews emerged on Steam to complain about the new update. Parts of these reviews explain the reasons why VRChat should not apply EAC, such as "disallows people to use mods, even mods for hard-of-hearing and deaf people that allow on-screen subtitles".

4.3 Hardware and Connection

This cluster contains discussions about VRChat's accessibility, including hardware requirement (T14 play with Oculus Quest, 0.9%; T31 high hardware requirement, 1.42%) and connection problems (T13 unable to log in, 2.03%; T9 banned by EAC, 1.64%; T41 unable to log in because of EAC, 1.8%).

When it comes to hardware issues, some consumers point out that VRChat limits some functions for Oculus Quest players and suggest linking it to a desktop to get a better gaming experience, such as "For Quest users I recommend getting the Virtual Desktop Streamer and a VR Link Cable, to get the most out of your experience". Other reviews mention that VRChat requests high hardware configuration ("This Game Takes Up Too Much GPU Resources, Makes The PC Hot, Especially For High-end GPUs"). There are also some reviews indicating connection problems, and most of them are caused by EAC ("I can't even play it anymore because of EAC, I use virtual desktop").

4.4 Recommendation

This cluster includes players' positive feedback on VRChat (T6 VRChat is the best, 7.72%; T17 VRChat is nice, 1.04%; T23 VRChat is fun, 4.25%; T33 VRChat is cool, 3.47%; T24 pog, 0.04%; T7 VRChat is good, 0.74%;), the reasons why they like VRChat (T42 fun to play with friends, 9.13%; T28 practising social skills, 4.24%), and prerequisite of having fun in the game (T38 desktop mode, 3.07%).

Most reviews in this cluster are simply showing their appraisals on VRChat without providing reasons, such as "This game is one of the best and funniest games i have ever played!". Two topics show reasons for appraisals, and both of them indicate social function is the main reason. Some said VRChat helps them to overcome social anxiety: "Good game to practice social skills, especially for people trying to overcome social anxiety like me".

5 Discussion

With the proliferation of applications utilizing head-mounted virtual reality to support their goals such as education and collaborative work [5], it is becoming increasingly relevant to understand the users' expectations and consequent attitudes towards them. Moreover, the consumer population of VR is evolving as the required hardware is becoming more affordable for individuals and institutions alike and the development of software is becoming increasingly diverse. Due to these developments, early studies of VR could rarely include more experienced consumers and the novelty effects of the technology were likely more prominent [7]. As consumers mature and diversify from early adopters, it is reasonable to assume that our pre-existing understanding of motivations, expectations, and experiences is becoming significantly outdated.

To understand this changing landscape of consumers it is necessary to examine existing practices in popular applications and utilize the wealth and breadth of daily global experiences of VR. Some such studies include for example interviews with users and investigations of various VR-specific phenomena [12, 13] and their communities and their interactions inside and outside of VR [22]. However, the existing literature is primarily concerned with the perspectives of *users as players* and related experiences, rather than examining users as *consumers* of a product and employing relevant approaches.

This study attempted at contributing to filling this gap by using a freely available and popular social VR application as the case study (namely, VRChat), applying topic modeling to its consumer reviews, and discussing them primarily through the lenses of the technology acceptance model (TAM; Venkatesh and Davis, 2000) and expectation-confirmation theory (ECT) [24] and needs satisfaction as outlined in the self-determination theory (SDT) [26]. Through our analysis, we devised the following themes: avatars and behaviors, complaints, hardware and connection, and recommendation. Finally, we discuss them from the perspectives of hardware and platform affordances and drawbacks, continuing with those relevant specifically to head mounted virtual reality uses, and in the end, we focus on the application's social aspects' influence on consumer attitudes.

5.1 Hardware and Platform

When intending to use VR applications, the first potential obstacles consumers encounter is related to the required hardware and specific bounds of the VR platform itself. Related to this and according to TAM, users' perceived ease of use of a given technology plays a significant role in their future intention to continue its use [23]. A notable number of anal-ysed reviews emphasised how a good experience requires very high-quality hardware, or having negative attitudes due to not being able to log into the application because of connection problems. These reviews show that these hardware problems impede some users from experiencing it simply and smoothly. These problems will significantly decrease users' intention to use VRChat. From our results, nearly 7% of the reviews are related to these problems, which is alarming to VRChat and other social VR application developers.

Another problem about the VRChat platform that was widely mentioned is Easy anti-cheat (EAC). From the topic model in the results, there are nine topics grouped into the EAC cluster and almost all the reviews in this cluster are negative. Most reviews show the leading reason for players' negative feedback on EAC is that it smothers their creative freedom, which can be related to motivational theories, such as the need for autonomy in the self-determination theory (SDT) [26]. Previous studies on SDT have found that the psychological demand for perceived autonomy is connected to user happiness and, as a result, predicts users' intentions to keep using virtual social applications [26]. The negative attitudes caused by EAC potentially emphasise the perceived de-centralized nature of virtual worlds and the assumed freedoms within them.

5.2 Virtual Reality Affordances

VRChat as a freely available social VR application on Steam provides users with a good opportunity to experience VR. However, some reviews show that it is not available to experience all the functions of the application with an Oculus Quest headset, they have to use some more advanced and expensive VR headsets to fulfill the configuration requirements. For users who do not have advanced VR devices, their perceived ease of use will decrease because they have to spend extra money on buying or upgrading devices, which negatively impacts their intention to use VRChat [23]. But users who own advanced VR devices will experience all the functions of the application. Some reviews indicated that they were satisfied with the full-body-tracking devices from their additional purchase. As the advanced devices can enhance users' experience such as improving presence in the application, their perceived usefulness will increase, which has a positive impact on the intention to use based on TAM [23]. So, VR affordances can make users who do not have advanced VR devices give up using the application, but give those who have VR devices more intention to use it.

5.3 Social Aspects

As a social VR application, users in VRChat need to meet other users in the virtual world and communicate with them. From the results, we found that many users' default expectations of other users are the same as they are in real life, including their avatars and behaviors. According to expectation-confirmation theory (ECT), users' confirmation of expectations of a product affects the degree of satisfaction and continuance intentions [24]. When other users' avatars are incongruous and inconsistent with some users' expectations, such as the avatar's gender mismatches the user's gender, or someone uses a non-anthropomorphic avatar, these users will have negative feelings and refuse to use VRChat. Some reviews also mentioned that others' impolite behaviors in the virtual world which are seldom seen in reality and inconsistent with social norms, can make users uncomfortable.

Our results also have positive findings on VRChat's social aspects. Some users found that avatars help them to overcome social anxiety when communicating with other players in VRChat. For example, one player said, "Good game to practice social skills, especially for people trying to overcome social anxiety like me." For these users, VRChat is a useful tool to practice social skills and therefore their intended use continuance might be based on this unintended, or tangential, function of the application. Therefore, it is to be expected that, with enough critical mass in terms of the number of consumers, they will likely find novel ways to transgress the normative use scenarios and essentially enrich the application and their experiences. However, these behaviors might not always be desirable and should be anticipated within the framing of the goal of the VR system.

6 Limitations and Future Works

Although informative on social VR consumer attitudes through multiple perspectives, as discussed above, it is important to consider this study's limitations in both explanatory power and generalization, as reflected through its scope, case study selection, data source and data wealth, and analysis methods.

Firstly, our framing presumes that the data collected stems from existing social VR users and that they, unless otherwise indicated, refer to attitudes about the application as experienced through a head-mounted virtual reality display. However, many of today's VR platforms and applications are versatile in terms of hardware required for accessing and using them and the one this study is based on is no different. Indeed, VRChat is available to users via a 2D computer screen and VR alike, rendering it impossible to always ascertain which experience the review is based on – immersive, non-immersive, or a combination of both. Whereas some experiences are only accessible through VR as they are a unique technological affordance of VR, such as naturalistic embodied interactions (e.g., T39) [22], others are accessible through both screen and VR display. Nevertheless, while this study reflects the attitudes of the VRChat consumers, as shared through *Steam* reviews, and is relevant to and to an extent generalizable to similar multi-platform applications, future studies should aim at examining whether certain themes are more prominent on one than the other platform.

Secondly, VRChat was deemed as a suitable case study due to being freely available for several use, with a wide user base, and diverse experiences due to users' freedom to essentially build their own small worlds within the application (e.g., games, night clubs, and nature retreats). However, its consumers' experiences are thus bound to the primarily voluntary and leisurely nature of interacting with the application, rendering these results not necessarily generalizable to serious contexts, such as education, simulation training, work collaboration, and mental or physical therapy applications. Future studies should thus expand the scope of investigation and contrast and compare the results so as to examine which consumer expectations are relatively universal, and which are context-specific. Thirdly, another context-specific constraint to generalizations is the source of reviews, as *Steam* is predominantly a platform for video games, including product distribution and facilitation of communities. As such, it is likely that reviews collected from the platform represent a specific population which might tend to have higher familiarity with interactive media and VR and distinct expectations of seemingly playful content (e.g., freedom for creativity and exploration). These results should thus be complemented with, for example, reviews collected directly within the application from a wide range of users.

Finally, while it is not reasonable to analyze approximately 100,000 reviews manually, the topic modeling approach presents its pitfalls when it comes to the non-explicit and more intricate mapping of consumer experiences. For example, in our analysis, we have encountered instances where implicit and culturally specific meaning was lost through clustering solely of the explicit content. Moroever, due to relying on explicit content, the modeling might even jeopardize the discriminant validity of the clusters. As such, these results should not be interpreted as providing a definitive and clear mapping of consumer experiences, but that the contribution is rather found in an extensive and broad representation of the scope and types of aspects that consumers find relevant to share.

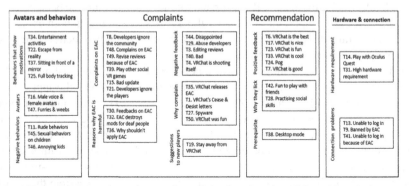

Fig. 1. Affinity Diagram: thematic grouping of the found topics. Titles with a dash are topics, boxes are groups or subgroups.

Acknowledgement. This study was funded by Tampere University (doctoral studies funding) and the Academy of Finland (342144; project 'POSTEMOTION').

References

1. Macey, A.L., Macey, J., Hamari, J.: Virtual reality in emotion regulation: a scoping review (2022)

2. Kilteni, K., Groten, R., Slater, M.: The sense of embodiment in virtual reality. Presence Teleoper. Virtual Environ. **21**(4), 373–387 (2012)
3. Liu, L., Kaplan, A.: No longer alone: finding common ground in collaborative virtual environments. In: Proceedings of the 33rd Annual ACM Symposium on Applied Computing, pp. 240–246, April 2018
4. Wei, X., Jin, X., Fan, M.: Communication in immersive social virtual reality: a systematic review of 10 years' studies. arXiv preprint arXiv:2210.01365 (2022)
5. Bujić, M., Macey, A.L., Järvelä, S., Hamari, J.: Playing with embodied social interaction: a thematic review of experiments on social aspects in gameful virtual reality. Interact. Comput. **33**(6), 583–595 (2021)
6. Xi, N., Hamari, J.: Shopping in virtual reality: a literature review and future agenda. J. Bus. Res. **134**, 37–58 (2021)
7. Kjeldskov, J., Graham, C.: A review of mobile HCI research methods. In: Chittaro, L. (ed.) Mobile HCI 2003. LNCS, vol. 2795, pp. 317–335. Springer, Heidelberg (2003). https://doi.org/10.1007/978-3-540-45233-1_23
8. Kang, H.N., Yong, H.R., Hwang, H.S.: A study of analyzing on online game reviews using a data mining approach: STEAM community data. Int. J. Innov. Manag. Technol. **8**(2), 90 (2017)
9. Lu, C., Li, X., Nummenmaa, T., Zhang, Z., Peltonen, J.: Patches and player community perceptions: analysis of no man's sky steam reviews. In: DiGRA 2020-Proceedings of the 2020 DiGRA International Conference. DiGRA (2020)
10. Latoschik, M.E., Roth, D., Gall, D., Achenbach, J., Waltemate, T., Botsch, M.: The effect of avatar realism in immersive social virtual realities. In: Proceedings of the 23rd ACM Symposium on Virtual Reality Software and Technology, pp. 1–10, November 2017
11. Rapuano, M., Sbordone, F.L., Borrelli, L.O., Ruggiero, G., Iachini, T.: The effect of facial expressions on interpersonal space: a gender study in immersive virtual reality. In: Esposito, A., Faundez-Zanuy, M., Morabito, F.C., Pasero, E. (eds.) Progresses in Artificial Intelligence and Neural Systems. SIST, vol. 184, pp. 477–486. Springer, Singapore (2021). https://doi.org/10.1007/978-981-15-5093-5_40
12. Freeman, G., Maloney, D.: Body, avatar, and me: the presentation and perception of self in social virtual reality. Proc. ACM Hum.-Comput. Interact. **4**(CSCW3), 1–27 (2021)
13. Freeman, G., Zamanifard, S., Maloney, D., Adkins, A.: My body, my avatar: how people perceive their avatars in social virtual reality. In: Extended Abstracts of the 2020 CHI Conference on Human Factors in Computing Systems, pp. 1–8, April 2020
14. Baowaly, M.K., Tu, Y.P., Chen, K.T.: Predicting the helpfulness of game reviews: a case study on the steam store. J. Intell. Fuzzy Syst. **36**(5), 4731–4742 (2019)
15. Lin, D., Bezemer, C.-P., Zou, Y., Hassan, A.E.: An empirical study of game reviews on the Steam platform. Empir. Softw. Eng. **24**(1), 170–207 (2018). https://doi.org/10.1007/s10664-018-9627-4
16. Busurkina, I., Karpenko, V., Tulubenskaya, E., Bulygin, D.: Game experience evaluation. A study of game reviews on the steam platform. In: Alexandrov, D.A., Boukhanovsky, A.V., Chugunov, A.V., Kabanov, Y., Koltsova, O., Musabirov, I. (eds.) DTGS 2020. CCIS, vol. 1242, pp. 117–127. Springer, Cham (2020). https://doi.org/10.1007/978-3-030-65218-0_9
17. Lu, C., Buruk, O.O., Hassan, L., Nummenmaa, T., Peltonen, J.:. "Switch" up your exercise: an empirical analysis of online user discussion of the Ring Fit Adventure exergame. In: CEUR Workshop Proceedings (2021)
18. Park, E.: User acceptance of smart wearable devices: an expectation-confirmation model approach. Telematics Inform. **47**, 101318 (2020)
19. Shadiev, R., Wang, X., Huang, Y.M.: Promoting intercultural competence in a learning activity supported by virtual reality technology. Int. Rev. Res. Open Distrib. Learn. **21**(3), 157–174 (2020)

20. Bujic, M., Hamari, J.: Satisfaction and willingness to consume immersive journalism: experiment of differences between VR, 360 video, and article. In: Proceedings of the 23rd International Conference on Academic Mindtrek, pp. 120–125, January 2020

21. Przybylski, A., Ryan, R., Rigby, C.: The motivating role of violence in video games. Pers. Soc. Psychol. Bull. **35**(2), 243–259 (2009)

22. Thibault, M., Bujic, M.: "Mirror Dwellers": social VR, identity and internet culture. In: DiGRA 2022–Proceedings of the 2022 DiGRA International Conference: Bringing Worlds Together. DiGRA Online Library (2022)

23. Venkatesh, V., Davis, F.D.: A theoretical extension of the technology acceptance model: four longitudinal field studies. Manag. Sci. **46**(2), 186–204 (2000)

24. Bhattacherjee, A.: Understanding information systems continuance: an expectation-confirmation model. MIS Q. **25**(3), 351–370 (2001)

25. Roberts, M.E., Stewart, B.M., Tingley, D.: stm: an R package for structural topic models. J. Stat. Softw. **91**, 1–40 (2019)

26. Deci, E.L., Olafsen, A.H., Ryan, R.M.: Self-determination theory in work organizations: the state of a science. Ann. Rev. Organ. Psychol. Organ. Behav. **4**, 19–43 (2017)

A Study of Consumer Purchase Intentions in E-Commerce Live Broadcast for Eye Health Products Based on Product and Host Discourse Attributes

Wang Zilong$^{(\boxtimes)}$ ⓘ, Zhang Wenkai ⓘ, and Liang Zecheng ⓘ

Guangdong University of Technology, No. 100, Waihuan West Road, Guangzhou University City, Panyu District, Guangzhou, China
garywang8096@163.com

Abstract. With changing lifestyles, increasing excessive eye use and rising consumer health awareness, the field of eye health products is expected to become a new blue ocean market. To identify the factors influencing the purchase intention of eye health products, by integrating the SOR model, TAM theory, persuasion theory, and health belief model, a theoretical framework for influencing consumer decisions is constructed from the perspective of product and anchor language characteristics, using e-commerce live broadcast as the information source. Questionnaire research was conducted with college students as the main research sample, and SEM models were constructed to verify the hypotheses and models. The results showed that: First, the perceived usefulness and perceived ease of use of eye health products, as well as the professionalism and authenticity of the anchor's language, positively influenced consumers' purchase intention, but the influence of the anchor's language charm on consumers' purchase intention was not significant. Second, consumer trust fully mediated between perceived ease of use and purchase intention, and partially mediated between perceived usefulness and purchase intention. Third, Consumer health beliefs fully mediated between anchor language professionalism and purchase intention, and partially mediated between anchor language truthfulness and purchase intentions.

Keywords: Eye Health · E-commerce live broadcast · Purchase intentions

1 Introduction

According to the World Vision Report released by the World Health Organization in 2019, at least 2.2 billion people worldwide are visually impaired or blind, and at least 1 billion of them have preventable or unresolved eye health problems. The outbreak of the COVID-19 pandemic in early 2020 has made "housebound" and "online" a major theme in people's daily lives.

Health products are effective in helping individuals improve their health. At present, research on health products is mainly focused on the technical implementation and functional exploration [1] of the products, but relatively little attention has been paid to

© The Author(s), under exclusive license to Springer Nature Switzerland AG 2023
Y. Tu and M. Chi (Eds.): WHICEB 2023, LNBIP 481, pp. 47–59, 2023.
https://doi.org/10.1007/978-3-031-32302-7_5

consumers' purchase intention, usage behavior, and their perception of health during the consumption process. In the field of eye health products, the research on the consumer is still in the initial stage. With the popularization of the Internet and the increase in the intensity of eye use among the general public, eye health products have ushered in a new "dividend period". Exploring the characteristics of consumers' consumption of eye health products in terms of product and marketing behavior is important for the development of this industry.

To fill the gap in this research area, this paper constructs a theoretical model based on SOR theory, TAM theory, health belief theory, and persuasion theory. Using e-commerce live streaming as a source of information for consumers, we explore the influence of product attributes of eye health products and language characteristics of e-commerce live streaming hosts on consumers' intention to purchase eye health products. This study attempts to answer the following research questions: First, how do the perceived usefulness and perceived ease of use of eye health products affect consumers' purchase intentions? Second, how do the charm, professionalism, and authenticity of the language of e-commerce live broadcast host influence consumers' purchase intentions? Third, health beliefs and the mechanism of trust influence in the process of consumer response. The findings of the study will help manufacturers in the eye health product industry chain to design targeted product designs and marketing programs, and help to popularize the concept of eye health.

2 Theoretical Basis

2.1 Eye Health Products

There are three main types of eye health products on the market today: myopia correction device products, eye medicine products for the treatment of serious eyes, and eye care products that focus on relieving visual fatigue and preventing myopia. The subjects of this study are eye care products that can be freely purchased in the market. The current eye health products market is still an emerging market with huge market potential. However, the popularity and the consumer acceptance of the product is relatively low. The market has not yet formed a sound industry norms. During the COVID-19 pandemic, the emergence of online production lifestyles accelerated the integration of the eye health product market, traditionally sold offline, with the e-commerce business.

2.2 Theoretical Framework of SOR

Stimulus-organism-response (SOR) theory suggests that a stimulus may originate from an external situation, and the stimulated organism will develop a certain mental state. The organism undergoes a series of mental activities that result in a behavioral response to the stimulus. The SOR theory based on Environment Psychology suggests that consumers' purchase intentions are stimulated by product attributes and marketing behaviors, which in turn influence consumers' psychological emotions to products and purchase activities. Eventually triggering consumers' willingness and behavior to buy. In the framework of SOR theory, the psychological state of the organism in response to external stimuli plays a mediating role in the generation of the final behavioral response [2]. In the context of live e-commerce live broadcast for eye health products, based on the product characteristics of eye health products and the marketing stimulus of the anchor's words, it remains to be explored what psychological state consumers need to experience to achieve a response to the stimulus in order to purchase.

2.3 Health Beliefs

Health beliefs are a system of perceptions that individuals hold about preventing disease, maintaining health, and striving to achieve optimal living, i.e., the perceptions of healthy living that people adhere to in their daily lives. The traditional characteristics of health beliefs by Glanz K et al. (1997) include individuals' perceived barriers, perceived benefits, perceived susceptibility, perceived severity, self-efficacy, and health consciousness. Based on this, a study by Beibei Liu et al. [3] found that consumers' intention to purchase nutritious food is positively influenced by perceived susceptibility, perceived benefits, consumer self-efficacy, and health beliefs. Health beliefs also motivate individuals to adopt health-friendly behaviors.

2.4 Hofland's Model of Persuasion and Aristotle's Rhetorical Techniques

Hovland's persuasion theory points out the role of four elements, including persuader, persuasive content, audience, and persuasive situation, in influencing the effect of persuasion. Among them, the persuader is the main external stimulus in the persuasion process and can have an impact on the audience's attitude. In specific persuasive situations, the persuader can bring about a change in the audience's attitude through textual descriptions, and ultimately lead to a difference in their behavior [4]. In Aristotle's book Rhetoric, the linguistic features of persuasion are divided into three modes, namely: appeal to personality, appeal to logic, and appeal to emotion. The use of different linguistic expression features convey different emotions and produce different persuasive effects. In the e-commerce live broadcast context, hosts as persuaders, their verbal factors can be divided into professionalism, charm, authenticity, and uniqueness [5]. This study focuses on the verbal persuasion factors of hosts during e-commerce live streaming. The verbal factors of live e-commerce hosts for eye health products are distinguished into charisma, professionalism, and authenticity to investigate which verbal characteristics of e-commerce hosts are more influential on consumer attitudes.

2.5 Technology Acceptance Model, TAM

The TAM model was originally used to study the scenarios of users' use of information systems [8]. While with the advancement of technology and the increase of new products and technologies, the application of the model was gradually expanded. Scholars introduced external variables such as perceived usefulness and perceived ease of use to explore the acceptance process of individuals for different technologies. Min Zhang et al. [6] identified the positive effects of perceived usefulness and perceived reliability on consumers' willingness to purchase health technology products from the perspective of product and consumer characteristics. Unlike traditional brick-and-mortar shopping, consumers perceive stronger risks during product purchases through e-commerce platforms. A study by Gefen D et al. showed that consumer trust in e-commerce influences consumers' purchase intentions more than trust in technology acceptance models. More studies have explored the impact of product characteristics of new products on purchase intentions and have used trust as an antecedent and mediating variable affecting consumer purchase intentions. As a product with relatively low public acceptance and popularity, it is worthwhile to investigate what product features affect consumers' purchase intentions and through what paths. Thus, this study classifies the product characteristics of eye health products into perceived usefulness and perceived ease of use, which can trigger consumer trust and increase purchase intention.

3   Research Hypothesis and Research Model

3.1   Product Attributes, Consumer Trust and Purchase Intention

Davis F D. defined perceived usefulness as the degree to which people perceive an improvement in their performance through the use of some new technology or letter system. Perceived usefulness is one of the variables often used by scholars to measure cognitive and affective factors of consumers, and it has been shown that consumers' perceived usefulness is an important factor influencing their attitude towards online shopping and can affect their final decision [7]. In studies on the purchase intention of health products, scholars have defined perceived usefulness as the extent to which individuals believe that using health technology products will improve their health status [6]. Substituting the consumption scenario of eye health products, this study defines perceived usefulness as the degree to which individuals believe that using eye health products will improve their own eye health.

This led to the hypothesis that:

H1a: Perceived usefulness positively affects consumers' intention to purchase eye health products

Perceived ease of use refers to the degree to which users think it is easy to use a system. In this study, perceived ease of use is defined as the degree to which consumers think they can easily use eye health products. Generally, whether consumers can use the purchased products better or not will directly affect consumers' purchase intention. The research of Lin Chao qun et al. [8] shows that convenient and fast operation of shopping websites can improve consumers' willingness to buy agricultural products.

The following assumptions are proposed:

H2a: Perceived ease of use positively affects consumers' intention to buy eye health products

Trust can reduce the risk and uncertainty in the transaction process. In the e-commerce environment, consumers do not have access to physical objects, so their shopping has high risk, and they need to build trust between buyers and sellers to reduce the uncertainty of consumption. Based on TAM theory model, consumers will judge things from their own perceived usefulness and perceived ease of use, which will also profoundly affect consumer trust. Numerous studies have shown that the perceived characteristics and trust inspired by consumers in the process of participating in e-commerce do not exist separately, and both perceived usefulness and perceived ease of use have a significant positive impact on consumer trust [9]. This leads to the hypothesis that:

H1b: Perceived usefulness positively affects consumer trust
H2b: Perceived ease of use positively affects consumer trust.

3.2 Language Characteristics of E-Commerce Live Broadcast Hosts, Consumer Health Beliefs and Purchase Intentions

Unlike the traditional online marketing model, the host in the e-commerce live streaming context can eliminate the time and space barrier between consumers and play a stronger persuasive effect. In this context, the language characteristics of hosts have an important impact on stimulating consumers' purchase intentions. The study by Liu Fengjun et al. [10] classified the characteristics of online red live broadcast's information sources as credibility, professionalism, interactivity, and attractiveness. Pointing out that the professionalism and interactivity of online red live broadcast's information sources positively affect consumers' purchase intention. A study by Gong Ting et al. [5] found that the charisma and authenticity characteristics of the host's language can positively influence consumers' purchase intentions. In this study, the popularity and acceptance of eye health products in the current market are relatively low. The professional explanation of the e-commerce live broadcast host can make consumers understand the product information faster, reduce the time cost and risk perception, and promote the purchase intention. The host's words of the product function of the real transmission, reduce the online shopping information asymmetry, improve the practical value of the product, and stimulate customers to buy. Charismatic hosts share their emotions and feelings in the process of information exchange, and convey healthy living concepts to consumers, triggering their emotional resonance and thus stimulating purchase intentions. This leads to the hypothesis that:

H3a: The charismatic nature of the host's language positively affects consumers' intention to purchase eye health products
H4a: The professionalism of the host's language positively affects consumers' intentions to purchase eye health products
H5a: The authenticity of the host's language positively affects consumers' intention to purchase eye health products

In e-commerce live broadcast, the language style of appealing to personality refers to the host conveying reliable information about the product to consumers by using professional language, proper nouns and knowledge and other linguistic expressions [11], which can be analogous to the professionalism of the host's language; appealing to logic mainly refers to the persuader ensuring the clarity and authenticity of the delivered information through logical arguments, and this persuasion style can be reflected through the authenticity of the host's language; appealing to emotion means that the persuader influences people's rational judgment by evoking their emotions, and even makes the audience produce reverse incentive, i.e., stimulating the urgency of demand by creating fear [12]. This persuasion style can be reflected by the charm of the host's language. The process of introducing product information to consumers by hosts in the e-commerce live broadcast of eye health products is also the process of popularizing health knowledge to consumers, helping them to exclude false product information. The live broadcast with strong emotional information may even trigger consumers' anxiety about their own eye health, thus stimulating the generation of consumers' health beliefs. This leads to the hypothesis that:

H3b: The charismatic nature of the host's language positively affects consumers' health beliefs
H4b: The professionalism of the host's language positively affects consumers' health beliefs
H5b: The authenticity of the host's language positively affects consumers' health beliefs.

3.3 Influence of Consumer Health Beliefs and Consumer Trust on Purchase Intention

Among the studies related to health beliefs, Jiang et al. [13] investigated the mediating effect of health beliefs in the effect of online information support on HPV vaccination intention. A study by Min Zhang et al. [12]showed that health beliefs positively moderated the effect of perceived usefulness on the willingness to purchase health technology products. This led to the hypothesis that:

H6: Consumer health beliefs positively affect eye health product purchase intention

Many literatures have highlighted the importance of trust in consumers' willingness to purchase online. Jarvenpaa's [14]study verified the ability of trust to influence consumers' online shopping intentions regardless of the culture they live in. A study by Yuntian Xie et al. [15] showed that trust positively influences consumers' behavior in purchasing green agricultural products. Wang et al. [16] explored the positive influence of consumer trust between the attributes of e-commerce hosts and consumers' purchase intentions. This led to the hypothesis that:

H7: Consumer trust positively affects purchase intention of eye health products.

3.4 The Mediating Role of Consumer Health Beliefs and Consumer Trust

In the e-commerce live broadcast of eye health products, hosts with verbal charisma can mobilize consumers' emotions and may even stimulate consumers' health beliefs by creating fear in order to achieve marketing goals, causing consumers to become anxious about eye health, form health beliefs and then become willing to buy. The hosts show their professionalism by talking about proper nouns and conveying professional knowledge to educate the market, which can help consumers form health beliefs that lead to purchase intentions. By telling the truth about the product, the host removes distracting information, reduces perceived barriers, and stimulates consumer's health beliefs, which leads to purchase intentions. This leads to the hypothesis that:

H8a: Consumer health beliefs mediate between the charismatic nature of the host's language and intention to purchase eye health products
H8b: Consumer health beliefs mediate the relationship between the professionalism of the host's language and the intention to purchase eye health products
H8c: Consumer health beliefs mediate between the authenticity of the host's language and intention to purchase eye health products

Eye health products are perceived by consumers to improve and help their eye health, creating trust in the product and then stimulating their willingness to purchase. When consumers are introduced to eye health products, they can feel that they have the ability to learn quickly and use the product correctly, which creates trust in the product and stimulates willingness to buy. This leads to the hypothesis that:

H9a: Consumer trust mediates the relationship between the perceived usefulness of eye health products and the intention to purchase eye health products
H9b: Consumer trust mediates the relationship between perceived ease of use and intention to purchase eye health products (Fig. 1).

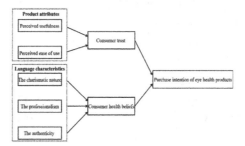

Fig. 1. Research model

4 Research Design

4.1 Samples and Data Collection

This study adopts the virtual scenario research method, in which the respondents are asked to read the research scenario first and then fill in the questionnaire. The survey was conducted on a group of college students aged 18–28. China's youth myopia rate is the highest in the world. According to the "China Eye Health White Paper" released by National Health Commission of the People's Republic of China in 2020, the overall prevalence of myopia among Chinese children and youth is 53.6%, and the overall prevalence among college students is over 90%. The eye health problems of college students are more prominent, and college students also have strong spending power, so it is representative to take college students as the main research target. The questionnaires of this study were selected and distributed within the WeChat groups of students in each school. 310 questionnaires were collected, and after excluding incomplete and regular questionnaires, 283 questionnaires were valid, with an efficiency rate of 91.3%. The following are the descriptive statistics of the sample.

The following are the descriptive statistics of the sample (Table 1).

Table 1. Sample characteristics

Variable	Indicator	Frequency	Percentage
Gender	Male	146	51.6
	Female	137	48.4
Age	<18	9	3.2
	18–28	262	92.6
	29–40	7	2.5
	>40	5	1.7
Education Level	Under the Bachelor-Degree Level	9	3.2
	Bachelor-Degree Level	269	95.1
	Master Degree Or Above	5	1.7
Feelings about eye health status	Very unhealthy	27	9.5
	Unhealthy	89	31.4
	Moderate	104	36.7
	Healthy	46	16.4
	Very healthy	17	6
Have you used eye health products	Yes	180	63.6
	No	103	36.4

4.2 Measurement Tools

Most of the constructs in the framework of this study were derived from existing studies, and some of them were modified and adjusted appropriately to fit the needs of the study. The perceived usefulness and perceived ease of use were based on the study by Davis F D. (1989), which included 6 items, and the scale was translated and adapted. The host language charisma referred to the study of Gong T. et al. [5] included a total of 3 items. The professionalism and authenticity of host language refer to Liu Fengjun et al.'s [10] study included a total of 6 items. Consumer trust reference Yang Q et al.'s (2015) study included a total of 2 items. Health beliefs refer to the study of Hojjati (2015) et al.

consisted of a total of 5 items. Purchase intentions refer to the scale developed by Dodds et al. (1991) consisted of 3 items. All questionnaire items were based on a 7-point Likert scale (7 = strongly agree and 1 = strongly disagree).

5 Data Analysis

5.1 Reliability and Validity

In our study, the questionnaire data were tested for reliability and validity using SPSS 28.0 and AMOS 28.0, and the test results are shown in Table 2. The reliability of the sample data was analyzed using Cronbach's alpha value and combined reliability (CR value), and the Cronbach's alpha values of each dimension of the variables were in the range of 0.778–0.902, and the results obtained were all greater than 0.700, indicating that the reliability of the scale meets the requirements; the CR values of each variable were in the range of 0.778–0.903, and the results obtained were all greater than 0.700, indicating that the scale's internal consistency is good, so the scale in our study has high reliability.

In our study, we drew on the established scales from domestic and international literature in designing the scale, and carried out the process of direct translation back translation and scenario transfer to ensure the semantic accuracy of the scale items. As the test results showed, the absolute values of the standardized loadings for each item were greater than 0.6 and showed significance, implying a good measurement relationship. All the AVE values corresponding to the total 8 factors were greater than 0.5, and all the CR values were higher than 0.7, implying that the data of this analysis had good convergent (convergent) validity.

5.2 Analysis Results

Results of Direct Effect. Our study used AMOS 28.0 to conduct multiple linear regression tests for direct effects, and the results showed that: perceived ease of use positively affected consumers' willingness to purchase eye health products ($\beta = 0.313, P < 0.01$) and positively affected consumers' trust ($\beta = 0.386, P < 0.01$), and hypotheses H1a and H1b were verified; perceived usefulness positively affected consumers' eye health product purchase intention ($\beta = 0.505, P < 0.01$) and positively affected consumer trust ($\beta = 0.431, P < 0.01$), hypotheses H2a and H2b were verified; the professionalism of e-commerce live broadcast host language positively affected consumer eye health product purchase intention ($\beta = 0.127, P < 0.01$) and positively affected consumer health beliefs ($\beta = 0.363, P < 0.01$), hypotheses H4a and H4b were verified; the authenticity of the language of the e-commerce live broadcast host positively affected consumers' willingness to purchase eye health products ($\beta = 0.666, P < 0.01$) and positively affected consumers' health beliefs ($\beta = 0.414, P < 0.01$), hypotheses H5a and H5b were verified; the charisma of the language of the e-commerce live broadcast host had no significant effect on consumers' willingness to purchase eye health product purchase intention was not significant ($\beta = 0.124, P > 0.05$), and the effect on consumer health beliefs was also not significant ($\beta = 0.042, P > 0.05$), and hypotheses H3a and H3b were not valid.

Table 2. The results of data's reliability and validity

Construct	Item	Loading	AVE	CR	Cronbach's alpha
Perceived usefulness	PU1	0.842	0.721	0.886	0.884
	PU2	0.848			
	PU3	0.857			
Perceived ease of use	PEU1	0.867	0.735	0.893	0.893
	PEU2	0.862			
	PEU3	0.843			
The charismatic nature	CHL1	0.781	0.648	0.846	0.848
	CHL2	0.795			
	CHL3	0.837			
The professionalism	PHL1	0.790	0.646	0.845	0.845
	PHL2	0.811			
	PHL3	0.809			
The authenticity	AHL1	0.802	0.684	0.866	0.863
	AHL2	0.848			
	AHL3	0.830			
Consumer trust	CT1	0.800	0.778	0.778	0.637
	CT2	0.796			
Consumer health beliefs	CHB1	0.686	0.854	0.857	0.546
	CHB2	0.807			
	CHB3	0.728			
	CHB4	0.748			
	CHB5	0.719			
Purchase intentions	PI1	0.862	0.902	0.903	0.755
	PI2	0.895			
	PI3	0.849			

Results of Moderation Effect. Our study used AMOS 28.0 to conduct multiple linear regression tests for mediating effects, and the results of the study showed that.

The effect of consumer trust on purchase intention was significant ($\beta = 0.631$, $p < 0.01$). After adding consumer trust, the effect of product usefulness on purchase intention decreases to 0.233, and this effect is significant and is partially mediated, indicating support for hypothesis H9a. After adding consumer trust, the effect of product ease of use on purchase intention decreases to 0.069, and this effect is not significant and is fully mediated, which does not support hypothesis H9b. The effect of consumer health beliefs on purchase intention was significant ($\beta = 0.382$, $p < 0.01$). After adding consumer health beliefs, the effect of professionalism of e-commerce live broadcast host language on purchase intention decreases to -0.012, and the effect is not significant, which is a full mediation, indicating support for hypothesis H9b; after adding consumer health beliefs, the effect of truthfulness of e-commerce live broadcast host language on purchase intention decreases to 0.508, and the effect is significant, which is a partial mediation, indicating support for hypothesis H8c. After adding consumer health beliefs, the effect of The charismatic nature of e-commerce live broadcast host language on purchase intention decreases to 0.108, and this effect is not significant, leading to insignificant mediation, which does not support hypothesis H9a.

6 Discussion

Based on SOR theory, TAM theory, health belief theory and persuasion theory, this study explored the path model affecting the purchase intention of eye health products in terms of product attributes and the amount of linguistic features of e-commerce hosts. The following conclusions were obtained: First, Product perceived usefulness and perceived ease of use positively affect consumers' purchase intention and consumer trust. The professionalism and authenticity of the language of the e-commerce live broadcast broadcast hosts positively affected consumers' purchase intention and consumers' health beliefs. However, the influence of the charm of the language of the e-commerce hosts on consumers' purchase intention, and the influence on consumers' health beliefs was not significant. Second, Consumer health beliefs and trust are important bridges between the characteristics of eye health products and the language characteristics of hosts to influence consumers' purchase intentions. In the process of live-streaming eye health products, the hosts' professional and authentic words can enhance consumers' health beliefs and make them willing to purchase their recommended products. The perceived usefulness and perceived ease of use of eye health products promote consumer trust, which leads to the willingness to purchase the products. The study also confirms that the charismatic nature of the host's language in the live broadcast does not influence health beliefs that lead to consumers' purchase intentions (Fig. 2).

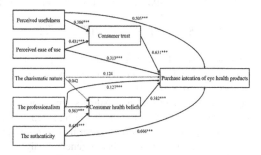

Fig. 2. Hypothesis testing results

Our study has some theoretical contributions. First, This paper takes eye health products, a product with low popularity and acceptance, as the research object, and enriches the research on health products and e-commerce live broadcast marketing. Second, our paper innovatively combines health beliefs and persuasion theories to explore the psychological mechanisms of consumers when making live e-commerce consumption decisions. Most of the previous studies on the purchase intention of health products have not studied consumers' health beliefs as the antecedent of external stimuli, but this paper combines this psychological concept with marketing theory to broaden the application area of health belief theory.

In terms of practical value, eye health products are undergoing a transition from offline sales to online sales, and live e-commerce has provided a new boost to the development of this industry. This study can provide theoretical support for the industrial transformation of eye health product merchants. The research on product attributes and language characteristics of live e-commerce hosts can provide a basis for product design of manufacturers and marketing strategy design of distributors in the industry chain.

This paper also has certain limitations. First, our research method is relatively single and has limitations. This paper only uses the questionnaire method for analysis, and future research can be further explored by combining experimental methods. Second, consumer purchasing behavior is a complex process, there may be other variables besides health beliefs and trust that influence purchasing behavior, and further research can be conducted on more individual consumer emotions in the future.

References

1. Li, C., Bi, X., Wang, Y.: The psychological mechanisms of personal health information management technologies for promoting users' health behavior: an empirical study based on smart wearable health products. Libr. Inf. Serv. **65**(19), 72–83 (2021). https://doi.org/10.13266/j.issn.0252-3116.2021.19.008
2. Wu, M., Li, S.: The inducing mechanisms of supplier innovation contribution in triadic sourcing context. Nankai Bus. Rev. **25**(02), 113–125 (2022)
3. Liu, B., Zhang, F., Cheng, L., Zhang, X.: Influencing factors of consumer nutritional food choice: based on an expanded model of health beliefs. J. Cent. China Normal Univ. (Nat. Sci.) **56**(06), 1074–1084 (2022). https://doi.org/10.19603/j.cnki.1000-1190.2022.06.019
4. 王伟, 陈伟, 祝效国, 王洪伟: 众筹融资成功率与语言风格的说服性——基于Kickstarter 的实证研究. 管理世界 **272**(05), 81–98 (2016). https://doi.org/10.19744/j.cnki.11-1235/f.2016.05.008
5. 龚婷, 周瑞芳, 郑明贵: 带货主播语言行为特征与消费者购买意愿关系分析. 商业经济研究 (18), 57–60 (2022)
6. Zhang, M., Luo, M., Nie, R.: Research on the purchase intention of health-technology products from the perspectives of product and consumer characteristics. Soft Sci. **31**(05), 94–98 (2017). https://doi.org/10.13956/j.ss.1001-8409.2017.05.21
7. Kao, T.D.: The impact of transaction trust on consumers' intentions to adopt M-commerce: a cross-cultural investigation. CyberPsychology Behav. **12**(2), 225–229 (2009)
8. Lin, C., Yu, H.: The influence of E-commerce platform promotion characteristics on the purchase intention of agricultural products: the heterogeneity analysis of promotion type. J. Commer. Econ. (08), 98–101 (2022)
9. Yu, K.Z., Song, Z.: An examination of the relationship between trust, TAM and online shopping. Theory Pract. Finance Econ. **26**(5), 5 (2005)
10. Fengjun, L., Meng, L., Siyun, C., Shen, D.: The impact of network celebrities' information source characteristics on purchase intention. Chin. J. Manag. **17**(01), 94–104 (2020)

11. Li, G., Zhang, Q.: Research on the influence mechanism of language characteristics on product sales in the context of E-commerce live broadcast. J. Commer. Econ. **847**(12), 77–80 (2022)
12. Qi, T., Liu, Q., Wang, T., Zhou, X.: The persuasive effect of linguistic styles in the description of paying for knowledge product-the moderating effect of knowledge producer's reputation. Nankai Bus. Rev. **23**(05), 159–170 (2020)
13. 蒋晓丽, 钟棣冰: 在线信息支持会增强HPV疫苗接种意愿吗?一个基于健康信念的中介模型. 新闻与写作 **453**(03), 79–88 (2022)
14. Jarvenpaa, S.L., et al.: Consumer trust in an internet store: a cross-cultural validation. J. Comput. Mediated Commun. **5**(2), JCMC526 (1999)
15. Xie, Y., Liu, L., Wang, X., Chen, C.: A study on the willingness of green agricultural products in the context of supply side reform: taking Zhangjiakou city as an example. Ecol. Econ. **34**(3), 5 (2018)
16. Wang, J., Wu, Y., Wang, Q., Li, J.: Esearch on the relationship between E-commerce anchor attributes, consumer trust and purchase intention—the moderating effect based on commodity price and reputation of e-commerce platform. Price Theory Pract. **450**(12), 151–154 (2021). https://doi.org/10.19851/j.cnki.CN11-1010/F.2021.12.469

Price and Service Decisions in a Joint Product Network Under Demand Uncertainty

Jiyuan Yu[1], Jun Ma[2(✉)], Yiming Jiang[3], and Yiliu (Paul) Tu[4]

[1] Tippie College of Business, University of Iowa, Iowa, IA 52242, USA
[2] Department of Business Technology Management, University of Calgary, Calgary, AB T2N 1N4, Canada
mjjun77@gmail.com
[3] School of Management, Shenyang University of Technology, Shenyang 110870, Liaoning, China
[4] Department of Mechanical and Manufacturing Engineering, University of Calgary, AB T2N 1N4, Canada

Abstract. This paper develops a stochastic equilibrium model for a joint product network under customer stockout aversion. The model is addressed in a two-echelon network topology where the producers simultaneously determine outputs and retail prices of joint products. Three features of our model are worth stressing: First, the model focuses on the pricing and output decisions of a joint product network. Joint pricing mode has been used to optimize the benefit of joint product supply chains. Second, the classical newsvendor model assumes unmet demand is lost. This assumption implies that customers are stockout neutral. In practice, it is usually unacceptable for firms to thoroughly lose the unmet demand. Considering the uncertain demand that depends on both price and service level, we introduce discrete choice models to characterize customer choice behaviors by assuming that customers are stockout aversion. Third, newsvendor model-based variational inequalities are used to formulate the equilibrium condition for a joint product network.

Keywords: Supply Chain Network Management · Joint Product · Network Equilibrium Model · Variational Inequality · Newsvendor Model

1 Introduction

The classical newsvendor model assumes unmet demand is lost (Petruzzi & Dada, 1999). Its assumption implies that customers are stockout neutral. In practice, it is usually unacceptable for firms to thoroughly lose the unmet demand, because those unsatisfied customers will attempt to purchase from their competitors (Feng & Zhang, 2017), even will not be back anymore. This study devotes to the inter supply chain competition, in which each firm in a supply chain maximizes the profits (or expected profits) and optimizes the probability of customers choosing a joint product, which depends on selling price and service level. The customers are assumed to be stockout aversion. We design

© The Author(s), under exclusive license to Springer Nature Switzerland AG 2023
Y. Tu and M. Chi (Eds.): WHICEB 2023, LNBIP 481, pp. 60–70, 2023.
https://doi.org/10.1007/978-3-031-32302-7_6

a two-echelon supply chain network of joint products, including raw material suppliers and joint product producers. Our results attempt to answer the following questions based on that customers are stockout aversion. "How are the firms' equilibria under affected by joint production under demand uncertainty?" and "How is the effect of the variance of demand fluctuation and customers service preference on the equilibria."

The demand uncertainty of one of joint products often impacts the demands and prices, even the cost of other joint products. The moderate cost of one of joint products affects the demands of the markets of chlorine and caustic soda in Canada (Shastitko & Shastitko, 2015). The price of soybean meal is influenced not only by the supply of soybean and the demand of soybean meal, but also by the demand of soybean oil. These phenomena are also quite common in petroleum refining industry (Griffin, 1972). The inconsistency of supply and demand fluctuation in the joint products markets causes dramatic waste and loss, specifically petroleum and perishable products. The newsvendor model is a common tool for uncertain demand, including known and unknown demand distributions (Lariviere & Porteus, 1999). Most literature focuses on the analysis of the impact on the production output of uncertain demand. However, they ignore it can influence the production cost, even the retail pricing (Granot & Yin, 2008). Moreover, the classical newsvendor model assumes unmet demand is lost (Petruzzi & Dada, 1999). Hence, some companies often decrease the sales of one of joint products or limit materials procurement to keep the sales of other joint products stable in practice (Shastitko & Shastitko, 2015). The common method in literature is to adopt a single penalty cost to offset the loss in the newsvendor model (Deng et al., 2014). This remains an issue in joint products that has not been considered in a setting with a supply chain network formed by two or more competing joint product supply chains. A main contribution to the literature and practice is a stochastic equilibrium decision for the joint product supply chains where customers are stockout aversion so as to reduce waste and loss. The energy savings potential for the only petroleum industry can be huge (Liu et al., 2013).

To our knowledge, our study first bridges joint product supply chains with a network equilibrium model under demand uncertainty. Special attention is given to the scenario where the producers' products are joint. On the one hand, the supply and demand of one of joint products jointly affect the supplies and demands of other joint products. On the other hand, the demand fluctuation of one of joint products brings additional surplus (inventory) risk for other joint products because of joint production. The interaction effect of supply-demand of joint products can offset the impact of commodity demands' augment by customers. Consequently, the profits of joint products in producers or retailers cannot be maximized in isolation. This also requires new methods because of the interaction effect of the supply-demand of joint products. In this study, a network equilibrium model incorporated with customer choice behavior is applied to optimize firms' decisions under inter supply chain competition of joint product setting. Integrating network equilibrium models with discrete choice models is a challenge with dimensionality augment. If customers consider more than two dimensions in their purchasing behavior in the model, the equilibrium conditions will be complicated, and computational speed will decrease exponentially. Therefore, customers are assumed to consider retail price and service level in their purchasing decision in the proposed model. Based on the equilibrium solutions, we can understand how various factors, such as competition, technology, and other joint products' supply-demand, influence the joint product flows among the supply chains, retail pricing, and surplus. Some valuable insights have been obtained from our proposed model. These results could potentially provide implications for governments and companies in making strategic decisions and policies, specifically for some industries that their demand is uncertain and the service level is a crucial factor on customer purchase behavior.

2 Model

2.1 Definitions and Assumptions

We develop a network equilibrium model for joint products under customer stockout aversion. The risk of demand is captured through the variance of demand fluctuation. We design a two-echelon joint product network constituted with suppliers and producers. Consider I joint products being produced by producer m, $m \in \{1, \cdots, M\}$ in a joint product network. Each producer purchases materials from supplier n, $n \in \{1, \cdots, N\}$ and sells end joint products to demand markets k, $k \in \{1, \cdots, K\}$. The market demands are uncertain, which is affected by many factors, including such things as weather, transportation, politics, and traffic accidents. The suppliers and producers are set to compete in a noncooperative fashion. In our model, we consider a fixed production ratio, and the range of the ratio fluctuation can be treated as a measure of producer m's technology, for example production line flexibility. Let γ_m^i denote the ratio of producer m producing joint product i. Then, if the output of one of joint products is decided, we can obtain other joint products' output,

$$q_{mk}^i = \frac{\gamma_m^i}{\gamma_m^j} \cdot q_{mk}^j, \forall i \neq j, \forall m. \tag{1}$$

2.2 Suppliers' Optimality Conditions

Each supplier makes decisions by controlling wholesale price p_{nm} and output q_{nm} to go for profit maximization, $(p_{nm}, q_{nm}) := argmax \, \pi_n(p_{nm}, q_{nm})$, where π_n is the profit function of supplier n. The output of supplier n is equal to the flows that supplier n delivers to all producers (Eq. (2)). Suppose supplier n has its production cost function f_n.

$$Q_n = \sum_{m=1}^{M} q_{nm}, \tag{2}$$

$$f_n = f_n(Q_n), \forall n. \tag{3}$$

Therefore, the optimization problem of supplier n can be formulated as function (4) that the revenue supplier n earned as a raw material provider minuses the production cost.

$$\max \sum_{m=1}^{M} p_{nm} \cdot q_{nm} - f_n(Q_n), \tag{4}$$

$$q_{nm} \geq 0, p_{nm} \geq 0, \forall n, m. \tag{5}$$

It is assumed that suppliers' production cost functions are continuous and convex. Therefore, the optimization function (4) for all suppliers constrained by function (5) can be further written as variational inequality (6) (Nash, 1950; Nash, 1951; Lions and Stampacchia, 1967; Nagurney and Dong, 2002; Nagurney, 2013).

$$\sum_{n=1}^{N} \sum_{m=1}^{M} \left[\frac{\partial f_n(q_n^*)}{\partial q_{nm}} - p_{nm} \right] \times \left[q_{nm} - q_{nm}^* \right] + \sum_{n=1}^{N} \sum_{m=1}^{M} \left[-q_{nm} \right] \times \left[p_{nm} - p_{nm}^* \right] \geq 0, \tag{6}$$
$$\forall q_{nm} \in R_+^{NM}.$$

where $\Omega = \{q_{nm} \geq 0, p_{nm} \geq 0\}$ is the feasible set of joint product suppliers' decision variables.

2.3 Producers' Optimality Conditions

Here, producer m makes its production decision and pricing of joint products, which is denoted by q_{mk}^i and p_{mk}^i. In the model, two decision variables are adopted by the producer to optimize its expected profit: (i) via retail price to match supply and demand and (ii) via its output (q_{mk}^i) to satisfy the uncertainty demand and influence the service level. The unsold products may bring back additional overage costs. Note that γ_m^i quantifies the ratios of the raw material is produced into joint products in the joint-production process. We assume that every producer goes for expected profit maximization by controlling retail price and output, $(p_{mk}^i, q_{mk}^i) := argmax\, \pi_m(p_{mk}^i, q_{mk}^i)$, where π_m is the expected profit function of producer m. If market demands are elastic price functions, and $I = 1$ (assembly supply chains), this model will become a classical network equilibrium model provided by Nagurney, Dong, et al. (2002).

The transaction cost of producers includes such things as production cost, transportation cost, discarding cost, and insurance. For security consideration, each producer purchases insurance from insurance companies. For example, in petroleum supply chains, producers purchase insurance from such banks as ING Bank, Royal Bank of Scotland, and Standard Chartered Bank. The total cost $\bar{c}_{mk}^i$ of joint product i between producer m and demand market k is combined with transaction cost tc_{mk}^i and allocated split-off cost $sc_m \cdot \theta_i$. Let c_{mk}^i denotes the marginal cost of joint product i between producer m and demand market k. The cost function of joint product i between producer m and demand market k is given by:

$$\bar{c}_{mk}^i = tc_{mk}^i + sc_m \cdot \theta_i, \forall m, k, i. \tag{7}$$

We utilize a multinomial logit function to model customer choice behavior purchasing joint products in a supply chain. In our model, price p^i and service level s^i of joint product i are two decision variables affected customers' choice behavior. The customer utility function choosing joint product i is given by the following:

$$U\left(p_{mk}^i, s_{mk}^i\right) = w^i - \alpha^i \cdot p_{mk}^i + \beta^i \cdot s_{mk}^i + \epsilon^i, \forall i \in I. \tag{8}$$

where w^i, α^i and β^i represent the intrinsic customer valuation, customer price and service preference coefficient of joint product i, respectively. The demand depends on the selling price and service level of the same joint products provided by all producers. Let N_k denotes the total customers mass at demand market k, and $P(U(i))$ represents the probability of customers choose joint product i of producer m at demand market k. According to the multinomial logit model, the probability of customers choosing joint product i of manufacturer m at demand market k can be listed as follows:

$$P(U(i)) = \frac{e^{U\left(p^i_{mk},s^i_{mk}\right)}}{1 + \sum\limits_{m=1}^{M} e^{U\left(p^i_{mk},s^i_{mk}\right)}} \tag{9}$$

Let D^i_{mk} denotes the true demand of joint product i from manufacturer m at demand market k. The demand of joint product i at the demand market k is described by the general and continuous cumulative probability distribution function (cdf) $F^i_{mk}(\cdot|p, s)$. Let $f^i_{mk}(\cdot|p, s)$ denote the probability density function of demand of joint product i at market k.

$$F^i_{mk}(\cdot|p, s) = F^i_{mk}\left(D^i_{mk} \leq N_k \cdot P^i_{mk}\right) = \int_0^{N_k \cdot P^i_{mk}} f^i_{mk}(\cdot|p, s)d_{D^i_{mk}}. \tag{10}$$

We assume that the uncertain demand follows a general, but known, continuous distribution, for example, normal and uniform distribution. Assuming that unsold joint products (surplus) in this selling season will bring back overage cost, and there is no shortage cost. Therefore, the service level s^i in this model is defined as the probability of the output of joint product i satisfying the random demand in a selling season, which is defined as α-service level in Schneider (1981).

The cost of joint products in a producer includes such things as the split-off cost of producers, transportation cost, insurance, and overage cost. Let cv^i_{mk} and v^i_{mk} denote the overage cost and expected surplus (inventory) of joint product i between producer m and demand market k. The expected surplus v^i_{mk} is the difference between the optimal output and expected demand. Each producer goes for expected profit maximization considering uncertain demands. Then, each producer has the following flow conservation,

$$N_k \cdot P(U(i)) + v^i_{mk} = q^{i*}_{mk}, ifp^i_{mk} > 0, \forall m, k, i. \tag{11}$$

Hence, the service level s^i in the model can be given as, $s^i_{mk} = \int_\omega^{q^i_{mk}} f(\cdot|p, s)d_{D^i_{mk}}$. Then the producers' optimization problem is to control selling price p^i_{mk} and service level s^i_{mk} to optimize the following expected profit functions. Based on the newsvendor model, the expected profit of producer m can be formulated by the difference between the price multiplied by the demand and the cost of raw material, overage, split-off, and transaction:

$$\begin{aligned}
max \sum_{k=1}^{K}\sum_{i=1}^{I}\int_0^{q^i_{mk}}\left(p^i_{mk} - c^i_{mk}\right)\cdot D^i_{mk}\cdot f^i_{mk}(\cdot|p, s)d_{D^i_{mk}} + \sum_{k=1}^{K}\sum_{i=1}^{I}\int_{q^i_{mk}}^{+\infty}\left(p^i_{mk} - c^i_{mk}\right)\cdot q^i_{mk}\cdot \\
f^i_{mk}(\cdot|p, s)d_{D^i_{mk}} - \sum_{k=1}^{K}\sum_{i=1}^{I}\int_{q^i_{mk}}^{+\infty} cv^i_{mk}\cdot\left(q^i_{mk} - D^i_{mk}\right)\cdot f^i_{mk}(\cdot|p, s)d_{D^i_{mk}} - \sum_{n=1}^{N} p_{nm}\cdot q_{nm},
\end{aligned} \tag{12}$$

$$s.t. \sum_{i=1}^{I} q_{mk}^i \le q_{nm} \cdot \varphi_m, \, q_{mk}^i \ge 0, \, p_{mk}^i \ge 0, \, \forall m, k, i. \tag{13}$$

where φ_m is the absorption coefficient (Erengüç et al., 1999). In this expression, the difference between the first and fourth items is the expected revenue of producer m, when the equilibrium outputs are above demands. The third item is the expected overage cost.

It is assumed that the cost function for each producer is continuous and convex. The equilibrium solutions of each producer reflect the stochastic equilibrium conditions that no customer can unilaterally improve their perceived utility, and no producer can unilaterally improve its expected profit. That is, $\left(q_{mk}^{i*}, p_{mk}^{i*}\right) \in$ arg max $U_m\left(q_{mk}^i, p_{mk}^i, D_{mk}^i\right), \forall x_{mk}^{i*} \in x_{mk}^i, \forall p_{mk}^{i*} \in p_{mk}^i$. If the quantitative or physical unit method is adopted as the cost allocations method of joint products, the optimization function (12) and the constrains (13) for all producers can be written as variational inequality (14) (Nash, 1950; Nash, 1951; Lions and Stampacchia, 1967; Nagurney and Dong, 2002; Nagurney, 2013).

$$\sum_{m=1}^{M} \sum_{k=1}^{K} \sum_{i=1}^{I} \left[c_{mk}^i - p_{mk}^i + \left(p_{mk}^i - c_{mk}^i + cv_{mk}^i \right) \cdot F_{mk}^i(\cdot|p, s) + \lambda_m + \delta_m^i \right] \times \left[v_{mk}^i - v_{mk}^{i*} \right] +$$
$$\sum_{m=1}^{M} \sum_{k=1}^{K} \sum_{i=1}^{I} \left[\left(c_{mk}^i - p_{mk}^i \right) \cdot N_k \cdot \frac{\partial P(i)}{\partial p_{mk}^{i*}} - N_k \cdot P_{mk}^i - \int_0^{q_{mk}^i} D_{mk}^i \cdot f_{mk}^i(\cdot|p, s) d_{D_{mk}^i} - v_{mk}^i + v_{mk}^i \cdot \right.$$
$$F_{mk}^i(\cdot|p, s) \bigg] \times \left[p_{mk}^i - p_{mk}^{i*} \right] + \sum_{m=1}^{M} \left[\sum_{i=1}^{I} \sum_{k=1}^{K} q_{mk}^i - q_{nm} \cdot \varphi_m \right] \times \left[\lambda_m - \lambda_m^* \right] + \tag{14}$$
$$\sum_{m=1}^{M} \sum_{k=1}^{K} \sum_{i=1}^{I} \left[q_{mk}^i - \frac{\gamma_{im}}{\gamma_{jm}} \cdot q_{mk}^i \right] \times \left[\delta_m^i - \delta_m^{i*} \right] + \sum_{n=1}^{N} \sum_{m=1}^{M} \left[q_{nm} \right] \times \left[p_{nm} - p_{nm}^* \right] +$$
$$\sum_{n=1}^{N} \sum_{m=1}^{M} \left[p_{nm} - \lambda_m \cdot \varphi_m \right] \times \left[q_{nm} - q_{nm}^* \right] \ge 0,$$

where $\Omega = \left\{ v_{mk}^i \ge 0, p_{mk}^i \ge 0 \right\}$ is the feasible set of joint product producers' decision variables. The term λ_m and δ_m^i are the Lagrange multiplier for producer m associated with constraint (1) and (13), respectively. According to KKT conditions, if q_{mk}^{i*} and p_{mk}^{i*} are the solutions of maximization problem (12), then there exist unique scalars λ_m for $m \in M$ and δ_m^i for $m \in M$, $i \in I$. The economic interpretations of Lagrange multiplier are revealed in much literature (see, Nagurney & Dong, 2002).

The equilibrium conditions in the entire joint product network must satisfy the sum of the variational inequalities (6) and (14). Therefore, considering the joint product flows conservation, the equilibrium conditions of the entire joint product network can be stated as a newsvendor model-based variational inequality formulation based on variational inequality theory.

$$\sum_{m=1}^{M} \sum_{k=1}^{K} \sum_{i=1}^{I} \left[c_{mk}^i - p_{mk}^i + \left(p_{mk}^i - c_{mk}^i + cv_{mk}^i \right) \cdot F_{mk}^i(\cdot|p, s) - \lambda_m - \delta_m^i \right] \times \left[v_{mk}^i - v_{mk}^{i*} \right] +$$
$$\sum_{m=1}^{M} \sum_{k=1}^{K} \sum_{i=1}^{I} \left[\left(c_{mk}^i - p_{mk}^i \right) \cdot N_k \cdot \frac{\partial p_{mk}^i}{\partial p_{mk}^{i*}} - N_k \cdot P_{mk}^i - \int_0^{q_{mk}^i} D_{mk}^i \cdot f_{mk}^i(\cdot|p, s) d_{D_{mk}^i} - v_{mk}^i + v_{mk}^i \cdot \right.$$
$$F_{mk}^i(\cdot|p, s) \bigg] \times \left[p_{mk}^i - p_{mk}^{i*} \right] + \sum_{m=1}^{M} \left[\sum_{i=1}^{I} \sum_{k=1}^{K} q_{mk}^i - q_{nm} \cdot \varphi_m \right] \times \left[\lambda_m - \lambda_m^* \right] + \tag{15}$$
$$\sum_{m=1}^{M} \sum_{k=1}^{K} \sum_{i=1}^{I} \left[q_{mk}^i - \frac{\gamma_{im}}{\gamma_{jm}} \cdot q_{mk}^i \right] \times \left[\delta_m^i - \delta_m^{i*} \right] + \sum_{n=1}^{N} \sum_{m=1}^{M} \left[\frac{\partial f_n(q_n^*)}{\partial q_{nm}} - \lambda_m \cdot \varphi_m \right] \times \left[q_{nm} - q_{nm}^* \right] \ge 0$$

where $\Omega = \{q_{nm} \geq 0, v_{mk}^i \geq 0, p_{mk}^i \geq 0\}$ is the feasible set of joint product suppliers' and producers' decision variables and λ_m and δ_m^i are the Lagrange multiplier for producer m associated with constraint (1) and (13), respectively. Variational inequality (15) also characterizes the stochastic equilibrium defined in Sect. 3.

3 A Numerical Example

In this example, we design a two-echelon dairy network topology. There are two dairy producers and two retailers in two markets (butter and cheese demand markets), respectively. The two dairy producers produce butter and cheese, which are substitutable and sold in these markets separately. The number of customers in both markets is $N_1 = N_2 = 1000$. Both producers provide logistic services in two demand markets. Suppose the demands of the butter and cheese are not correlated with each other. The joint cost allocation after the split-off point they used is the quantitative or physical unit method. The cost data of the dairy network are listed in Table 1. The output ratios (γ) of the butter and cheese after the split-off point are 0.107:0.103 for producer 1 and 0.105:0.101 for producer 2. The absorption coefficients are 0.21 and 0.206 for producer 1 and producer 2, respectively. The overage cost in $cv_{11}^1 = 1$, $cv_{21}^1 = 1$, $cv_{12}^2 = 1$, and $cv_{22}^2 = 1$. Considering two different scenarios, each scenario has special issues, including technology update, service level improvement, and inventory management. The customer utility function of joint product i as follows:

$$U\left(p^i, s^i\right) = w^i - \alpha^i \cdot p^i + \beta^i \cdot s^i + \epsilon^i, i = 1, 2,$$

where the intrinsic customer valuation $w^i, i = 1, 2$, the customer price and service preference coefficients $\alpha^i, i = 1, 2$, and $\beta^i, i = 1, 2$ follow a Normal distribution, $w^1 = N\left(9, 1^2\right)$, $w^2 = N\left(6, 1^2\right)$, $\alpha^1 = N\left(0.5, 0.1^2\right)$, $\alpha^2 = N\left(0.5, 0.1^2\right)$, $\beta^1 = N\left(0.3, 0.08^2\right)$, and $\beta^2 = N\left(0.3, 0.08^2\right)$. Ma et al. (2020) elaborated a method to estimate the parameters in customer utility function from the customers' sales record using maximum-likelihood estimation (MLE), respectively (Fig. 1).

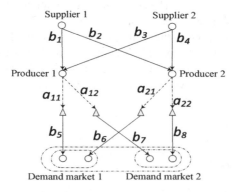

Fig. 1. The dairy network topology.

Table 1. Link cost functions in the dairy network.

Cost function	Cost function
$tc_{b1} = 0.15x_{b1} + 0.000045x_{b1}^2$	$tc_{b3} = 0.2x_{b3} + 0.000045x_{b3}^2$
$tc_{b2} = 0.15x_{b1} + 0.000032x_{b2}^2$	$tc_{b4} = 0.1x_{b3} + 0.000032x_{b4}^2$
$tc_{b5} = 2.8x_{b5} + 70$	$tc_{b6} = 3.0x_{b6} + 70$
$tc_{b7} = 2.2x_{b7} + 60$	$tc_{b8} = 2.0x_{b8} + 60$
$sc_{a1} = 2.05(x_{b1} + x_{b3}) + 60$	$sc_{a2} = 2(x_{b2} + x_{b4}) + 60$

Considering each scenario's particularity, we utilize the parameters in Table 1 to compute the equilibrium solutions. Following this, the outputs, prices and expected surpluses yielded by the modified projection method in two demand markets at the equilibrium pattern can be found. Based on the equilibrium solutions, the profits of SC_{11}, SC_{21}, SC_{12}, and SC_{22} are also provided in Table 2.

Scenario 1: The variances of demand distributions of joint product 1 and 2 in this scenario are given as: $\sigma_1^2 = 50^2$ and $\sigma_2^2 = 50^2$. The equilibrium solutions, including equilibrium prices, flows, service level, and expected profits, are reported in Table 2. Due to the need of the service level sensitive customers, there necessarily exists butter and cheese surplus in producer 1 and producer 2 in this scenario.

Scenario 2: Recalling that the output ratio γ can be treated as a measure of producers' technology. The decision maker in producer 2 intends to improve the output ratios of butter and cheese from 0.105:0.101 to 0.108:0.106 and the absorption coefficients from 0.206 to 0.214, respectively. A higher cost is charged for the new technology resulting in the new output ratios of butter and cheese. The new split-off cost function of producer 2 become:

$$sc_{a2} = 2.08(x_{b2} + x_{b4}) + 60$$

As the split-off cost becomes higher on link a_2 than before, the equilibrium flows, profits, and selling prices on path SC_{21} and SC_{22} change largely. Although the equilibrium flows on supply chain SC_{22} increases due to the variation of output ratios, the service levels and the expected profits of supply chain SC_{21} and SC_{22} decrease because of the higher the split-off cost of butter and cheese. It is worth to note that selling prices and service levels on path SC_{21} and SC_{22} change inversely, because of the selection of the cost allocations of joint products. Although only producer 2 improves its output ratios of butter and cheese, the expected profits of supply chain SC_{11} and SC_{12} increase from the selection of producer 2's new technology because of competition.

We find the variance of demand distribution σ^2 and the customer service preference coefficient β are key parameters to affect the fluctuations of the equilibrium solutions, including equilibrium flows, prices, service level, and expected surplus. To better discuss and analyze the impact of the variance of demand, we assume that the variance σ^2 of demand distribution and customers service preference coefficient β of joint product 1 vary from 40^2 to 50^2 and 0.31 to 0.40, respectively. The sensitivity of equilibrium prices, outputs, service level, expected surpluses, and in demand markets are depicted as

Table 2. Equilibrium solutions to Scenario 1–2. ($\rho = 0.001, \varepsilon = 0.0001$)

	Scenario 1 ($\sigma_1^2 = 50^2, \sigma_2^2 = 50^2$)	Scenario 2 ($\sigma_1^2 = 50^2, \sigma_2^2 = 50^2$)
x_{b1}	2826.06	2777.31
x_{b2}	2316.53	2209.48
x_{b3}	2260.85	2221.85
x_{b4}	3088.71	2945.98
x_{a11}	544.30	534.91
x_{a21}	567.55	556.79
x_{a12}	523.96	539.90
x_{a22}	545.94	562.10
x_{b5}	488.50	488.88
x_{b6}	507.74	505.99
x_{b7}	466.84	471.85
x_{b8}	489.77	495.26
p_{11}	8.79	9.38
p_{21}	8.72	9.33
p_{12}	7.77	7.22
p_{22}	7.67	6.97
s_1	86.78%	82.14%
s_2	88.42%	84.52%
s_3	87.34%	91.32%
s_4	86.94%	90.94%
π_{sc11}	2,105.3	2421.0
π_{sc21}	2,890.7	2294.2
π_{sc12}	2,341.7	2706.6
π_{sc22}	3,058.2	2638.1

in sensitivity analysis. We analyze the impact of the variance σ^2 of demand distribution and customer service preference coefficient β on the equilibrium prices, outputs, and service level and get some meaningful observations from the sensitivity analysis.

4 Conclusions

Stockout aversion customer behavior has overly been ignored in newsvendor problems. This paper fills the gap from several perspectives in the risk management of the joint product network: (1) In our model, the producer's products are joint. The proposed model and computational framework are widely applicable in joint product network management.

The model can be used to deal with competition between joint product supply chains and optimize the profit of joint products' producers and providers, for example, petroleum refining firms in petroleum supply chains, coal producers in coal supply chains, and dairy producers in dairy supply chains. (2) An assumption is generalized and relaxed by incorporating customer choice behavior into the joint product network. The assumption that customers are stockout aversion is adopted in our model. Service level (α-type service level) is a key influence factor on customers purchasing behavior. In practice, many industries that customers are stockout aversion may employ this network equilibrium model to optimize the profit and service level. Based on the above assumption, our analytical and numerical analyses reveal the effects of the variance of uncertain demand and customer preference coefficient on the equilibrium solutions of the joint product network. These findings may provide valuable insights to the producers, retailers, and 3PLs in a supply chain network when adjusting their strategies, including risk control and customer service management. (3) Behavior-based market analysis models that currently worked as intelligent business tools in some internet companies can easily connect with supply chains. Introducing customer choice behavior into a supply chain network is also an attempt to connect intelligent business and supply chain management. This model may seamlessly and efficiently connect with the behavior-based market analysis models and intelligent business.

References

Petruzzi, N.C., Dada, M.: Pricing and the newsvendor problem: a review with extensions. Oper. Res. **47**(2), 183–194 (1999)

Feng, T., Zhang, Y.: Modeling strategic behavior in the competitive newsvendor problem: an experimental investigation. Prod. Oper. Manag. **26**(7), 1383–1398 (2017)

Shastitko, A., Shastitko, A.: Markets of joint products: a theoretical model and policy implications. Russ. J. Econ. **1**(2), 199–216 (2015)

Griffin, J.M.: The process analysis alternative to statistical cost functions: an application to petroleum refining. Am. Econ. Rev. **62**(1/2), 46–56 (1972)

Lariviere, M.A., Porteus, E.L.: Stalking information: Bayesian inventory management with unobserved lost sales. Manag. Sci. **45**(3), 346–363 (1999)

Granot, D., Yin, S.: Price and order postponement in a decentralized newsvendor model with multiplicative and price-dependent demand. Oper. Res. **56**(1), 121–139 (2008)

Deng, T., Shen, Z.J.M., Shanthikumar, J.G.: Statistical learning of service-dependent demand in a multiperiod newsvendor setting. Oper. Res. **62**(5), 1064–1076 (2014)

Liu, X., et al.: An assessment of the energy-saving potential in China's petroleum refining industry from a technical perspective. Energy **59**, 38–49 (2013)

Nash, J.F.: Equilibrium points in n-person games. Proc. Natl. Acad. Sci. U.S.A. **36**(1), 48–49 (1950)

Nash, J.F.: Non-cooperative games. Ann. Math. Second Ser. Ann. Math. **54**(2), 286–295 (1951)

Lions, J., Stampacchia, G.: Variational inequalities. Commun. Pure Appl. Math. **20**(3), 493–519 (1967)

Nagurney, A., Dong, J., Zhang, D.: A supply chain network equilibrium model. Transp. Res. Part E Logist. Transp. Rev. **38**(5), 281–303 (2002)

Nagurney, A.: Network Economics: A Variational Inequality Approach, vol. 10. Springer. Dordrecht (2013). https://doi.org/10.1007/978-94-011-2178-1

Research on the Influence of Anchors' Characteristics on Consumers' Impulse Buying from the Perspective of Emotional Contagion

Xiaoting Chen and Li Li[✉]

School of Economics and Management, Nanjing University of Science and Technology,
Nanjing 210094, China
Lily691111@126.com

Abstract. Based on the S-O-R model, the structural equation model is constructed to study the driving mechanism of the e-commerce anchors' characteristics on consumers' impulse buying behavior, and to further explore whether the audience activity plays a moderating role in it. Through the empirical analysis of 327 valid data, the results showed that the similarity, attraction, professionalism and interactivity of anchors all have significant positive effects on consumers' pleasure emotions. Among them, similarity, attraction and professionalism positively affect the impulsive buying behavior of consumers through the mediating effect of pleasure emotion. Audience activity negatively moderates the influence of similarity and attraction on consumers' pleasure emotion. Now, anchors not only need to further improve their work skills, but also need to build more attractive live broadcast room according to their own characteristics to attract the attention of consumers and stimulate them to buy products, which is particularly important for the live broadcast rooms with low audience activity.

Keywords: E-commerce · Anchor's Characteristics · Impulse Buying Behavior

1 Introduction

In recent years, due to its real-time interaction and immersive entertainment, ecommerce live broadcasting has been rapidly promoted in the Internet consumer market, which market size is expected to exceed 26 billion yuan in 2025 [1]. With the rapid growth of the scale of e-commerce live broadcasting, a large number of people swarm into this industry, the types of anchors become more diversified, consumers' attention is more dispersed, and the characteristics of anchors gradually become an important factor affecting consumers' shopping decisions [2]. Therefore, e-commerce anchors and e-commerce enterprises have explored strategies to strengthen the characteristics of e-commerce anchors in order to stimulate their desire to buy to the maximum extent. At the same time, the increasingly diversified consumer psychology also put forward more requirements for anchors. Therefore, it is necessary to further study the subdivision of the characteristics of e-commerce anchors.

Y. Tu and M. Chi (Eds.): WHICEB 2023, LNBIP 481, pp. 71–82, 2023.
https://doi.org/10.1007/978-3-031-32302-7_7

Compared with traditional e-commerce, e-commerce live streaming has more impulsive consumption. Impulse buying refers to an individual's immediate purchase response after perceiving strong external stimuli without the prior purchase intention to buy a certain or a certain type of product [3]. According to a survey conducted by China Consumers Association, 44.1% of consumers believe that they have made impulse buying in live streaming shopping [4]. But at present, few scholars have analyzed the influence of anchor characteristics on consumers' impulse buying behavior. Most studies on anchor characteristics focus on the analysis of purchase intention or behavior [5], while those on impulse buying behavior are more focused on the overall stimulus of broadcast room [6]. In addition, some scholars have found that audience behavior in broadcast room can also significantly affect consumer perception, resulting in a herd effect. In fact, other viewers can not only play part of the role of anchors, but also influence consumers' judgment on the ability and quality of anchors through group evaluation. Therefore, the number of viewers may have a regulating effect on the stimulation of anchors' characteristics on consumers, but now there is little discussion on this point. Therefore, this study aims to explore which characteristics of e-commerce anchors will stimulate the generation of consumer attitudes and purchasing decisions. And whether audience activity in the broadcast room has any effect on these effects?

2 Theoretical Background and Hypotheses Development

2.1 Anchor's Characteristics

The anchor's characteristics is refer to the characteristics of anchors in the livestream shopping scenario. Most scholars classify the characteristics of anchors into whether they can be trusted, whether they are professional with rich knowledge, and whether they can attract the interest of consumers [5]. Some scholars have further explored the subdivision dimension of anchor characteristics. Liu [7] interviewed 55 interviewees and found that it also included the interactivity of communication between anchors and audiences. Liu [1] found that consumers tend to choose anchors similar to their own in terms of viewing vision, interest and morality, and summarized the dimension of similarity. In the scenario of livestream shopping, Anchors should have a more comprehensive and in-depth understanding of products or services, and be able to market the audience through strong social skills and communication skills. And from the perspective of personal characteristics, distinctive and attractive anchors are more likely to attract consumers' attention and stand out from the crowd. Meanwhile, some anchors will also convey similar style preferences and aesthetic tastes to consumers to attract them. Therefore, based on the above analysis, this paper divides the characteristics of e-commerce anchors into similarity, popularity, attraction, professionalism and interactivity.

Similarity refers to the degree of similarity between anchors and themselves perceived by consumers in terms of style, aesthetics, values, etc. The principle of similar attraction in psychology indicates that the more similar others are to themselves, the more easily they are attracted [6]. When consumers perceive the similarity between the anchor and themselves in some aspect, they will have a favorable impression on the anchor. Some scholars have pointed out that anchors create similarities in vision, interest and morality, which can make consumers feel familiar and intimate [1]. Hu pointed out that the perception of similarity among peers in social shopping websites can affect their judgment on whether the information is credible [8]. However, there are few studies to verify whether similarity has a significant impact on consumers' impulse buying behavior. Based on the above analysis, this study proposes the following hypothesis:

H1: The similarity between anchors and consumers positively affects consumers' pleasure emotion.

Anchor attraction refers to the attractiveness of anchor's internal traits, professional skills and other personal charm. Studies have shown that consumers tend to believe that the information provided by highly attractive celebrities is more convincing, which is more conducive to the audience's love and recognition of anchors and their products [1]. Kim's research shows that the attractiveness of anchors can significantly affect the flow experience of consumers [9]. Zhu subdivides the attractiveness of anchors and finds that both physical and social attractiveness of anchors can significantly affect consumers' emotional trust [10]. Therefore, the following hypothesis is proposed in this study:

H2: The attractiveness of anchors positively affect consumers' pleasure emotion.

The professionalism of e-commerce anchors refers to the professionalism of ecommerce anchors in terms of relevant knowledge, experience or skills [7]. For consumers with purchase intention, by watching the professional display and recommendation of anchors, they can quickly and effectively grasp the professional information related to products, reduce the cost of searching for suitable products and improve the pleasure of the purchase process [1]. For consumers who do not have clear purchase intention, e-commerce anchors can highlight the use value of products, so that consumers can trigger their cognition of their own potential needs, and be more willing to participate in the live broadcast [11]. Accordingly, the following hypothesis is proposed:

H3: The professionalism of anchors has a positive impact on consumers' pleasure emotion.

Anchor interactivity refers to the degree of effective interaction between anchors and consumers. The interaction between e-commerce anchors and audience can not only satisfy consumers' cognitive needs for products, but also satisfy their emotional needs such as participation desire and sense of belonging, forming a deeper emotional connection [5]. Liu [7]found that frequent interactions between anchors and audiences can create a sense of immersion for consumers and enhance the perceived hedonic shopping value. Chen [12] found that the building of social presence of consumers in ecommerce live streaming can be achieved through the interaction between customers and merchants. This study proposes the following hypothesis.

H4: The interactivity of anchors positively affect consumers' pleasure emotion.

2.2 Emotional Contagion Theory

Emotional contagion refers to the process by which a person or group influences the emotions or behaviors of another person or group by inducing emotion and behavior. Hoffman believes that emotion contagion is an "association-learning" mechanism, that is, when people face positive or negative emotions induced by others, they will produce similar feelings to others through association [13]. And as people continue to imitate and learn from this emotional experience, they will be further induced to feel similar experiences or indirectly make them recall similar experiences in the past, thus creating a deeper emotional resonance. In the scenario of livestream shopping, when consumers feel the stimulation from the anchor's language, expressions and behavior, their inner emotional experience will produce two levels of psychological changes in the chain [14].When anchors describe and display their products through warm, friendly words and behaviors, they will awaken the audience's positive emotional experience and generate pleasant emotions. In addition, under the emotional induction of the anchor, the audience will resonate with the scene described by the anchor and further generate emotional trust. Therefore, the following hypotheses are proposed in this study:

H5: Consumers' pleasure emotion will positively influence their emotional trust.

2.3 Consumers' Emotion and Impulse Buying Behavior

Impulse buying is a strong reactive behavior produced by individuals after receiving external stimuli, which is dominated by emotion. Zheng [11] found that consumers' own positive emotions in online live shopping would have a positive impact on impulse buying intention or behavior. Zhou [6] verified that emotional trust can be used as an intermediary variable to stimulate the purchase intention of e-commerce live streaming consumers. On this basis, Meng [14] through empirical analysis found that consumers' positive emotions and emotional trust can significantly positively influence their impulse purchase intention. Based on the above research results, the following hypotheses are proposed in this study:

H6: Consumers' pleasure emotion positively affect their impulse buying behavior.
H7: Consumers' emotional trust positively affect their impulse buying behavior.
H8: Consumers' pleasure emotion plays a mediating role in the interaction between anchors' characteristics and consumers' impulse buying behavior.

2.4 Audience Activity

In this study, audience activity is defined as the degree to which consumers perceive audience interaction in other broadcast rooms. From the perspective of interpersonal interaction, the larger the number of audience, the more interaction between consumers, and the influence of each other can lead to the herd effect [15]. Studies have shown that when consumers have doubts about online sellers or advertisements, they are more inclined to rely on the shopping information of friends or even strangers for reference [16]. With the frequent exposure of dishonest and immoral events of caller anchors in recent years, consumers now will refer to the feedback of others in the scenario of live broa casting. Based on this, the following hypothesis is proposed in this study:

H9: Activity plays a moderating role in the influence of anchor characteristics on pleasure emotion.

2.5 Stimuli-Organism-Response Model

Stimuli-Organism-Response (SOR) model is the most common research model in Ecommerce live streaming studies, which refers to that when a person receives external stimuli, it affects his or her internal emotional state or cognition, thereby causing an individual to react with attitudes or behaviors [17]. This paper also builds a theoretical model based on this framework. The research model is shown in Fig. 1.

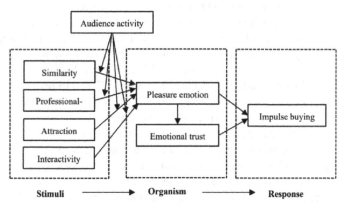

Fig. 1. Study model

3   Theoretical Background and Hypotheses Development

3.1 Measurement Development

The design of the survey items was based on the previous literature. The questionnaire is composed of 32 questions, slightly modified from the previous literature to make it more applicable to the research background of livestreaming e-commerce. The items for measuring item were adapted from those in the previous study (Table1). A five-point Likert scale was applied to each item, with one being 'strongly disagree' and five being 'strongly agree'. In the questionnaire, respondent were asked to recall the latest e-commerce live shopping situation, and then check the relevant options of the questionnaire according to their personal situation.

Table 1. Variable item Source

Variable	Mark	Source	Variable	Mark	Source
Similarity	S	Li, et al. [1]	Pleasure emotion	PE	Zhou et al. [6]
Interactivity	IN	Chen, et al. [12]	Emotional trust	ET	Meng et al. [14]
Professionalism	BP	Zheng, et al. [11]	Audience activity	AA	Kuan et al. [15]
Attraction	BA	Zhu, et al. [10]	Impulse buying behavior	IB	Zheng, et al. [11]

3.2 Data Collection and Sampling

The sample of the survey was limited to customers who had livestream shopping experiences to investigate the influence of anchors' characteristics on consumers' impulse buying intention. First, we did a pilot test, targeted at 82 participants. Then adjustments were made to clarify survey questions. The online survey on the wenjuanxing website (www.wjx.cn) lasted from 25 August 2022 to 14 September 2022 with the hyperlink published on social media such as WeChat. There were 327 of 415 responses were collected. The valid rate of questionnaire collection was 78.80%, with a gender distribution of 26.30% and 73.30% for men and women, respectively. The main range of the age group was mainly between 18 and 30 years old, accounting for 88.68% of the total sample. The distribution between 31 and 40 years old accounting for 6.73%. Additionally, the distribution of watching live streaming more than once a week on average, accounting for 67.58%. The above questionnaire survey results are consistent with the statistical characteristics that Chinese e-commerce live streaming consumers are mainly female, young and middle-aged people. At the same time, the subjects are active in live streaming shopping behavior, and 81.65% of the them had e-commerce live streaming shopping in the past six months. Therefore, distribution of samples collected in this study is in line with the reality.

4 Results

4.1 Reliability and Validity Tests

In this study, the exploratory factor analysis was conducted using SPSS 21.0, showing that Kaiser-Meyer-Olkin (KMO) was 0.910, more than 0.8, and the eight factor finally extracted is consistent with the original research model, indicating that the questionnaire design is reasonable. Then, as shown in Table 2, the Cronbach's alpha coefficients of all dimensions in the questionnaire were over 0.7, indicating that the good reliability of the questionnaire. And the average variance extracted (AVE) and combined reliability (CR) of variables were greater than 0.5 and 0.7, respectively, which belongs to the acceptable level.

According to Table 3, the square root of AVE of each latent variable is greater than the correlation coefficient with other latent variables, showing good discriminative validity.

Table 2. Result of reliability and validity tests

Variable	Cronbach's alpha	CR	AVE	Variable	Cronbach's alpha	CR	AVE
S	0.712	0.723	0.467	PE	0.750	0.751	0.504
IN	0.835	0.835	0.559	ET	0.740	0.745	0.494
BP	0.853	0.853	0.598	AA	0.803	0.808	0.584
BA	0.829	0.829	0.621	IB	0.781	/	/

In summary, the reliability and validity of the scale designed in this study all meet the requirements, so modeling and analysis can be continued.

Table 3. Result of discriminative validity tests

Variable	ET	IN	IB	PE	P	BA	S
ET	**0.703**						
IN	0.561	**0.788**					
IB	0.270	0.193	**0.764**				
PE	0.640	0.625	0.396	**0.710**			
P	0.660	0.679	0.172	0.638	**0.773**		
BA	0.611	0.696	0.279	0.699	0.670	**0.748**	
S	0.555	0.401	0.216	0.573	0.497	0.553	**0.683**

4.2 Common Method Biases

The unrotated exploratory factor analysis showed that the explanatory variance of the first common factor was 34.462%, which was less than the required critical value. The common method latent factor method was used for further test. After the common method deviation variable was added, the change value of RMSEA was only 0.009, no more than 0.05, and the change of fitting index of the model was no more than 0.1. It can be seen that there was no serious homology deviation in the data collected.

4.3 Comparison of Measurement Models

In this study the maximum likelihood method was used to examine the normal distribution of the measured variables, and AMOS 24.0 was used to estimate the parameter. The overall results of the fitting evaluation are as follows: RMSEA = 0.041 (0.05 or below), CFI = 0.904 (0.9 or more), CFI = 0.959 (0.9 or more), The detailed information is shown in Table 4. According to the structural models of this study, most values were close to or completely in accordance with the standard values. That is to say, the model fitting is sufficient.

Table 4. Model fitting results

Fitting index	χ^2	df	$\chi^2/$df	GFI	AGFI	CFI	NFI	TLI	RMESA
idea state	/	/	< 2	≥ 0.9	≥ 0.8	≥ 0.9	≥ 0.8	≥ 0.8	< 0.05
Fitting result	473.191	304	1.557	0.904	0.881	0.959	0.894	0.952	0.041

4.4 Test of Hypotheses

The standardized path coefficients and hypothesis testing results of the model are shown in Table 5, and *, **, *** means $p < 0.05$, $p < 0.01$, $p < 0.001$ respectively. For Hypothesis 1, anchors' similarity in the scenario of livestreaming e-commerce was found to be positively correlated with consumers' pleasure emotion ($\beta = 0.251$, $p < 0.001$), and thus hypothesis 1 is supported. In the same way, as shown in the Table 5, Hypothesis 2 ($\beta = 0.297$, $p < 0.01$), Hypothesis 3 ($\beta = 0.236$, $p < 0.01$), Hypothesis 4 ($\beta = 0.176$, $p < 0.05$) are all supported, anchors' attraction, professionalism and interactivity were found to be positively correlated with consumers' pleasure emotion. Hypothesis 5 ($\beta = 0.745$, $p < 0.001$), Hypothesis 6 ($\beta = 0.394$, $p < 0.001$) are supported too, Consumers' pleasure emotion will positively influence their emotional trust and impulse buying behavior. For Hypothesis 7, emotional trust wasn't found to be positively correlated with their impulse buying behavior ($\beta = -0.035$, $p > 0.05$). It may have more influence on consumers' other purchasing behaviors, such as repurchase intention.

In conclusion, the attractiveness, similarity, professionalism and interactivity of anchors can all have a significant positive impact on the happy emotions of consumers, among which the most influential feature of anchors is attractiveness. When consumers perceive the stimulation of anchors, they will be infected, thus awakening their potential purchase needs and joining in the live shopping activities.

Table 5. Results of path coefficient

Hypothesis	Path	Standardized β	T value	Result
H1	**S → P**	0.251	***	Support
H2	BP → PE	0.297	0.009**	Support
H3	P → PE	0.236	**0.004****	Support
H4	IN → PE	0.176	0.045*	Support
H5	PE → ET	0.745	***	Support
H6	PE → IB	0.394	***	Support
H7	ET → IB	-0.035	0.756	Not support

For Hypothesis 8, in this study, 2000 samples were tested by Bootstrap ML method, the bootstrapping program was used to construct a 95% confidence interval for the bias correction of the indirect effect, the results are shown in Table 6. The mediation of the impact of anchor's similarity, attraction and professionalism on consumer's impulse buying behavior was found to be realised by consumers' pleasure emotion.

Table 6. Mediation effect test

Path	Effect value	SE	Bias-corrected 95% CI			Result
			Lower	Upper	P	
S → PE → IB	**0.119**	0.070	0.022	0.310	0.011	Support
BA → PE → IB	0.128	**0.099**	0.008	0.414	0.032	Support
BP → PE → IB	0.091	0.052	0.020	0.241	0.005	Support
IN → PE → IB	0.088	0.066	-0.011	0.247	0.071	Not support

For Hypothesis 9, In order to show the moderating effect of audience activity more directly, regression analysis was carried out using process v3.3. The subjects were divided into two groups according to the standard deviation of upper and lower (+1SD/-1SD), and a simple effect graph was drawn according to the output data. The results showed (Fig. 2) that audience activity had a moderating effect on the influence of anchor's similarity and attraction on pleasure emotion. When audience activity is low (M-1SD), anchor's similarity ($t = -1.955$, $p < 0.1$) and attraction ($t = -2.040$, $p < 0.05$) had more significant effect on their pleasure emotion.

According to the moderating effect test, audience activity has a significant moderating effect on anchors' personal characteristic attributes (similarity and attractiveness), but has no significant moderating effect on anchors' personal skill attributes (professionalism and interactivity). The lower the audience activity, the stronger the influence of anchor similarity and attraction on consumers' happy emotions. Thus, in the broadcast room with low audience activity, anchors should highlight their personal charm more to attract consumers' interest in watching, so as to mobilize their enthusiasm to participate in the live broadcast. However, in the broadcast room with high audience activity, more attention should be paid to observing the content of bullet screen interaction of the audience in the broadcast room and guiding them consciously.

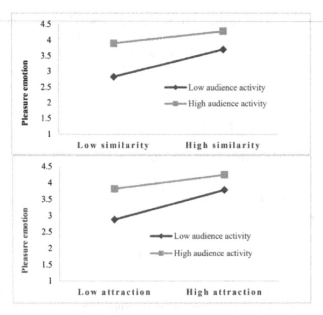

Fig. 2. Moderating effect breakdown drawing

5 Discussion

5.1 Research Conclusion

In this paper, the S-O-R paradigm is used to explore whether anchor characteristics have a significant impact on consumer impulse buying behavior. Finally, the following conclusions are reached:

First, the similarity, professionalism, attraction and interactivity have a significant positive impact on pleasure emotion, thus stimulating consumers' impulse buying behavior. Among them, attraction is the greatest influence on pleasure emotion, followed by similarity. Pleasure emotion plays a significant role in mediating similarity, attraction, professionalism and impulse buying behavior. E-commerce anchors, as the most important link between consumers and merchants (or products), can arouse similar emotional experience and association of audience through language and other ways, thus triggering consumers' desire to buying impulsively.

Second, audience activity negatively moderates the relationship between anchor attraction, similarity and pleasure emotion, while the moderating effect on anchor's professionalism and interactivity is not significant. In the broadcast room with high audience activity, consumers are less influenced by the similarity and attraction of anchor. Obviously, bullet screen is used to conduct frequent real-time interaction among consumers. Which will distract consumers' attention from e-commerce anchor and replace part of the attractiveness and similarity of anchors to meet consumers' demand for interest and resonance when watching live broadcasts. Therefore, anchors should pay attention to the guidance of the audience discussion of bullet screen.

5.2 Suggestion

For the merchants and e-commerce anchors with live broadcasting business, they can focus on anchor's attractiveness, similarity, professionalism and interactivity, and prove it according to their own conditions and needs. Among them, attraction is particularly important. Anchor should continue to strengthen the knowledge and create their own style of live streaming according to their own advantages, so as to make customer more willing to participate in live shopping. Anchors can also highlight their similarities with consumers and set up a variety of interactive ways to crease consumers' interest and trigger their potential purchase demand. In addition, pay attention to the number of audience in the living room is important. In addition, when the audience activity is low, anchors can show more attraction and similarity, and when the audience activity is high, they should put more energy on the interaction and feedback with the audience, so as to gain insight into consumer needs.

For consumers of e-commerce live streaming, this study can let them better understand the reasons for their impulse buying in e-commerce live streaming. When they in the livestream shopping scenario in the future, they can consciously control impulse buying after receiving the similarity, attraction, professionalism and interactive stimulation of the anchors, so that keep a clear mind and place an order to their actual needs and combined with the information of product quality and objective evaluation of others.

5.3 Limitations and Future Research

The questionnaire data in this study were filled in by the respondents based on their experience. Therefore, there may be a discrepancy between cognition and actual behavior. In future studies, scenario experiment method or crawler and other technologies can be used to collect data. Secondly, the data used in this model construction is obtained through snowball sampling, and the sample situation is relatively simple. In the future, the sample size can be expanded to collect more samples of different age groups and income levels for analysis. Finally, the types of e-commerce anchors are very rich, and their influences on consumers' impulsive buying behavior are not the same. So grouping can be considered to conduct heterogeneity test to further explore whether different anchors have different influences on consumers' impulsive buying behavior.

Acknowledgement. This research was supported by the National Natural Science Foundation of China under Grant 71771122.

References

1. Li, Y., Li, X., Cai, J.: How attachment affects user stickiness on live streaming platforms: a socio-technical approach perspective. J. Retail. Consum. Serv. **60**, 102478 (2021)
2. Han, X., Xu, Z.: The impact of e-commerce anchor attributes on consumers' online purchase intention: based on grounded theory. Foreign Econ. Manage. **10**, 62–75 (2020). (in Chinese)
3. Beatty, S.E., Ferrell, M.E.: Impulse buying: modeling its precursors. J. Retail. **74**(2), 169–191 (1998)

4. China Consumers Association. https://www.cca.org.cn/jmxf/detail/29533.html. Accessed 29 Aug 2022

5. Meng, L., Liu, F., Chen, S., et al.: May i arouse you: a study on the influence mechanism of different types of live streaming celebrities' information source characteristic/s on consumers' purchase intention. Nankai Manage. Rev. **01**, 131–143 (2020). (in Chinese)

6. Zhou, R., Tong, L.: A study on the influencing factors of consumers' purchase intention during livestreaming e-commerce: the mediating effect of emotion. Front. Psychol. **13**, 903023 (2022)

7. Liu, F., Meng, L., Chen, S., et al.: Study on the influence of online celebrity live streaming on consumers' purchase intention and its mechanism. J. Manage. Sci. **01**, 94–104 (2020). (in Chinese)

8. Hu, X., Huang, Q., Zhong, X., et al.: The influence of peer characteristics and technical features of a social shopping website on a consumer's purchase intention. Int. J. Inf. Manage. **36**(6), 1218–1230 (2016)

9. Kim, M., Kim, H.M.: What online game spectators want from their twitch streamers: flow and well-being perspectives. J. Retail. Consum. Serv. **66**, 102951 (2022)

10. Zhu, L., Li, H., Nie, K., et al.: How do anchors' characteristics influence consumers' behavioural intention in livestream shopping? A moderated chain-mediation explanatory model. Front. Psychol. **12**, 730636 (2021)

11. Zheng, S., Chen, J., Liao, J., et al.: What motivates users' viewing and purchasing behavior motivations in live streaming: a stream-streamer-viewer perspective. J. Retail. Consum. Serv. **72**, 103240 (2023)

12. Chen Y., Gao X., Wen Y.: A study on the mutual trust between buyers and sellers in online broadcast shopping mode. China Manage. Sci. **02**, 228–236 (2021). (in Chinese)

13. Hoffman., M.L.: How automatic and representational is empathy, and why. Behav. Brain Sci. **25**(1), 38–39 (2002)

14. Meng., L.M., Duan, S., Zhao, Y., et al.: The impact of online celebrity in livestreaming ecommerce on purchase intention from the perspective of emotional contagion. J. Retail Consum. Serv. **63**, 102733 (2021)

15. Kuan., K.K., Zhong, Y., et al.: Informational and normative social influence in group buying: evidence from self-reported and EEG data. J. Manage. Inf. Syst. **30**(4), 151–178 (2014)

16. Chang, Y.T., Yu, H., Lu, H.P.: Persuasive messages, popularity cohesion, and message diffusion in social media marketing. J. Bus. Res. **68**(4), 777–782 (2015)

17. Ming, J., Jianqiu, Z., Bilal, M., et al.: How social presence influences impulse buying behavior in live streaming commerce? The role of SOR theory. Int. J. Web Inf. Syst. **17**(4), 300–320 (2021)

Developing IT Ambidexterity: Insights from Knowledge Interaction Between CIO and TMT

Yiwen Zhang, Nianxin Wang[✉], and Hao Hu

Jiangsu University of Science and Technology, Zhenjiang, China
wangnianxin@163.com

Abstract. Literature has shown that IT ambidexterity can significantly enhance organizational agility or performance. However, little attention has been paid to how to foster IT ambidexterity. Through the lens of CIO-TMT knowledge interaction, this paper empirically examines the effects two different types of CIO-TMT knowledge interaction mechanisms (i.e., structural and social systems of knowing) on IT ambidexterity and the moderating effects of environmental dynamism. Data analysis and model estimation are performed on matched-pair survey of 347 Chinese shipbuilding firms by applying structural equation model. Results show that both structural and social systems of knowing positively affect IT ambidexterity and serve as substitutes. Environmental dynamism positively moderates the relationship between social systems of knowing and IT ambidexterity, but has no moderating impact on the structural systems of knowing and IT ambidexterity. Moreover, the three-way interaction among environmental dynamism, structural and social systems of knowing also suggests that the substitution effect between structural and social systems of knowing will be weakened in dynamic environments. This study extends the IT ambidexterity literature by examining its antecedents through the lens of knowledge interaction between CIO and TMT, which makes a significant contribution to both IS research and practice.

Keywords: IT ambidexterity · CIO-TMT knowledge interaction · structural systems of knowing · social systems of knowing · three-way interaction

1 Introduction

In today's changing business environment, the business activities of firms are more dependent on the application and management ability of information technology (IT). In the practice of business management, firms have two different focuses on the application and management of IT. One is the exploration of new IT resources and practices, so as to cultivate new capabilities and create new competitive advantages. The second is the use of existing IT resources and practices to enhance firms' capabilities and support or simplify current business processes. However, if firms only focus on exploration, they may fall into the trap of failure, and if they only focus on exploitation, they will fall into the trap of success. Therefore, firms need to have the ability to explore and exploit IT

Y. Tu and M. Chi (Eds.): WHICEB 2023, LNBIP 481, pp. 83–95, 2023.
https://doi.org/10.1007/978-3-031-32302-7_8

resources and practices simultaneously (i.e., IT ambidexterity) to meet the ever-changing business requirements under the dynamic environments [1].

The pursuit of IT ambidexterity is a highly complex process that involves tremendous uncertainty and thus requires adequate information processing by top management teams to mitigate the complexity and tension underlying IT exploration and IT exploitation. Organizational information processing is mainly carried out by senior managers through the explanation of business events, strategic decision-making and formulation of action plans, which requires them to coordinate among different business departments and share and integrate information and knowledge [2]. Thus, the top management of firms must integrate and understand business and IT knowledge to enhance the common understanding of the role of IT in the organization [3]. In particular, the CIO (chief information officer), as the leader of a firm's IT department, has more prominent IT knowledge than other senior executives, while the TMT (top management team, TMT), especially the CEO (chief executive officer), is responsible for the business operation. They are well versed in firms' business strategies and objectives, and thus their business knowledge is extensive. As the main body of firm IT strategy planning and implementation, both CIO and TMT should thus participate in the decision-making process of IT ambidexterity and their knowledge should be integrated to process information and mitigate the uncertainties. Thus, in this study, we propose that the knowledge sharing and integration mechanism (i.e., knowledge interaction mechanism) between the CIO and TMT will inevitably affect the cultivation of IT ambidexterity.

2   Conceptual Background

2.1   IT Ambidexterity

IT ambidexterity is derived from the concept of organizational ambidexterity. IT ambidexterity has been typically defined in the information systems (IS) literature as a firm's ability to simultaneously pursue explorative and exploitative use of its IT resources and practices [1]. IT exploration refers to the experimentation with new IT resources or new practices with existing IT resources. It is related to a firm's ability to understand emerging ITs, evaluate advantages and disadvantages of a set of alternatives, and select the one that is most likely to bring operational and strategic benefits to the firm. In contrast, IT exploitation refers to the efficient leverage and refinement of existing IT resources through known practices. It is related to a firm's ability to make use of its current portfolio of IT resources, to assimilate them in different business processes based on proven methods, and to acquire complementary technologies to improve its efficiency. The ambidextrous development of IT capability can not only make full use of existing IT resources and enhance potential value but also bring new IT resources for firms to create and maintain competitive advantages. Firms with higher IT ambidexterity will respond more successfully to customer needs and develop new capabilities, thus achieving higher organizational performance and greater profitability.

While organizational ambidexterity has been studied for more than two decades and resulted in a large body of literature [4, 5], research on IT ambidexterity is just burgeoning. Existing literature has fully explored the influence mechanism of IT ambidexterity on organizational agility [1, 6, 7], performance [8, 9] or innovation capability [10, 11], emphasizing and confirming the business value of IT ambidexterity. However, little attention has been paid to examining the antecedents of IT ambidexterity. The IS field has not yet formed a systematic and clear understanding of which antecedent variables can affect the cultivation of IT ambidexterity. In order to fill this research gap, this paper explores the antecedents of IT ambidexterity based on the perspective of knowledge interaction mechanism between the CIO and TMT.

2.2 CIO-TMT Knowledge Interaction Mechanism

CIO-TMT knowledge interaction refers to the process of transferring, communicating and sharing IT and business knowledge among senior executives. Its purpose is to improve the CIO's business knowledge and TMT's IT knowledge, to promote the generation of shared domain knowledge between the CIO and TMT, and to achieve the shared understanding about the role of IT in the firm. Since the pursuit of IT ambidexterity involves tremendous uncertainty and equivocality and requires organization-wide information interpretation and sensemaking to address those challenges, we thus believe that information processing and knowledge sharing within the firm has the most profound impact on IT ambidexterity. Systems of knowing (SK), refer to the organizational arrangements for information communication and exchange [2, 12] among executives, will enable knowledge sharing and integration between the CIO and TMT [13].

There are two different types of SK based on formal working and informal social relationship and interaction mechanisms [14]. We use structural SK and social SK to represent formal and informal organizational communication mechanism respectively. Structural SK are based on formal organizational structure and working relationship, allowing structured and formal interaction. As a result, top managers can share and integrate business and IT knowledge. Based on informal social relations, social SK can realize informal contact, communication and socialization activities to promote efficient information flow and rich communication between the CIO and TMT. It is also helpful to establish a relationship of trust between the two sides and promote the development of the CIO's business knowledge, TMT's IT knowledge, as well as common language and understanding between them [14].

Prior research on IT strategic management has suggested that both structural and social SK play important roles in developing shared and knowledge between the CIO and TMT [14]. Thus, in this study, we regard structural and social SK as potential antecedents and explore their effects on IT ambidexterity.

2.3 Environmental Dynamism

Environmental dynamism refers to the volatility and unpredictability of a firm's external environment. These uncertainties include customer demand, competitor actions, and technological improvement. In stable environments, firms contend with less radical changes and don't need to adjust internal operations rapidly. While in dynamic environment, firms contend with radical changes which require innovative responses and IT solutions [15]. Next, we explore how environmental dynamism moderates the effects of SK on IT ambidexterity.

3 Research Model and Hypotheses Development

This paper aims to explore the potential influence of CIO-TMT knowledge interaction mechanism on IT ambidexterity, and constructs a three-way interaction model of structural SK, social SK, environmental dynamism and IT ambidexterity, as shown in Fig. 1. The model emphasizes the influence of structural SK, social SK and their interaction effects on IT ambidexterity under different environmental dynamism.

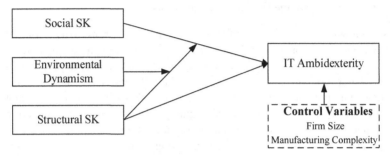

Fig. 1. Research model

3.1 Systems of Knowing and IT Ambidexterity

The CIO and TMT work together within a formal structure to develop processes, policies, incentives and penalties to ensure that the desired level of IT capability can be achieved. Prior studies have suggested that the CIO and CEO with a smaller hierarchical distance are able to understand the intention of the TMTS more accurately; CIO involved in TMT can not only have a better understanding of their firm's business and direction but also provide valuable information for TMT's decision-making. Also, free from the constraints of formal hierarchies, social SK can enable the CIO and TMT to increase mutual understanding, reduce communication costs, and stimulate them to coordinate with each other to address challenges in the development of IT ambidexterity.

Prior studies have shown that formal and informal organizational communication mechanisms [16] and integration mechanisms [17] contribute to the development of organizational ambidexterity. Therefore, we propose that both structural SK and social SK can enhance information processing, knowledge sharing and integration between the CIO and TMT so that they can better understand how the firm's existing IT resources can support current business strategies and how emerging IT can support new business strategies [13]. Based on this, we propose the following hypotheses:

Hypothesis 1a: Structural SK is positively associated with IT ambidexterity.
Hypothesis 1b: Social SK is positively associated with IT ambidexterity.

3.2 Social SK and IT Ambidexterity: Moderating Effect of Structural SK

Armstrong et al. (1999) has showed a positive correlation between the social SK and the CIO-CEO hierarchy distance, while a negative correlation between structural SK and social SK, because a greater hierarchy distance implies a lower structural SK. For CIOs who are structurally close to the CEO, they will have more formal reporting opportunities and thus informal interaction is not needed. In addition, CIOs who participate in TMT can communicate and exchange more equally and effectively with other TMT members, which can also reduce the dependence on informal communication to some extent. In contrast, CIOs with larger hierarchical distance and less formal interaction with the CEO need more informal interaction to express their views and obtain the approval of the CEO. Thus, we propose that structural SK and social SK have substitution effect in the process of enabling IT ambidexterity, and propose the hypothesis:

Hypothesis 2: Structural SK negatively moderates the relationship between social SK and IT ambidexterity.

3.3 Moderating Effect of Environmental Dynamism

In stable environments, firms enter the market in a relatively simple way and the frequency of competitive behavior is low. The conventional business processes and IT utilization lead to a reduced reliance on CIO-TMT knowledge interaction. However, in more dynamic environments, rapid changes of business processes and iterative updates of IT may cause previously developed functions of firms to fail to keep up with frequent changes of product, and excessive use of existing processes or capabilities will reduce the flexibility to make effective adjustments [18]. Thus, firms' demand for knowledge interaction across different departments will increase, and more high-frequency and effective knowledge interaction can effectively support the foster of IT ambidexterity. In this context, the flexible and efficient interaction mode represented by social SK will have an increased positive impact on IT ambidexterity, while the mechanical and rigid interaction mode represented by structural SK will have a reduced positive impact on IT ambidexterity. Thus, we propose the following hypotheses:

Hypothesis 3a: Environmental dynamism negatively moderates the relationship between structural SK and IT ambidexterity.
Hypothesis 3b: Environmental dynamism positively moderates the relationship between social SK and IT ambidexterity.

3.4 Three-Way Interaction Among Environmental Dynamism, Structural SK and Social SK on IT Ambidexterity

When firms' external environment becomes more unpredictable, it will bring more ambiguity and uncertainty to the simultaneous exploration and exploitation of IT [19]. Because the greater the uncertainty of the task, the greater the amount of information that decision-makers have to deal with during the execution of the tasks [12]. Thus, there will be an increasing need for TMT to integrate business and IT knowledge in a more dynamic environment. At this point, a single interaction mechanism is not enough to meet the TMT's demand for knowledge sharing and integration.

In this sense, environment dynamism may impose different requirements on SK. In stable environments, a high degree of structural SK may substitute the effect of social SK on IT ambidexterity, and they don't need to exist simultaneously. While in dynamic environments, high degree of social SK can help CIO and TMT establish a relationship of trust. Also, high structural SK can promote CIO's business knowledge, TMT's IT knowledge and the development of common understanding, thus enhancing IT ambidexterity. Therefore, we propose that the substitution effect between structural and social SK will be weakened in dynamic environments:

Hypothesis 4: The moderating effect of structural SK on the relationship between social SK and IT ambidexterity is positively moderated by environmental dynamism.

4 Methodology

4.1 Data Collection

Our study was tested using a matched-pair survey of business-IT executive. We developed two questionnaires: the first targeted at senior IT executives and the second targeted at the CEO. Structural SK; social SK and IT ambidexterity were measured by IT executive; whereas environmental dynamism was measured by business executive. Before large-scale data collection, two IS professors, two CIOs and three CEOs were invited to revise the face validity of the questionnaire measurement items. We randomly selected 12,086 Chinese shipbuilding companies from the list of China Shipbuilding Industry Association and sent questionnaires to 2,000 of them by E-mail. After tracking and reminding the companies that did not reply in time, a total of 355 questionnaires were collected, with a recovery rate of 17.75%. Due to the lack of individual questionnaire filling, 8 questionnaires were deleted and 347 valid questionnaires were obtained.

To assess non-response bias, we compared differences between early and late respondents based on revenue and number of employees. The T-test results revealed no significant difference between the first 87 (25%) and the last 87 questionnaires in these two demographic variables. Thus, non-response bias is not a concern in this study.

4.2 Measurement Development

The measures for all constructs were adapted from the literature, as shown in Table 1. The constructs in the model were measured using 7-point Likert scales.

Following general practice in the literature on ambidexterity, the measure of IT Ambidexterity was typically an item-level interaction mathematically computed as a multiplication of IT exploration and IT exploitation. We also controlled for the effect of firm size and manufacturing complexity on IT ambidexterity. Firm size was measured using the natural logarithm of the number of employees. Manufacturing complexity was measured according to the industry classification code of the responding firm.

Table 1. Measurements items and sources

Constructs	Items	Sources
Structural SK	1. I am often involved in major decision makings with CEO 2. I interact with TMT members on a formal basis (e.g., official meetings, work-related phone calls, etc.) 3. I often directly report to the CEO	Preston and Karahanna (2009); Liang et al. (2022)
Social SK	1. I often have informal contact with CEO 2. I socialize with the CEO 3. I have informal exchanges with CEO	
IT exploration	1. Explore new IT resources for future business models 2. Explore new IT resources for future products/services 3. Explore new IT resources for future business processes 4. Commit sufficient funding for experimentation of next generation IT 5. Acquire new IT resources and practices 6. Experiment with new IT resources and practices	Lee et al. (2015); Liang et al. (2022)
IT exploitation	1. Utilize existing IT resources for current business models 2. Utilize existing IT resources for current business processes 3. Utilize existing IT resources for current IT service capability 4. Reuse existing IT components, such as hardware and network resources 5. Reuse existing IT applications and services 6. Reuse existing IT skills	
Environmental dynamism	1. Market activities of your key competitors 2. The tastes and preferences of your customers in your principal industry 3. Rate of innovation of new operating processes and new products or services in your principal industry	Karimi et al. (2004);

5 Results

5.1 Measurement Evaluation

Before testing the model, we evaluated the validity and reliability of the measures. As Table 2 shows, we tested the validity of the measures through two procedures. First, the square root of each construct's average variance extracted (AVE) is much greater than the construct's correlations, suggesting sufficient discriminant validity. Second, factor loadings and cross loadings were calculated. The loading of each item is over 0.80, suggesting sufficient convergent validity. Also, each item's factor loading is much higher than its cross-loadings, confirming the sufficiency of discriminant validity. The reliability was examined by computing composite reliability and Cronbach's α coefficients. All scores exceed Nunnally's (1978) recommended cut-off of 0.70.

Table 2. Inter-construct correlations

	CA	CR	1	2	3	4	5	6	7
1.Firm size	1.000	1.000	**1.000**						
2.Manufacturing complexity	1.000	1.000	0.000	**1.000**					
3.Envir.dynamism	0.915	0.940	−0.098	−0.080	**0.893**				
4.Social SK	0.904	0.939	0.030	0.114^*	-0.110^*	**0.915**			
5.Structural SK	0.959	0.973	−0.028	0.026	−0.013	-0.457^{**}	**0.961**		
6.IT exploration	0.960	0.968	-0.110^*	0.044	−0.040	0.171^{**}	0.007	**0.913**	
7.IT exploitation	0.968	0.974	0.019	0.012	−0.073	0.128^*	0.238^{**}	0.008	**0.930**

Note: The diagonal elements are the square roots of AVEs. $** \ p < 0.01$, $* \ p < 0.05$

5.2 Common Method Variance Analysis

Although we collected paired data from business and IT executives, a single method and paper-based survey was used and thus could lead to common method variance (CMV) [20]. We carried out the Harmon's one factor test by following Podsakoff et al. (2003). The items of the five theoretical constructs were entered into a principal component analysis. Five factors were identified and the first factor of the unrotated solution explains only 25.21% of the total variance, showing no existence of CMV.

5.3 Hypothesis Testing

As our sample size is relatively small, we used smart PLS 3.0 to test our model. We show the step-by-step analysis in Table 3. In Model 1, we examined the effects of control variables on IT ambidexterity. In Model 2, we added the direct effect of structural SK and social SK. In Model 3, we added their interaction. In Model 4, we tested the moderating effects of environmental dynamism on structural SK and social SK. In Model 5, we

Table 3. Hieratical data analysis

Controls	Impact on IT Ambidexterity				
	Model 1	Model 2	Model 3	Model 4	Model 5
Firm size	−0.073	−0.073	0.082†	0.083†	0.084†
Manufacturing complexity	0.051	−0.007	−0.002	−0.019	−0.022
Direct effects					
Social SK(SO)		0.388**	0.464**	0.402**	0.428**
Structural SK(ST)		0.332**	0.249**	0.334**	0.321**
Environmental Dynamism (ED)				−0.024	0.084
Moderation effects					
ST•SO			−0.142**		
ED•SO				0.058†	0.035
ED•ST				0.032	0.047
ED•ST•SO					0.185*
R^2	0.008	0.148	0.178	0.165	0.179

Note: $\dagger$ p < 0.1; * p < 0.05; ** p < 0.01

tested the three-way interaction effects of structural SK, social SK, and environmental dynamism on IT ambidexterity.

Direct Effects of Systems of Knowing. The results of Model 2 showed that the path coefficients between structural SK and IT ambidexterity ($\beta = 0.332$, $p < 0.01$) and between social SK and IT ambidexterity ($\beta = 0.388$, $p < 0.01$) were positive and significant. So, both H1a and H1b are supported.

Two-Way Interaction Effects. We adopted the approach of Chin et al. (2003) and standardized the indicator to generate the interaction term. In Model 3, the moderating effect of structural SK on the relationship between social SK and IT ambidexterity was negatively significant ($\beta = -0.142$, $p < 0.01$). Figure 2 displays the simple slope of the moderating effect. At lower levels of structural systems of knowing (1SD below the mean), IT ambidexterity increases rapidly with the increase of social SK. However, at higher levels of structural SK, the effect of social SK on IT ambidexterity was minor because the slope changes little with the increase of social SK. Therefore, H2 is supported.

The moderating effect of environmental dynamism on the relationship between social SK and IT ambidexterity (Model 4) was positively significant ($\beta = 0.058$, $p < 0.1$). Figure 3 displays the simple slope to show the moderating effect. At lower levels of environmental dynamism (1SD below the mean), IT ambidexterity increases with the increase of social SK. At higher levels of environmental dynamism, the effect of the social SK on IT ambidexterity is enhanced. Therefore, H3a is supported. However, the moderating effect of environmental dynamism on the relationship between the structural SK and IT ambidexterity was not significant, H3b is not supported.

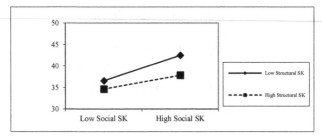

Fig. 2. Moderating Effects of Structural Systems of Knowing

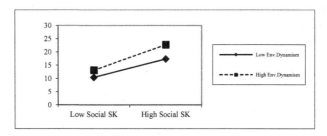

Fig. 3. Moderating Effects of Environmental Dynamism

Three-Way Interaction Effect. The interaction item between environmental dynamism, structural SK, and social SK (Model 5) is positively significant ($\beta = 0.185$, $p < 0.05$), thus supporting H4. The three-way interaction between structural SK, social SK, and environmental dynamism can be illustrated by plotting the relationship between social SK and IT ambidexterity at high and low degree of environmental dynamism and structural SK. Figure 4 Plot (4), which represents the relationship between social SK and IT ambidexterity in both low degree of environmental dynamism and structural SK, reveals that IT ambidexterity will rise with the increase of social SK. However, Fig. 4 Plot (3), which represents the relationship between social SK and IT ambidexterity in low degree of environmental dynamism but high degree of structural SK, reveals that higher levels of social SK can't enhance IT ambidexterity. We calculated the slope difference based on the study of Dawson and Richter (2006). Plots (3) and (4) are significantly different from each other (t = 2.034, p < 0.05). In high environmental dynamism, structural SK no longer moderates the relationship between social SK and IT ambidexterity, because social SK can always enhance IT ambidexterity (plots (1) and (2) are not significant different). In addition, under the context of stable environment and high structural SK, the slope of the relationship between social SK and IT ambidexterity is significantly different from the slopes in other three conditions. These results further support H4.

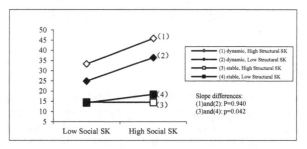

Fig. 4. Three-way Interaction among environmental dynamism, structural SK, and social SK

6 Discussion

With continuous investment in IT, the ambidextrous applications of IT are playing an increasingly important role in firms' business operations. Thus, IT ambidexterity has attracted a lot of attention from IS scholars who explore its impact on agility or other performance. However, little attention has been paid to how to develop IT ambidexterity. In this study, we endeavor to fill this gap by exploring the antecedents of IT ambidexterity from the perspective of knowledge interaction between the CIO and TMT.

6.1 Implications for Research

First, from the perspective of the CIO-TMT knowledge interaction, we establish a theoretical model by considering the effects of different CIO-TMT interaction mechanisms on IT ambidexterity, and confirm that structural and social SK are two important antecedents of IT ambidexterity. By exploring the causal relationship between SK and IT ambidexterity, we have contributed to the IT ambidexterity literature. Second, by examining the moderating effect of environmental dynamism, we focus on the influence of structural and social SK and their interaction effects on IT ambidexterity, which expands the research context of the effects of SK on IT ambidexterity. Finally, the empirical results confirm that there is a substitution effect between different types of SK, and this substitution effect is moderated by environmental dynamism, that is, the substitution effect between structural and social SK only exists in the stable environment.

6.2 Implications for Practice

Firms should consciously improve and provide different types of communication mechanisms to strengthen the knowledge interaction and sharing between the CIO and TMT. Through the design of appropriate organizational structure to improve the level of the CIO or the CIO become formal TMT members to enhance structural knowledge interaction, or encourage the CIO and TMT members to establish informal social relations, to participate in social activities to enhance social knowledge interaction. In addition, firms should also consider the influence of external environment to avoid the negative impact caused by the substitution effect between structural and social knowledge interaction mechanism. Specifically, in the dynamic environments, firms need more integrated information and knowledge in the decision-making process, in this context, the knowledge interaction between structural and social mechanisms will not be negatively affected by the substitution effect.

6.3 Limitations

This paper has some limitations. First, the data are from Chinese shipping industry, and economic or environmental factors in the same industry may limit the generalizability of the findings. Second, our results rely on perception binary data from two respondents in each firm's business and IT domains, which may lead to bias. Third, developing IT ambidexterity is an ongoing process influenced by numerous elements. Besides systems of knowing, other antecedents should also be identified to gain a deeper understanding.

7 Conclusion

In this paper, we examine the effects of structural and social SK and their interaction on IT ambidexterity under different environmental dynamism. Through empirical analysis of the matched-pair data from 347 firms, the results support most of our hypotheses and lead to the following conclusions. First, both structural and social SK can positively affect IT ambidexterity and have a substitution effect, that is, under the high degree of structural SK, the positive influence of the social SK on IT ambidexterity will be weakened. Second, environmental dynamism positively moderates the relationship between social SK and IT ambidexterity, but has no moderating effect on the relationship between structural SK and IT ambidexterity. Third, the results of the three-way interaction show that the substitution effect between structural SK and the social SK will be weakened in the dynamic environment. That is, the substitution effect between structural and social SK only exists in the stable environment. As the dynamics of the environment improve, the substitution effect diminishes.

Acknowledgement. This research was supported by the National Natural Science Foundation of China under Grant 71971101.

References

1. Lee, O.-K., Sambamurthy, V., Lim, K.H., et al.: How does it ambidexterity impact organizational agility? Inf. Syst. Res. **26**(2), 398–417 (2015)
2. Daft, R.L., Lengel, R.H.: Organizational information requirements, media richness and structural design. Manag. Sci. **32**(5), 554–571 (1986)
3. Heavey, C., Simsek, Z.: Distributed cognition in top management teams and organizational ambidexterity: the influence of transactive memory systems. J. Manag. **43**(3), 919–945 (2017)
4. Gibson, C.B., Birkinshaw, J.: The antecedents, consequences, and mediating role of organizational ambidexterity. Acad. Manag. J. **47**(2), 209–226 (2004)
5. Raisch, S., Birkinshaw, J., Probst, G., et al.: Organizational ambidexterity: balancing exploitation and exploration for sustained performance. Organ. Sci. **20**(4), 685–695 (2009)
6. Liang, H., Wang, N., Xue, Y.: Juggling information technology (it) exploration and exploitation: a proportional balance view of it ambidexterity. Inf. Syst. Res. **33**(4), 1386–1402 (2022)

7. Syed, T.A., Blome, C., Papadopoulos, T.: Impact of it ambidexterity on new product development speed: theory and empirical evidence. Decis. Sci. **51**(3), 655–690 (2020)
8. Mithas, S., Rust, R.T.: How information technology strategy and investments influence firm performance: conjecture and empirical evidence1. MIS Q. **40**(1), 223–246 (2016)
9. Steelman, Z.R., Havakhor, T., Sabherwal, R., et al.: Performance consequences of information technology investments: implications of emphasizing new or current information technologies. Inf. Syst. Res. **30**(1), 204–218 (2019)
10. Zheng, J., Liu, H., Zhou, J.: High-performance work systems and open innovation: moderating role of it capability. Ind. Manage. Data Syst. **120**(8), 1441–1457 (2020)
11. Guinea, A.O.D., Raymond, L.: Enabling innovation in the face of uncertainty through it ambidexterity: a fuzzy set qualitative comparative analysis of industrial service SMEs. Int. J. Inf. Manage. **50**, 244–260 (2020)
12. Galbraith, J.R.: Organization design: an information processing view. Interfaces **4**(3), 28–36 (1974)
13. Armstrong, C.P., Sambamurthy, V.: Information technology assimilation in firms: the influence of senior leadership and it infrastructures. Inf. Syst. Res. **10**(4), 304–327 (1999)
14. Preston, D.S., Karahanna, E.: Antecedents of is strategic alignment: a nomological network. Inf. Syst. Res. **20**(2), 159–179 (2009)
15. Xue, L., Ray, G., Sambamurthy, V.: Efficiency or innovation: how do industry environments moderate the effects of firms' it asset portfolios?. MIS Quart. **36**, 509–528 (2012)
16. Jansen, J.J.P., Van Den Bosch, F.A.J., Volberda, H.W.: Exploratory innovation, exploitative innovation, and performance: effects of organizational antecedents and environmental moderators. Manag. Sci. **52**(11), 1661–1674 (2006)
17. Jansen, J.J.P., Tempelaar, M.P., Bosch, F.A.J.V.D., et al.: Structural differentiation and ambidexterity: the mediating role of integration mechanisms. Organ. Science **20**(4), 797–811 (2009)
18. Wang, H., Li, J.: Untangling the effects of overexploration and overexploitation on organizational performance: the moderating role of environmental dynamism. J. Manag. **34**(5), 925–951 (2008)
19. Wang, N., Liang, H., Zhong, W., et al.: Resource structuring or capability building? An empirical study of the business value of information technology. J. Manag. Inf. Syst. **29**(2), 325–367 (2012)
20. Podsakoff, P.M., MacKenzie, S.B., Lee, J.-Y., et al.: Common method biases in behavioral research: a critical review of the literature and recommended remedies. J. Appl. Psychol. **88**(5), 879 (2003)

How Chatbots' Anthropomorphism Affects User Satisfaction: The Mediating Role of Perceived Warmth and Competence

Tianqi Zheng, Xingyu Duan, Kang Zhang, Xiangcheng Yang, and Yi Jiang[✉]

China University of Geosciences, Wuhan 430078, Hubei, China
jiangy@cug.edu.cn

Abstract. Chatbots are widely employed in various areas as an important product of artificial intelligence techniques because they can simulate human conversations and satisfy business demands in various circumstances. However, users do not always appear to be satisfied with chatbot anthropomorphism. This study proposes a dual pathway by which the anthropomorphism of chatbots affects user satisfaction from a theoretical perspective of task technology fit, and explores the key boundary conditions of individual characteristics and task characteristics in shaping user satisfaction. To test our study hypotheses, we conducted a social survey and a laboratory experiment. We evaluated the parallel mediation effect of perceived warmth and perceived competence via an online survey. In addition, users with high social phobia can enhance the effect of anthropomorphism on perceived warmth. In the laboratory study, we used 2 (anthropomorphic: high anthropomorphic vs. low anthropomorphic) x 2 (task creativity: high creative vs. low creative) between subjects who were asked to buy clothes via an e-commerce platform chatbot designed specifically for this study. They then completed an online survey to evaluate their experience. The results showed that the anthropomorphic chatbot induced higher perceptual abilities when performing creative tasks. The current study not only contributes to the literature on AI user satisfaction but also provides directions for the application of task-technology fit theory to human-computer interaction.

Keywords: Anthropomorphism · User Satisfaction · Chatbot · Task Technology Fit

1 Introduction

AI technologies are now incorporated in products and services in ways that provide four user experiences: data capture, classification, delegation, and social [1]. AI is expected to replace people in many jobs, and chatbots, also known as conversational agents, are one of the most prevalent applications. A chatbot is considered as "a machine dialogue system that interacts with human users through natural conversational language" [2]. However, user acceptance of chatbots has been mixed. According to the Expectancy Confirmation Theory (ECT), users' willingness to buy a product again or continue using a service is largely determined by their satisfaction with previous use of that product or service [3]. Improving user satisfaction will therefore lead to the continued use of chatbots and is key to the success of artificial intelligence.

Anthropomorphism refers to giving users a humanized experience by imitating human language, behavior, or social signals, or even convincing them that they are communicating with real people [4]. Although previous studies have already discussed that anthropomorphism has a positive impact on behavioral outcomes such as user satisfaction and persistent use intentions, there are still some studies to suggest that individuals may be unsatisfied when there is a mismatch between what users expect and how satisfied they actually experience. Furthermore, research have shown that a high level of anthropomorphism might cause the "Uncanny Valley" effect, which makes users feel threatened and afraid. Existing research cannot determine the boundaries of technology use and how to provide tailored services to meet user needs.

RQ1. How the anthropomorphism of chatbots shapes user satisfaction?

AI technology transforms human-computer interaction from passive and structured input and output to active and adaptive. Chatbots can extract information about users from their surroundings and context and understand the messages they send. So users no longer accept a one-size-fits-all service model. Chatbots should dynamically adjust their technical strength to suit the needs of specific individuals for specific tasks, exhibiting tailored responses and services to enhance user perceptions and outcomes.

RQ2. How does the path from anthropomorphism to user satisfaction for chatbots change when dealing with different users in different tasks?

We extend task-technology fit theory and stereotype content model to explore how anthropomorphism of chatbot shapes user satisfaction. We propose an intermediate process with two dimensions of warmth and competence that argues that users are satisfied only when their task requirements are matched with chatbots' technical capabilities. In addition, we explore whether different personalities of users and different types of tasks have an impact on this fitting process. A social survey and a between-groups experimental design in an e-commerce context have been investigated.

This study contributes to the formation of user satisfaction in the field of human-computer interaction in two ways. First, previous studies solely stressed the instrumental value of technology and ignored the emotional appeal of users caused by anthropomorphism [5]. By introducing the stereotype content model, we provide an integrated perspective to analyze users' perceptions of how well anthropomorphic matches their task needs in terms of both warmth and competence. Moreover, we propose an interaction among social personality, task creativity and technical features based on the task technology fit theory to provide a reference for future research on the application of task technology fit models in the context of artificial intelligence.

2 Literature Background and Theory Development

2.1 Anthropomorphism and User Satisfaction

Anthropomorphism refers to the human-like characteristics, behaviors, or emotions tendency that chatbots exhibit when conversing with users [6]. Chatbots can act as "companions" when they communicate with users using human-like names and anthropomorphic language and manage and share information in a specific format [7].

Anthropomorphism has been found to yield a number of outcomes, improving the quality of user-chatbot interactions and facilitate social and emotional connections. Of these results, user satisfaction is our main concern. User satisfaction is the feeling of pleasure an individual receives when some need is satisfied. It reflects the relative relationship between individuals' prior expectations of a product, technology or service and how they actually feels after using it [8]. In fact, chatbots' capacity to recommend accuracy, convenience, customization, and efficiency allows them to convey broad and reliable information to users, thereby increasing satisfaction. Meanwhile, anthropomorphism allows chatbots to behave more like human agents, evoking positive user attitudes toward chatbots with humanized names and social language.

However, it is unclear whether a higher level of anthropomorphism would always result in a better user experience and satisfaction. Because users have higher expectations and demands for anthropomorphic chatbots, it is challenging to generate user satisfaction and willingness to continue using them if they discover that the chatbots' services and capabilities do not yet satisfy their particular needs or initial expectations. For example, Davenport et al. found that users prefer to interact with real humans in more complex tasks [8]. Additionally, too much anthropomorphism might cause uneasiness. When chatbots resemble humans to a certain degree, they may be perceived as uncanny by users, causing feelings of discomfort and revulsion, which is what robotics expert Masahiro Mori proposed in his "Uncanny Valley" theory.

It is thus unclear how the effectiveness achieved by anthropomorphism fits users' expectations and generates satisfaction. Most of prior user satisfaction studies have concentrated on influencing factors such as system quality, information quality, perceived usefulness, and perceived ease of use [8]. However, anthropomorphism allows chatbots to provide users with a humanized service experience by using human-like language, appearance, and names, causing users to have various perceptions similar to those in human interactions. User satisfaction may no longer be solely based on the system's functional performance, but should also consider emotional needs. Thus, we will discuss the mechanisms of anthropomorphism on user satisfaction.

2.2 Warmth and Competence

Warmth and competence, two basic concepts in the stereotype content model, have been used to indicate individuals' perceptions of various social behaviors in interpersonal relationships [9]. Prior research has shown that people are hardly motivated to feel warmth when faced with a bot service and merely perceive an increase in competence traits. However, the application of anthropomorphism to chatbots allows them to deliver emotional value in addition to solving user-specific tasks potentially leading to higher perceptions of warmth and competence. In summary, we jointly explore the influence path from anthropomorphism to user satisfaction in terms of the two dimensions of perceived warmth and competence.

Firstly, perceived warmth refers to the degree to which individuals perceive intelligent assistants to be friendly, kind, and caring [10]. Anthropomorphism allows chatbots to be defined as conversational agents with emotional functions, prompting users to develop emotional attachments [11]. Specifically, chatbot anthropomorphic cues like name, voice, and linguistic style can increase user session participation. Users will then generate warm comments like caring, kind, and friendly. Secondly, perceived competence refers to an individual's perception of the intelligence, effectiveness and efficiency of an intelligent assistant in task solving [10]. It has been shown that anthropomorphism makes users tend to believe that it has the same human problem-solving abilities to accomplish the task at hand. As users' task requirements are realized, their view of the technology's value rises automatically, resulting in an improved perception of the system's capabilities.

Furthermore, users' perceived warmth can maintain and improve their harmonious relationships with chatbots, thus obtaining higher satisfaction. Meanwhile, users reported greater satisfaction with their interaction with the chatbot once they felt it had the ability to meet their current needs for smooth problem-solving. Thus, we propose the hypothesis that: H1. Perceived warmth mediates the relationship between anthropomorphism and user satisfaction. H2. Perceived competence mediates the relationship between anthropomorphism and user satisfaction.

2.3   Task-Technology Fit in Chatbots

In previous work, scholars have neglected to address whether technology matches the user task and user characteristics in a given situation. Goodhue and Thompson (1995) proposed the task-technology fit model to quantify the interaction between the user's perceived task, technology and individual [5]. The core of the model is to measure how the technology embedded in an information system product is adapted to the task at hand and thus enhances user evaluation [5]. Therefore, to investigate how chatbots should use anthropomorphism within appropriate boundaries, we introduce a task-technology fit model to explore the adaptation between anthropomorphic technology, tasks and individual characteristics, in an attempt to more fully understand the beliefs and attitudes of different individuals towards AI technology in different task contexts. We propose two moderating variables, individual and task characteristics.

Social phobia is a recurrent feeling of anxiety or fear in social or performance situations [12]. Firstly, interactions with chatbots become a form of safe behavior for high-socially-phobic users seeking to avoid face-to-face contact. The more intelligent and anthropomorphic the robot is, the more they are attracted to it because it not only does not judge or reject them negatively, but also helps the user solve problems without any surprises, thus, the perceived competence of the user is greatly increased. Secondly, high-socially-phobic users who feel isolated or lack social connection, can recover this social pain and increase perceived warmth by interacting with anthropomorphic chatbots. Thus, we propose the hypothesis that: H3. For users with high social phobia, the effect of anthropomorphism on perceived warmth (H3a) and perceived competence (H3b) is higher.

Social butterfly refers to being cheerful and bold in social aspects, being able to get acquainted with strangers, being willing to express oneself. In one possibility, users with high social butterfly have higher social needs, so when the chatbot's language style or behavioral state is closer to that of human, the warmth and competence perceived by users is also higher [13]. In another possibility, high social butterfly users do not worry or fear negative comments. They are less sensitive to the resulting changes in sociality even if chatbots become more anthropomorphic, and thus may not affect the perceived warmth and competence of the user. Thus, we propose the hypothesis that: H3. Individual's social butterfly moderates between anthropomorphism and perceived warmth (H3c)/perceived competence (H3d).

The measures of task creativity are novelty and utility [14]. Creative tasks require divergent thinking, intelligence, personality and other innovative thinking to propose novel solutions to such relatively subjective, complex and ill-defined problems [15]. It is often believed that robots can only be used to perform non-creative tasks with objective, clear answers. So in highly creative task scenarios, users are more likely to prefer the help of a human attendant. When a chatbot performs more closely to a human, users may be more likely to perceive it as having human-like abilities and to perceive more warmth. Thus, we propose that: H4. When the user chatbot's interaction is to execute high-creative tasks rather than low-creative tasks, the effect of anthropomorphism on perceived warmth (H4a) and competence (H4b) is stronger.

3 Study 1

3.1 Construct Measurement

All constructs were measured with multi-item, 7-point Likert scales.

Anthropomorphism (A). Chatbots talk to me: with human-like names/voice/greeting; at a rate similar to that of a human; with onomatopoeia similar to human words.

Perceived warmth (PW). When I talk to chatbots: there is a sense of "concern"/"affability"/"friendliness"/"human warmth"/"sociability".

Perceived Competence (PC). In the course of helping me on my task: chatbots are quick/efficient/powerful/skilled.

Social Phobia (SP). I get nervous in the street when people stare at me; I get nervous if I'm sitting on someone in a car; I get nervous in the lift if someone is looking at me; I often worry that I might do something to draw attention; When people look at me, I'll be shaking with nerves; I feel conspicuous when I stand in a row.

Social Butterfly (SB). I like to talk to a lot of different people at parties; I feel comfortable when there are a lot of people around; I enjoy being the center of attention in a crowd; I like to initiate conversations with strangers; I love being on stage and performing; I can find something to talk about with anyone.

User satisfaction (US). After talking to a chatbot: I feel very satisfied/happy/relieved/willing to use; I would recommend it to my friends.

3.2 Participants and Data Collection

The survey data were collected via paper file and online. Finally, 751 responses were received, including 615 valid responses. The participants consisted of 41.6% males and 58.4% females. 82.9% of them had a college or higher education. Additionally, more than 71.5% of them use chatbots more than once a month. Thus, the respondents' understanding of the questionnaire and the results are convincing.

3.3 Results

We analyze the reliability and validity of the measurement model by using SPSS 26 and Smart PLS 3.0. The results show that our research model demonstrated satisfactory validity and reliability. The value of SRMR is 0.052, suggesting a good fit.

Collinearity among the predictor variables was not a concern since all VIF values were below 2. The paths test was performed in PLS and the results are shown in Fig. 1. The anthropomorphism of chatbots significantly facilitates users' perceived warmth (b = 0.385, p < 0.001) and perceived competence (b = 0.411, p < 0.01). Both perceived warmth (b = 0.576, p < 0.001) and perceived competence (b = 0.255, p < 0.01) have a positive effect on user satisfaction. In addition, perceived warmth has a stronger impact on user satisfaction than perceived competence.

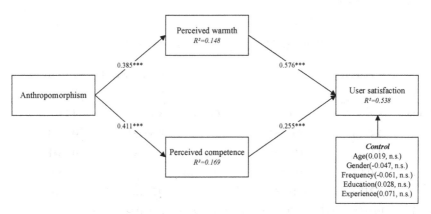

Fig. 1. PLS results test

We investigate the mediating role of perceived warmth and perceived competence in the effect of anthropomorphism on user satisfaction. The result in Table 1 indicated that the 95% confidence intervals for the mediating effects of perceived warmth and perceived competence between anthropomorphism and user satisfaction did not contain zero, confirming the mediating role of the above two variables, sup-porting H1 and H2.

Also, these two variables play a full mediating role in the effect of anthropomorphism on user satisfaction. Particularly, the indirect effect of perceived warmth is significantly stronger than that of perceived competence (effectPW-effectPC = 0.1267, BootCI = [0.0635 ~ 0.1931]).

Table 1. Results of mediating effect testing

Paths	Direct effect				Indirect effect				Results
	effect	BootSE	LLCI	ULCI	effect	BootSE	LLCI	ULCI	
PW	.0614	.0324	.0589	−.0023	.2273	.0297	.1715	.2871	Full
PC	.0614	.0324	.0589	−.0023	.1006	.0194	.0638	.1396	Full

We tested the extent to which social phobia and social butterfly moderated the main effects of anthropomorphism. As shown in Table 2, anthropomorphism × social phobia interaction had a positive significant effect on perceived warmth. In contrast, none of the moderation effects of perceived competence were significant. Therefore, of the moderating hypotheses, only hypothesis 3b was supported. The moderation graph in the left half of Fig. 2 further shows whether the effect of anthropomorphism on perceived warmth changes under different levels of social phobia. As predicted, at high levels of social phobia, the positive effect of anthropomorphism on perceived warmth is stronger, i.e., as anthropomorphism increases, perceived warmth increases more (low SP: b = 0.2732, p < 0.001, BootCI = [0.1703~0.3761]; high SP: b = 0.5695, p < 0.001, BootCI = [0.4507~0.6884]).

Table 2. Results of moderating effect testing

	social phobia			social butterfly		
	PW	PC		PW	PC
Constant	3.7763***	4.7699***	Constant	3.7884***	4.7703***
A	0.4214***	0.4234***	A	0.3693***	0.3971***
SP	0.1837***	0.0889**	SB	0.3519***	0.1888***
A × SP	0.1001***	0.0357	A × SB	0.0491	0.0304
R2	0.2187	0.1843	R2	0.2715	0.2105
Int CI	[0.049,0.151]	[−0.013,0.084]	Int CI	[−0.004,0.102]	[−0.021,0.082]

4 Study 2

4.1 Experimental Design

In order to test the fit effect between anthropomorphism and tasks with different levels of creativity, a 2 (high-anthropomorphic vs. low-anthropomorphic chatbot) × 2 (high-creative vs. low-creative task) between-subjects design was employed. We developed a text-based chatbot to replicate the context of online purchasing interactions between users and intelligent customer service. Participants were asked to communicate with a text chatbot to complete the designated tasks. Finally, participants were asked to fill in a questionnaire based on their true feelings.

The anthropomorphic chatbot was designed to interact with participants using a hu-man-like name (Xiao Zheng) and conversational cues similar to humans (such as greeting and modal words). When participants send a message to the chatbot, a cue indicating that the chatbot is typing a message will appear in the interface promptly, and the chatbot will respond after a period of delay. The non-anthropomorphic chatbot was designed to interact with participants in a stiff conversational style, using a non-human name (Intelligent Customer Service # 1) and stereotypically indifferent words. When participants give messages to the chatbot, the chatbot will respond without delay. Participants who were given the high-creative task setting manipulation were asked to talk to the chatbot and ask for suggestions about the style of T-shirts. And the participants in the low-creative task group were asked to ask for information about T-shirt sizes.

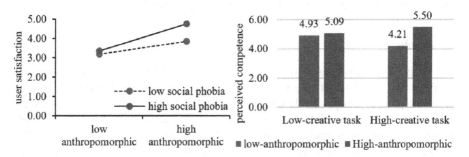

Fig. 2. The moderation graph

4.2 Participants and Procedure

We recruited 138 participants to join this experiment over a two-week period. They had an average age of 20.41 years (SD = 2.09), with 82 (59.4 percent) being female. At the beginning of the experiment, participants were asked to view a 15-s overview of the experiment to clarify their assigned task. Participants in the high-creative task group spoke with intelligent customer service about their recommended T-shirt, and intelligent customer service asked a few questions about their style preferences; participants in the low-creative task group were asked to provide their height and weight information to obtain size recommendations. After completing the experiment, participants were asked to complete an online survey.

4.3 Measures

We used the same scales as in Study 1 to measure perceived warmth, perceived competence, and user satisfaction. Anthropomorphism was measured on the same scale as in Study 1 for manipulation checks, but the "I think the intelligent assistant and I have a similar voice" item was excluded because the chatbot in the experiment was text-based. In addition, manipulation check questions for anthropomorphism and task creativity were included in the survey: "I think intelligent customer service is similar to humans" and "The task of asking intelligent customer service to recommend size/style to me is creative".

4.4 Manipulation Check

An independent t-test was used to check the manipulation for anthropomorphism and task creativity. According to the results, the degree of anthropomorphism in the anthropomorphic chatbot group ($M = 5.37$, $SD = 1.46$, $p < 0.001$) was much higher than in the non-anthropomorphic chatbot group ($M = 3.24$, $SD = 1.92$, $p < 0.001$). Thus, the anthropomorphism manipulation was successful. In addition, the degree of creativity was significantly higher in the high-creative task group than in the low-creative task group. The manipulation question was answered with an average of 5.84 ($SD = 1.32$) by participants in the style recommendation task, while participants in the size recommendation task responded with an average of 3.14 ($SD = 1.88$). It showed a significant difference ($t = 9.735$, $p < 0.001$). The task creativity manipulation was successful.

4.5 Results

A two-way ANOVA was used to test the interaction effects of anthropomorphism and task creativity. The interaction effect of anthropomorphism and task creativity on perceived competence was positively significant ($F = 4.485$, $p < 0.05$). The two-way interactions are in Fig. 2. In the high-creative group, perceived competence increases significantly as anthropomorphism increases(Anthropomorphic: $M = 5.50$, $SD = 1.21$; Non-anthropomorphic: $M = 4.21$, $SD = 1.89$). In contrast, in the low-creative group, perceived competence did not change significantly with increasing anthropomorphism (Anthropomorphic: $M = 5.09$, $SD = 1.46$; Non-anthropomorphic: $M = 4.93$, $SD = 1.67$). However, the interaction effect of anthropomorphism and task creativity on perceived warmth was not significant. Therefore, only hypothesis 4b was supported.

5 Discussion

5.1 Summary of Findings and Discussion

This study was to figure out how chatbot anthropomorphism influences user satisfaction, and to see if tasks with varying levels of creativity and individuals with varying social personalities have an impact on the outcome. To test our hypotheses, we conducted a survey and an experiment, and the results supported the majority.

First, the findings indicated that perceived competence and perceived warmth play a fully mediating role in the relationship between anthropomorphism and user satisfaction. Specifically, only by stimulating the user's perception of warmth and competence can chatbots with anthropomorphic features acquire user satisfaction. Furthermore, we discovered that users are more satisfied when they sense more warmth rather than perceived competence, implying that consumers demand more human attention from anthropomorphic beings than traditional information systems can give.

Second, the findings also provide interesting insights into the moderating role of social phobia and social butterfly. The results suggest that only social phobia positively moderates the relationship between anthropomorphism and perceived warmth. Our interpretation of this finding is that users with social phobia are afraid of real-world interactions and adopt avoidance behaviors, when conversations with human-like chatbots can compensate for their missing social feelings in reality. Thus, for people with high social phobia, their expectation of participating in a kind and pleasant session can be satisfied to a greater extent, and thus they can perceive more warmth. However, an individual's level of social phobia has no effect on their perceived competence, possibly because social phobia is unrelated to the user's initial expectations about the chatbot's functionality, i.e., if the chatbot fails to solve the user's problem, perceived competence does not increase even for users with high social phobia.

Third, the findings provide an empirical evidence for the effect of specific tasks on perceived task technology fit. The findings of Study 2 show that when users employ a chatbot to perform a creative task, anthropomorphism is more likely to boost their perceptions of chatbot capabilities. However, the relationship between anthropomorphism and perceived warmth was not influenced by task creativity. This finding can be explained by the fact that while executing a more challenging class of tasks requiring high creativity and complexity, consumers choose human help over machine help. Thus, an anthropomorphic chatbot makes users feel that it is more like a real human and has human-like abilities to solve problems, make suggestions, etc.

5.2 Theoretical Implications

First, this study extends the application of task-technology fit model in the context of artificial intelligence from an anthropomorphic lens. Prior research on traditional IT, based on the task-technology fit model, has focused on the problem-solving capability of IT, which may only provide a limited interpretation for human-like chatbots' jobs. We proposed an integrated dual-fit model based on the warmth-competence, because the user's attitude is not entirely determined by the efficiency and utility of task solving. The most significant feature of AI-powered chatbots is their anthropomorphic design, which transforms them from instrumental assistants to social participants, with an emphasis on bringing emotional comfort to users. Thus, the dual-fit model can fully explain the relationship between anthropomorphism and user satisfaction.

Secondly, this study introduced two new individual characteristic variables, social butterfly and social phobia, to investigate their interaction with anthropomorphism, and found that social-phobic users gain more warmth in their interactions with the chatbot. Previous studies have confirmed that relevant individual characteristics such as personality and Internet ability affect users' psychological perception in human-computer interaction. However, users currently care more about the social experience in their interactions than about problem solving, and the threshold of social need varies from person to person. We found that social phobia affects the emotional experience of users during their interaction with chatbots, providing a new entry point for exploring the influence of users' personal qualities on human-chatbot interactions.

Finally, this paper proposed a task characteristic variable to clarify the application boundary of anthropomorphic technology in chatbot. Current research on chatbots shows that users' attitudes toward anthropomorphism remain mixed. Few studies have empirically examined the interaction between task characteristics and AI technologies. This study focuses on task creativity and finds that in highly creative tasks, users tend to perceive anthropomorphic chatbots as more capable, which in turn generates higher satisfaction. The findings of this paper provide an explanation for the controversy of previous studies at the task level and lay a foundation for further research on the effects of task characteristics on human-computer interaction.

5.3 Managerial Implications

This research also provides three managerial implications for both chatbot designers and managers. Firstly, an increasing number of developers have previously worked on enhancing algorithms that allow chatbots to identify and solve a wide range of problems, resulting in increased user satisfaction. On this foundation, this study found that anthropomorphism not only enhances the user's perceived competence, but also gains user satisfaction by satisfying their emotional needs and giving them a sense of warmth. In brief, service providers should focus their design on the two goals of improving the competence and warmth of chatbots, and use anthropomorphism properly to stimulate users to be infected by the intelligence and warmth of chatbots.

Secondly, our findings reveal that persons who are socially phobic have unique perceptions of human-computer interaction. Developers can use social phobia as part of a user's personality label and mine information about the user's behavior to determine the user's social phobia level, allowing them to target specific marketing to people with different personalities. Chatbot developers should stress the social participant role of chatbots for users with high social phobia, emphasizing their kind and compassionate human-like features to suit users' needs for warm social interactions.

Thirdly, we find that the use boundary of chatbot anthropomorphism is related to the type of task. We suggest that marketers concentrate on activities that are more suited to their abilities and leave to AI those on which they underperform. This article introduces task creativity to distinguish between different types of tasks. To take e-commerce scenario as an example, when chatbots perform high-creative tasks such as product recommendations, customer complaints, and price negotiation, the developers and suppliers should intentionally emphasize the anthropomorphism of chatbots, making them close to real human service providers, so as to enhance users' perception of chatbots' capabilities and thus improve their satisfaction.

5.4 Limitations and Future Research

This study also has some limitations that need to be addressed in future research. First, the anthropomorphism we discuss is based on text-based chatbots, and there-fore involves elements that do not include vocal and visual cues. Previous studies have shown that anthropomorphic visual, identity, and conversation design cues all produce positive behavioral outcomes. Future research can be extended to other types of chatbot applications. Second, There are more potential variables that can be measured at the emotional level to reflect the user's perception of task technology fit, such as social presence and perceived empathy. Finally, individual personality traits are very complex, and there are many unstudied variables, such as emotional instability and affinity, which will be a future direction to explore.

Acknowledgement. This research was supported by the National Natural Science Foundation of China under Grant 71702176.

References

1. Puntoni, S., Reczek, R.W., Giesler, M., Botti, S.: Consumers and Artificial Intelligence: an experiential perspective. J. Mark. **85**(10), 131–151 (2021)
2. Shawar, B.A., Atwell, E.S.: Using corpora in machine-learning chatbot systems. Int. J. Corpus Linguist. **10**(4), 489–516 (2005)
3. Anderson, E.W., Sullivan, M.W.: The antecedents and consequences of customer satisfaction for firms. Mark. Sci. **12**(2), 125–143 (1993)
4. Murtarelli, G., Gregory, A., Romenti, S.: A conversation-based perspective for shaping ethical human-machine interactions: the particular challenge of chatbots. J. Bus. Res. **129**, 927–935 (2021)
5. Goodhue, D.L.: Development and measurement validity of a task - technology fit instrument for user evaluations of information system. Decis. Sci. **29**(1), 105–138 (1998)
6. Li, X.G., Sung, Y.J.: Anthropomorphism brings us closer: the mediating role of psychological distance in user-ai assistant interactions. Comput. Hum. Behav. **118**, 106680 (2021)
7. Westerman, D., Cross, A.C., Lindmark, P.G.: I believe in a thing called bot: perceptions of the humanness of "Chatbots." Commun. Stud. **70**(3), 295–312 (2019)
8. Li, Y., Zhao, P., Jiang, Y.: A literature review of information system user satisfaction: a case study of ERP system. Technol. Econ. **33**(3), 119–131 (2014). (in Chinese)
9. Fiske, S.T., Cuddy, A.J., Glick, P.: Universal dimensions of social cognition: warmth and competence. Trends Cogn. Sci. **11**(2), 77–83 (2007)
10. Aaker, J., Vohs, K.D., Mogilner, C.: Nonprofits are seen as warm and for-profits as competent: firm stereotypes matter. J. Consum. Res. **37**(2), 224–237 (2010)
11. Glikson, E., Woolley, A.W.: Human trust in artificial intelligence: review of empirical research. Acad. Manag. Ann. **14**(2), 627–660 (2020)
12. Aburoomi, R.J., Malak, M.Z.: Evaluation of social phobia among Syrian refugees' youth in Jordan. Psychiatr. Q. **92**(3), 1175–1185 (2021). https://doi.org/10.1007/s11126-021-09901-2
13. Mimoun, M.S.B., Poncin, I., Garnier, M.: Animated conversational agents and e-consumer productivity: the roles of agents and individual characteristics. Inf. Manag. **54**(5), 545–559 (2017)
14. Barron, F.: The disposition toward originality. Psychol. Sci. Public Interest **51**(3), 478 (1955)
15. Edmonds, E., Candy, L.: Creativity, art practice, and knowledge. Commun. ACM **45**(10), 91–95 (2002)

The Effect of Key Opinion Leader Type on Purchase Intention: Considering the Moderating Effect of Product Type

Rongkai Zhang[1], Bingni Ma[1], Yingyan Li[1], Fuping Chen[1], Jianan Yan[1], Yuxi Lin[1(✉)], and Yifan Wu[2]

[1] College of Management, Shenzhen University, Shenzhen 518060, China
`linyuxi2200@163.com`
[2] Sino-Mac International Academy, Shenzhen, China

Abstract. Virtual KOL (Key Opinion Leader) is gradually gaining acceptance as a new form of marketing. In this study, we investigate the influence of virtual KOL and real KOL on consumers' purchase intentions in different product types (search goods and experience goods) concerning the SOR model and using perceived trust and consumer identification as mediating variables. We collected 248 valid data through questionnaires and used SPSS and Process model 4 to conduct regression and mediation analysis to test the hypothesis. This study identifies for the first time the emerging marketing approach of virtual KOLs and examines the differences in marketing effectiveness and mechanisms of action between real and virtual KOLs.

Keywords: Key Opinion Leader · Consumer Purchase Intentions · Search Goods · Experience Goods

1 Introduction

In the age of self-media, the internet is increasingly becoming a method for acquiring knowledge and sharing life. When consumers choose to make purchases online, they are faced with the dilemma of not being able to observe and touch the actual product, so they tend to actively search for and obtain information about the product and use it as a basis for their purchase. At this time, KOLs (Key Opinion Leaders) can play a central role in the group to guide and influence others. They can use their expertise to actively participate in discussions in online communities, for example, by sharing real experiences and feelings, announcing product information, driving community members to participate in discussions and interactions, arousing cognitive and emotional resonance among followers [1].

At the same time, as digital connectivity continues to improve and VR technology is constantly being updated, virtual characters have their unique advantages over real people. Previous research has shown that virtual characters are customizable, easy to shape, and adaptable. It is easier to avoid scandals associated with brands and products due to their adverse public opinion [2]. At this stage, most of the research on virtual characters focuses on analyzing the impact of virtual spokespersons on brands and the technological development and innovation of virtual characters. There is little research comparing the relationship between virtual KOL and real KOL on consumers' purchasing behavior and their influence mechanisms.

We consider that consumers' ability to obtain information for different types of products is different; for example, products can be classified as experience goods and search goods according to whether consumers can obtain information about product quality before purchase [3]. Through scenario simulation experiments, this study aims to use perceived trust and consumer identification as mediating variables to explore the mechanisms of virtual and real KOL in virtual communities on consumers' purchase intention under different product types (search goods and experience goods). This study is not only an extension of the research field related to KOL and virtual characters but also can help companies better select the right KOL for their product attributes, further highlight the business value of virtual characters, thus increasing the sales and profits of companies and promoting the deeper development of the KOL industry.

2 Theoretical Foundation

2.1 Virtual KOLs

Virtual spokespeople are virtual characters created by companies to present brand attributes, connotations and values to consumers, and to build strong brand relationships and brand perceptions [4]. The characteristics of virtual spokespeople, such as attractiveness, professionalism, relevance, and nostalgia, have an impact on consumers' attitudes and purchase intentions [5].

Compared to traditional virtual spokespersons, virtual KOLs are more anthropomorphic in terms of appearance, and their appearance, body shape, and clothing are more realistic in terms of setting and are no longer limited to virtual worlds such as anime, film and television, or simple advertising design. Through daily operations, the avatars are brought into the real world, participating in current social events and grasping trends, expressing opinions and attitudes, giving them personality and emotional expression, and creating a three-dimensional and rich character image.

2.2 Product Type

Product type is an important factor that affects consumer perceptions and behaviors. From the perspective of product information access, products can be divided into search goods and experience goods [3]. Search goods refer to products whose quality and applicability can be objectively assessed based on the information searching behavior before purchase, with a low degree of information asymmetries, such as cell phones and computers. Experience goods refer to products whose quality can't tell only by information searching behavior before product purchasing but rely more on subjective experience after use to assess product quality, with a high degree of information asymmetry, such as perfumes [6].

Different products with different types of spokespersons have different marketing effects. However, the relationship between virtual opinion leaders and search goods and experience goods has not yet been studied.

2.3 Consumer Identity

The basic concept of consumer identity is that people express the sameness or difference between themselves, and others utilizing consumption and assign themselves to a specific social group, thus positioning and categorizing themselves socially [7]. In real marketing activities, for consumers to gain a sense of social identity and depict a lifestyle, companies invite idols and celebrities to endorse them according to their type.

2.4 Perceived Trust

Perceived trust is when a person trusts and is comfortable deciding his or her actions based on information provided by others. Studies have shown that the professional and interactive nature of KOLs facilitates the formation of perceived trust. Based on SOR theory, perceived trust as a consumer psychological perception has an important influence on consumer behavioral decisions such as purchasing [8].

3   Theoretical Models and Hypotheses

3.1   Theoretical Framework

Our study considers that the external stimuli and influence paths may differ under different product types. Therefore, this paper investigates the differences in consumers' purchase intentions when different types of KOLs are used as stimuli for consumers under different product type conditions, using consumer identification and perceived trust as mediating variables. The model is shown in Fig. 1.

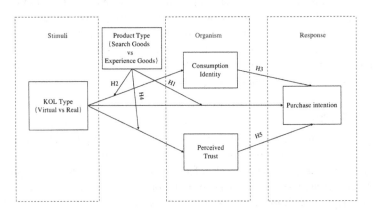

Fig. 1. Theoretical model.

3.2 Interaction of KOL Type and Product Type

In past studies, the effectiveness of celebrity endorsement advertising has been found to vary by product type, reflecting the importance of the fit between celebrity and product [9]. Nelson classifies product types as search products and experience products by the degree to which consumers perceive product quality information before purchasing a product [3].

When a product is an experience product, consumers focus on the experience and details of the product due to the lack of objective criteria, and therefore they will process the information available to them in greater depth to obtain enough useful information to increase their trust in the product. In this case, external influences such as product popularity will play a more important role in the consumer's purchase decision [10]. When the product is a search product, the search product's KOL is more of a showcase and a matchmaker, building images and scenarios to highlight the product's desired characteristics and style. Therefore, when subjective feelings are no longer the focus of consumers' attention, the characteristics of virtual KOLs often provide a better match with products. In summary, the following hypotheses are proposed.

H1: The interaction between the KOL and the product type affects consumers' purchase intention.
H1a: When the products are experienced goods, real KOLs can give consumers more positive purchase intentions compared to virtual KOLs.
H1b: When the products are search goods, the virtual KOL makes consumers more willing to buy than the real KOL.

3.3 The Mediating Role of Consumer Identity

Consumer identity is the perception of the degree of similarity between a particular individual and one's personality traits, including values and emotions. Studies have shown that KOLs use their expertise to participate in discussions that can elicit cognitive and emotional resonance from followers and build online community identity [11].

When the product is an experience good, consumers make judgments with the help of external cues obtained during the shopping process. Consumers are more likely to have emotional resonance, develop a sense of love and identity, and eventually follow to produce purchase behavior. When the product is a search good, its practical value is often realized through the characteristics and attributes of the product itself. Consumers can fully understand the product quality through the Parameter information in the advertisement content [12] and thus form their judgment of the product. With the use of virtual KOLs, consumers are less disturbed by emotional factors of KOLs. Hence, consumers' choice is more based on their initial judgment of product-related parameters and choose the product that is consistent with their own identity, thus generating a higher sense of consumer identification.

According to consumer behavior, consumers' emotions and perceptions are the basis for their purchase intentions. The increase in consumer identification will increase the level of Consumer Preferences and thus lead to consumer purchase behavior. Therefore, this study proposes the following hypothesis.

H2: Under different product types, KOL types affect consumer identity differently.
H2a: When the product is an experience good, consumers have higher consumer identification with real KOLs than virtual KOLs.
H2b: When the product is a search good, consumers have higher consumer identification with virtual KOLs than real KOLs.
H3: Consumer identification has a positive effect on consumers' purchase intention.

3.4 The Mediating Role of Perceived Trust

Consumers' trust in products is a critical factor in their purchase decisions, and a high level of trust can accelerate the consumer consumption process. The professionalism of KOLs is an essential factor in establishing trust influence, where professionalism can be judged based on their knowledge background, social identity, and the professionalism and authority of their published statements [13].

When the product is an experience good, consumers can only know the attributes of the product after using it, and they will perceive the product through the experience, thus influencing the consumption experience and purchase decision. According to the research, authenticity can improve consumers' trust in the brand and make them form a positive attitude toward the brand [14]. When the product is a search good, its quality can be directly judged by search attributes, which is generally based on objective criteria and is less difficult to judge. Most studies have shown that virtual KOLs and consumers are more often a type of interaction like social interaction with less interaction and feedback mechanisms between them when consumers are more willing to trust the relevant attributes provided by the merchant itself about the search item, thus generating a higher perceived trust in it.

McKnight found that perceived trust makes consumers willing to share personal information and make purchases. Therefore, we propose the following hypothesis.

H4 Under different product types, KOL types affect perceived trust differently.
H4a When the product is an experience good, consumers have higher perceived trust in real KOLs than in virtual KOLs.
H4b When the product is a search good, consumers have higher perceived trust in virtual KOLs than in real KOLs.
H5 Perceived trust has a positive impact on consumers' purchase intentions.

4 Research Design

This study used a situational simulation experiment with a 2(KOL type: real vs. virtual) × 2 (product type: search goods vs. experience goods) between-group factorial experimental design. The data required for the study was collected through an online survey agency (www.wjx.cn). A total of 248 valid questionnaires were collected.

The formal questionnaire was divided into four parts, and in the first part the subjects were guided through the stimulus material into scenarios of different KOL types and product types. Subjects were asked to enter the corresponding procedure. Then, subjects saw pictures of the KOL and her presentation of the product, and subjects in different type groups saw different product presentations with control variables. To ensure the consistency of other variables, the poster design and lay-out were kept the same, and the distinction was made by labeling the real KOL and the virtual KOL.

The second part of the questionnaire was conducted to test the manipulation of relevant variables and the measurement of confounding factors. The perception of KOL type was measured by asking subjects whether they perceived the KOL as a real character or a virtual character, respectively, and to avoid subjects' preference for the type of product offered in the experiment itself, the product attractiveness was measured in this paper using a seven-point Likert scale. The product type was perceived by informing the subjects of the definition of search goods and experience goods and then asking them to rate the related products (1 = search goods, 7 = experience goods).

The third part of the questionnaire measures consumer identification, perceived trust, and purchase intention. The scale was adapted from the established scales of previous scholarly research. (The above measurements were made on a 5-point Likert scale, where 1 = strongly disagree; 5 = strongly agree).

The fourth part of the questionnaire measured the subjects' demographic characteristics, including gender, age group, education, occupation, and monthly income.

5 Data Analysis

5.1 Fundamental Analysis

This study tested whether the manipulation of product type was successful by independent sample t-test. The results showed a significant difference between consumers' perceptions of search and experience goods ($M_{search\ goods} = 3.24$; $M_{experience\ goods} = 5.28$, $p < 0.01$), indicating that the manipulation of product type was successful in this experiment. This study tested whether the manipulation was successful for virtual characters by independent samples t-test. The results showed significant differences in consumers' perceptions of virtual KOLs ($M_{virtual} = 2.56$; $M_{real} = 4.13$, $p < 0.01$), indicating the success of this experiment on whether the manipulation was successful for virtual characters (Table 1).

Table 1. Adjusting the results of the directed attribute manipulation test

latent variable	Variables	Sample size	Average	Standard Deviation (SD)	p
KOL Types	virtual KOL	2.56	1.530	133	0.00
	real KOL	4.13	2.203	115	
Product Types	Search goods	3.24	2.090	121	0.00
	Experience goods	5.28	1.567	127	

In addition, to test the existence of the effect of different product types on consumers' product attractiveness, this study was verified using ANOVA, which showed that, $p = 0.107 > 0.05$, different levels of changes in the control variables did not have a significant effect on the observed variables.

To confirm the reliability and validity of the questionnaire, this study used SPSS statistical software to analyze the data of the questionnaire for reliability, and the Cronbach's alpha coefficient of each scale was greater than 0.8, and the total Cronbach's alpha coefficient was 0.958, indicating that the questionnaire had excellent reliability in the formal research. In the KMO and Bartlett tests, the total KMO value is 0.927, which is greater than 0.7, indicating that the questionnaire has high validity.

5.2 Interaction Test

In this study, we use hierarchical regression. From the analysis of the results of Model II, it can be seen that the coefficient of the interaction term between product types and KOL types is significant at the 0.001 level, indicating that product types play a significant moderating role in the relationship between KOL types and purchase intention. Then, we used linear regression to examine the main effects under the conditions of experience goods and search goods, respectively (Table 2).

Table 2. Results of linear regression analysis

Variables	Experience goods	Search goods
KOL Types	0.276**	0.269**
R^2	0.069	0.064
F	10.338**	9.252**

Note: $* * * p < 0.001, * p < 0.05, * * p < 0.01$

For experience goods, the effect of the real KOL on purchase intention was significantly higher than that of the virtual KOL (M $_{real}$ = 2.9333; M $_{virtual}$ = 2.3234, p = 0.002); for search goods, the effect of virtual KOL on purchase intention was significantly higher than that of real KOL (M $_{real}$ = 2.4121; M $_{virtual}$ = 3.0152, p = 0.003). In summary, hypotheses H1, H1a, and H1b held.

5.3 Mediating Effects Test

Consumer Identity. Under experience products, the predictive effect of KOL types on purchase intention was significant (β = 0.5514, t = 3.2153, p = 0.002). The positive predictive effect of KOL type on consumer identification was significant (β = 0.6326, t = 3.7378, p < 0.001), and the positive predictive effect of consumer identification on purchase intention was also significant. In addition, real KOLs better promoted the formation of consumer identification. Under search products, the results showed that the predictive effect o KOL types on purchase intention was significant (β = -0.5372, t = -3.0418, p = 0.003). The negative predictive effect of KOL types on consumer identification was significant ($\beta = -0.4917, t = -2.76655, p = 0.007$), while the positive predictive effect of consumer identification on purchase intention was also significant. In addition, virtual KOLs better promoted the formation of consumer identification, hypothesesH2a, H2b and H3 held (Tables 3 and 4).

Table 3. Mediating model test results of consumer identity

Predictive variables	Result Variables	β	Direct Effects					β	Indirect Effect			
			Standardized β	SE	t	95%CI			Standardized β	SE	95%CI	
KOL types(EG)	Consumer identity	0.6637***	0.6326***	0.1776	3.7378	0.3123	1.0151					
Consumer Identity(EG)	Purchase intention	0.8487***	0.805***	0.0583	14.5619	0.7333	0.9641					
KOL types(EG)	Purchase intention	0.61**	0.5514**	0.1897	3.2153	0.2345	0.9854	0.0467	0.0422	0.122	0.122	0.2881
KOL types(SG)	Consumer identity	−0.5657**	−0.4917**	0.2045	−2.7665	−0.9705	−0.1608					
Consumer identity(SG)	Purchase intention	0.828***	0.8485***	0.0465	17.8169	0.7359	0.9199					
KOL types(SG)	Purchase intention	−0.603**	−0.5372**	0.1982	−3.0418	−0.9956	−0.2105	−0.1347	−0.12	0.1069	−0.3465	0.077

Note: N = 127; ***p<0.001, *p < 0.05, **p < 0.01; Based on 5000 bootstrap samples

Table 4. Mediating model test results of perceived trust

Predictive variables	Result Variables	Direct Effects						Indirect Effect				
		β	Standardized β	SE	t	95%CI		β	Standardized β	SE	95%CI	
KOL types(EG)	perceived trust	0.4933**	0.4646**	0.1843	2.677	0.1286	0.8581					
Perceived trust(EG)	Purchase intention	0.909***	0.873***	0.0433	20.9975	0.8237	0.9951					
KOL types(EG)	Purchase intention	0.61**	0.5514**	0.1897	3.2153	0.2345	0.9854	0.1613	0.1458	0.0918	−0.0203	0.3429
KOL types(SG)	perceived trust	−0.0348	−0.0302	0.2116	−0.1647	−0.4539	0.3842					
Perceived trust(SG)	Purchase intention	0.545***	0.5608***	0.0701	7.7774	0.4065	0.6842					
KOL types(SG)	Purchase intention	−0.603**	−0.5372**	0.1982	−3.0418	−0.9956	−0.2105	−0.584***	−0.5203***	0.1619	−0.9046	−0.2634

Note: N = 127; $* * * p < 0.001$, $* * p < 0.05$, $* * p < 0.01$; Based on 5000 bootstrap samples.

Perceived Trust. Under experience products, the predictive effect of KOL types on purchase intention was significant ($\beta = 0.5514$, $t = 3.2153$, $p = 0.002$). The positive predictive effect of KOL type on perceived trust was significant (β, $t = 2.677$, $p = 0.008$), as was the positive predictive effect of perceived trust on purchase intention. In addition, real KOLs better promoted the formation of consumers' perceived trust. Under search goods, the predictive effect of KOL types on purchase intention was significant ($\beta = -0.5372$, $t = -3.0418$, $p = 0.003$). The negative predictive effect of KOL types on perceived trust was not significant ($\beta = -0.0302$, $t = -0.1647$, $p = 0.870$), while the positive predictive effect of perceived trust on purchase intention was significant. In addition, perceived trust did not play a mediating role in KOL types on purchase intention, hypothesis H4b did not hold and H4a, H5 held.

6 Conclusion and Discussion

This study explores the specific effects of different KOLs (real and virtual) on consumer purchase intentions under different product types (search and experience products) and their mechanisms of action. Firstly, there are significant differences between the two different KOLs on consumer identification and purchase intention in different product type contexts. For search products, the recommendations of virtual KOLs generate higher levels of consumer identification and purchase intentions than those of traditional real-life KOLs; for experience products, consumers have higher levels of consumer identification and purchase intentions for the recommendations of real-life KOLs with greater empathy and authenticity than those of emerging virtual KOLs. At the same time, the study also verified the mediating mechanism of consumer identification in the influence of KOLs on consumer purchase behavior. Perceived trust is only significantly mediated in the generation of purchase intentions for experiential products, but not for search products.

The theoretical contribution of this study is to identify for the first time the emerging marketing method of virtual KOLs and to investigate the differences in the marketing effects and mechanisms of action between real and virtual KOLs. It also proposes a theoretical model of the influence of consumers' purchase intentions in different product types (search products and experience products), deepens the understanding of consumers' motivation in different product types, explains the mediating function of perceived trust and consumer identification in the mechanism of action of KOLs, and provides a useful addition to the existing theoretical research system in this field.

In practice, companies should use different KOLs to recommend their own products and should distinguish whether their products are search products or experience products and adopt different marketing strategies. Companies should avoid blindly following the trend and analyze their products rationally. If they are search products, they should actively try virtual KOLs to help reduce marketing costs and increase online consumers' willingness to buy. When designing the appearance of virtual KOLs, designers or companies should match their intended persona. This will enable consumers to empathize and gain a higher level of perceived trust and consumer identification, leading to better marketing results.

This paper extends the research on KOLs to a certain extent, but it still has certain limitations due to the research conditions. This study only distinguishes between real and virtual KOLs and does not examine the personality characteristics and product relevance of virtual KOLs. In the future, data mining and other methods will be used to analyze social platform data to further explore the effects of different characteristics.

Acknowledgments. This work has been partly supported by the National Natural Science Foundation of China (Grant No. 71901150), National Natural Science Foundation of Guangdong Province (Grant No. 2022A1515012077), Shenzhen Higher Education Support Plan (Grant No. 20200826144104001), Guangdong Province Innovation Team "Intelligent Management and Interdisciplinary Innovation" (Grant No. 2021WCXTD002).

References

1. Koh, J., Kim, Y.G., Butler, B., et al.: Encouraging participation in virtual communities. Commun. ACM **50**(2), 68–73 (2007)
2. Till, B.D., Shimp, T.A.: Endorsers in advertising: the case of negative celebrity information. J. Advert. **27**(1), 67–82 (1998)
3. Nelson, P.: Information and consumer behavior. J. Polit. Econ. **78**(2), 311–329 (1970)
4. Callcott, M.F., Phillips, B.J.: Observations: elves make good cookies: creating likable spokes-character advertising. J. Advert. Res. **36**(5), 73 (1996)
5. Kassymbayeva, A.: The impact of spokes-characters on customer loyalty. Int. J. Bus. Manag. **12**(7), 162–173 (2017)
6. Klein, L.R.: Evaluating the potential of interactive media through a new lens: search versus experience goods. J. Bus. Res. **41**(3), 195–203 (1998)
7. Jiang, W., Song, Y.: Mobile shopping during COVID-19: the effect of hedonic experience on brand conspicuousness, brand identity and associated behavior. Int. J. Environ. Res. Public Health **19**(8), 4894 (2022)
8. Gefen, D., Karahanna, E., Straub, D.W.: Trust and TAM in online shopping: an integrated model. MIS Q. **27**, 51–90 (2003)
9. Friedman, H., Friedman, L.: Endorser effectiveness by product type. J. Adv. Res. **19**(5), 63–71 1979
10. Lee, S.H.M.: The role of consumers' network positions on information-seeking behavior of experts and novices: a power perspective. J. Bus. Res. **67**(1), 2853–2859 (2014)
11. Pahnila, S., Warsta, J.: Online shopping viewed from a habit and value perspective. Behav. Inf. Technol. **29**(6), 621–632 (2010)
12. Nazlan, N.H., Tanford, S., Montgomery, R.: The effect of availability heuristics in online consumer reviews. J. Consum. Behav. **17**(5), 449–460 (2018)
13. Pornpitakpan, C.: The persuasiveness of source credibility: a critical review of five decades' evidence. J. Appl. Soc. Psychol. **34**(2), 243–281 (2004)
14. Erdem, T., Swait, J.: Brand credibility, brand consideration, and choice. J. Consum. Res. **31**(1), 191–198 (2004)

Examining the Relative Importance of Factors Influencing Perinatal Anxiety in Different Perinatal Periods During the Covid-19 Pandemic: A Random Forest-Based Approach

Xiaobing Gan[1], Ting Guo[1], Yang Wang[1(✉)], Zhenzhen Zhu[1], and Yongjie Zhou[2]

[1] College of Management, Shenzhen University, Shenzhen, China
wangyanghim@szu.edu.cn
[2] Shenzhen Kangning Hospital, Shenzhen, China

Abstract. Perinatal anxiety disorders are associated with adverse outcomes for mothers and children. However, most studies investigating perinatal anxiety, especially during the Covid-19 pandemic, have focused on pregnancy symptoms at a certain time. This study aimed to describe the prevalence of anxiety in four perinatal periods and to determine the relative importance of factors influencing anxiety in different perinatal periods during the Covid-19 pandemic. This cross-sectional study recruited 2030 women from February 28 to April 26, 2020, in Wuhan, Beijing, and Lanzhou, China. A random forest model was used to identify factors affecting anxiety during four perinatal periods, and the Shapley Additive explanation (SHAP) method was used to further interpret the results. The results show that during the Covid-19 pandemic, the prevalence of anxiety in the four trimesters of pregnancy was 21.5%, 19.2%, 21.6%, and 27.2%, respectively. Depression, insomnia, and worries or fears during childbirth are all important factors affecting maternal anxiety, among which depression is the most important factor. However, the relative importance of factors in different stages of pregnancy is different, so precise intervention should be implemented in time to alleviate the occurrence of maternal anxiety.

Keywords: Perinatal Anxiety Disorders · Covid-19 · Random Forest · Shapley Additive explanation

1 Introduction

Since December 2019, Covid-19 has spread rapidly and widely around the world and quickly became a global pandemic. In a high-risk and stressful environment caused by infectious disease outbreaks, people tend to feel fear and uncertainty and are prone to a range of psychological problems and physical symptoms [1]. During the Covid-19 pandemic, the public was found to have more severe mental health problems than before, with a relatively high prevalence [2]. Due to changes in the level and function of the endocrine system during pregnancy, pregnant women are prone to physical and

Y. Tu and M. Chi (Eds.): WHICEB 2023, LNBIP 481, pp. 119–130, 2023.
https://doi.org/10.1007/978-3-031-32302-7_11

psychological stress reactions, and psychological stress reactions will lead to different degrees of fear, tension, and other emotions, and these negative emotions will make pregnant women more psychological disorders such as stress, anxiety, and depression are prone to occur, which have a great impact on the physical and mental health of pregnant women and fetuses. Mei et al. [3] found a higher prevalence of anxiety and depression in pregnant women during the Covid-19 epidemic than before the epidemic. In contrast, a cross-sectional study of 156 participants showed that pregnant women had the same rates of anxiety as before the pandemic and significantly higher rates of depression; Pregnant women living in Wuhan have no higher levels of depression or anxiety than those in other areas [4]. The impact of the COVID-19 pandemic on maternal mental health outcomes has not been fully elucidated. Therefore, after the outbreak of the new coronavirus, we conducted a survey of maternal mental health in different provinces in China, including Wuhan (the first city of the outbreak, with the largest number of confirmed cases), Beijing (the number of confirmed cases was moderate), Lanzhou (the number of confirmed cases was relatively less). Demographic and COVID-19-related characteristics, such as age, degree of education, and economic loss, were also collected to analyze the mental health status of pregnant women during the Covid-19 pandemic.

Perinatal mental health is an important public health issue because of its negative impact on maternal and fetal health and its significant economic cost to society if not addressed and treated. Common mental health problems that women experience during the perinatal period include anxiety, depression, insomnia, etc. Symptoms of perinatal depression have been extensively studied, but perinatal anxiety has received limited attention from researchers and health professionals [5]. The research suggests that maternal prenatal and postnatal anxiety may contribute to an increased risk of adverse maternal sequelae, including higher negative somatic symptoms, postpartum depression, and increased risk of suicide [6]. At the same time, there is evidence that the prevalence of anxiety varies widely between different perinatal periods (0.9% to 22.9%) [7]. However, most research on anxiety during pregnancy, especially during the Covid-19 pandemic, has focused on anxiety in one or two trimesters, such as the second and third trimesters [7]. Investigating potential clinical risk factors and associated factors for different perinatal anxiety disorders may help to more precisely target preventive interventions in at-risk mothers.

Random forests (RF) provide a natural way to measure feature importance with average feature impurity reduction [8]. Feature importance measurement using random forests has attracted more and more attention in many fields [9]. The advantage of using random forests instead of multiple linear regression methods is that it allows for non-linearities and interactions between the data without explicitly identifying them [8]. Random forests are suitable for the problem of small sample data and are robust to unbalanced data. It can achieve higher prediction accuracy without rescaling and modifying the data [10]. Although random forests can provide good classification and prediction accuracy, the best performance models belong to very complex or ensemble models that are very difficult to explain (black box) [11]. Diagnosis or treatment decisions that rely on black-box machine models violate the principles of evidence-based medicine because there is no explanation of reasoning or reason for a particular decision in an individual case [11]. Hu et al. [12] used XGBoost, logistic regression (LR), and random forests (RF) to build a prediction model to predict the mortality of critically ill influenza patients, and then used SHAP to visualize the impact of selected features on mortality. Therefore, this study introduces the interpretable machine learning SHAP (Shapley Additive exPlanation) method to further analyze the results of random forests and enhance the interpretability of the model. This study aimed to analyze maternal anxiety in different perinatal periods, and use machine learning algorithms to determine the differences and importance of the influencing factors of anxiety disorders in different pregnancy and postpartum periods during the Covid-19 pandemic.

2 Materials and Methods

2.1 Participants

From February 28 to April 26, 2020, a cross-sectional study was conducted in Beijing, Wuhan, and Lanzhou, China. Participants were recruited by staged sampling. In the first stage, cities were selected for cross-sectional study according to the severity of the epidemic (Wuhan, Beijing, Lanzhou) and economic development (Beijing, Wuhan, Lanzhou). In the second phase, self-assessment questionnaires were sent to investigators in the three cities, who then sent them to local obstetric health facilities. Finally, a self-assessment questionnaire was completed by those who attended the obstetric health facility.

A total of 2236 participants were recruited to complete the self-assessment questionnaire, and 2030 questionnaires were included in the study after analysis of the questionnaire filling situation. The population of Beijing, Wuhan, and Lanzhou in 2020 is 21.893 million, 12.448 million, and 4.384 million respectively. According to the population difference between the three cities, the sample numbers of Beijing, Wuhan, and Lanzhou are 824, 764, and 442 respectively. The criteria for inclusion were: (1) Participants were adult pregnant women (no less than 18 years old); (2) Only participants in Beijing, Wuhan, and Lanzhou were studied; (3) During pregnancy or within 8 weeks after delivery.

2.2 Demographic and Clinical Characteristics

Demographic and clinical characteristics of the participants in three aspects, physical, psychological, and social, were collected. A total of 19 characteristics were selected as the influencing factors of maternal anxiety in different pregnancy periods analyzed in this study, including Age, Marital status, Place of residence(indicates the severity of the impact of the epidemic), Degree of education, Annual household income, Financial loss in Covid-19, Number of pregnancies, Parity, Smoking, Drinking, Nausea and vomiting during pregnancy, Daily attention to fetal movement, Contractions, Stomach ache, Impact of pregnancy on the action, Any worries or fears during childbirth, Depression, Insomnia, and Be take care of.

2.3 Anxiety

Participants' anxiety was assessed using the Generalized Anxiety Disorder Scale (GAD-7). The GAD-7 was developed by Spitzer et al. [13]. This single-dimension scale is a seven-item self-assessment tool with a 4-point Likert scale ranging from 0 (never) to 3 (almost every day). The scale was used to measure how often the participants experienced anxiety in the past two weeks. The Generalized Anxiety Disorder Scale (GAD-7) has a total score of 21, with 0 to 4 indicating no anxiety, 5 to 9 indicating mild anxiety, 10 to 13 indicating moderate anxiety, 14 to 18 indicating moderate to severe anxiety, and 19 to 21 indicating severe anxiety. The Cronbach's alpha of the scale was 0.92 in our study. Therefore, in this study, 5 points of the cut-off score were used to classify participants with and without anxiety.

2.4 Random Forest Classification

The random forest model first randomly samples data and features and uses the extracted data and features to build a decision tree and form a combined classifier [14]. In this study, four random forest models were established for samples of different gestational periods to identify the influencing factors of maternal anxiety. Use the open-source sci-kit-learn library in Python to implement the random forest algorithm and train the model.

2.5 Model Interpretation

Random forests can automatically generate relatively important scores for features, but this score can only be used for variable interpretation, and the extent and direction of the impact of features cannot be known. Therefore, an interpretable machine learning SHAP method is introduced to further explain random forest results. SHAP is an additivity explanation model inspired by Shapley values, which belongs to the post hoc explanation method of models. The core idea of SHAP is to calculate the marginal contribution of features to the model output, and then explain the "black box model" from the global and local levels. Global interpretability reflects the positive or negative impact of each feature on the target variable, while local interpretability evaluates the contribution of features in each sample to explain the specific output of each instance. To further explain our research model, this study employs TreeSHAP, which is developed based on the tree model in the Python SHAP package.

3 Results

3.1 Demographic Characteristics of Participants

Information on specific demographic characteristics for the four trimesters is provided in the Appendix. A total of 2030 maternal data were collected, with a total anxiety rate of 21.23%. There were 461 samples in the first trimester, with an anxiety rate of 21.5%; there were 449 samples in the second trimester and an anxiety rate of 19.2%; the largest number of samples in the third trimester of pregnancy was 1039, with an anxiety rate of 21.6%; the smallest number of women in the postpartum period was 81 and the anxiety rate was 27.2%.

3.2 Testing Prediction Accuracy of Random Forest

To explore the influencing factors of maternal anxiety in different pregnancy periods, four random forest models were established for analysis. Using grid search to optimize the parameters of the established random forest model can ensure that the parameters with the highest accuracy can be found within the specified parameter range, and find the optimal parameters shown in Table 1. The performance of the random forest classifier was then evaluated using 10-fold cross-validation, and the results showed that the accuracy of the first trimester was 0.84 with AUCs of 0.83; the accuracy of the second trimester was 0.84 with AUCs of 0.86; the accuracy of the third trimester was 0.87 with AUCs was 0.92; the accuracy of the postpartum model was 0.84, and the AUCs were 0.88 (see Fig. 1. And Table 1.).

Table 1. Parameters of the Random Forest Model.

Hyper-parameter	Range	First trimester	Second trimester	Third trimester	Postpartum
n_estimators	[10,100,1000]	10	1000	1000	10
min_saples_split	[2, 5, 10, 12]	5	12	12	12
max_features	[2, 5, 8, 10, 12]	8	12	8	5
max_depth	[2, 3, 5, 8, 10]	8	8	3	3
accuracy		0.84	0.84	0.87	0.84
AUCs value		0.83	0.86	0.92	0.88

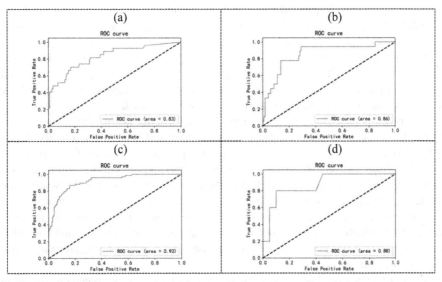

Fig. 1. ROC curves for four perinatal periods. (a) First trimester, (b) Second trimester, (c) Third trimester, and (d) Postpartum.

3.3   Importance Ranking of Machine Learning

The random forest model determines the importance of features by the average impurity reduction value, and the importance of the features is automatically distributed by the model, but it cannot quantify the contribution of each feature to the model output. To determine the positive and negative effects of features and give a quantitative description of these effects, we use the SHAP method to analyze the factors that affect the output of the machine learning model, which further improves the interpretability of the model. Figure 2.a shows the feature importance results obtained from the random forest model for the first trimester by SHAP. It was found that the top five important factors affecting the anxiety of pregnant women in the first trimester were depression, insomnia, place of residence, any worries or fears during childbirth, and the impact of pregnancy on the action. Depression was the most important factor affecting anxiety in the first trimester, changing the absolute probability of predicting anxiety by an average of 32 percentage points. Insomnia and place of residence changed by 9% and 7% respectively. SHAP summary plot combines feature importance and feature impact, depicting the corresponding contribution of each factor to the outcome variable. Each point on the summary plot is the Shapley value of a feature and an instance, where the red and blue points reflect high and low feature values respectively, and the distribution of the Shapley value of each feature can be understood through the summary plot. For pregnant women in the first trimester, most factors have a negative impact on anxiety. The SHAP summary plot shows that fewer depression and insomnia scores are associated with a lower risk of anxiety, and higher scores are associated with a higher risk of anxiety. Pregnant women with worries and fears of childbirth are at higher risk of anxiety. The greater the impact of pregnancy on the action, the higher the risk of anxiety. Factors that alleviate the anxiety of pregnant women in the first trimester include the place of residence, financial loss in COVID-19, and whether there is someone to take care of their daily life. Those who lived in areas that were more severely affected by the epidemic (Wuhan), suffered more financial loss in COVID-19, and took care of pregnant women's daily life more, had a lower risk of anxiety (see Fig. 2.b).

Figure 2.c shows the results of the feature importance analysis performed on the data of pregnant women in the second trimester. For pregnant women in the second trimester, depression, insomnia, financial loss in COVID-19, place of residence and any worries or fears during childbirth are the top five important factors affecting anxiety. Among them, depression is the most important influencing factor, which changes the probability of predicting anxiety by 35% on average, and insomnia and financial loss in COVID-19 change by 15% and 6%, respectively. Figure 2.d shows that depression, insomnia, financial loss in COVID-19, and any worries and fears during childbirth have a facilitative effect on anxiety. The higher the scores of depression and insomnia, the greater the financial loss in COVID-19, the pregnant women who live in areas with more serious epidemics (Wuhan), and the pregnant women who have worries and fears during childbirth, the higher the risk of anxiety. Older, pregnant women, who have higher annual family income, and have more severe nausea and vomiting during pregnancy have a lower risk of anxiety.

It can be seen from Fig. 2.e that the top five factors affecting pregnant women in the third trimester of pregnancy are depression, insomnia, any worries or fears during childbirth, the impact of pregnancy on the action, and financial loss in COVID-19. As in the first and second trimesters, depression and insomnia were the two most important factors affecting maternal anxiety, changing the mean predicted probability by 27% and 12%, respectively. Figure 2.f shows that the higher the depression and insomnia scores, the greater the worries or fears during childbirth, the greater the impact of pregnancy on actions, and the greater financial loss in COVID-19, the greater the risk of anxiety.

The top five influencing factors affecting postpartum anxiety are depression, worries or fears during childbirth, insomnia, financial loss in COVID-19, and age (see Fig. 2.g). As with pregnancy, depression was the most important factor affecting anxiety in postpartum women, changing the mean predicted probability by 19%. Any worries or fears during childbirth and insomnia changed the mean predicted probability of anxiety by 15% and 8%, respectively. Figure 2.h shows that depression, worries or fears during childbirth, insomnia, financial loss in COVID-19, and age are risk factors for anxiety in pregnant women, and the impact of pregnancy on action has a mitigating effect on anxiety.

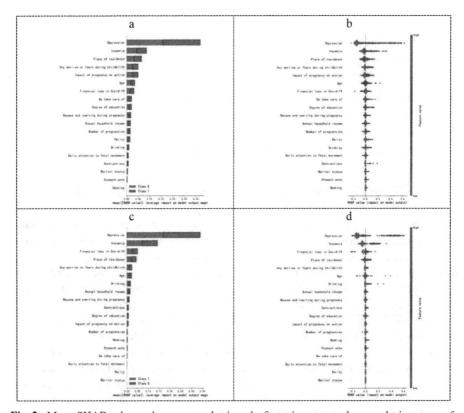

Fig. 2. Mean SHAP value and summary plot in a, b: first trimester, c, d: second trimester, e, f: third trimester, g, h: postpartum

126   X. Gan et al.

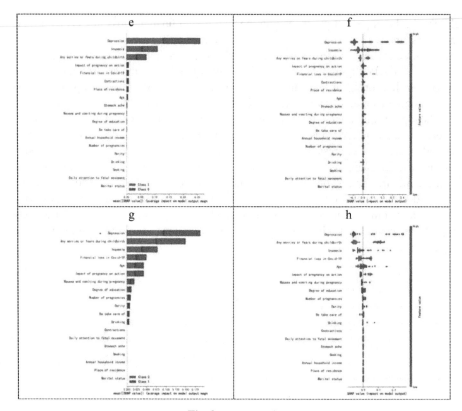

Fig. 2. (*continued*)

According to Fig. 2., the order of the importance of the characteristics affecting maternal anxiety during the four pregnancy periods is shown in Table 2. Comparing the importance rankings of influencing factors on anxiety in different pregnancy periods, it was found that there were differences in the factors affecting anxiety in different pregnancy periods. The impact of place of residence on anxiety during pregnancy is more important, but for postpartum women, the importance of the place of residence is relatively low. The impact of pregnancy on action is an important factor in the three trimesters except for the second trimester, and the ranking of importance in the second trimester is relatively low. Some factors are relatively important in the characteristics of individual periods. For example, whether there is someone to take care of is relatively important in the first trimester, annual family income and drinking have a greater impact on pregnant women in the second trimester, contractions and stomach aches are the most important in the third trimester, and the number of pregnancies has a greater impact on postpartum women's anxiety than other periods. Depression was the most important influencing factor for maternal anxiety in all periods, and insomnia and worries or fears during childbirth were also the most important influencing factors. In contrast, marital status was less important for maternal anxiety in all periods, as was daily attention to fetal movement and smoking.

Table 2. Ranking of feature importance of anxiety in different pregnancy periods.

Attribute names	First trimester	Second trimester	Third trimester	Postpartum
Depression	1	1	1	1
Insomnia	2	2	2	3
Place of residence	3	4	4	18
Any worries or fears during childbirth	4	5	3	2
Impact of pregnancy on action	5	12	4	6
Age	6	6	8	5
Financial loss in COVID-19	7	3	5	4
We take care of	8	16	12	11
Degree of education	9	11	11	8
Nausea and vomiting during pregnancy	10	9	10	7
Annual household income	11	8	13	17
Number of pregnancies	12	13	14	9
Parity	13	18	15	10
Drinking	14	7	16	12
Daily attention to fetal movement	15	17	18	14
Contractions	16	10	6	13
Marital status	17	19	19	19
Stomach ache	18	15	9	15
Smoking	19	14	17	16

4   Discussion

Random forest models were used to predict maternal anxiety and to assess the importance of influencing factors affecting anxiety in different trimesters of pregnancy. The experimental results show that the random forest model has high predictive performance and discriminative ability, and it is effective in identifying maternal anxiety. However, as a black-box model, random forest lacks an explanation of the prediction process and results. Therefore, we conduct an in-depth analysis through the SHAP method to quantify the influence of factors to explore how these factors affect maternal anxiety.

The study shows that the total anxiety rate of pregnant women is 21.23%, and the anxiety rates of the four pregnancy periods are 21.5%, 19.2%, 21.6%, and 27.2%, respectively. Anxiety prevalence was lowest in the second trimester and highest in postpartum women. Farrell et al. [15] believe that women's concern about new family members makes postpartum women's anxiety rate significantly higher than that of pregnant women. In the second trimester, the fetus develops more smoothly, the growth rate is relatively fast, and the overall symptoms of the mother are relatively stable [16]. Based

128   X. Gan et al.

on this, it is reasonable that the prevalence of anxiety in the first and third trimesters is higher than in the second trimester.

For different pregnancy periods, depression and insomnia are the most important factors affecting maternal anxiety, and they all have a positive impact on anxiety, that is, the higher the scores of depression and insomnia, the higher the risk of maternal anxiety. Depression and anxiety are highly comorbid, and it is generally believed that anxiety and depression are closely related [17]. Insomnia, a stable marker of anxiety and depression, is one of the common symptoms of both disorders [18]. In addition to depression and insomnia, any worries or fears of childbirth is also high in all trimesters of pregnancy, especially in the postpartum and third trimesters, possibly because these two periods are closer to labor and more intuitive to the mother. Hu et al. [19] found that worries and fears about childbirth were independent factors affecting mental health during pregnancy.

The place of residence is more important to the anxiety of women during pregnancy, which may be due to the different epidemic blockade measures implemented in Lanzhou, Beijing, and Wuhan, and the degree to which women can receive routine prenatal care to determine the health of the fetus and themselves [20]. Since this study was conducted in China, there is a custom of "confinement". Postpartum women stay at home regardless of whether there is an epidemic or not and are less affected by the epidemic blockade policies in different regions. The influence of place of residence on postpartum women's anxiety may also be related to the imbalance of postpartum women collected in this study in the three cities. In the second trimester, the condition of the fetus and the pregnant woman itself is relatively stable, and the mobility of the pregnant woman will not be restricted too much [16].

The study found that the feature importance of maternal anxiety is different in different gestational periods. In addition to depression, insomnia, and any worries or fears during childbirth, attention needs to be paid to women in the first trimester who live in areas with relatively backward economic development (such as Lanzhou) and whose pregnancy status has a greater impact on their actions. For women in the second trimester, special attention needs to be paid to women who have suffered greater economic losses due to the epidemic, live in areas with severe epidemics (such as Wuhan), and younger women who have drinking habits. For women in the third trimester, it is also necessary to pay attention to the impact of pregnancy on the action, greater losses due to the epidemic, and increased frequency of contractions have a greater risk of anxiety. Among postpartum women, the more worries or fears of childbirth, the greater the economic loss, and the older they are, the more likely they are to suffer from anxiety disorders. The results of the study show that there are similarities and differences in the feature importance of maternal anxiety during different pregnancy periods, and more attention should be paid to important factors (such as depression, insomnia, and worries or fears during childbirth) for intervention.

This study has some limitations. First of all, this study adopts a cross-sectional design, which makes it difficult to compare the changes in the incidence of anxiety before and after the outbreak of Covid-19. At the same time, the cross-sectional design can only explore relevant factors, but it is difficult to draw causal conclusions. Secondly, this study uses Chinese multi-center data samples, which can provide some references for related research in China, but cannot provide sufficient reference significance for other regions. Finally, the postpartum data collected in this study are relatively small, and there may be insufficient research on postpartum anxiety. This study also has some strengths. First of all, unlike previous studies on a certain period of pregnancy, our study analyzes maternal anxiety throughout the prenatal and postpartum periods, which has stronger integrity and generalization. Second, this study uses a random forest model to analyze maternal anxiety, which enriches the research in this field. Our study also introduced the SHAP method to further explain the precise impact of each factor on maternal anxiety at different gestational trimesters.

5   Conclusion

This study combined the random forest and SHAP methods to identify and analyze factors affecting maternal anxiety in different gestation periods. Random forest was used to analyze the demographic factors of pregnant women, but due to the "black box" nature of the random forest model, the SHAP method was introduced to further explain the influence of various factors on maternal anxiety. Our results showed that during the COVID-19 pandemic, the prevalence of anxiety varied across pregnancies, with the highest prevalence occurring during the postpartum period. Therefore, the public should pay more attention to the occurrence of women's postpartum anxiety. In addition, similarities and differences were found in the feature importance of maternal anxiety in different trimesters. Depression, insomnia, and worries or fears of childbirth were important factors for maternal anxiety in all trimesters, especially depression. Certain factors are more important to the anxiety of pregnant women in a specific pregnancy, such as place of residence, daily life with care, and annual family income. Based on this, different interventions can be taken in different pregnancy periods to alleviate the occurrence of maternal anxiety.

Acknowledgement. This research was supported by the National Natural Science Foundation of China under Grant 72004072.

References

1. Usher, K., Durkin, J., Bhullar, N.: The COVID-19 pandemic and mental health impacts. Int. J. Mental Health Nurs. Early View. 29(30), 315 (2020)
2. Heymann, D.L., et al.: COVID-19: what is next for public health?. Lancet 10224, 395 (2020)
3. Mei, H., et al.: Depression, anxiety, and stress symptoms in pregnant women before and during the COVID-19 pandemic. J. Psychosom. Res. 149, 110586 (2021)
4. Dong, H., et al.: Investigation on the mental health status of pregnant women in China during the Pandemic COVID-19. Arch. Gynecol. Obstet. 303(2), 463-469 (2021)
5. Morris, J.R., et al.: Early pregnancy anxiety during the COVID-19 pandemic: preliminary findings from the UCSF ASPIRE study. BMC Pregnancy Childbirth 22(1), 1–12 (2022)
6. Alder, Dr. P.J., et al.: Depression and anxiety during pregnancy: a risk factor for obstetric, fetal and neonatal outcome? A critical review of the literature (2007)

7. Dennis, C.L., Falah-Hassani, K., Shiri, R.: Prevalence of antenatal and postnatal anxiety: Systematic review and meta-analysis. Br. J. Psychiatry J. Mental Sci. **210**(5), 315 (2017)

8. Gromping, U.: Variable importance assessment in regression: linear regression versus random forest. Amer Statist **63**(4), 308–319 (2009)

9. Strobl, C., et al.: Bias in random forest variable importance measures: Illustrations, sources and a solution. Bmc Bioinf. **8**(1), 1–21 (2007)

10. Daga, S., et al.: Decision tree and random forest models for outcome prediction in antibody incompatible kidney transplantation. Biomed. Signal Process. Control **37**(10), 1025–1042 (2002)

11. London, A.J.: Artificial intelligence and black-box medical decisions: accuracy versus explainability. Hastings Cent. Rep. **49**(1), 15–21 (2019)

12. Hu, C.A., et al.: Using a machine learning approach to predict mortality in critically ill influenza patients: a cross-sectional retrospective multicentre study in Taiwan. BMJ **10**(2), e033898 (2020)

13. Spitzer, R.L., et al.: A brief measure for assessing generalized anxiety disorder: the GAD-7. Arch. Intern. Med. **166**(10), 1092–1097 (2006)

14. Breiman, L.: Random forests. Mach Learn **45**(1), 5–32 (2001)

15. Farrell, T., et al.: The impact of the COVID-19 pandemic on the perinatal mental health of women (2020)

16. Kiserud, T., et al.: The world health organization fetal growth charts: concept, findings, interpretation, and application. Am. J. Obstet. Gynecol. **218**(2), S619 (2018)

17. Zbozinek, T.D., et al.: Diagnostic overlap of generalized anxiety disorder and major depressive disorder in a primary care sample. Depression Anxiety **29**(12), 1065–1071 (2012)

18. Neckelmann, D., Mykletun, A., Dahl, A.A.: Chronic insomnia as a risk factor for developing anxiety and depression. Sleep **30**(7), 873 (2007)

19. Hu, M., et al.: The prevalence and correlates of peripartum depression in different stages of pregnancy during COVID-19 pandemic in China. BMC Pregnancy Childbirth **22**(1), 1–13 (2022)

20. Cheng, B., Chen, J., Wang, G.: Psychological factors influencing choice of prenatal diagnosis in Chinese multiparous women with advanced maternal age. J. Matern. Fetal. Neonatal. Med. **32**(14), 2295–2301 (2019)

Research on Information Anxiety in Different Epidemic Prevention and Control States of Public Health Emergency – Based on Information Task Perspective

Quan Lu[1]([✉]), Xiaoying Zheng[1], Yutian Shen[1], and Jing Chen[2]

[1] School of Information Management, Wuhan University, Wuhan 430072, China
mrluquan@whu.edu.cn
[2] School of Information Management, Central China Normal University, Wuhan 430079, China

Abstract. This paper explored the information anxiety of community residents in different prevention and control states from the perspective of information tasks, and provided suggestions on information service for future public health emergency. Through in-depth interviews, the information anxiety scale of community residents in five prevention and control states was constructed. The information tasks and information anxiety of residents in each prevention and control state were investigated through questionnaires, and the differences and causes were analyzed. Our research found that information anxiety was highest when residents were isolated at home, and lowest when they were in centralized isolation. The anxiety of information environment, information quality and quantity were the highest in the case of home isolation and community isolation. The highest degree of information anxiety due to the heaviest burden of information tasks in home isolation, and there is a positive correlation between the two. Residents' information anxiety is positively correlated with the proportion of material/life tasks, and is negatively correlated with the proportion of daily epidemic notification tasks.

Keywords: Information Anxiety · Prevention and Control States · Public Health Emergency · Information Task

1 Introduction

During the outbreak of the COVID-19 pandemic, massive epidemic information, false news and negative reports will cause anxiety and panic among some people, and "infodemic" has brought unprecedented challenges [1]. To control the spread of the pandemic, modern quarantine strategies have proven to be highly effective means of reducing exposure rates. China had taken very active and precise prevention and control measures to reduce the spread of infectious diseases and protect the lives of the public. Different quarantine strategies had been adopted for groups with different transmission risks to achieve precise prevention and control. This not only controlled the spread of the disease, but also minimized the inconvenience caused by the quarantine measures to the

Y. Tu and M. Chi (Eds.): WHICEB 2023, LNBIP 481, pp. 131–143, 2023.
https://doi.org/10.1007/978-3-031-32302-7_12

public life. Although isolation is necessary for public health emergency, it also have an impact on people's mental health [2]. According to the precise quarantine strategies, the living state of residents can be divided into several different types. Different lifestyles caused by quarantine strategies also change the information behavior of the residents, which is reflected in the information tasks under different prevention and control states. For example, residents under home isolation are unable to go out to purchase materials, thus generating special information tasks in this situation, such as searching material information online and so on. Extra information tasks brought by quarantine strategies also increase information anxiety [3]. The living mode and information task of residents under different prevention and control states are generally different, which may lead to different information anxiety.

This raises an important question for us, that is, does information anxiety present different characteristics under different prevention and control states? How can we reduce information anxiety by effectively providing information services in different states? However, existing research on information anxiety in the context of public health emergency regard the epidemic prevention and control as the overall background, and rarely further classify it, ignoring the change of information anxiety caused by the difference of information tasks under different states. Therefore, it is necessary to explore the epidemic-related information tasks and corresponding information anxiety of community residents under different epidemic prevention and control states, and summarize precise suggestions to alleviate information anxiety. This could provide recommendations for information anxiety relief and information services delivery during future pandemics and enrich the theory of information anxiety under public health emergency. The objectives of this study are as follows: (1) To explore the information anxiety of community residents under different prevention and control states. (2) Analyze the difference of information anxiety types of community residents under different prevention and control states. (3) To understand the burden and composition of information tasks of community residents under different prevention and control states, and to discuss the causes of information anxiety from the perspective of information tasks.

2   Literature Review

The concept of information anxiety was first proposed by Wurman, who believed that information anxiety is a black hole between data and knowledge, and a state of stress resulting in anxiety when the required information cannot be accessed, understood and utilized [4]. Information anxiety is a state in which negative emotions such as irritability and anxiety occur in the process of searching, understanding, selecting, collecting and utilizing information to meet specific information needs.

Some scholars have studied information anxiety under public health emergencies. Past research mainly analyzed the influencing factors of information anxiety, including information behavior, information factors and individual factors. Then corresponding measures to relieve information anxiety were put forward. Qiong Wang et al. found that there was a positive correlation between information overload and anxiety in the context of public health emergencies, which was moderated by Confucian responsibility thinking [5]. Compared with traditional information channels such as official websites and newspapers, obtaining information about public health emergencies from social media channels is more likely to aggravate information anxiety [6]. The overuse of social media caused by isolation also contributes to information anxiety [7]. Although past research had considered the special impact of quarantine strategies on information anxiety in public health emergencies, few research have differentiated between different prevention and control states. As a result, the proposed measures to relieve information anxiety are not precise.

Task-based information search theory puts forward that information task is one of the motivations of many users' information search behavior. Task prompts users to generate information needs, and the types of tasks are diverse [8]. Scholars generally classify tasks into different types from different perspectives based on research purposes and needs [9]. In addition, information tasks are closely related to users' working and living situations, and the complexity of information tasks is closely related to users' experience of information anxiety [10]. Community residents under different epidemic prevention and control states have unique information task characteristics which cause different information anxiety. Therefore, this paper chose information task as the theoretical perspective to explore information anxiety under different prevention and control states.

3   Methodology

In this paper, based on previous literature, the existing information anxiety scale was revised according to the research scene and interview data. The information anxiety scale includes 4 dimensions, 19 sub-dimensions and 19 items. Through questionnaire survey, information tasks characteristic and information anxiety of community residents under different epidemic prevention and control states were investigated. Based on the results, the causes of information anxiety were discussed, and corresponding mitigation strategies were proposed. The questionnaire was mainly divided into five parts: basic demographic information, epidemic prevention and control status, epidemic related information task burden, main information task types proportion and information anxiety scale.

3.1   Questionnaire Preparation

By reviewing China's COVID-19 prevention and control policies, the state of epidemic prevention and control was divided into the following five types according to the restrictions of residents' range of activity: (1) Centralized isolation: centralized management organized by the government in designated places. (2) Home isolation: health monitoring at one's own home. (3) Community isolation: Partition isolation of residential districts and grid management in communities. (4) Regional control: control administrative regions at all levels to restrict the flow of people. (5) Social control: On the premise of not affecting the normal production and life order, reduce population mobility without additional compulsory measures.

This paper classified the information tasks under the state of prevention and control according to the content of the tasks. Through interviews with community residents under different state of prevention and control, five types of epidemic-related information which mainly searched and browsed by people was classified. They are materials/life, health, community notification, daily epidemic notification, and other. Questionnaire items were designed to investigate the proportion of time spent by residents to complete each type of information in all related information, as the proportion of such information tasks among residents.

3.2   Revised Information Anxiety Scale

Most of the existing studies are based on the five influential factors in Wurman's information anxiety theory. Starting from the different stages of information processing and the influential factors of information anxiety, the measurement scale is developed and revised. Due to the different research context, the construction of dimensions is also different. Based on information anxiety theory, this study constructed an interview outline and selected eight community residents by random sampling from three cities of Wuhan, Shanghai and Shanxi in China to conduct semi-structured interviews. The respondents were from different epidemic prevention and control states, and ranged in age from 18 to 60. The questions outlined in the interview included: (1) Information tasks during the epidemic prevention and control period. (2) Whether there had been information anxiety and the reasons for the process. (3) Difficulties in finding, obtaining and using epidemic-related information. (4) Suggestions on information services. Combined with the scale dimension results of literature research, according to the steps and methods of topic analysis [11], the interview results were artificially transcribed. After two rounds of back-to-back coding and expert opinion consultation, the 4 dimensions and 20 sub-dimensions of information anxiety in this research scenario were preliminary determined. Some of the coded data are shown in Table 1. The dimensions of the scale formulated in the existing literature mainly include information quality and quantity, information literacy, information environment, information technology and retrieval system quality, personal traits, information access and so on. Most of the dimensions and sub-dimensions were established with reference to previous studies [12, 13], while passive reception and information channels are unique sub-dimensions in epidemic prevention and control scenarios obtained from the interview results.

Table 1. Coded data of partial interviews with community residents.

Dimension	Sub-dimension	Partial original statement
Information quality and quantity anxiety	accuracy	P6: Concerned about whether the number of cases in the community is accurate
	authenticity	P5: Videos of rumors and rumors are a little uncomfortable to watch
	usefulness	P7: There is no list of more helpful information for citizens

(continued)

Table 1. (*continued*)

Dimension	Sub-dimension	Partial original statement
	authority	P6: Kind of distrust the current information, no one channel has enough authority to publish
	timeliness	P2: Our community does not publish very timely, always publish not timely
	Lack of information	P6: Local neighborhood committees do not release information
	Excessive amount of information	P8: Epidemic information accounts for a very large proportion of browsing information, nearly half of it
Information acquisition anxiety	Passive reception	P7: I can't take the initiative to get the information I want through wechat group, so I can only accept it passively
	Information channel	P1: There is no unified channel to publish notices
	Missing information	P3: I'm afraid of missing the information inside buying group
	Information selection	P6: You have to figure out which information is reliable and which is needed
	Time cost	P6: It takes up a lot of time
Information environment anxiety	Information disorganization	P2: The information organization and typesetting in wechat group is quite chaotic
	Negative information	P5: Some negative information on the Internet can actually cause people anxiety
	Behavior of others	P1: Some people stock up on a lot of supplies, and when you read this news, you will stock up on some supplies, which may cause some panic
	Rapid change of information	P1: Local policy information changes too much, too often

(*continued*)

Table 1. (*continued*)

Dimension	Sub-dimension	Partial original statement
Information literacy anxiety	Discriminating ability	P2: Search information is also not very good at identifying its true extent
	Search capability	P4: I don't know where to search for the results I want. Sometimes I can't find the results I want
	Ability to understand and analyze	P2: The voice on the Internet is more extreme, you have to analyze yourself
	Software capability	P4: Don't know how to use QR codes

Based on the 4 dimensions identified, the initial scale of 20 items was compiled. Using the Likert five-point scale from "completely disagree" to "completely agree". The questionnaire was pretested by online random sampling method, and 282 questionnaires were collected. KMO and Bartlett sphericity tests were performed on the questionnaire scale. KMO value was 0.925 and P value was less than 0.05, indicating that the questionnaire scale was suitable for factor analysis. The maximum variance orthogonal rotation was used to extract four factors, and the cumulative variance interpretation rate after factor rotation was 69.061%. The factor loading coefficient after rotation was analyzed, and the inappropriate items are deleted, that is, the timeliness of information quality and quantity anxiety. The factor loading coefficient of the remaining items were greater than 0.4. Combined with the opinions of three experts in the field of information science, the four main factors that should be included in the scale were determined. Cronbach reliability analysis was used. The α coefficient of the scale was 0.886 and α coefficient of each dimension was between 0.5 and 0.9, indicating good reliability of the questionnaire.

Through the naming of factors, the four dimensions of information anxiety in this study were defined as follows: (1) Information quality and quantity anxiety: The quality of information received by residents is too low, and the amount of information is not within a reasonable range, resulting in anxiety. Including all kinds of fake, unavailable spam, too much information or missing information. (2) Information acquisition anxiety: It refers to the anxiety of community residents caused by poor information collection and selection in the process of information acquisition, such as high time cost and lack of official unified information channels. (3) Information environment anxiety: Anxiety is caused by factors in the information environment, such as negative information transmission and bad information behaviors of others. (4) Information literacy anxiety: The ability to use, search, identify, analyze and understand is insufficient, resulting in anxiety and irritability. Compared with previous studies, the scale constructed in this paper is more applicable to epidemic prevention and control scenarios, with a wider range of research objects, not limited to specific information media.

3.3 Questionnaire Data Collection

The object of this study is the community residents under different epidemic prevention and control states. A total of 557 questionnaires were collected through online distribution, and 538 effective questionnaires with an effective rate of 96.5% were obtained by excluding the ones with short response time. The distribution characteristics of questionnaire samples are shown in Table 2. The sample data covers all regions and age groups, which is extensive and representative.

KMO and Bartlett sphericity tests were performed on the questionnaire scale of the formal experiment. The KMO value was 0.923 and the P value was less than 0.05. The questionnaire scale was suitable for factor analysis. Four factors were extracted by maximum variance orthogonal rotation, and the cumulative variance interpretation rate was 68.3% after factor rotation. The factor loading coefficient after rotation was analyzed. The factor loading coefficient of the question items were greater than 0.4, and the questionnaire item and factor reached a reasonable corresponding relationship, and the questionnaire validity was good. Cronbach reliability analysis was used, the α coefficient of the scale was 0.89, and the α coefficient of each dimension was between 0.5 and 0.9, indicating good reliability of the questionnaire.

Table 2. Sample distribution characteristics.

Attribute	Category	Sample number	Percentage
Age	Below 18	46	8.6%
	18–30	382	71%
	31–45	66	12.3%
	46–60	42	7.8%
	Over 60	2	0.4%
State of prevention and control	Centralized isolation	55	10.4%
	Home isolation	98	18.2%
	Community isolation	95	17.7%
	Regional control	139	25.8%
	Social control	150	27.9%

4 Results and Discussion

4.1 General Situation of Information Anxiety of Community Residents Under Different Prevention and Control States

The overall situation and variance analysis of information anxiety under the five prevention and control states are shown in Fig. 1 and Table 3. The results show that there are significant differences in the degree of information anxiety of community residents under different prevention and control states. Residents under home isolation state had the highest degree of information anxiety, while those under centralized isolation state had the lowest degree of information anxiety. The restriction of home isolation and community isolation was relatively strict, and residents were most troubled by information anxiety, and it is urgent to focus on improving their information services.

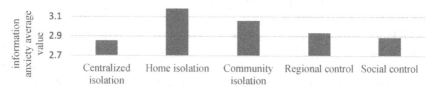

Fig. 1. Information anxiety degree under different prevention and control states.

Table 3. Variance analysis of information anxiety under different prevention and control states.

Centralized isolation	Home isolation	Community isolation	Regional control	Social control	F value
2.854	3.184	3.058	2.935	2.888	0.003

4.2 Analysis of Information Anxiety Types of Community Residents Under Different Prevention and Control States

The distribution of information anxiety types of residents under five prevention and control states is shown in Fig. 2. The information environment anxiety, information quality and quantity anxiety were higher under home isolation and community isolation. Under regional control and social control, residents had the highest anxiety about information environment and the lowest anxiety about information acquisition. In the centralized isolation state, information environment anxiety and information acquisition anxiety were higher.

Information environment anxiety in all states presented a high level, indicating that the adverse network information environment had caused a relatively large impact on all residents. It is the focus of relief and improvement. Studies have shown that receiving too much negative information is a risk factor for aggravating anxiety and panic [14]. Residents obtain a large amount of negative information through the media network, resulting in negative information overload, which amplifies the risk and aggravates anxiety and panic. Therefore, it is crucial to timely shift people's attention to negative information, conduct positive guidance, improve the social media environment and spread positive information.

The residents in the state of home isolation also had difficulty in the quality and quantity of information. It's hard to guarantee the quality of information on social media [15]. An important source of information during home quarantine was wechat groups based on communities or buildings. However, such information is mainly communicated orally and it's difficult to control the quantity and guarantee the quality of information. In the interview with the residents who had been isolated at home, "There is a lot of information and confusion in the group buying group" (P5). In addition, due to the high demand for information in the range of activity under home isolation and community isolation, it is difficult for the information server to release all aspects, and there was a lack of relevant information. Residents who had been quarantinable at home mentioned: "The official release of information lacks some information needed by residents" (P7). Therefore, there are many problems in the community and building wechat group information release mechanism, and it is critical to provide high-quality and comprehensive information based on residents' range of activity. Residents under centralized isolation, home isolation and community isolation also had certain difficulties in obtaining information, and it is necessary to further improve the information acquisition channel and release mechanism under specific prevention and control states.

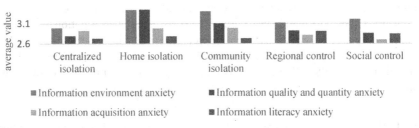

Fig. 2. Distribution of information anxiety types under different prevention and control states.

4.3 Causes of Community Residents' Information Anxiety in Different Prevention and Control States from the Perspective of Information Task

The Influence of Different Information Task Burden on Information Anxiety.
In our research, the burden of epidemic-related information tasks under different prevention and control states was investigated, and 84.4% of community residents felt the burden. The information task burden was heaviest in the home isolation state, while the regional control and social control were light. The material support supply at the centralized isolation points effectively reduced the information task burden. Figure 3 shows that as the epidemic-related information task burden increases, the degree of information anxiety increases significantly and presents a significant positive correlation. It can be inferred that the restrictions under the state of prevention and control lead to a heavier burden of related information tasks among residents, which leads to a higher degree of information anxiety.

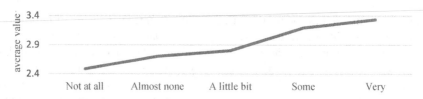

Fig. 3. Information anxiety changed with the epidemic-related information task burden.

As shown in Table 4 and Fig. 4, residents with different burden levels had significant differences in information environment anxiety, information quality and quantity anxiety, and information acquisition anxiety. There are significant positive correlations between them. The deeper the burden level, the higher the degree of these three types of information anxiety. There was no significant difference in information literacy anxiety among different epidemic information task burden levels, and the correlation was not significant, indicating that residents' anxiety caused by inadequate information literacy was not affected by information task burden. The reason is that information literacy is the inherent ability of residents, and residents' perception of self-information literacy ability defects will not increase due to the large task burden. Therefore, the resolution of information literacy anxiety still needs to rely on the improvement of residents' information ability.

Table 4. Variance analysis and correlation of different types of information anxiety under different burden.

Type	F value	P value	Correlation coefficient
Information anxiety	22.850	0.000**	0.368**
Information environment anxiety	24.815	0.000**	0.383**
Information quality and quantity anxiety	17.943	0.000**	0.337**
Information acquisition anxiety	15.903	0.000**	0.317**
Information literacy anxiety	2.281	0.059	−0.08

note: *, $p < 0.05$, * ** *$p < 0.01$

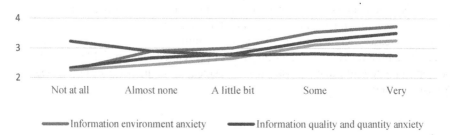

Fig. 4. Different types of information anxiety change with the epidemic-related information task burden.

The Influence of Different Information Task Types on Information Anxiety.
In order to further explore the influence of different types of information tasks on information anxiety, this paper classified information tasks according to their contents and investigated the proportion of relevant tasks, See Fig. 5. In order to ensure the life of families and individuals during the isolation period, the main information task of the residents under home and community isolation was to obtain and use material/life information, accounting for 30.73% and 25.49%. Material/life task burden of centralized isolation were the least, in which residents were provided with living supplies by quarantine points, accounting for only 17.36% of the total. In the three states of centralized isolation, home isolation and community isolation, the range of activity was severely limited, and the task of obtaining community information was relatively large.

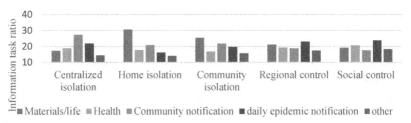

Fig. 5. The proportion of each information task type under different prevention and control states.

Pearson correlation analysis was conducted on residents' information anxiety degree and the proportion of each information task type. Table 5 shows that there is a significant positive correlation between material/life information task proportion and the level of information anxiety. The more material/life information tasks occupy, the more likely to aggravate the generation of information anxiety, including information environment anxiety, information quality and quantity anxiety, information acquisition anxiety. The provision of living materials at the centralized isolation point effectively reduces the proportion of material/life information tasks, which can be considered as one of the reasons for the low level of information anxiety of residents in the centralized isolation state. However, there was a significant negative correlation between daily epidemic notification task proportion and information anxiety. Therefore, it can be inferred that providing convenient and high-quality material and life information for residents under home isolation and strengthening residents' attention to official information can reduce the degree of information anxiety.

Table 5. Correlation analysis between the proportion of different information task types and information anxiety.

Correlation coefficient	Materials/life	Health	Community notification	daily epidemic notification	other
Information anxiety	0.157**	−0.018	−0.048	−0.089*	−0.032
Information environment anxiety	0.113**	−0.034	−0.066	−0.052	−0.009
Information quality and quantity anxiety	0.178**	−0.011	−0.071	−0.095*	−0.036
Information acquisition anxiety	0.109**	0.001	−0.022	−0.074	−0.070
Information literacy anxiety	0.003	−0.015	−0.015	−0.011	0.032

note: $*, p < 0.05, ***p < 0.01$

5 Conclusion

In the case of public health emergencies with quarantine strategies, the change of life mode will change daily information tasks of residents accordingly, which lead to all kinds of information anxiety. Taking the prevention and control of COVID-19 in China as an example, this paper explored the information tasks and anxiety of community residents under different prevention and control states from the perspective of information tasks. On the one hand, the research results are helpful for providing experience and suggestions for improving information services during the prevention and control period of future public health emergencies.

According to the results of the study, there are great differences in information anxiety under different prevention and control states. It is worth noting that the anxiety of the information environment has caused a huge pressure, indicating the importance of information environment in the context of public health emergencies. It is essential to maintain a positive information environment during public health emergency. Because the excessive burden of information tasks will further aggravate information anxiety, it is suggested that the improvement of information services should focus on enhancing its convenience. Residents' information anxiety is positively correlated with the proportion of material/life tasks, and is negatively correlated with the proportion of daily epidemic notification tasks. Therefore, the material/life information services under home and community isolation need to be improved, and directing the public to pay more attention to the official information can reduce the generation of information anxiety.

Acknowledgement. This research was supported by the National Social Science Fund of China (No: 20ATQ008).

References

1. Zarocostas, J.: How to fight an infodemic. lancet. **395**, 676 (2020)
2. FACMHN, K.U.A.R.P., Bhullar, N.: Life in the pandemic: social isolation and mental health (2020)
3. Ebrahim, A., Saif, Z., Buheji, M., AlBasri, N., Al-Husaini, F., Jahrami, H.: COVID-19 information-seeking behavior and anxiety symptoms among parents. OSP J. Health Care Med. **1**, 1–9 (2020)
4. Wurman, R.S., Sume, D., Liefer, L., Whitehouse, A.K.: Information Anxiety 2. Kybernetes **31** (2001)
5. Wang, Q., Luo, X., Tu, R., Xiao, T., Hu, W.: COVID-19 information overload and cyber aggression during the pandemic lockdown: The mediating role of depression/anxiety and the moderating role of Confucian responsibility thinking. Int. J. Environ. Res. Publ. Health **19**, 1540 (2022)
6. Soroya, S.H., Farooq, A., Mahmood, K., Isoaho, J., Zara, S.: From information seeking to information avoidance: Understanding the health information behavior during a global health crisis. Inf. Process. Manage. **58**, 102440 (2021)
7. Catedrilla, J., et al.: Loneliness, boredom and information anxiety on problematic use of social media during the COVID-19 pandemic. In: Proceedings of the 28th International Conference on Computers in Education, pp. 52–60. Asia-Pacific Society for Computers in Education (2020)
8. Vakkari, P.: Task-based information searching. Annu. Rev. Inf. Sci. Technol. (ARIST). **37**, 413–464 (2003)
9. Cole, C.: A theory of information need for information retrieval that connects information to knowledge. J. Am. Soc. Inform. Sci. Technol. **62**, 1216–1231 (2011)
10. Wang, Y.: Task-based information seeking in different study settings. In: Proceedings of the 2018 Conference on Human Information Interaction & Retrieval, pp. 363–365 (2018)
11. Braun, V., Clarke, V.: Using thematic analysis in psychology. Qual. Res. Psychol. **3**, 77–101 (2006)
12. Wang, L., Ma, Z.: Research on information anxiety of university students' under the epidemic of COVID-19—from the perspective of stress disorder. J. Mod. Inf. **40**, 14–24 (2020). (in Chinese)
13. Shen, Y., Lu, Q., Cao, G., Chen, J.: Exploring the changes of user information anxiety at different stages in the process of academic information seeking. Inf. Sci. **39**, 143–151 (2021). (in Chinese)
14. Rudaizky, D., Basanovic, J., MacLeod, C.: Biased attentional engagement with, and disengagement from, negative information: independent cognitive pathways to anxiety vulnerability? Cogn. Emot. **28**, 245–259 (2014)
15. Agarwal, N., Yiliyasi, Y.: Information quality challenges in social media. In: ICIQ (2010)

A Systematic Literature Review of Digital Transformation of Manufacturing Enterprises: Bibliometric Analysis and Knowledge Framework

Zhiwei Zhang, Ning Zhang[✉], and Jiayi Gu

School of Information, Central University of Finance and Economics, Beijing, China
zhangning@cufe.edu.cn

Abstract. How manufacturing companies can achieve digital transformation is an important issue of concern in theory and practice. The research results of digital transformation of manufacturing enterprises are rich and the research topics are diverse, but it is still necessary to systematically summarize previous achievements and build a relatively complete knowledge framework to provide support for subsequent research. This paper analyzes the digital transformation literatures of manufacturing enterprises by knowledge map with CiteSpace. First, identify the research topics and key documents of digital transformation of manufacturing enterprises based on co-citation analysis; Secondly, the research frontiers and research hotspots are identified based on keyword co-occurrence analysis; Finally, the knowledge framework of digital transformation research of manufacturing enterprises is constructed. In the knowledge framework, six research themes are identified, i.e., digital technology, dynamic capability, circular economy, digital servitization, lean manufacturing and maturity model. Several cross-topic research results were found, providing ideas for future research in the field of digital transfor-mation of manufacturing enterprises.

Keywords: Manufacturing Enterprise · Digital Transformation · Knowledge Map · Bibliometric · CiteSpace

1 Introduction

The main part of the real economy is the manufacturing industry, and the digital transformation of industrial enterprises is quite significant. But digital transformation is a complicated process that involves not only technical issues but also organizational and management changes (Verhoef et al., 2021), which is both an opportunity and a challenge for manufacturing companies. At this point, both business managers and scholars are interested in how manufacturing enterprises can achieve digital transformation.

In the existing research on the digital transformation of manufacturing enterprises, scholars have focused on technology adoption (Agostini and Nosella, 2020), digital (Abou-foul et al., 2021), business model (Chen et al., 2018; Caputo et al., 2021)

Y. Tu and M. Chi (Eds.): WHICEB 2023, LNBIP 481, pp. 144–155, 2023.
https://doi.org/10.1007/978-3-031-32302-7_13

and ecosystems (Kohtamäki et al., 2019) from different perspectives. In general, the research results of digital transformation of manufacturing enterprises are rich, and the research topics are diverse, but it is still necessary to systematically summarize previous achievements, build a relatively complete knowledge framework, and provide support for subsequent research.

Systematically summarizing previous research results, identifying research frontiers and hotspots, and establishing a knowledge framework for the digital transformation of manufacturing companies will help researchers understand the field from a more complete point of view and find new directions for future research. Based on the knowledge map method, this paper uses CiteSpace to do bibliometric analysis: (1) Study the collaboration of authors, and the distribution of disciplines; (2) Use co-citation analysis to cluster and identify research topics and find key knowledge; (3) Use a co-occurrence analysis of keywords to find research frontiers and hotspots; (4) Based on the above, develop a knowledge framework for the digital transformation of manufacturing enterprises.

2   Materials and Methods

2.1   Research Methods

Knowledge map is the main method of bibliometric visualization, which can comprehensively analyze the research status in various fields, examine development trends and frontier areas. In this paper, the software CiteSpace 6.1R6 is used as a bibliometric and visual analysis tool in the field of digital transformation of manufacturing enterprises, which can perform co-citation analysis, co-word analysis, burst detection and cluster analysis.

2.2   Data Processing

This article focuses on the digital transformation of manufacturing enterprises based on the definition of three sets of search keywords, using data from the Web of Science core database, principally SCI-EXPANDED and SSCI, from 2011 to 2021, in English.

- **Group 1: digital keywords**, namely "digital transformation" or "digital products" or "digital servitization" or "digital services" or "digital platform" or "digital technology" or "digital organization" or "digital enterprise" or " digital strategy" or "digital innovation" or "digitalization" or "digitalisation" or "digitization" or "robot" or "ict" or "information communication technology" or "cloud computing" or "big data" or "iot" or " internet of things" or "artificial intelligence" or "ai" or "machine learning" or "virtual reality" or "augmented reality".
- **Group 2: keywords related to manufacturing characteristics**, namely "manufacturing" or "manufacture" or "manufacturer" or "manufacturers" or "flexible production" or "lean production" or "mass production" or "customized production".
- **Group 3: enterprise keywords**, namely "enterprises" or "enterprise" or "business" or "businesses" or "firm" or "firms" or "companies" or "company" or "corporate" or "corporates" or "smes".

Combining the above three groups of keywords with "AND", 2130 records were obtained by subject screening in the web of science core database. On this basis, the screening conditions were based on literature category papers, review papers, and conference proceedings papers, and editorials were excluded Materials, book chapters and letters, etc., finally got 2084 records.

3 Results

3.1 Publication Trends and Authors Analysis

In general, from 2011 to 2015, the growth of the publication number was relatively stable. Since 2016, the growth has been very rapid, and in 2021, 698 documents were published, indicating that more scholars are focusing on manufacturing enterprise digital transformation.

The centrality of all authors is less than 0.1, indicating that the authors cooperation network is still relatively scattered, and a core group of authors has not yet formed. CiteSpace analyzed the information of co-cited authors. Tao F and Zhong RY appear as authors with high publication number and also as highly cited authors, which shows that some prolific authors not only pay attention to the number of papers, but also pay attention to the research quality.

3.2 Co-citation Analysis

Reference co-citation cluster network (Fig. 1) includes co-cited reference and clustering information. In this paper, the clustering Modularity Q value is 0.8994, indicating that the clustering results are well; the average value of Silhouette is 0.9673, indicating that the clustering results have high reliability.

In reference co-citation cluster network map, the cluster labels are obtained by extracting the keywords of the citing articles using the logarithmic likelihood algorithm (LLR). A total of 18 clusters (see Fig. 1) were obtained for the cited articles in this paper. Each cluster represents a research topic, in which each node is a cited article, and the size of the node represents the degree of importance. The cited literatures included in the cluster constitutes the research basis of this field. Among these clusters, except for the cluster "#0 industry 4.0" as the background information and the cluster "#13 digital transformation" as the keyword search, the other clusters with a cluster size greater than 20 were merged as shown in Table 1, which shown six Thematic Area such as maturity models, circular economy, lean manufacturing, dynamic capabilities, digital servitization, and digital technologies.

The cited frequency and centrality represent the importance of the literature, and the literature with centrality greater than 0.1 is generally a pivotal node that inspires cross-domain research. The literature published by Liao YX in 2017 was the most cited, with 110 citations; the rest of most cited references were Frank et al. (2019a) (98 citations), Xu et al. (2018) (98 citations), Lee et al. (2015) (81 citations). These highly cited references mainly discuss the development and future research topics of Industry 4.0 and related technologies, transformation paths, and intelligent manufacturing (Lee et al.,

2015; Kang et al., 2016; Liao et al., 2017; Zhong et al., 2017; Xu et al., 2018; Frank et al., 2019a), which are cited as background literature for research on digital transformation of manufacturing enterprises. Among the top 10 references with a centrality greater than 0.1, apart from background documents such as Industry 4.0 and intelligent manufacturing, they mainly involve servitization (Kowalkowski et al., 2015; Opresnik and Taisch, 2015), business models (Mueller et al., 2018), cloud manufacturing (Thames and Schaefer, 2016) and other topics. These literatures have laid the foundation for the research on the digital transformation of manufacturing enterprises.

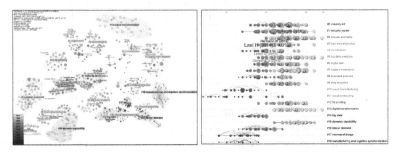

Fig. 1. Reference co-citation cluster network and timeline network.

Table 1. Research topics based on co-citation analysis

Clusters	Size	Silhouette	Mean (Year)	Thematic Area
#1 maturity model	51	0.961	2016	maturity model
#2 circular economy	48	0.993	2018	circular economy
#3 lean manufacturing	41	0.962	2017	lean manufacturing
#15 dynamic capability	22	0.965	2019	dynamic capabilities
#4 servitization	41	0.95	2015	digital servitization
#7 digital servitization	35	1	2017	
#11 cloud computing	27	0.945	2010	digital technologies
#5 big data analytics	40	0.968	2018	
#9 data analytics	30	0.968	2017	
#14 big data	23	0.846	2013	
#17 internet of things	22	0.956	2012	
#6 digital twin	40	0.994	2017	
#10 cloud manufacturing	28	0.983	2012	

3.3   Co-occurrence Analysis

Keywords

Keyword co-occurrence analysis is mainly to statistically analyze the occurrence frequency, centrality, and burst of keywords in citing articles, which can intuitively analyze research topics and research hotspots. Figure 2 is a keyword co-occurrence network map, which is composed of 560 keywords in the citing literatures (nodes in the figure). The size of the node indicates the frequency of keyword occurrence; the nodes in the purple outer circle represent the higher centrality of the keyword, play a pivotal role.

In the keyword co-occurrence network, the top 10 keywords in the past five years are future (178 times), smart manufacturing (140 times), capability (82 times), business model (79 times), digital twins (67 times), smart (59 times), data analytics (58 times), circular economy (55 times), research agenda (48 times) and logistics (47 times), to some extent represent the focus of current research, which can be summarized as intelligent manufacturing, dynamic capabilities, business models, circular economy, digital technology and logistics, etc. Keywords with a centrality greater than 0.1 include "absorptive capacity", "competition", "adoption", "ahp", "network", "service", "cloud manufacturing", "growth", "manufacturing system", and "product development"; from the average year, these keywords cannot fully represent the latest developments, but they had played a pivotal role in the research on the digital transformation of manufacturing enterprises.

Fig. 2. Keyword co-occurrence network.

Keyword Citation Bursts

Keyword burst detection can reflect changes in research hotspots within a certain period of time, and can also observe emerging research topics. According to the results of burstiness detection, in this paper 45 keywords were selected with strong bursts (Fig. 3). From 2011 to 2021, the research frontier of digital transformation in manufacturing enterprises has changed over time. "Competition" has a high burst and lasts the longest (2012–2019), which is the external driving force for manufacturing companies to carry out digital transformation. Other keywords with strong bursts and long duration are "cloud manufacturing", "cloud computing", "information technology" and "ict" (2011–2017), all of which are related to digital technology. In recent years, the keywords with strong bursts are "service innovation" and "research agenda". "service innovation" mainly discusses digital servitization (Frank et al., 2019b; Paiola and Gebauer, 2020); "research agenda" includes digital technology (Dwivedi et al., 2021), digital servitization (Paschou et al., 2020), circular economy(Cricelli and Strazzullo, 2021), etc.

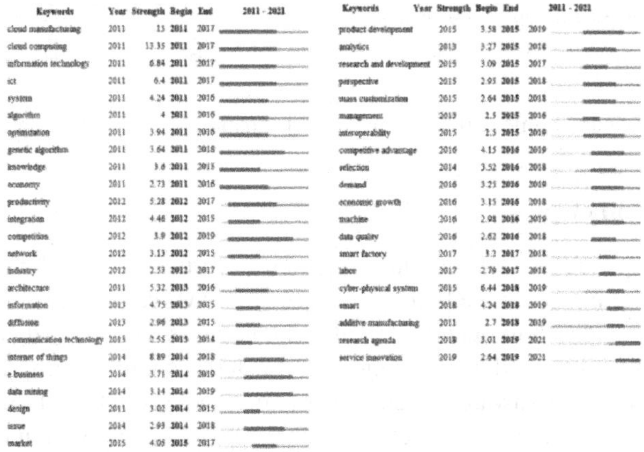

Fig. 3. Top 45 keywords with citation bursts.

4   Knowledge Framework

In view of the complexity and exploratory nature of the digital transformation of the manufacturing industry, it is necessary to build a relatively complete knowledge framework to provide a reference for future research.

Based on the analysis and processing of cooperation network, co-citation network and keyword co-occurrence, this paper builds a knowledge framework for the digital transformation of manufacturing enterprises. As shown in Fig. 4, the knowledge framework of the digital transformation of manufacturing enterprises reflects the interdisciplinary characteristics of this field, and presents the key research topics and contents. Generally speaking, the digital transformation of manufacturing enterprises is a process in which digital technology continuously empowers the management and business of manufacturing enterprises (such as circular economy, lean management, digital servitization, etc.). Whether the transformation can be successful depends on whether the manufacturing enterprise can build dynamic capabilities; during the transformation process, it is necessary to constantly evaluate the level of digital maturity, and dynamically feedback and adjust. According to the knowledge framework, this paper divides the digital transformation of manufacturing enterprises into the following six research themes.

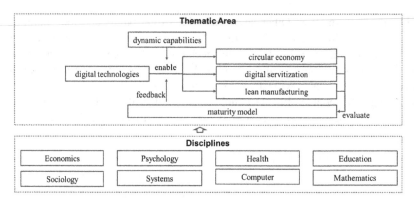

Fig. 4. Knowledge framework for digital transformation of manufacturing enterprises.

4.1 Digital Technologies

Digital technology are the drivers behind digital transformation. The digital transformation of manufacturing under the Industry 4.0 scenario involves a large number of digital technologies. In addition to general digital technologies such as cloud computing, big data, Internet of Things, and blockchain, it also includes manufacturing-related Digital technologies, such as hardware-driven technologies such as 3D printing and robotics, and software-driven technologies such as blockchain (Hahn, 2020). Some scholars also divide the digital technologies related to Industry 4.0 into three categories based on the purpose of use: (1) smart data collection, storage, analysis and sharing technologies; (2) shop floor technologies, such as virtual reality and augmented reality; (3) integrated technologies, such as Physical Information System (CPS), etc. (Kamble et al., 2020) and summarized the characteristics of digital technologies related to Industry 4.0 (Ciano et al., 2021).

4.2 Dynamic Capabilities

Dynamic capability is a company's strategic ability to integrate, build and reconfigure internal and external resources to cope with and possibly shape a rapidly changing business environment (Teece, 2012), including stages such as sensing opportunities, seizing opportunities, and continuously renewal (Teece, 2014). Based on the early concept of dynamic capability foundation, scholars have integrated dynamic capability theory with resource-based theory, resource orchestration theory, and contingency theory to form a new theoretical framework. Using this as a micro-theoretical basis to study new issues in new scenarios, specifically, scholars use dynamic capabilities and their extended theories to study the impact of digital transformation capabilities (Sousa-Zomer et al., 2020), digital manufacturing capabilities (Savastano et al., 2021), big data (Dubey et al., 2020) on corporate performance, and the impact of digital capabilities on new product development (Pan et al., 2021), etc. In addition, some scholars pay attention to big data and lean management, and study the dynamic capability effect of big data (Wamba et al., 2017), and the synergy between dynamic capabilities, big data and lean management (Gupta et al., 2020).

4.3 Circular Economy

Research on circular economy is always related to concepts such as Industry 4.0 and sustainability. Due to the rapid population growth and the continuous consumption of natural resources, there is a need to make optimal use of resources using the principles of sustainable development, in contrast to the "one-off" philosophy of the traditional linear economy towards recycling, which is known as the circular economy (Sahu et al., 2022).Among the papers with the highest citation frequency, the research mainly discusses the mutually beneficial relationship between Industry 4.0 and related digital technologies and circular economy in the context of Industry 4.0 (de Sousa Jabbour et al., 2018b), business models for reusing and recycling waste materials such as scrap metal or e-waste(Nascimento et al., 2018), sustainable supply chains, sustainable manufacturing based on digital technologies (Machado et al., 2020) et al.

4.4 Lean Manufacturing

The main goal of lean management is to produce on demand and reduce waste. In the digital environment of Industry 4.0, scholars mainly study how lean manufacturing and digitalization are integrated (Jing et al., 2021; Rossini et al., 2021a), and the impact on corporate performance (Buer et al., 2021). Driven by digital technologies related to Industry 4.0, scholars have also paid attention to lean automation (Rossini et al., 2021b), lean supply chain management (Núñez-Merino et al., 2020) and the impact on performance. Some scholars have studied the impact of digital technologies on lean management (Abd Rahman et al., 2021; Anosike et al., 2021), and summarized the corresponding relationship between digital technology and lean production technologies (such as VSM and JIT, etc.) (Gupta et al., 2020; Ciano et al., 2021). In addition, some scholars have studied digital technologies and lean management (Ciano et al., 2021), lean management, digital technologies (such as big data analysis) and circular economy (Belhadi et al., 2020) across topics.

4.5 Digital Servitization

The topic of digital servitization mainly focuses on digital servitization and value co-creation, and discusses how manufacturing enterprises can promote service-oriented transformation through digitalization, so as to realize value co-creation. The research in this topic is mainly divided into three categories. First, the basic concept of digital servitization is defined, and digital servitization is considered to be the process of developing new services or improving existing services through the use of digital technology (Paschou et al., 2020). Second, discuss how digitalization can promote the service-oriented transformation of manufacturing enterprises. Some authors have explored the role of digitalization in the service-oriented transformation of manufacturing enterprises (Rymaszewska et al., 2017; Ardolino et al., 2018). Finally, some authors' research on digital servitization focuses on digitization and business models, and explains the dynamic relationship between digitalization and servitization in the process of shaping business models from different perspectives (Frank et al., 2019b; Kohtamäki et al., 2019).

4.6 Maturity Model

On the basis of the definition of Industry 4.0 and its related concepts (Lasi et al., 2014; Liao et al., 2017; de Sousa Jabbour et al., 2018a), scholars use literature review and other methods to propose maturity models from different perspectives, and give the dimensions, indicators and maturity levels of maturity model evaluation.

Most of these maturity models include multiple dimensions such as technology and management (Pirola et al., 2020; Santos and Martinho, 2020), and some only include technology dimension (Pacchini et al., 2019). For the completeness of the maturity model, Dikhanbayeva et al. (2020) gave an evaluation method based on eight principles of digital transformation design.

5 Conclusions

This paper uses CiteSpace to conduct a visual analysis of the literatures on the digital transformation of manufacturing enterprises from 2011 to 2021, and from the perspectives of cooperation network, co-citation analysis and co-occurrence analysis, and to a certain extent comprehends the research frontiers and hotspots in this field. This paper draws the following findings from the analysis: (1) The research in this field is interdisciplinary. The author cooperation network is still relatively scattered, and the core author group has not yet formed; (2) Through the analysis of reference co-citation clustering and summarizing 6 research themes of maturity model, circular economy, lean manufacturing, dynamic capability, digital servitization and digital technologies; (3) Through keyword co-occurrence analysis, it is found that smart manufacturing, dynamic capability, business model, circular economy, digital technology and logistics are the research hotspots. "Service innovation" is the keyword of strongest burst in recent years, and it will be a major focus of future research. The themes and directions of research that came out of the co-citation analysis and the keyword co-occurrence analysis are mostly the same.

This research is innovative to a certain extent. First, it classifies the research topics of digital transformation of manufacturing enterprises, laying a knowledge base for subsequent research; secondly, it identifies the research hotspots of digital transformation of manufacturing enterprises, and makes suggestions for future research directions; Finally, a knowledge framework for the digital transformation of manufacturing enterprises is integrated, which includes six research themes: maturity model, circular economy, lean manufacturing, dynamic capabilities, digital servitization and digital technologies. It also finds the phenomenon of cross-subject research.

Nonetheless, this study still has certain drawbacks. This study did not do a full-text analysis; instead, it relied solely on bibliometric analysis based on titles, keywords, and abstracts. There is a certain shortage of information; second, there are too many documents and too much information; and further interpretation is required.

References

Abd Rahman, M.S., Mohamad, E., Abdul Rahman, A.A.: Development of IoT—enabled data analytics enhance decision support system for lean manufacturing process improvement. Concurr. Eng. **29**(3), 208–220 (2021)

Abou-foul, M., Ruiz-Alba, J.L., Soares, A.: The impact of digitalization and servitization on the financial performance of a firm: an empirical analysis. Prod. Plann. Contr. **32**(12), 975–989 (2021)

Agostini, L., Nosella, A.: The adoption of industry 4.0 technologies in SMEs: results of an international study. Manag. Decis. **58**(4), 625–643 (2020)

Anosike, A., Alafropatis, K., Garza-Reyes, J.A., et al.: Lean manufacturing and internet of things-a synergetic or antagonist relationship? Comput. Ind. **129**, 103464 (2021)

Ardolino, M., Rapaccini, M., Saccani, N., et al.: The role of digital technologies for the service transformation of industrial companies. Int. J. Prod. Res. **56**(6), 2116–2132 (2018)

Belhadi, A., Kamble, S.S., Zkik, K., et al.: The integrated effect of big data analytics, lean six sigma and green manufacturing on the environmental performance of manufacturing companies: the case of North Africa. J. Clean. Prod. **252**(2020)

Buer, S.-V., Semini, M., Strandhagen, J.O., et al.: The complementary effect of lean manufacturing and digitalisation on operational performance. Int. J. Prod. Res. **59**(7), 1976–1992 (2021)

Caputo, A., Pizzi, S., Pellegrini, M.M., et al.: Digitalization and business models: where are we going? A science map of the field. J. Bus. Res. **123**, 489–501 (2021)

Chen, J., Zhang, R., Wu, D.: Equipment maintenance business model innovation for sustainable competitive advantage in the digitalization context: connotation, types, and measuring. Sustainability **10** (2018)

Ciano, M.P., Dallasega, P., Orzes, G., et al.: One-to-one relationships between industry 4.0 technologies and lean production techniques: a multiple case study. Int. J. Prod. Res. **59**(5), 1386–410 (2021)

Cricelli, L., Strazzullo, S.: The economic aspect of digital sustainability: a systematic review. Sustainability **13**(15), 8241 (2021)

Xu, L.D., Xu, E.L., Li, L.: Industry 4.0: state of the art and future trends. Int. J. Prod. Res. **56**, 2941–62 (2018)

Dikhanbayeva, D., Shaikholla, S., Suleiman, Z., et al.: Assessment of industry 4.0 maturity models by design principles. Sustainability **12**(23), 9927 (2020)

Dubey, R., Gunasekaran, A., Childe, S.J., et al.: Big data analytics and artificial intelligence pathway to operational performance under the effects of entrepreneurial orientation and environmental dynamism: a study of manufacturing organisations. Int. J. Prod. Econ. **226** (2020)

Dwivedi, Y.K., Hughes, L., Ismagilova, E., et al.: Artificial Intelligence (AI): multidisciplinary perspectives on emerging challenges, opportunities, and agenda for research, practice and policy. Int. J. Inf. Manag. **57** (2021)

Frank, A.G., Dalenogare, L.S., Ayala, N.F.: Industry 4.0 technologies: implementation patterns in manufacturing companies. Int. J. Prod. Econ. **210**, 15–26 (2019a)

Frank, A.G., Mendes, G.H., Ayala, N.F., et al.: Servitization and industry 4.0 convergence in the digital transformation of product firms: a business model innovation perspective. Technol. Forecast. Soc. Change **141**, 341–51 (2019b)

Gupta, S., Modgil, S., Gunasekaran, A.: Big data in lean six sigma: a review and further research directions. Int. J. Prod. Res. **58**(3), 947–969 (2020)

Hahn, G.J.: Industry 4.0: a supply chain innovation perspective. Int. J. Prod. Res. **58**(5), 1425–41 (2020)

Jing, S., Feng, Y., Yan, J.: Path selection of lean digitalization for traditional manufacturing industry under heterogeneous competitive position. Comput. Industr. Eng. **161** (2021)

Kamble, S., Gunasekaran, A., Dhone, N.C.: Industry 4.0 and lean manufacturing practices for sustainable organisational performance in Indian manufacturing companies. Int. J. Prod. Res. **58**(5), 1319–37 (2020)

Kang, H.S., et al.: Smart manufacturing: past research, present findings, and future directions. Int. J. Prec. Eng. Manuf.-Green Technol. **3**(1), 111–128 (2016). https://doi.org/10.1007/s40684-016-0015-5

Kohtamäki, M., Parida, V., Oghazi, P., et al.: Digital servitization business models in ecosystems: a theory of the firm. J. Bus. Res. **104**, 380–392 (2019)

Kowalkowski, C., Windahl, C., Kindström, D., et al.: What service transition? Rethinking established assumptions about manufacturers' service-led growth strategies. Ind. Mark. Manage. **45**, 59–69 (2015)

Lasi, H., Fettke, P., Kemper, H.-G., et al.: Industry 4.0. Bus. Inf. Syst. Eng. **6**(4), 239–42 (2014)

Lee, J., Bagheri, B., Kao, H.-A.: A cyber-physical systems architecture for industry 4.0-based manufacturing systems. Manuf. Lett. **3**, 18–23 (2015)

Liao, Y., Deschamps, F., Loures, E.D., et al.: Past, present and future of industry 4.0 - a systematic literature review and research agenda proposal. Int. J. Prod. Res. **55**(12), 3609–29 (2017)

Machado, C.G., Winroth, M.P., Ribeiro Silva, E.H.D: Sustainable manufacturing in Industry 4.0: an emerging research agenda. Int. J. Prod. Res. **58**(5), 1462–84 (2020)

Mueller, J.M., Buliga, O., Voigt, K.: Fortune favors the prepared: how SMEs approach business model innovations in Industry 4.0. Technol. Forecast. Soc. Change **132**, 2–17 (2018)

Nascimento, D.L., Alencastro, V., Quelhas, O.L., et al.: Exploring Industry 4.0 technologies to enable circular economy practices in a manufacturing context (2018)

Núñez-Merino, M., Maqueira-Marín, J.M., Moyano-Fuentes, J., et al.: Information and digital technologies of Industry 4.0 and Lean supply chain management: a systematic literature review. Int. J. Prod. Res. **58**(16), 5034–5061(2020)

Opresnik, D., Taisch, M.: The value of big data in servitization. Int. J. Prod. Econ. **165**, 174–184 (2015)

Pacchini, A.P., Lucato, W.C., Facchini, F., et al.: The degree of readiness for the implementation of Industry 4.0. Comput. Indust. **113**, 103125 (2019)

Paiola, M., Gebauer, H.: Internet of things technologies, digital servitization and business model innovation in BtoB manufacturing firms. Ind. Mark. Manage. **89**, 245–264 (2020)

Pan, X., Oh, K.-S., Wang, M.: Strategic orientation, digital capabilities, and new product development in emerging market firms: the moderating role of corporate social responsibility. Sustainability **13** (2021)

Paschou, T., Rapaccini, M., Adrodegari, F., et al.: Digital servitization in manufacturing: a systematic literature review and research agenda. Ind. Mark. Manage. **89**, 278–292 (2020)

Pirola, F., Cimini, C., Pinto, R.: Digital readiness assessment of Italian SMEs: a case-study research. J. Manuf. Technol. Manag. **31**(5), 1045–1083 (2020)

Rossini, M., Cifone, F.D., Kassem, B., et al.: Being lean: how to shape digital transformation in the manufacturing sector. J. Manuf. Technol. Manag. **32**(9), 239–259 (2021a)

Rossini, M., Costa, F., Tortorella, G.L., et al.: Lean production and Industry 4.0 integration: how lean automation is emerging in manufacturing industry. Int. J. Prod. Res. **60**(21), 6430–50 (2021b)

Rymaszewska, A., Helo, P., Gunasekaran, A.: IoT powered servitization of manufacturing - an exploratory case study. Int. J. Prod. Econ. **192**, 92–105 (2017)

Sahu, A., Agrawal, S., Kumar, G.: Integrating Industry 4.0 and circular economy: a review. J. Enterpr. Inf. Manag. **35**(3), 885–917 (2022)

Santos, R.C., Martinho, J.L.: An Industry 4.0 maturity model proposal. J. Manuf. Technol. Manag. **31**(5), 1023–43 (2020)

Savastano, M., Cucari, N., Dentale, F., et al.: The interplay between digital manufacturing and dynamic capabilities: an empirical examination of direct and indirect effects on firm performance. J. Manuf. Technol. Manag. **33**(2), 213–238 (2021) de Sousa Jabbour, A.B.L., Jabbour, C.J., Foropon, C., et al.: When titans meet – Can industry 4.0 revolutionise the environmentally-sustainable manufacturing wave? The role of critical success factors. Technol. Forecast. Soc. Change **132**, 18–25 (2018a)

de Sousa Jabbour, A.B.L., Jabbour, C.J., Godinho Filho, M., Roubaud, D.: Industry 4.0 and the circular economy: a proposed research agenda and original roadmap for sustainable operations. Ann. Oper. Res. **270**(1–2), 273–286 (2018b). https://doi.org/10.1007/s10479-018-2772-8

Sousa-Zomer, T.T., Neely, A., Martinez, V.: Digital transforming capability and performance: a microfoundational perspective. Int. J. Oper. Prod. Manag. **40**(7/8), 1095–1128 (2020)

Teece, D.J.: Dynamic capabilities: routines versus entrepreneurial action. J. Manage. Stud. **49**(8), 1395–1401 (2012)

Teece, D.J.: The foundations of enterprise performance: dynamic and ordinary capabilities in an (economic) theory of firms. Acad. Manag. Perspect. **28**(4), 328–352 (2014)

Thames, L., Schaefer, D.: Software-defined cloud manufacturing for Industry 4.0. Procedia CIRP **52**, 12–17 (2016)

Verhoef, P.C., Broekhuizen, T., Bart, Y., et al.: Digital transformation: a multidisciplinary reflection and research agenda. J. Bus. Res. **122**, 889–901 (2021)

Wamba, S.F., Gunasekaran, A., Akter, S., et al.: Big data analytics and firm performance: effects of dynamic capabilities. J. Bus. Res. **70**, 356–365 (2017)

Zhong, R.Y., Xu, X., Klotz, E., et al.: Intelligent manufacturing in the context of Industry 4.0: a review. Engineering **3**(5), 616–30 (2017)

The Influence of the Thematic Coherency of CSR Activities on Users' Purchase Intention on E-Commerce Platforms

Xvyuge Peng and Jundong Hou[✉]

China University of Geosciences, Wuhan 430078, China
houjundong@cug.edu.cn

Abstract. Digital technology has reshaped the business landscape, E-Commerce platform enterprises are becoming a new organizational vehicle, and their social responsibility has attracted extensive discussions. However, most of the existing studies focused on the connotation, boundaries, lack of responsibility and alienation motives and management countermeasures of CSR in e-commerce platform enterprises, and little research has clearly pointed out whether e-commerce platform enterprises should choose to focus on a fixed theme to carry out high coherence CSR activities or invest in diversified themes to carry out low coherence CSR activities, and whether different coherence CSR activities will have different effects on users' purchase intention. Drawing on the social identity theory and SOR theory, the present research develops the underlying mechanism through which thematic consistency of CSR activities influences the purchase intention by including consumer-company identification as a mediator. A theoretical model proposed to describe the hypothesized relationships was tested by the method of questionnaire survey and experiment. The results shown that consumer-company identification partially mediates the relationship between thematic coherency and users' purchase intention and that the theme coherency of CSR activities of e-commerce platform firms has a favorable influence on users' buy intention. The results point to the need for e-commerce platform companies to implement thematic coherence strategies in order to stimulate consumers' more favorable purchasing intents and to achieve the best possible thematic coherence strategies for social responsibility initiatives.

Keywords: E-commerce platform enterprise · corporate social responsibility · thematic consistency · users' purchase intention

1 Introduction

With the booming development of digital intelligence technology, e-commerce platform enterprises play an important role in digital intelligence-enabled high-quality development, and also gradually become an active force in promoting China's economic transformation and development. The absence and alienation of corporate social responsibility (CSR) will aggravate the damage to various stakeholders and reduce the overall welfare level of society. Therefore, it has become an inevitable requirement for the high-quality development of e-commerce platform enterprises to actively undertake CSR. As a new type of organization in the era of Internet economy, the openness, extensibility, virtuality and bilateral nature of e-commerce platform enterprises determine that compared with traditional enterprises, the subjects and objects of CSR of e-commerce platform enterprises are more special and their specific responsibility contents are more complicated. Therefore, it is of certain practical significance to conduct CSR-related research on e-commerce platforms.

One of the platform companies' goals of carrying out CSR is to show responsible social image to users, which could establish a pro-social connection. Although the positive effects of CSR activities have been repeatedly proven, practical results show that not all CSR activities can directly achieve the expected results, and the final effect of the activities will be influenced by a variety of factors. Therefore, how to maximize the utility of limited resources has become a realistic problem for e-commerce platform companies. Through the practical observation of CSR activities of e-commerce platforms, there are distinct differences in the consistency of the CSR themes of most e-commerce platform enterprises, as shown by the fact that some e-commerce platform enterprises choose to keep a high degree of thematic consistency, but some decide to maintain a strong thematic diversity.

Therefore, this study focuses on the issue of CSR consistency under the thematic strategy of e-commerce platforms, i.e., the continuity of e-commerce platform companies' commitment to their chosen themes when carrying out CSR activities. This study explored whether companies should maintain higher thematic consistency or stronger thematic diversity to stimulate users' stronger purchase intention, and introduced consumer-company identity to study its impact on the path of CSR thematic consistency and users' purchase intention. This article attempted to provide theoretical basis and practical guidance for platform companies to optimize their socially responsible thematic consistency strategies with the method of questionnaire survey and experiment.

2 Literature Review

2.1 Corporate Social Responsibility

CSR has been defined in various ways in the literature. CSR was first described by Sheldon as a company's obligation to consider how its operations affect other people and the environment while advancing its own financial goals. Carroll defined CSR as involving the economic, legal, ethical, and discretionary expectations that society has on an organization at a given time [1]. On this basis, scholars have proposed that CSR is a comprehensive responsibility undertaken by companies from the perspective of stakeholders and society as a whole, i.e., the active management activities and responsible behaviors adopted by companies to meet the needs of consumers at the social, environmental and ethical levels. The ability of businesses to go above and beyond what they were initially required to do or chose to do, and to engage in activities that contribute to the betterment of society whenever possible, out of a general social need, is now a more comprehensive definition of corporate social responsibility. Nowadays, more research is examining the impact of CSR on customer attitudes and actions. CSR activities influence various consumer behavioral outcomes like purchase intention [2], consumer brand preference [3], corporate reputation [4], recommendations and brand equity [5]. However, according to Deng, "positive deeds are not always rewarded" by businesses, and "unappealing" circumstances do occur [6]. When companies engage in CSR activities with a lower brand match and more passive time selection, it stimulates the creation of consumer psychological contract violation, which promotes consumer boycott behavior [7]. In conclusion, the majority of current studies concentrate on how CSR affects consumer behavior and offer suggestions on whether to participate in CSR. In reality, more study is required to fully understand how businesses engage in CSR because the results of current studies are not clear regarding the effects of CSR actions.

2.2 Consumer-Company Identification

According to Bhattacharya [8], consumer-company identification is a state of connection, proximity or similarity of perception between consumer and company. The perception is brought about by a subjective comparison process between the organization's identity and the consumer's own identity, where shared values play a very important role in influencing the process [9]. Bergami found that consumer-company identification is not a purely cognitive structure, but also includes an affective and evaluative component [10]. Regarding the impact of consumer-company identification, previous scholars have also agreed on this; the higher the level of consumer-company identification, the stronger the connection between the firm and the consumer, and the more positive the consumer response to the firm. Lee stated that when consumer-company identification is significant, it has an impact on individuals' judgments, choices, behaviors, and performance, and that judgments based on identification are not easily changed [11]. This is due to the fact that the formation of consumer-company identification implies that the individual's sense of self achieves some alignment with the firms' perceptions, and thus consumers tend to establish their moral superiority and sense of belonging through their purchase behavior out of self-expression or reinforcement needs.

2.3 Thematic Consistency of CSR Activities

Coherency, which is frequently used to describe the fluidity or duration of an event, instead refers to the consistency of a company's commitment to social responsibility when used to define CSR. Although there is no clear definition, scholars have repeatedly categorized CSR activities into high and low coherence strategies from the perspective of corporate practice based on time. According to Barnes CSR activities can be divided into continuous activities and short-term one-off activities [12]. Existing studies suggest that the coherence of CSR themes can be categorized into two strategies: "digging deeper" and "digging more" according to the type of activity themes. Based on the above clear delineation of the thematic coherence of social responsibility activities, existing studies link social responsibility thematic strategies to consumer behavior and explore the relationship between the two from different perspectives. Companies should adopt a high-match continuous CSR theme strategy to achieve the most positive impact on consumers.

3   Hypotheses Development

3.1   Thematic Consistency of CSR Activities on E-Commerce Platforms and Users' Purchase Intention

The impact of the theme of CSR activities on e-commerce platforms, the subject of this study, on users' purchase intentions can be explained in the following two ways. On the one hand, congruity theory suggests that people tend to achieve a balanced, harmonious and highly consistent state when they perceive things. As a result, the content of CSR information received by users in highly coherent activities is more consistent, and users are more likely to respond positively because they have to pay less to obtain CSR-related information. At the same time, the cue consistency theory states that the more consistent the information that consumers receive from multiple leads, the more beneficial they can be. Therefore, when the theme of CSR activities conducted by e-commerce platform enterprises is more coherent, more coherent information with strong correlation is delivered to users, and at this time, the information of social responsibility activities with the same theme will be deepened and strengthened in users' minds, eventually forming a longer-acting and more impressive cognition of social responsibility activities, which further has a positive impact on users' purchase intention.

On the other hand, according to the theory of multi-attribute attitude, individuals' behavioral attitudes, which in turn determine their behavioral intents, are formed by their appraisals of the impacts and results of their activity. This means that anticipated impacts of a company's social responsibility efforts also affect how users respond to those efforts [13], and if users are optimistic about the expected effects of the social responsibility activities, they will show more positive attitudes and behaviors. Users tend to form a clearer and more positive perception of the results of the CSR activities when the theme is more cohesive, which makes them more willing to make positive comments about the company and further generates more positive purchase intentions. Users also tend to believe that the company will be more likely to help solve a public concern given the large number of focused resources. Accordingly, our first hypothesis is as follows:

H1. Thematic Consistency of CSR Activities on e-commerce Platforms Has a Significant Positive Association with Users' Purchase Intention.

3.2   Thematic Consistency of CSR Activities on E-Commerce Platforms and Consumer-Company Identification

It has been repeatedly shown that company commitment to CSR has a beneficial effect on customer identification. Compared with the low coherence activities, when the CSR activities carried out by e-commerce platform enterprises have a high coherence, the CSR activities of enterprises can be more easily defined as a long-term commitment. At this time, users' suspicion of the ultimate purpose of the social activities of e-commerce platform enterprises is greatly reduced, and social responsibility activities have a stronger voluntary color, thus being defined as an act of pursuing the overall interests of society. This increases users' sense of corporate identity by fostering positive perceptions of corporate social responsibility and overall corporate performance. With low thematic consistency, users are more likely to attribute CSR activities conducted by e-commerce platforms as "promotional CSR" [14], the main purpose of which is to help companies accomplish publicity and hype, thus failing to have a positive effect on consumer-company identification.

Through social responsibility initiatives, companies also try to present an image of a pro-social organization to consumers [15], which further trigger a closer connection with consumers and thus make them more inclined to identify with the organization. Whether the corporate image information conveyed by e-commerce platform companies through social responsibility activities can be well perceived and interpreted by consumers will also have a crucial impact on the positive corporate image. In the context of a high degree of coherence, e-commerce platform companies provide more time for users to understand the connection between themselves and public welfare events, and users can also more easily distinguish information about the company's social responsibility activities from its daily promotional information, resulting in improved user reception and interpretation of CSR information. On this basis, it is also easier for users to build a responsible image of the e-commerce platform as a company that cares about social welfare, thus creating a stronger consumer-company identity. Thus, we hypothesize:

H2. Thematic consistency of CSR activities on e-commerce platforms has a significant positive association with consumer-company identification.

3.3 Thematic Consistency of CSR Activities on E-Commerce Platforms, Consumer-Company Identification, and Users' Purchase Intention

The prerequisite for CSR to have an impact on consumer decisions is that it appeals to the consumer's self-concept, i.e., it gains the consumer's approval. Existing studies found that when consumers perceive that a company cares about the well-being of its stakeholders and takes the initiative to be socially responsible, consumers will have a higher sense of identification with the company and thus increase their willingness to purchase the company's products or services.

E-commerce platform enterprises build digital transaction and interaction interfaces with the help of platforms, and complete the creation of economic and social values by linking buyers and sellers or multiple parties [16]. The transaction activities of e-commerce platform enterprises also have prominent features such as the absence of experiential links, the virtual nature of transactions, the separation of physical and information, and the separation of payment and delivery. Therefore, compared with traditional purchasing behavior, platform users have a more limited right to know before purchasing products or services from e-commerce platforms, and it is difficult for users to make in-depth assessments of product characteristics and quality with only the product information displayed on the platform. Therefore, users are more inclined to make purchases based on their attitudes and emotions toward the e-commerce platform company, so organizational identity, once generated, will have a more positive impact on user behavior.

Organizational identity theory suggests that when consumers experience an emotional connection with a platform company, they form a deeper psychological connection with the company, develop a strong sense that they belong to the organization, and perceive that they have common interests with the organization [17]. Thus, users with a stable consumer-firm identity have a stronger connection to the e-commerce platform company and are more likely to generate positive behavior toward the company. The main behavior that individuals can exercise as users of e-commerce platform companies is the purchase of the company's products or services, and brand commitment based on consumer-firm identity needs to be better expressed through this behavior. Purchasing the products of the company they identify with becomes an act of expression and projection of self, and the best way for users to demonstrate their alignment with the company's goals and preference for that company. Thus, we hypothesize:

H3. Consumer-company identification mediates the relationship between thematic consistency of CSR activities on e-commerce platforms and users' purchase intention.

Figure 1 presents the theoretical framework in this study.

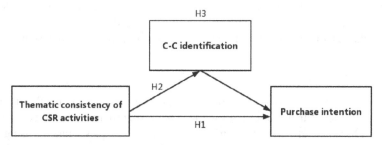

Fig. 1. The proposed theoretical framework and hypothesis.

4   Data and Research Design

4.1   Data Collection Instrument

All of the constructs in the conceptual model were adapted from past research. We measured consumer-company identification using four items from Einwiller. We measured users' purchase intention using three items from Wang and Moon. We measured thematic consistency of CSR activities using four items from Ellen. A five-point Likert scale, ranging from "1 = strongly disagree" to "5 = strongly agree" was used to measure all items.

4.2   Experiment Design

High and low levels of coherence were set up in the experimental design for this investigation. The CSR activities of e-commerce platforms in both contexts were set as social responsibility activities with high matching in this study to avoid the interference of activity matching. In the pre-experimental stage, based on the actual situation of social responsibility activities carried out by current e-commerce platform companies, themes such as "e-commerce for agriculture", "green logistics", "intellectual property protection", "youth development support", "non-traditional culture preservation" and "women's empowerment" were selected. Twenty university students were invited to rate how well the above activities matched the e-commerce platform companies.

Finally, "E-Commerce for Agriculture" and "Green Logistics" were selected as the social responsibility activities with a good match.

During the experiment, first, the subjects were asked to read the materials in different contexts. The CSR activities' themes vary in their degree of thematic consistency as follows: company A is an e-commerce platform enterprise that actively undertakes social responsibility activities, and has carried out social responsibility activities like "public welfare live event" for ten consecutive years. The low consistency group is described as company B is an e-commerce platform enterprise that actively undertakes social responsibility activities, and has engaged in various types of social responsibility activities for ten consecutive years. After then, participants were asked questions about the thematic coherence of the business's CSR initiatives in order to assess the validity of the experimental manipulation. Finally, the subjects were asked to complete the questions related to consumer-company identification and purchase intention in turn. Demographic characteristics such as gender, age, and occupation were also measured.

4.3 Data Collection

Data was collected from users of e-commerce platform. The study mainly distributed and collected questionnaires through sojump, a platform providing functions equivalent to Amazon Mechanical Turk. The distribution of completed questionnaires using social media platforms like WeChat, QQ, and Weibo. Ultimately, 158 were returned, but 8 questionnaires were excluded due to incomplete responses or incorrect selection of polygraph questions. The remaining 150 questionnaires were used for final data analysis and thus the effective rate was 94.9%. Male respondents accounted for 47.3% of the sample. The highest percentage of respondents in this survey was full-time students, totaling 62.0%.

5   Results

5.1   Measurement Model

Before testing the proposed theoretical model, all the constructs and their corresponding subscales were assessed to ensure their validity and reliability with the assistance of SPSS 26. Results showed that the Cronbach's alpha for thematic consistency, consumer-company identification, and users' purchase intention were 0.864, 0.848, and 0.768, respectively, which were all greater than 0.7, and the overall reliability of the questionnaire was also greater than 0.8. This indicates that the scales used in this questionnaire have good reliability.

This research also examined the content validity and construct validity. All measurement scales were referred to existing mature scales at home and abroad, and appropriate adjustments were made to ensure the content validity of the scales to a certain extent. An exploratory factor analysis (EFA) together with a confirmatory factor analysis (CFA) was performed to examine the construct validity in this study. The value of KMO = 0.834 was far greater than the standard value of 0.7. Meanwhile, the results from Bartlett's test also indicated good significance based on the value of the approximate chi-square = 675.515 and p = 0.

The convergent validity and discriminant validity were tested. The results imply that the factor loadings are all greater than 0.7, indicating that each latent variable is highly representative of the topic to which it belongs. The reliability CR of each variable combination is greater than 0.7, and the average variance extracted AVE is greater than 0.5, which indicates good questionnaire aggregation validity. The discriminant validity emphasizes the uniqueness of each construct from its other counterparts. The statistics illustrates the good discriminant validity.

5.2 Experimental Validity Testing

To verify the rationality of the experimental design and the validity of the manipulation, the questionnaire asked the subjects to rate the thematic coherence of CSR activities in companies A and B respectively. Independent-sample test was used to test the validity of the experimental manipulation. The test results clearly showed that the subjects' perceived thematic coherence of CSR activities was significantly higher in the continuous context than in the interrupted context ($t = 21.390$, $p < 0.001$), which indicates that the material manipulation of the experimental setup regarding the thematic coherence of activities was successful and both contexts had the expected impact on the subjects.

5.3 Hypothesis Testing

This study uses one-way ANOVA to test the difference of users' purchase intention under the two thematic coherence levels, and the test results show that users' purchase intention is significantly higher under the "high coherence" strategy than under the "low coherence" strategy ($F = 35.978$, $p < 0.001$). That is, high theme coherence is more likely to enhance users' purchase intention compared with low theme coherence. These results support H1.

Secondly, a one-way ANOVA was also used to verify the differences in consumer-company identification under different levels of thematic consistency, and the test results showed that consumer-company identification was significantly higher under the "high coherence" thematic strategy than under the "low coherence" thematic strategy ($F = 35.188$, $p < 0.001$). That is, when e-commerce platform companies carry out CSR activities, high theme coherency is more likely to enhance the consumer-company identification. These results support H2.

5.4 Mediation Analysis

In order to test the proposed mediation effects (i.e., hypotheses 3), We used the process plug-in v3. 3 of SPSS 26.0 and selected model 4 of the Bootstrap test for the mediation effect. In this process, the thematic coherency of CSR activities was selected as the independent variable, users' purchase intention as the dependent variable, and consumer-company identification as the mediating variable. **Table 1** shows that the model has good fitting effect with a 95% bootstrap confidence interval. Specifically contains a linear regression fit of the mediating variable ($R^2 = 0.210$, $F = 39.345$, $p < 0.001$) and a linear regression fit of the dependent variable ($R^2 = 0.249$, $F = 24.344$, $p < 0.001$).

Table 1. Results of mediation role model testing.

		coeff	SE	95% CI		R^2	F-value	P-value
				Lower	Upper			
CCI	Constants	2.825	0.152	2.524	3.125	0.210	39.345	0.000
	Thematic Consistency	0.283	0.045	0.194	0.372			
PI	Constants	1.543	0.321	0.909	2.176	0.249	24.344	0.000
	CCI	0.361	0.095	0.174	0.548			
	Thematic Consistency	0.203	0.059	0.087	0.319			

The results of the intermediate effect test show that the total effect of thematic consistency on users' purchase intention is 0.305 with a 95% bootstrap confidence interval (CI.95 = 0.197,0.413). The results show that the mediating effect value of consumer-company identification is 0.102 with a 95% bootstrap confidence interval (CI.95 = 0.034, 0.227). And after controlling for mediating variables control, the value of the direct effect of thematic coherence on users' purchase intention is 0.203 with a 95% bootstrap confidence interval (CI.95 = 0.087,0.319). It indicates that the direct effect of thematic consistency on users' purchase intention remains significant, i.e., there is a partial mediating role of consumer-company identification between thematic consistency of CSR activities of e-commerce platform and platform users' purchase intention. These results support H3. The results are presented in **Table 2**.

Table 2. Results of mediating effect between CSR thematic consistency and users' purchase intention.

	Effect	SE	BootLLCI	BootULCI
Direct effect	0.203	0.059	0.087	0.319
Indirect effect	0.102	0.049	0.034	0.227
Total effect	0.305	0.059	0.197	0.413

6   Conclusions and Discussion

Consistency of CSR activities on e-commerce platforms positively relates to users' purchase intention. The higher the consistency of the themes chosen by companies in their social responsibility activities, the stronger the willingness of users to purchase the products or services. The reason for this may be that when e-commerce platform companies choose to invest in social responsibility activities with the same theme, a large number of social responsibility activities with strong correlation and high consistency will be deepened and strengthened in users' minds, and it is easier to prompt users to form deep knowledge of social responsibility activities. Furthermore, when a large number of resources for social responsibility activities are pooled together, users tend to think that e-commerce platform companies are more sustainable in solving social problems in this area, which will have a more positive impact on purchase intention.

Consumer-company identification partially mediates the relationship between the thematic coherency of CSR activities on e-commerce platforms and users' purchase intentions. This shows that although there is not a single relationship between the coherency of CSR activities on e-commerce platforms and users' purchase intention, the long-term commitment to a fixed theme of social responsibility activities is the key to promoting users' corporate identity and thus forming a positive willingness to purchase.

6.1 Theoretical Contribution

This research made different theoretical contributions to the extant literature. First, this study extended the existing literature through examining and validating the conceptual framework and exploring the role of CSR activities of e-commerce platform companies in influencing users' purchase intention. Only a little research has been done on the outcomes of the CSR activities on e-commerce platforms, especially concerning the thematic consistency of CSR activities on e-commerce platforms. Thus, to our best knowledge, the present study extends the literature on the underlying mechanism through which e-commerce platforms' CSR activities consistency is associated with positive behavioral outcomes and result in a high consumer-company identification. Second, a few studies have examined the impact of CSR theme matching on users' purchase intention, ignoring the importance of coherence. Therefore, this research filled the gap by examining the role of CSR topic coherence on users' purchase intention. Finally, this study built empirical support for the proposed model that the consistency of CSR activities of e-commerce platforms influences users' purchase intentions through mediating.

6.2 Managerial Implications

Our research findings have significant managerial implications. First of all, e-commerce platform companies should further clarify the importance of social responsibility activities and consider social responsibility strategies comprehensively. For e-commerce platform companies, the fulfillment of social responsibility cannot be achieved simply by investing in any social responsibility activities, and the effect that can be achieved by carrying out social responsibility activities will be influenced by many factors, such as the company itself, the external environment and consumers. Therefore, how to consider environmental factors and their own resource conditions, propose a better solution to the theme of social responsibility, and finally achieve both economic and social benefits is a realistic problem that enterprises need to solve.

Second, e-commerce platform companies should allocate activity resources reasonably according to their own reality to maximize the utility of CSR activity resources. As the complexity of the current external environment and the subjective initiative of consumers continue to increase, the resources available to companies are increasingly limited, and the effects of social responsibility are increasingly restricted. In the actual operation process, if an enterprise has already carried out social responsibility activities on a certain theme in the early stage, in order to make the limited activity resources have a more positive impact on users, it can continue to increase the resources invested in the theme activities. If an enterprise has not yet engaged in social responsibility activities, it should fully consider the current market environment and its own actual situation, and later choose a fixed theme of social responsibility activities for long-term investment as far as possible, so as to finally realize the long-term development of its own business and social cause.

Finally, e-commerce platform companies should integrate CSR into user relationship management, fully recognizing the good role that CSR plays in maintaining the relationship between companies and users. For e-commerce platform companies, actively carrying out highly coherent social responsibility activities can help users form a higher level of consumer-enterprise identity, and the close relationship between companies and users is derived from the high level of user identification with the company.

6.3 Limitations and Future Research

The present study has some limitations. First, the impact that a company's social responsibility activity can have on consumer behavior can be influenced not only by the subject of the action, but also by external environmental conditions and consumers' own factors. Therefore, future studies can further refine the research model along this direction. Second, the study's sample has some limitations. For example, the subjects are primarily full-time students who are geographically restricted, and the sample's representativeness needs to be improved. Future studies should broaden the user sample, and in addition to covering different occupational types and age groups, the sample should try to cover multiple regions or cities. Finally, we only considered e-commerce platform companies. Because organizational structures and culture differ by industry, the conclusions are limited to e-commerce platform companies.

Acknowledgement. This research was supported by the National Natural Science Foundation of China under Grant 72274185 and 71874163, and this research was funded by Major Program of Social Science Planning in Fuzhou, China under grant number 2022FZA01.

References

1. Carroll, A.B.: A three-dimensional conceptual model of corporate performance. Acad. Manag. Rev. **4**(4), 497–505 (1979)
2. Liu, X.P., Mao, L.J., Deng, W.X.: The influence of consumer mindset and corporate social responsibility on purchase intention. Soc. Behav. Pers. **46**(10), 1647–1656 (2018)
3. Hwang, J., Cho, S., Kim, W.: Philanthropic corporate social responsibility, consumer attitudes, brand preference, and customer citizenship behavior: older adult employment as a moderator. Soc. Behav. Person. **47**(7) (2019). UNSP e8111
4. Gras-Gil, E., Manzano, M.P., Fernandez, J.H.: Investigating the relationship between corporate social responsibility and earnings management: evidence from Spain. Bro-Bus. Res. Quart. **19**(4), 289–299 (2016)

5. He, Y., Lai, K.K.: The effect of corporate social responsibility on brand loyalty: the mediating role of brand image. Total Qual. Manag. Bus. Excell. **25**(3–4), 249–263 (2014)
6. Deng, X.M.: Understanding consumer's responses to enterprise 's ethical behaviors: an investigation in China. J. Bus. Ethics **107**(2), 159–181 (2012)
7. Deng, X.M., Long, X., Liu, Y.: Can good deeds always lead to rewards? A study on the mechanism of consumers' boycott to CSR. Nankai Bus. Rev. Int. **20**(06), 129–139 (2017)
8. Bhattacharya, C.B., Sen, S.: Consumer-company identification: a framework for understanding consumers relationships with companies. J. Mark. **67**(2), 76–88 (2003)
9. Hunt, S.D., Wood, V.R., Chonko, L.B.: Corporate ethical values and organizational commitment in marketing. J. Mark. **53**(3), 79–90 (1989)
10. Bergami, M., Bagozzi, R.P.: Self-categorization, affective commitment and group self-esteem as distinct aspects of social identity in the organization. Br. J. Soc. Psychol. **39**, 555–577 (2000)
11. Lee, J.Q., Liu, F.J.: A study on the relationship between corporate social responsibility characteristics and consumer response-concurrently discuss the mediating and moderating effect of consumer-company identification. Collect. Ess. Fin. Econ. (1), 85–94 (2017). (in Chinese)
12. Barnes, N.G., Fitzgibbons, D.A.: Business-charity links: is cause related marketing in your future? Bus. Forum **16**(4), 20–23 (1991)
13. Knoblich, G., Flach, R.: Predicting the effects of actions: interactions of perception and action. Psychol. Sci. **12**(6), 467–472 (2001)
14. Pirsch, J., Gupta, S., Grau, S.L.: A framework for understanding corporate social responsibility programs as a continuum: an exploratory study. J. Bus. Ethics **70**(2), 125–140 (2001)
15. Du, S., Bhattacharya, C.B., Sen, S.: Reaping relational rewards from corporate social responsibility: the role of competitive positioning. Int. J. Res. Mark. **24**(3), 224–241 (2007)
16. Xiao, H.J., Lee, P.: Ecological governance of platform enterprises' CSR. Manag. World **35**(04), 120–144+196 (2019). (in Chinese)
17. Dukerich, J.M., Golden, B.R., Shortell, S.M.: Beauty is in the eye of the beholder: the impact of organizational identification, identity, and image on the cooperative behaviors of physicians. Adm. Sci. Q. **47**(3), 507–533 (2002)

Investment Strategies of Digital Music Copyright in Uncertain Environment

Xixi Wang and Nan Zhang[⊠]

Harbin Institute of Technology, Harbin, People's Republic of China
wangxixi5587@126.com, andyzhang@hit.edu.cn

Abstract. Online contents providers such as music platforms (e.g., Netease Cloud Music, QQ Music, etc.) generally adopt the mode that free users can listen to part of the music library, and paying users can listen to all the music. This paper takes online music platform as the research subject and takes the instability of network environment and the uncertainty of digital music copyright playing effects into consideration to study the copyright investment decisions of digital assets. Firstly, this paper takes the playback effects of different levels of digital music copyright and the operation cost of online music platforms as uncertain variables, and then constructs an uncertain digital music copyright portfolio model considering the constraints of income, cost, and risk of the platform. Secondly, based on the uncertainty theory, the uncertainty model is transformed into the corresponding deterministic form. Finally, this paper calculates the optimal choice of music tracks belonging to different levels through numerical examples, verifies the effectiveness and practicability of the model and algorithm, and further explores the influence of investment preference on investment decisions.

Keywords: Digital Music Copyright · Copyright Investment · Uncertain Variable · Uncertain Programming

1 Introduction

With the progress of society and the development of information technology, people's demand for spiritual and cultural consumption is growing. More and more consumers begin to obtain news, videos, music, knowledge, and other online contents through the Internet [1]. Digital music is the digital format of a piece of music that based on network technology and can be transmitted and downloaded through the Internet. Depending on the platforms and media, digital music can be further divided into wireless music and online music. The formation of online music industry is based on Internet and mobile technology. iiMedia Research data shows that the scale of online music users and market will continue to expand under the strong support of 5G, AI, and other cutting-edge technologies[1].

At the end of the 20th century, after the online music appeared in China, the public's copyright awareness of music was awakened gradually. In 2015, the National Copyright

---

[1] Source: iiMedia Report 2020 China Online Music Industry Development Research Report.

Administration issued the Notice on Ordering Online Music Service Providers to Stop Unauthorized Dissemination of Music Works, and according to the notice, all major music platforms removed all uncopyrighted music, and online music industry of China officially entered the era of copyright. At the same time, with the increasing depth and breadth of consumers' access to the Internet, the competition for copyright among online platforms is becoming increasingly fierce. Copyright protection policies have been strengthened, online contents copyright owners and platforms actively safeguard their legitimate rights and interests, and the investment environment for digital copyright has been rapidly improved [2].

The rapidly rising cost of copyright investment has made it the biggest operating expense for online music platforms. At the same time, more and more users are willing to pay for high-quality online contents, and rich library resources become the basis of payment and the key to user retention [3]. Copyright investment affects the revenue models and pricing strategies of the platforms to some extent. After entering the copyright period, the major online music platforms try to gain a competitive advantage by buying as many Copyrights as possible. In this situation, the investment choice of digital music copyright is extremely important for the healthy and orderly development of online music platforms. Digital assets are getting more and more attentions. Many scholars have begun to investigate portfolio strategies for digital assets [4]. Petukhina et al. assess the out-of-sample performance of eight portfolio allocation strategies relative to the naive 1/N rule applied to traditional and crypto-assets investment universe [5]. Nevertheless, to our best knowledge, there is a lack of research on digital copyright investment strategies.

Further, with the rapid development of mobile Internet in recent years and the impact of COVID-19 on the network environment, the instability of social network environment and the uncertainty of music copyright value have been greatly enhanced. For example, a negative personal event of the singer of a musical track may affect the playing effect of the music copyright. At this point, online music platforms cannot judge the future data of music tracks according to the music playing data in the previous network environment. These uncertain factors lead to decision-makers having nothing to rely on, and uncertainty theory provides a theoretical framework for analyzing such situations.

Uncertainty theory was put forward by Liu [6] in 2007, which is the theoretical basis for solving subjective uncertainty. Nowadays, the uncertainty theory has been widely used in finance [7–12], the vehicle routing problem [13, 14], the intensive production plan [15], social media marketing [16] and other fields, to solve the uncertainty influences in the areas mentioned above. In the copyright investment process, the product we are investing in is usually new. Currently, we do not have enough historical data to determine the probability distribution, so it is incomplete for us to consider uncertain factors as random variables. The uncertainty theory is precisely a theory that uses reliability to measure the possibility of events when the sample size is small. At this point, we can determine the uncertain distribution that the variable satisfies. Therefore, in this paper, the uncertain factors in investment process are considered as uncertain variables.

In view of digital copyright investment behavior, this paper regards the uncertain factors in copyright investment as uncertain variables. In this paper, we treat the online content service provider as the decision-making party, the copyright portfolio involved in the copyright process as the background, the digital music copyright playing effect, and the cost of the decision-making party as the uncertain variables, the copyright income effect, investment cost and investment risk as the constraints of promotion decision optimization problem, the copyright investment decision of online music platform.

The remaining components of this paper are shown below. In the second section, an uncertain music copyright portfolio model is established, which considers investment income (playing effect), investment cost and investment risk. In Sect. 3, the uncertain model is transformed into an equivalent deterministic model. In Sect. 4, numerical simulation experiments are carried out to demonstrate the effectiveness and practicability of the model. In section five, conclusions and prospects are given. Finally, in the appendix (available upon request), basic concepts in uncertainty theory are reviewed.

2 Uncertain Digital Music Copyright Investment Model

How to rationally invest in digital music copyright for platform vendors? Before answering the question, we put forward two assumptions based on the realistic situation and research purpose.

Assumption 1: Digital music copyright levels are from grade 1 to grade n.

Online music platforms, as the decision-making party, grade digital music Copyrights according to the music type of the music track, the audience type and the creator and singer of the music, which affects the music played. For example, "Netease Music Cloud", as an important music service platform, classifies the digital music copyright according to the degree of the audience's preference of the composer and singer of a music track, as well as the relevant data of previous similar music.

Assumption 2: Digital music Copyrights of the same grade have the same value, and the cost for decision makers to invest in digital music Copyrights of the same grade is also the same.

Since the playing effect of digital music is subject to uncertain factors such as the Internet environment and the popularity of the singer across the time, the existing data is not enough to explain the future playing effect (such as the number of music tracks played, likes, and comments). Therefore, in this paper, the expected revenue effect of digital music copyright of different levels is expressed by uncertain variables as $\xi_1, \xi_2, \cdots, \xi_n$.

Before deciding, decision makers will have a certain expectation of the benefits. At this point, the expected playback effect of the digital copyright is the expected income of decision makers. The decision maker should ensure that the average expected return reaches at least one level, which is set as α. Accordingly, the constraint conditions are proposed, expected income constraint:

$$E[\xi_1 x_1 + \xi_2 x_2 + \cdots + \xi_n x_n] \geq \alpha \tag{1}$$

Among them, E represents the expected value of uncertain variable. The proportion of the digital music copyright from the level i is $x_i (x = 1, 2, \cdots, n)$, which satisfies $x_1 + x_2 + \cdots + x_n = 1$. x_i is the decision variable and α is the lowest income expectation given by the decision maker in advance.

The copyright investment process generates costs. The cost to decision makers is directly proportional to the performance of digital assets. Since the playing effect of music copyright is an uncertain variable, the cost to be paid by the decision maker should also be an uncertain variable. Let's assume that the cost of the decision maker for copyrights at level i is c_i, $i = 1, 2, \cdots, n$. Accordingly, the constraint conditions are proposed cost constraint:

$$M\{c_1x_1 + c_2x_2 + \cdots + c_nx_n \geq Y\} \leq \beta \tag{2}$$

Among them, M is called the uncertainty measure. Y is the ratio of the maximum cost that decision makers can pay to the total number of the digital music copyright, that is, the highest average cost from the decision maker. β indicates the maximum tolerance of the decision maker for exceeding the cost budget.

Decisions are accompanied by risks. It is assumed that the fluctuation of the expected return of each decision is a risk. Therefore, the measure of risk can be measured by variance. Decision makers should ensure that the risk of product promotion is not too large, that is, it does not exceed the level λ. Accordingly, the constraint conditions are proposed, risk constraint:

$$V[\xi_1x_1 + \xi_2x_2 + \cdots + \xi_nx_n] \leq \lambda \tag{3}$$

Among them, V indicates the variance of the expected communication effect. λ is the maximum average risk tolerance given by the decision maker in advance.

The goal of decision makers is to maximize benefits and minimize risks. However, because the units of benefit and risk are not consistent, decision makers often consider minimizing risk on a per-unit basis. Therefore, this paper takes V/E minimization as the decision-making objective, that is, minimizing the risk on the basis of unit return, which also means maximizing the return when the risk is fixed. Therefore, the objective function is,

$$min \frac{V[\xi_1x_1 + \xi_2x_2 + \cdots + \xi_nx_n]}{E[\xi_1x_1 + \xi_2x_2 + \cdots + \xi_nx_n]} \tag{4}$$

To sum up, the uncertain digital music copyright investment model which considers investment returns, investment costs and investment risks (Uncertain Digital Music Copyright Investment Model, UDMCI-model):

$$\begin{cases} min \frac{V[\xi_1x_1 + \xi_2x_2 + \cdots + \xi_nx_n]}{E[\xi_1x_1 + \xi_2x_2 + \cdots + \xi_nx_n]} \\ s.t. \\ E[\xi_1x_1 + \xi_2x_2 + \cdots + \xi_nx_n] \geq \alpha \\ M\{c_1x_1 + c_2x_2 + \cdots + c_nx_n \geq Y\} \leq \beta \\ V[\xi_1x_1 + \xi_2x_2 + \cdots + \xi_nx_n] \leq \lambda \\ x_1 + x_2 + \cdots + x_n = 1 \\ x_i \geq 0 \\ i = 1, 2, \cdots, n. \end{cases} \tag{5}$$

3 Model Transformation

Formula (5) is the general form of the UDMCI-model, and decision-makers cannot obtain the optimal choice of copyright levels according to model (5). In order to facilitate the solution of model (5), this paper gives the equivalent form of model (5) according to the uncertainty theory.

Assume that play effect is an independent normal uncertainty variable. In this case, has a continuous monotonically increasing uncertain distribution function. Assume that, cost as an independent normal uncertainty variable. In this case, has a continuous monotonically increasing uncertain distribution function. Therefore, model (5) can be transformed into the following form:

$$
\begin{cases}
\min \left(\sum_{i=1}^{n} \sigma_i x_i\right)^2 \bigg/ \sum_{i=1}^{n} \mu_i x_i \\
s.t. \\
\quad \sum_{i=1}^{n} \mu_i x_i \geq \alpha \\
\quad \sum_{i=1}^{n} x_i (e_i + \frac{\sqrt{3}\delta_i}{\pi} \ln \frac{\beta}{1-\beta}) \leq Y \\
\quad \left(\sum_{i=1}^{n} \sigma_i x_i\right)^2 \leq \lambda \\
\quad x_1 + x_2 + \cdots + x_n = 1 \\
\quad x_i \geq 0 \\
\quad i = 1, 2, \cdots, n.
\end{cases}
\tag{6}
$$

The formula has been proven to have a unique solution [6]. According to Liu [6], ξ_i is an uncertain variable, $\xi_i \sim N(\mu_i, \sigma_i)$, $i = 1, 2, \cdots, n$. Therefore, the income constraint in model (5) is

$$
E[\sum_{i=1}^{n} x_i \xi_i] = \sum_{i=1}^{n} x_i E[\xi_i] = \sum_{i=1}^{n} x_i \mu_i.
$$

Therefore, in the same way, according to Liu [6], there are

$$
\sqrt{V[x_1 \xi_1 + x_2 \xi_2 + \cdots + x_n \xi_n]} = x_1 \sqrt{V[\xi_1]} + x_2 \sqrt{V[\xi_2]} + \cdots + x_n \sqrt{V[\xi_n]}
$$
$$
= x_1 \sigma_1 + x_2 \sigma_2 + \cdots + x_n \sigma_n
$$
$$
= \sum_{i=1}^{n} x_i \sigma_i.
$$

Therefore, the risk constraint in model (5) is

$$
V[\sum_{i=1}^{n} \xi_i x_i] = (\sum_{i=1}^{n} \sigma_i x_i)^2 \leq \lambda.
$$

c_i is a normal uncertain variable, $c_i \sim N(e_i, \delta_i)$, $i = 1, 2, \cdots, n$. According to Liu [6], the uncertain inverse distribution function of $\sum_{i=1}^{n} c_i x_i$ at β is:

$$\sum_{i=1}^{n} x_i \Psi_i^{-1}(\beta).$$

According to the monotonicity of uncertain variable c_i, the cost constraint in the model (5) can be written as follows:

$$\sum_{i=1}^{n} x_i \Psi_i^{-1}(\beta) \leq Y,$$

$$\sum_{i=1}^{n} x_i (e_i + \frac{\sqrt{3}\delta_i}{\pi} \ln \frac{\beta}{1-\beta}) \leq Y.$$

Therefore, the transformation of model (5) into model (6) can be proved.

4 Numerical Example

4.1 Experiment

In order to make decision makers better apply the UDMCI-model considering the constraints of benefits, costs, and risks in practice, a numerical example is used to illustrate the application of the model. To keep things simple, decision makers have divided digital music rights into eight levels. The playing effect of music tracks is affected by many factors, and it is impossible to predict the future playing effect based on the existing data. Therefore, this paper adopts the expert experiences method in the uncertainty programming theory [17], in which experts estimate the final playing effect and investment cost according to their own knowledge, ability and social network environment, and then obtain the corresponding normal uncertainty distribution. Then, the least square method [6] in the uncertainty theory is used for parameter estimation. The final parameter results are shown in Table 1.

Table 1. Uncertain distribution of expected play effect and cost.

Level i	μ_i	σ_i	e_i	δ_i
1	25000	50	3000	30
2	50100	100	4500	87
3	100000	150	9900	56
4	350000	310	20000	77
5	1100000	360	110000	90
6	8800000	510	780000	97
7	15000000	750	1500000	125
8	38000000	1000	3000000	200

Suppose the decision maker decides to select a total of 50 music tracks for digital music copyright investment, the expected playing effect (number of plays, likes and comments) is 620 million, and the expected total cost is 90 million RMB. It is assumed that decision makers use model (6) to deal with the above problems. The specific model is:

$$
\begin{cases}
\min \ \left(\sum_{i=1}^{8} \sigma_i x_i\right)^2 \Big/ \sum_{i=1}^{8} \mu_i x_i \\
s.t. \\
\quad \sum_{i=1}^{8} \mu_i x_i \geq 31000000 \\
\quad \sum_{i=1}^{8} x_i \left(e_i + \frac{\sqrt{3}\delta_i}{\pi} \ln \frac{0.1}{1-0.1}\right) \leq 4500000 \\
\quad \left(\sum_{i=1}^{8} \sigma_i x_i\right)^2 \leq 3000000 \\
\quad x_1 + x_2 + \cdots + x_8 = 1 \\
\quad x_i \geq 0, i = 1, 2, \cdots, 8.
\end{cases}
\tag{7}
$$

Among them, the lowest limit of average expectation is $\alpha = 31000000$. The maximum tolerance of average risk is $\lambda = 3000000$. The cost constraint threshold value acceptable to decision makers is $Y = 4500000$, and the reliability that exceeds the threshold value β cannot exceed 0.1.

By running Matlab R2018a and using fmincon solver, the optimal solution of the model is 0.0244. At this time, the distribution ratio of different levels is shown in Table 2.

At this point, when the number of Copyrights selected by the decision maker at each level is (2, 2, 2, 2, 2, 2, 36), the decision can well meet the expected income, and the cost is reasonable and the risk is low enough. The results in Table 2 show that: when making copyright investment decisions, the highest level of copyright should be the one to focus on, and multiple levels copyright should also be involved. This can not only

Table 2. Allocation ratio.

Level	Allocation ratio
1	0.0241
2	0.0243
3	0.0238
4	0.0234
5	0.0238
6	0.0305
7	0.0382
8	0.8121

ensure the final investment returns, but also increase the diversity of platform repertoire styles, which can better adapt to the different needs of the vast audience.

4.2 The Effectiveness of the Fmincon

The iterative convergence of the objective function value (OFV) is shown in Fig. 1. It can be easily seen from Fig. 1 that the convergence speed of fmincon solver is very fast. In addition, it stops when the number of iterations reaches 20, indicating that fmincon solver is an effective method for solving this model.

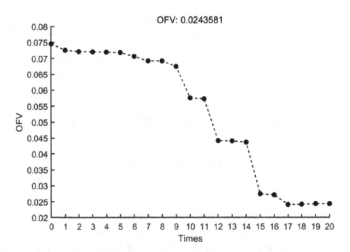

Fig. 1. Fmincon's iterative convergence graph of objective function value.

4.3 The Effectiveness of the Model

In this section, this paper changes the value of α, λ, and Y to describe different preferences of decision makers, including expected playing effect preference, risk preference and cost preference. The simulation results are analyzed to explore the influences of different investment preferences on portfolio decision, to verify the effectiveness of the model.

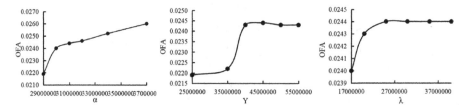

Fig. 2. OFV changing with $\alpha \lambda$ Y

Table 3. The optimal selection proportions for different α

α	Optimal selection strategy x^*	OFV
29000000	$x_1 = 0.1014, x_2 = 0.0587, x_3 = 0.0282, x_4 = 0.013,$ $x_5 = 0.0119, x_6 = 0.0142, x_7 = 0.0107, x_8 = 0.7618$	**0.0219**
30000000	$x_1 = 0.0300, x_2 = 0.0297, x_3 = 0.0285, x_4 = 0.0264,$ $x_5 = 0.0265, x_6 = 0.0336, x_7 = 0.0387, x_8 = 0.7867$	**0.0240**
31000000	$x_1 = 0.0241, x_2 = 0.0243, x_3 = 0.0238, x_4 = 0.0234,$ $x_5 = 0.0238, x_6 = 0.0305, x_7 = 0.0382, x_8 = 0.8121$	**0.0244**
32000000	$x_1 = 0.0218, x_2 = 0.0217, x_3 = 0.0210, x_4 = 0.0199,$ $x_5 = 0.0200, x_6 = 0.0256, x_7 = 0.0305, x_8 = 0.8396$	**0.0246**
34000000	$x_1 = 0.0133, x_2 = 0.0135, x_3 = 0.0133, x_4 = 0.0133,$ $x_5 = 0.0136, x_6 = 0.0176, x_7 = 0.0228, x_8 = 0.8927$	**0.0252**
37000000	$x_1 = 0.0032, x_2 = 0.0035, x_3 = 0.0033, x_4 = 0.0032,$ $x_5 = 0.0035, x_6 = 0.0043, x_7 = 0.0056, x_8 = 0.9734$	**0.0260**

Table 3 describes the optimal selection under different expected playback effect preferences and calculates the corresponding objective function values. As shown in Fig. 2, high return is accompanied by high risk. The higher the return, the greater the increase of risk. Therefore, the larger the value, the larger the value of the objective function (Table 3).

Table 4 describes the optimal choice of investment decision under different risk preferences. Under a certain risk threshold, the higher the risk threshold that decision makers can bear, the greater the increase of risk under unit return, which is consistent

Table 4. The optimal selection proportions for different λ.

λ	Optimal selection strategy x^*	OFV
1700000	$x_1 = 0.0284, x_2 = 0.0280, x_3 = 0.0271, x_4 = 0.0260,$ $x_5 = 0.0264, x_6 = 0.0341, x_7 = 0.0103, x_8 = 0.8196$	**0.0240**
2000000	$x_1 = 0.0241, x_2 = 0.0244, x_3 = 0.0239, x_4 = 0.0233,$ $x_5 = 0.0238, x_6 = 0.0306, x_7 = 0.0378, x_8 = 0.8120$	**0.0243**
2500000	$x_1 = 0.0236, x_2 = 0.0238, x_3 = 0.0234, x_4 = 0.0231,$ $x_5 = 0.0235, x_6 = 0.0301, x_7 = 0.0403, x_8 = 0.8122$	**0.0244**
3000000	$x_1 = 0.0241, x_2 = 0.0243, x_3 = 0.0238, x_4 = 0.0234,$ $x_5 = 0.0238, x_6 = 0.0305, x_7 = 0.0382, x_8 = 0.8121$	**0.0244**
3500000	$x_1 = 0.0241, x_2 = 0.0243, x_3 = 0.0238, x_4 = 0.0234,$ $x_5 = 0.0238, x_6 = 0.0305, x_7 = 0.0382, x_8 = 0.8121$	**0.0244**
4000000	$x_1 = 0.0241, x_2 = 0.0243, x_3 = 0.0238, x_4 = 0.0234,$ $x_5 = 0.0238, x_6 = 0.0305, x_7 = 0.0382, x_8 = 0.8121$	**0.0244**

with the target value shown in Table 4. As shown in Fig. 2, when the risk threshold is below 2500000, with the increase of the risk threshold, the value of risk under unit return will be larger. However, when the risk threshold is set too high, the risk value under unit income will not change basically. Therefore, the model is reasonable and effective.

Table 5. The optimal selection proportions for different Y

Y	Optimal selection strategy x^*	OFV
2500000	$x_1 = 0.0302, x_2 = 0.0299, x_3 = 0.0282, x_4 = 0.0354,$ $x_5 = 0.0189, x_6 = 0.0259, x_7 = 0.0275, x_8 = 0.8041$	**0.0219**
3500000	$x_1 = 0.0156, x_2 = 0.0103, x_3 = 0.0070, x_4 = 0.0031,$ $x_5 = 0.0027, x_6 = 0.0031, x_7 = 0.0023, x_8 = 0.8155$	**0.0222**
4000000	$x_1 = 0.0258, x_2 = 0.0257, x_3 = 0.0247, x_4 = 0.0232,$ $x_5 = 0.0233, x_6 = 0.0297, x_7 = 0.0348, x_8 = 0.8128$	**0.0243**
4500000	$x_1 = 0.0241, x_2 = 0.0243, x_3 = 0.0238, x_4 = 0.0234,$ $x_5 = 0.0238, x_6 = 0.0305, x_7 = 0.0382, x_8 = 0.8121$	**0.0244**
5000000	$x_1 = 0.0257, x_2 = 0.0255, x_3 = 0.0246, x_4 = 0.0231,$ $x_5 = 0.0232, x_6 = 0.0297, x_7 = 0.0349, x_8 = 0.8134$	**0.0243**

High investment leads to high returns. Moreover, when the cost input is high enough, the risk can be avoided to a certain extent. Therefore, at a certain cost threshold, the value at risk per unit of revenue increases. When the cost threshold is high enough, some risks can be avoided, so there is no significant change in risk. This is consistent with the target value results shown in Table 5 and Fig. 2. When the cost input is too high, the value at risk will no longer change significantly.

In summary, the experimental results presented in this section confirm the rationality and effectiveness of the model.

5 Conclusion

Digital music copyright is a powerful tool for online music platforms to gain profits as well as the industry competitiveness. High-quality investment decisions are conducive to the sustainable development of the platform. Under the condition of limited cost expenditure, online music platform should minimize the promotion risk on the basis of satisfying the expected playback effect, so as to make the optimal investment decision reasonable. Considering the instability of the network environment and the uncertainty of the playing effect of music tracks, this paper innovatively introduces the uncertainty theory to build the digital music copyright portfolio model under the uncertain environment, which is expected to fill in the gap of investment strategy research in the field of digital music copyright. The research results of this paper can provide a theoretical basis for the scientific decision of copyright investment in online music platforms, and have a guiding role in the rationalization of copyright investment in such platforms.

The main contributions of this paper are as follows: Firstly, the uncertainty theory is applied to the research of digital music copyright for the first time. Secondly, the portfolio strategy of digital music copyright under uncertain environment is studied. Thirdly, the paper explores the influence of decision makers' investment preference on digital music copyright investment.

As digital music copyright investment involves the issue of trade secrets, this paper uses the simulation value as an example in the simulation experiment, but there is a certain deviation from the actual situation. In the future, we hope to obtain real data from online music platforms through different channels and technical means to achieve better fitting effect. In addition, this paper takes music copyright in digital copyright as an example to build a single objective uncertain portfolio model. The next research direction is to consider the investment process of digital copyright, conduct a detailed study, and propose an optimal investment plan for multi-objective digital copyright investment. Finally, digital music copyright investment has a variety of copyright investment methods, including obtaining exclusive copyright, copyright sublicense, etc., which have different characteristics and are subject to different factors. It is an important research direction to use different ways of copyright investment to make portfolio decision. The model can be further improved according to different combinations of copyright investment ways to better adapt to the actual needs of the platform.

Acknowledgement. This research was supported by the National Natural Science Foundation of China under Grant 72121001 and 72131005, and Shanghai Pudong Development Bank under spdbheb-20220415.

References

1. Abhishek, V., Jerath, K., Zhang, Z.J.: Agency selling or reselling? Channel structures in electronic retailing. Manage. Sci. **62**(8), 2259–2280 (2015)
2. Sundararajan, A.: Managing digital piracy: pricing and protection. Inf. Syst. Res. **15**(3), 287–308 (2004)
3. Rutz, O.J., Bucklin, R.E.: From generic to branded: a model of spillover in paid search advertising. J. Mark. Res. **48**(1), 87–102 (2011)
4. Glas, T.: Asset Pricing and Investment Styles in Digital Assets: A Comparison with Traditional Asset Classes. Springer Nature, Berlin (2022)
5. Petukhina, A., Sprünken, E.: Evaluation of multi-asset investment strategies with digital assets. Dig. Fin. **3**(1), 45–79 (2021). https://doi.org/10.1007/s42521-021-00031-9
6. Liu, B.: Uncertainty Theory. In: Uncertainty Theory Laboratory 5th edn (2021)
7. Liu, B.: Some research problems in uncertainty theory. J. Uncert. Syst. **3**(1), 3–10 (2009)
8. Yu, S., Ning, Y.: An interest-rate model with jumps for uncertain financial markets. Physica A **527**, 121424 (2019)
9. Huang, X., Di, H.: Uncertain portfolio selection with mental accounts. Int. J. Syst. Sci. **51**(12), 2079–2090 (2020)
10. Chang, J., Sun, L., Zhang, B., Peng, J.: Multi-period portfolio selection with mental accounts and realistic constraints based on uncertainty theory. J. Comput. Appl. Math. **377**, 112892 (2020)
11. Xue, L., Di, H., Zhao, X., Zhang, Z.: Uncertain portfolio selection with mental accounts and realistic constraints. J. Comput. Appl. Math. **346**, 42–52 (2019)
12. Li, B., Zhang, R.: A new mean-variance-entropy model for uncertain portfolio optimization with liquidity and diversification. Chaos, Solitons Fractals **146**, 110842 (2021)
13. Li, Y., Peng, R., Kucukkoc, I., Tang, X., Wei, F.: System reliability optimization for an assembly line under uncertain random environment. Comput. Ind. Eng. **146**, 106540 (2020)
14. Ning, Y., Su, T.: A multilevel approach for modelling vehicle routing problem with uncertain travelling time. J. Intell. Manuf. **28**(3), 683–688 (2014). https://doi.org/10.1007/s10845-014-0979-3
15. Ning, Y., Pang, N., Wang, X.: An uncertain aggregate production planning model considering investment in vegetable preservation technology. Math. Probl. Eng., 8505868 (2019)
16. Jin, M., Ning, Y., Li, B., Liu, F., Gao, C., Gao, Y.: Uncertain KOL selection with multiple constraints in advertising promotion. IEEE Access **9**, 142869–142878 (2021)
17. Liu, B.: Uncertainty Theory: A Branch of Mathematics for Modeling Human Uncertainty. Springer-Verlag, Berlin (2010)

Role of Channel Characteristics of the New Retail Model on Brand Loyalty

Chunliu Gu and Tianmei Wang[✉]

School of Information, Central University of Finance and Economics, Beijing, China
wangtianmei@cufe.edu.cn

Abstract. This paper explores the influence of two channel characteristics on brand loyalty, namely, the vividness of online information presentation and offline travel distance perception and the moderating effects of haptic perception demand and price consistency in the new retail model based on the dual system theory of decision making. A total of 537 valid samples were collected for model testing. Results showed that the vividness of online information presentation had a significant positive effect on customer behavior loyalty and attitude loyalty; offline travel distance perception only had a significant negative effect on customer attitude loyalty; haptic perception needs negatively moderated the relationship between vividness of information presentation and customer behavior loyalty; and price consistency positively moderated the relationship between travel distance perception and customer attitude loyalty. The findings have implications for different experience-based FMCG brands to break out the "traffic" dilemma in new retail.

Keywords: New Retail Model · Vividness of Information Presentation · Travel Distance Perception · Brand Loyalty

1 Introduction

New retail is a novel model that realizes the synergy and integration of traditional and e-commerce retails with the help of digital technologies such as big data and artificial intelligence to provide customers with a seamless shopping experience (Lee et al., 2021). Popular clothing, shoes, hats, and bags are both experience-based and FMCG products, and customers have a strong need to purchase both the experience of being present and the convenience of repeated purchases. On one hand, the increasing number of new brands and the diversification of purchase channels make it easy for old customers to be attracted by other brands and to be "lost" in the process of repeated purchase. On the other hand, the fierce competition also makes it costly for companies to obtain new customers. The cost of "traffic" of new customers is increasing. These "traffic" dilemmas have become obstacles to optimizing brand loyalty building. Studies have highlighted the importance of omnichannel management (Lee et al., 2021) and the impact of channel integration on service satisfaction (Fisher et al., 2019). Research has also explored the impact of specific factors on purchase decisions in a single channel (Kim et al., 2019), and others have discussed customer channel preferences in omnichannel

Y. Tu and M. Chi (Eds.): WHICEB 2023, LNBIP 481, pp. 180–193, 2023.
https://doi.org/10.1007/978-3-031-32302-7_16

operations (Luo et al. 2020). Few studies have explored in depth the impact of online and offline channel characteristics on brand loyalty in the channel integration process of new retail. Therefore, breaking through the dilemma of customer "traffic" loss and optimizing brand loyalty in the experience-based FMCG industry are important for new retailers by effectively implementing omnichannel management, deeply exploring the different channel characteristics of online and offline channels in omnichannel, and exploring their internal influence mechanisms on brand loyalty.

2 Literature Review

An important driver of customer loyalty is customer satisfaction, based on expectation confirmation theory (ECT). While, with the diversification of sales channels in retail scenarios, studies have been conducted to explore other key factors affecting brand loyalty from online or offline channels, respectively. For offline channels, the influence of store atmosphere, brand image, corporate social responsibility, customer's attitude, confidence, and relationship with brand loyalty was discussed from the perspective of social image and emotional relationship with the brand (Jung et al., 2020; Iglesias et al., 2020). By contrast, for online sales channels, the influence of brand identity, brand rewards, personalization of advertising messages, and perceived value of information on brand loyalty was analyzed from the perspective of emotional relationship and marketing approach of brands (Kaur et al., 2020; Shanahan et al., 2019).

The omnichannel of the new retail model consists of two types of channels, namely, online and offline. Most existing studies have explored the effects of specific factors of a single channel on channel integration, purchase behavior, and pro-social behavior. The offline channel remains the main channel of the new retail model, which aims to satisfy customers' needs for on-the-spot experiences through stores. Early studies have focused on service quality, store atmosphere, and travel factors (Francioni et al., 2018; Grewal et al., 2012; Luo et al., 2020). The online channel is another feature of the new retail model, which presents product information with the help of virtual digital technology. Studies have analyzed the effects of information presentation in online channels from two perspectives: local and overall feature. Based on local feature, existing studies have explored the effects of information presentation characteristics such as picture content, color, and size (Luo et al., 2021). Based on overall feature, existing studies have explored the effects of information presentation methods, such as static pictures, zoomed images, and rotated videos (Jai et al., 2021).

In summary, existing studies have mostly focused on the characteristics of only one channel in new retail model, and information presentation effect and travel distance has become key factors influencing customer decisions in offline or online channels, respectively. For information presentation, customers' judgment of product value is not only based on the local characteristics of information presentation but also depends on the overall characteristics of information presentation. Although some studies have explored the overall characteristics, they have not yet fully discussed its influence on customers' brand loyalty. For travel distance, studies have discussed the influence of travel factors on channel integration and purchase decisions, however, most studies have ignored the difference between spatial travel distance and cognitive travel distance, and its impact on customer loyalty. It has important theoretical value to study the impact of different characteristics of the two channels on customer loyalty, and has practical guidance for FMCG band to break out the customer "traffic" loss dilemma.

3   Research Hypothesis

Studies have shown that brand loyalty can be finely measured in terms of attitude and behavior loyalties (Chaudhuri et al., 2001). In the new retailing model, behavior loyalty can improve the repeat purchase of old customers, while willingness to recommend of attitude loyalty has a word-of-mouth effect and can help companies reduce the cost of acquiring new customers. Therefore, both behavior and attitude loyalties are important elements to focus on. From the perspective of brands and customers, both of them always expect online and offline channels are complementary. Similarly, in the new retail model, omnichannel is the key to influence customers' purchase decision, and correspondingly channel characteristics become an important factor affecting brand loyalty.

The Dual-system theory believes that human decision making has two modes: intuitive heuristic and rational analytical processing; the heuristic system relies on intuition to deal with problems, processing speed is faster, more partial information is extracted for processing, and decision bias is easily produced; whereas the analytical processing system requires conscious effort to deal with problems, systematic information processing, processing speed is slower, and decision bias can be somewhat avoided (Evans et al., 2013). Customers have the tendency to use simple heuristics for decision making when making repeated purchases and relatively unimportant decisions. This paper argues that in the new retail model, customers are free to choose online or offline channels, the vividness of information presentation is the evaluation of the overall display of product information in online channels, and the travel distance perception is the customer's cognitive judgment of the spatial distance when purchasing in offline channels. Both of them affect the customer's choice of information processing mode in the decision-making process. The conceptual model of this paper sees Fig. 1.

Online channels do not allow customers to touch and experience products on the spot but rather display product information with digital technology, and the effect of product information presentation in online channels also affects customers' decisions. According to the principle of perceptual organization, humans are more likely to understand and remember things from a holistic visual perspective in an unconscious state (Jimenez et al., 2017), and the vividness of information presentation makes it easier for customers to understand and remember product information without extra cognitive effort. For brands with low vividness of information presentation, customers need to mobilize their analytical processing systems more to sort out, discriminate, and understand product information, which requires additional cognitive effort. By contrast, for high vividness of information presentation, customers can stimulate their visual nerves more effectively and complete most cognitive tasks heuristically and autonomously, which makes information processing less difficult and increases customers' willingness to purchase and recommend the brand. Kim et al. (2019) showed that positive image processing can increase customers' willingness to buy; Yu et al. (2017) found that online information presentation forms with visual and interactive features are more likely to trigger customers' online presence, which in turn stimulates customers' willingness to purchase and recommend. Therefore, the vividness of information presentation significantly affects behavior and attitude loyalty. In summary, the following hypotheses are proposed:

H1: Vividness of information presentation significantly and positively affects customers' (a) behavior loyalty and (b) attitude loyalty.

Cognitive distance is the perception of distance between locations that are distant and invisible to each other in a large-scale space (Ankomah et al., 1995), and customers' perception of travel distance to offline stores is also a form of cognitive distance. According to existing retail store location studies, the closer the physical distance to the brand's store, the lower the travel cost and the greater the likelihood of customer repurchase. However, actual distance is only the basis of perceived distance, and customers may use perceived distance rather than actual distance when choosing a destination (Raghubir et al., 1996). As the actual distance increases, the customer's estimate of the perceived distance also increases and produces some cognitive bias (Ankomah et al., 1995). In this paper, we argue that for brands with perceived distant travel distances, customers need to invest extra cognitive effort to process a large amount of travel information, and decision inaccuracy and difficulty increase. By contrast, for brands with perceived close travel distances, customers need to process less spatial distance information, completing decisions through heuristic system, and more willing to purchase and recommend the brand. Lin et al. (2008) found that cognitive distance estimates do not directly predict tourists' intention to visit but indirectly predict customers' intention to visit through the inaccuracy of cognitive distance; Raghubir et al. (1996) demonstrated that in the case of map navigation, the cognitive distance formed is automatically used by the customer's heuristic system, and is more accessible and accurate than the actual distance and therefore is more likely to be preferred by customers' recommendations. Therefore, travel distance perception significantly affects behavior and attitude loyalty. In summary, the following hypotheses are proposed:

H2: Travel distance perception significantly and negatively affects customers' (a) behavior loyalty and (b) attitude loyalty.

Compared with offline channels, online channels have difficulty providing haptic experiences similar to those of physical stores through sensory systems. This lack of sensory cues can cause hesitation among customers to shop in online channels. Haptic perception needs can be defined as the preference of customers to access product information through the haptic sensory system, which allows for obtaining a cognitive evaluation of the product, establishing an emotional bond with the product, and thus influencing customer attitudes and behaviors (Peck et al., 2006). De Canio et al. (2021) found that customers with strong haptic characteristics prefer offline physical and mobile channels that provide direct touch interfaces (e.g., touch screens, touch pads). Manzano et al. (2016) used the fashion apparel industry as an example and found that customers who chose online channels showed lower haptic demand than those who chose offline channels. This paper argues that customers with low haptic perceptual demand prefer digital information presentation, and those with high haptic perceptual demand prefer to experience product information in person. Therefore, haptic perceptual demand weakens the impact of vividness of online information presentation on behavior customer and attitude loyalty. In summary, the following hypotheses are proposed:

H3: Haptic perception needs play a negative moderating role between vividness of information presentation and customers' (a) behavior loyalty and (b) attitude loyalty.

Price consistency is defined as the customer's perception of the difference in product prices between offline and online channels. Chu et al. (2008) found that households are more price sensitive to offline channels than online channels, and the closer the household is to the brand's offline store, the higher the customer's price sensitivity. In new retailing model, price is more likely to significantly influence customers' shopping choices in offline channels, and the closer the travel distance is perceived, the more significant the effect to be. Price is an important signal of product quality, and price inconsistency between online and offline is likely to lead customers to judge the quality of the brand's products as bad, thus reducing customers' trust in the brand. Mookherjee et al. (2021) showed that pricing inconsistency between online and offline influences repurchase or retention behavior through customer regret and disappointment. This paper argues that online and offline price consistency can enhance customer trust and positive emotions toward the brand's products, thus strengthening the impact of offline travel distance perception on customer behavior and attitude loyalty. In summary, the following hypotheses are proposed:

H4a: Price consistency plays a positive moderating role between travel distance perception and customers' (a) behavior loyalty and (b) attitude loyalty.

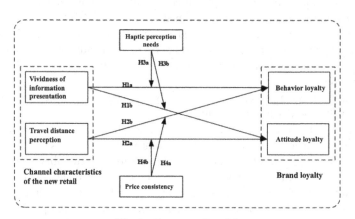

Fig. 1. Conceptual model

4 Study Design

In this study, data were collected via an online questionnaire, and the respondents were customers who had visited both online and offline stores of a clothing brand within the last three months. The data collection was divided into two stages: pre-survey and formal survey. A total of 700 questionnaires were distributed, and invalid questionnaires with failed attention check, incomplete, and abnormal answer time were excluded. Finally, a total of 537 valid questionnaires were obtained, with a valid recovery rate of 76.7%.

To improve the content validity of the scales, all scales used in existing studies were used to measure the variables, and the vividness of information presentation was referred to the scale of Yu et al. (2017), travel distance perception was referred to the studies of Ankomah et al. (1995) and Lin et al. (2008) using the inverse measurement scale, haptic perceived need was referred to the scale of De Canio et al. (2021), price consistency was referred to Mookherjee et al. (2021), time pressure with reference to Hamermesh et al. (2007), brand satisfaction with reference to Jung et al. (2020) and Francioni et al. (2018), and brand loyalty with reference to Chaudhuri et al. (2001) and Jung et al. (2020). The questionnaire items were also adapted to the study scenario. Each variable was measured on a 7-point Likert scale. In addition, customers' gender, age, income, number of online shopping trips, time pressure, and brand satisfaction affect brand loyalty, and related to online information presentation and travel distance perception. Thus, these variables are used as control variables.

5 Data Analysis and Results

5.1 Descriptive Statistics

Table 1 summarizes the descriptive statistical analysis of the survey sample. The proportion of female samples is slightly higher than that of male samples, which is in line with the current situation of female customers in the apparel industry.

Table 1. Demographics Summary

Variable	Classification	Number	Percent (%)
Gender	Female	328	61.1
	Male	209	38.9
Age (years)	0–20	18	3.4
	21–30	293	54.6
	31–40	177	33.0

(*continued*)

Table 1. (*continued*)

Variable	Classification	Number	Percent (%)
	41–50	29	5.4
	>50	20	3.7
Degree	High school and below	16	3.0
	Specialist	63	11.7
	Undergraduate	401	74.7
	Graduate	57	10.6
Income	Less than 1000 RMB	10	1.9
	1001–3000RMB	89	16.6
	3001–5000RMB	75	14.0
	5001–8000RMB	172	32.0
	More than 8000 RMB	191	35.6
Times of online purchases Nearly a month	Less than 3 times	8	1.5
	3–5 times	55	10.2
	6–10 times	121	22.5
	More than 10 times	353	65.7

5.2 Reliability Analysis and Common Method Bias Test

In this study, SPSS 22.0 and AMOS 20.0 were used to test the reliability and validity of each variable, and Table 2 gives a summary. First, the Cronbach's Alpha value of each variable of the questionnaire in this study was higher than 0.6, and the overall Cronbach's Alpha value was approximately 0.8. The composite reliability (CR) of each variable was higher than 0.6, and the quality of data reliability was good. In addition, the factor loadings and the average variance extracted (AVE) values of each variable showed that the factor loadings of each variable were greater than 0.6. The average variance extracted (AVE) of each variable was more than 0.5, which indicated that the convergent validity of the scale was good. Meanwhile, the square root of AVE values was greater than the correlation coefficient of each variable, which indicates that the scale has good discriminant validity as shown in Table 3.

The study conducted a factor analysis of all question items for each latent variable of brand satisfaction, brand loyalty, vividness of information presentation, travel distance perception, and haptic perception demand and time pressure. It then obtained an unrotated first principal component with a variance explained of 24.35%, with no significant common method bias.

Table 2. Reliability tests and AVE values for each variable

Construct	Items	Factor loading	CR	AVE
Information presented by Vividness (PV)	PV3	0.726	0.71	0.55
	PV5	0.763		
Traveling Distance Perception (DS)	DS1	0.917	0.94	0.79
	DS2	0.921		
	DS3	0.798		
	DS4	0.912		
Haptic perception needs (TC)	TC2	0.844	0.93	0.76
	TC3	0.885		
	TC4	0.873		
	TC5	0.892		
Price Consistency (CN)	CN2	0.771	0.84	0.72
	CN3	0.920		
Brands Satisfaction (SA)	SA1	0.704	0.67	0.51
	SA2	0.719		
Time pressure (TP)	TP1	0.896	0.95	0.84
	TP2	0.917		
	TP3	0.931		
	TP4	0.924		
Behavior Loyalty (LYB)	LYB1	0.765	0.77	0.53
	LYB2	0.655		
	LYB3	0.749		
Attitude Loyalty (LYT)	LYT1	0.784	0.82	0.60
	LYT2	0.771		
	LYT3	0.770		

Table 3. Pearson correlation with AVE square root values

	PV	DS	TC	CN	SA	TP	LYB	LYT
PV	**0.745**							
DS	0.183	**0.888**						
TC	−0.052	0.070	**0.874**					
CN	0.255	0.230	0.108	**0.849**				
SA	0.428	0.217	0.046	0.157	**0.712**			
TP	−0.106	−0.126	0.165	−0.082	−0.121	**0.917**		
LYB	0.413	0.209	−0.039	0.169	0.638	−0.186	**0.725**	
LYT	0.454	0.275	0.017	0.302	0.644	−0.109	0.641	**0.775**

Note: Diagonal numbers are AVE square root values.

5.3 Hypothesis Testing

The main research variables were centered prior to formal regression analysis using SPSS 20.0 software. In addition, the VIF values of the research model were below 5.0, indicating that the model in this study does not have serious multicollinearity problems. According to the regression results in Table 4, the baseline Model 1 indicates that customer age, income level, channel preference, shopping time pressure, and brand satisfaction significantly affect customers' behavior loyalty to the brand; whereas gender, education level, and number of online purchases in the last month have no significant effect; the baseline model 5 indicates that customer education level, income level, and brand satisfaction significantly affect customers' attitude loyalty to the brand, whereas gender, age, number of online purchases in the last month, channel preference, and time pressure have no significant effect.

Model 2 indicates that vividness of information presentation has a significant positive effect on behavior loyalty ($\beta = 0.144$, $p < 0.01$). Travel distance perception has no significant effect on behavior loyalty. The regression results supported hypothesis H1a but did not support hypothesis H2a. Models 3 and 4 further added moderating variables and moderating interaction terms and found that haptic perceived demand negatively moderated the effect of vividness of information presentation on behavior loyalty ($\beta = -0.089$, $p < 0.01$), and price consistency did not significantly moderate the effect of travel distance perception on behavior loyalty, supporting hypothesis H3a but not hypothesis H4a.

Model 6 indicates that vividness of information presentation and travel distance perception have a significant negative effect on attitude loyalty (travel distance perception using the inverse measurement scale, $\beta = 0.182$, $p < 0.01$; $\beta = 0.111$, $p < 0.01$), supporting Hypotheses H1b and H2b. Models 7 and 8 further added moderating variables and moderating interaction terms and found that price consistency significantly and positively moderated the effect of travel distance perception on attitude loyalty ($\beta = 0.058$, $p < 0.1$). Haptic perceived need did not significantly moderate the effect of vividness of information presentation on attitude loyalty, which did not support hypothesis H3b but supported hypothesis H4b.

Table 4. Results of hierarchical regression analysis

Variables	LYB				LYT			
	Model 1	Model 2	Model 3	Model 4	Model 5	Model 6	Model 7	Model 8
Control variables								
Gender	−0.003 (−0.099)	−0.005 (−0.154)	−0.008 (−0.242)	−0.002 (−0.046)	−0.027 (−0.796)	−0.030 (−0.925)	−0.039 (−1.210)	−0.037 (−1.140)
Age	−0.090** (−2.385)	−0.091** (−2.459)	−0.089** (−2.407)	−0.099*** (−2.671)	−0.032 (0.846)	−0.034 (−0.931)	−0.021 (0.0590)	−0.024 (−0.667)
Education level	−0.052 (−1.502)	−0.042 (−1.228)	−0.040 (−1.179)	−0.047 (−1.387)	−0.084** (−2.435)	−0.072** (−2.162)	−0.063* (−1.925)	−0.065* (−1.991)
Income level	0.146*** (3.816)	0.115*** (3.005)	0.114*** (2.972)	0.127*** (3.302)	0.174*** (4.572)	0.128*** (3.403)	0.123*** (3.340)	0.131*** (3.533)
Number of online purchases	0.035 (1.035)	0.043 (1.298)	0.043 (1.282)	0.039 (1.155)	−0.038 (−1.129)	−0.030 (0.906)	−0.034 (−1.047)	−0.037 (−1.141)
Channel Preference	0.056* (1.680)	0.045 (1.340)	0.035 (0.952)	0.035 (0.967)	0.012 (0.361)	0.005 (0.166)	0.015 (0.424)	0.016 (0.440)
SA	0.593*** (17.158)	0.531*** (14.344)	0.533*** (14.342)	0.522*** (14.055)	0.605*** (17.503)	0.518*** (14.283)	0.516*** (14.452)	0.509*** (14.194)
TP	−0.097*** (−2.900)	−0.085*** (−2.576)	−0.078** (−2.269)	−0.076** (−2.227)	−0.017 (−0.511)	0.001 (0.043)	0.007 (0.225)	0.011 (0.340)
Independent variables								
PV		0.144*** (3.936)	0.137*** (3.672)	0.151*** (4.021)	0.182*** (5.066)	0.147*** (4.091)	0.151*** (4.147)	0.182*** (5.066)
DS		0.045 (1.323)	0.041 (1.207)	0.054 (1.464)	0.111*** (3.354)	0.087*** (2.621)	0.109*** (3.073)	0.111*** (3.354)
Moderating variables								
TC			−0.032 (−0.884)	−0.010 (−0.270)			−0.020 (−0.576)	−0.012 (−0.337)
CN			0.026 (0.771)	0.008 (0.224)			0.154*** (4.679)	0.142*** (4.222)
Moderating effects								
PV* TC				−0.089*** (−2.631)				−0.031 (−0.960)
DS* CN				0.033 (0.963)				0.058* (1.734)
R2	0.442	0.461	0.462	0.470	0.442	0.482	0.503	0.507
Adjusted R2	0.434	0.451	0.450	0.456	0.434	0.472	0.492	0.493
F−value	52.350***	45.019***	37.569***	33.122***	52.340***	48.971***	44.183***	38.291***

Note: *** indicates $p < 0.01$, ** indicates $p < 0.05$, * indicates $p < 0.1$.

To further verify the moderating effect mechanism, this paper also dichotomizes the haptic perceived demand, price consistency variables for simple slope test. The test results again prove the moderating effect of hypotheses H3a and H4b as shown in Fig. 2 and 3.

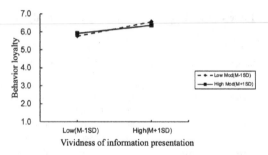

Fig. 2. Moderating effect of haptic perception needs on the vividness of information presentation and customer behavior loyalty

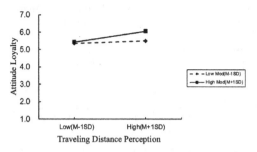

Fig. 3. Moderating effect of price consistency on travel distance perception and customer attitude loyalty

6   Conclusion and Insights

6.1   Research Findings

Based on the new retail model, this paper constructs a research model affecting customer loyalty from the perspective of online and offline channels; explores the influence of two channel characteristics, vividness of information presentation, and travel distance perception on brand loyalty; and analyzes the moderating effects of customers' haptic perception needs and online and offline price consistency. The vividness of online information presentation was found to have a significant positive effect on customers' behavior and attitude loyalty to the brand, indicating that the holistic presentation effect of product information can indeed strengthen customers' memory and understanding of the brand and then form long-term purchase intention and emotional preference. This finding indicates that with the realization of omnichannel, the influence of travel distance perception on customers' own purchase decision is weakening. This phenomenon is probably due to the fact that customers in the near distance can buy via online or offline channels, and customers in the far distance prefer to buy through online channels. Therefore, the distance is no longer a key factor. This finding is in line with Luo et al. (2020) who found complementary views of online and offline channels. The study also found that haptic perception demand has a negative moderating effect on the relationship between vividness of information presentation and behavior loyalty, and price consistency has a positive moderating effect on the relationship between travel distance perception and attitude loyalty, indicating individual differences about the influence of channel characteristics on brand loyalty.

6.2 Theoretical Contributions and Practice Insights

This paper reveals the influence mechanism of different channel characteristics on brand loyalty. Firstly, the new retail model seamlessly integrates online and offline channels. However, most previous studies have analyzed the influencing factors of brand loyalty in a single channel, ignoring the difference effect of channel characteristics on brand loyalty. This paper bridges this gap, enriching the research on brand loyalty and new retail models. Secondly, based on dual-system decision theory, this paper explores the influence of online information presentation vividness and offline travel distance perception on customers' behavior willingness. it complements the research on the holistic characteristics of information presentation and further reveals the influence mechanism of information presentation effect on customers' behavior decision. Meanwhile, using subjective perception instead of objective measurement to measure travel distance is more consistent with the regular of customers' decision, and expands the measurement of travel distance in retail location research. Finally, this paper gains insight about the mechanisms of different channel characteristics on brand loyalty by dividing it into two dimensions: behavior and attitude loyalties. The findings show that perceived travel distance has no significant effect on behavior loyalty, whereas it has a significant effect on attitude loyalty. The latter may be due to the fact that individuals' behavior of recommending is a dominant endorsement behavior and needs to like the product more and have more credible information. Thus, they are more willing to choose brands with perceived proximity.

The findings of the study also have implications for new retailers to break out the "traffic" dilemma. New retail enterprises can divide customers into four groups according to two indicators of haptic perception demand and price consistency sensitivity in omnichannel operation and formulate operation strategies by combining customers' travel distance perception and individual deviation: for two groups of customers with high haptic perception demand, provide travel convenience information for their offline store shopping, among which customers have long travel distance and high price consistency sensitivity. For the two types of customers with low haptic perception needs, we focus on vivid advertisements such as online live events or e-magazines to strengthen customers' brand memory and give travel coupons to customers with long travel distance and high price consistency sensitivity. The limitation of this paper is that only the apparel industry is selected as an example for model construction and validation. Future research can be conducted for different experience-based FMCG products to further verify the applicability of the findings of this study.

Acknowledgement. This research was supported by the National Natural Science Foundation of China under Grant 72072194.

References

Ankomah, P.K., Crompton, J.L., Baker, D.A.: A study of pleasure travelers' cognitive distance assessments. J. Travel Res. **34**(2), 12–18 (1995)

Chaudhuri, A., Holbrook, M.B.: The chain of effects from brand trust and brand affect to brand performance: the role of brand loyalty. J. Mark. **65**(2), 81–93 (2001)

Childs, M., Jin, B., Tullar, W.L.: Vertical versus horizontal line extensions: a comparison of dilution effects. J. Prod. Brand Manag. **27**(6), 670–683 (2018)

Chu, J., Chintagunta, P., Cebollada, J.: Research note-a comparison of within-household price sensitivity across online and offline channels. Mark. Sci. **27**(2), 283–299 (2008)

De Canio, F., Fuentes-Blasco, M.: I need to touch it to buy it! How haptic information influences consumer shopping behavior across channels. J. Retail. Consum. Serv. **61**, 102569 (2021)

Evans, J.S.B.T., Stanovich, K.E.: Dual-process theories of higher cognition: advancing the debate. Perspect. Psychol. Sci. **8**(3) (2013)

Fisher, M.L., Gallino, S., Xu, J.J.: The value of rapid delivery in omnichannel retailing. J. Mark. Res. **56**(5), 732–748 (2019)

Francioni, B., Savelli, E., Cioppi, M.: Store satisfaction and store loyalty: the moderating role of store atmosphere. J. Retail. Consum. Serv. **43**(C), 333–341(2018)

Grewal, D., Kopalle, P., Marmorstein, H., et al.: Does travel time to stores matter? The role of merchandise availability. J. Retail. **88**(3), 437–444 (2012)

Hamermesh, D.S., Lee, J.: Stressed out on four continents: time crunch or yuppie kvetch? Rev. Econ. Stat. **89**(2), 374–383 (2007)

Iglesias, O., Markovic, S., Bagherzadeh, M., et al.: Co-creation: a key link between corporate social responsibility, customer trust, and customer loyalty. J. Bus. Ethics **163**(1), 151–166 (2020)

Jai, T.M.C., Fang, D., Bao, F.S., et al.: Seeing it is like touching it: unraveling the effective product presentations on online apparel purchase decisions and brain activity (An fMRI Study). J. Interact. Mark. **53**, 66–79 (2021)

Jimenez, M., Montoro, P.R., Luna, D.: Global shape integration and illusory form perception in the absence of awareness. Conscious. Cogn. **53**, 31–46 (2017)

Jung, J., Kim, S.J., Kim, K.H.: Sustainable marketing activities of traditional fashion market and brand loyalty. J. Bus. Res. **120**, 294–301 (2020)

Kaur, H., Paruthi, M., Islam, J.U., et al.: The role of brand community identification and reward on consumer brand engagement and brand loyalty in virtual brand communities. Telematics Inform. **46**, 101321 (2020)

Kim, M.: Digital product presentation, information processing, need for cognition and behavioral in-tent in digital commerce. J. Retail. Consum. Serv. **50**, 362–370 (2019)

Lee, S.Y., Son, Y., Oh, W.: Effectiveness of integrated offline-and-online promotions in omnichannel targeting: a randomized field experiment. J. Manag. Inf. Syst. **38**(2), 484–516 (2021)

Lin, C.H., Morais, D.B.: The spatial clustering effect of destination distribution on cognitive distance estimates and its impact on tourists' destination choices. J. Travel Tour. Mark. **25**(3–4), 382–397 (2008)

Luo, Y., Tang, L.R., Kim, E.: A picture is worth a thousand words: the role of a cover photograph on a travel agency's online identity. Int. J. Hosp. Manag. **94**, 102801 (2021)

Luo, X., Zhang, Y., Zeng, F., et al.: Complementarity and cannibalization of offline-to-online Targeting: a field experiment on omnichannel commerce. MIS Q. **44**(2), 957–982 (2020)

Manzano, R., Ferrán, M., Gavilan, D., et al.: The influence of need for touch in multichannel purchasing behaviour. An approach based on its instrumental and autotelic dimensions and consumer's shopping task. Int. J. Mark. Commun. New Media **4**(6), 48–68 (2016)

Mookherjee, S., Lee, J.J., Sung, B.: Multichannel presence, boon or curse?: a comparison in price, loyalty, regret, and disappointment. J. Bus. Res. **132**, 429–440 (2021)

Peck, J., Wiggins, J.: It just feels good: customers' affective response to touch and its influence on persuasion. J. Mark. **70**(4), 56–69 (2006)

Raghubir, P., Krishna, A.: As the crow flies: bias in consumers' map-based distance judgments. J. Consum. Res. **23**(1), 26–39 (1996)

Shanahan, T., Tran, T.P., Taylor, E.C.: Getting to know you: social media personalization as a means of enhancing brand loyalty and perceived quality. J. Retail. Consum. Serv. **47**, 57–65 (2019)

Sujan, M., Dekleva, C.: Product categorization and inference making: some implications for comparative advertising. J. Consum. Res. **14**(3), 372–378 (1987)

Yu, X., Xu, Z.L., Guo, W.J.: Research on the influence of online merchants' product information presentation on consumers' behavioral intentions–a model construction based on social presence theory. Intell. Theory Pract. **40**(10), 80–84 (2017)

Research on the Introduction of Private Brand for E-commerce Platform Under Mixed Channels of Manufacturer

Honglin Zhang, Shizhong Ai[✉], and Rong Du

School of Economics and Management, Xidian University, Xi'an 710126, China
shzhai@mail.xidian.edu.cn

Abstract. With the rapid development of e-commerce and the intensified competition between platforms and that between platforms and manufacturers, private brand strategy has become the key for e-commerce platforms to gain competitive advantages. Under the premise that the manufacturer relies on the e-commerce platform to sell commodities through wholesale channel and platform channel, basic decision model (without introducing private brand) and platform introduction decision model (introducing private brand) are established. Applying backward induction to analyze the influence of channel preference, platform commission rate and the quality of private brand commodity on equilibrium profit and optimal decision, we can come to the conclusion that: (1) When consumer's platform channel preference is high or the commission rate is high, the e-commerce platform should introduce private brand to enhance its competitiveness and increase revenue; (2) After the introduction of private brand into e-commerce platform, the wholesale price, sales price and revenue of manufacturer will be reduced; (3) After the introduction of private brand into e-commerce platform, with the improvement of the quality of private brand commodity, the revenue of e-commerce platform may decrease.

Keywords: E-commerce platform · Private brand · Channel competition · Product quality

1 Introduction

With the advent of the era of e-commerce, consumers' shopping behavior has undergone great changes. The gradually normalized online shopping not only meets the daily life needs of consumers, but also becomes a kind of spiritual dependence for consumers. At the same time, browsing and buying commodities on e-commerce platforms has become the mainstream online shopping method for consumers. Through the diversified integration of e-commerce platforms with social applications, their operating models have become increasingly rich [1]. On the one hand, e-commerce platforms attract manufacturers to enter e-commerce platforms by charging platform usage fees (commissions) to sell commodities directly to customers. At this point, the ownership of the commodity still belongs to the manufacturer [2]. For example, the official flagship stores of merchants on e-commerce platforms. On the other hand, manufacturers can also resell their goods to e-commerce platforms, which sell them to customers. For example, the self-operated channels of e-commerce platforms.

While allowing manufacturers to sell commodities through the platform, e-commerce platforms will also consider establishing their own brands ("private brands" in this paper) to enhance their competitiveness. In the past two decades, private brands have been discovered rapidly and achieved remarkable results, and have become an effective way for e-commerce platforms to enhance their competitiveness [3]. The development of private brands in other countries is much earlier than that in China. According to the survey data of Nielsen in 2005, private brands account for about 16% of sales and grow at an annual rate of 7% [4]. Private brands in the fashion and electronics sectors have grown particularly fast. In 2009, the sales volume of electronic products of Best Buy, the largest electronic products retailer in North America, reached 40% [5]. In 2018, according to Nielsen data, the sales of private brand commodities in major retail channels in the United States reached $129 billion, up 4.4% year on year, and the growth rate was four times that of manufacturers' brands [6]. In China, with the rapid development of e-commerce in recent years, more and more e-commerce platforms have begun to introduce their private brands. Walmart has launched 13 series of its own brand in China, and Tesco has developed nearly 2,000 kinds of its own brand goods for the Chinese market [7]. In addition, e-commerce platforms such as Jing Dong and Dang Dang have also become the main force of private brands under the pressure of intensified competition and driven by supply-side reform. For example, Jing Dong currently has a number of its private brands such as Jing Zao, Jia Bai and Ba Xiang Shi.

As a new sales channel, private brand can not only enrich the sales channels of e-commerce platform, but also attract consumers with its lower price and brand effect. In the mixed channels of manufacturer, the revenue of e-commerce platform is passive and limited by the manufacturer. The manufacturer's wholesale channel (on the e-commerce platform) can bring sales revenue to the e-commerce platform and the platform channel can bring commission revenue to the e-commerce platform. After the introduction of private brand, the e-commerce platform can carry out differentiated competition with manufacturer, build its own brand, manage them from a strategic perspective, and avoid homogeneous competition. Furthermore, the e-commerce platform can strive for more initiative in the negotiations with manufacturers. The introduction of private brand is bound to intensify channel competition and change the revenue of manufacturers and e-commerce platforms.

Based on the above real-life contexts in practice, this paper constructs an online sales system including a manufacturer and an e-commerce platform to explore the following research questions. (1) Under what circumstances is the e-commerce platform inclined to introduce its private brand? (2) What is the impact on the manufacturer and the e-commerce platform after the introduction of private brand? (3) How does the product quality of private brand affect the revenue of the e-commerce platform?

2 Literature Review

This paper conducts the literature review from two aspects: one is the research on channel competition of private brand in the sales system, and the other is the research on the quality of private brand products.

The research on the channel competition of private brands in the sales system can be carried out from multiple perspectives such as the game between private brands and manufacturer brands, retailers' overall profits and consumers' preferences. There are relatively many related studies on private brand and manufacturer brand games. Chintagunta et al. [8] found that the introduction of private brands by retailers will increase their bargaining power with manufacturers, thus affecting their pricing decisions and commodity demand. Jin et al. [9] studied the interaction between the manufacturer's channel strategy and the retailer's private brand introduction strategy under wholesale price discrimination and uniform wholesale price, and found that under wholesale price discrimination, retailers are less motivated to introduce private brands in a single channel, while under uniform wholesale price, retailers are less motivated to introduce private brands in a dual channel. Choi et al. [10] studied the influence of power structure on the decision-making of each participant in the supply chain for a supply chain composed of one manufacturer and two retailers with private brands, and found that retailers should maximize the difference between private brands and other brands, and manufacturers can obtain higher benefits by cooperating with retailers with smaller power positions. Li et al. [11] constructed a model in which retailers introduce private brand in the context of two manufacturers and one retailer, and analyzed the impact of introducing private brand on the market performance of retailers and manufacturers under the conditions of indirect channel and mixed channel. From consumers' preferences, Seenivasan et al. [12] found that the introduction of private brands by retailers can increase consumer loyalty. From the perspective of retailers' overall earnings, Ailawadi et al. [13] found that retailers selling private brands have lower prices and higher profit margins, but it is not desirable to sell too many private brands at the expense of manufacturer brands, and retailers need to balance the quantity of private brands and manufacturer brands.

In addition, a considerable part of the research on private brand focuses on product quality. Wang et al. [14] considered that whether retailers can achieve the goal of developing their own brands depends on how to make pricing decisions on their own brand products, and the actual product quality and consumers' perceived quality are the key to this problem. According to this, the Stackelberg game model with the coexistence of manufacturer brand, manufacturer brand and retailer's private brand are constructed. Jiang et al. [15] sorted out the private brand product quality management mode from multiple perspectives, analyzed the key points of private brand product management collaboration, and put forward management suggestions for retailers' private brand product quality collaboration practice. In the industry where product quality accidents cause consumer trust crisis, high-end private brands become an important means for retailers to use their own reputation to alleviate information asymmetry. Zhao [16] considers that in the supply chain composed of retailers and manufacturers, there is a competitive relationship between private brand and manufacturer's brand products, so retailers need to take incentive measures to control the quality of private brand products, so as to achieve the coordination, stability and mutual benefit of the supply chain.

However, few papers have considered the impact of product quality on the decision to introduce private brands and the impact on the revenue of e-commerce platforms after the introduction of private brands. This paper differs from the above literature in the following two aspects. Firstly, the manufacturer in this paper has two sales channels (wholesale channel and platform channel) through the e-commerce platform, and therefore, the manufacturer's relationship with the e-commerce platform is competitive and cooperative. The e-commerce platform can obtain revenue from both the manufacturer's wholesale channel and the platform channel. Secondly, in addition to comprehensively considering the impact of commission rate, channel preference and product quality on the decision to introduce private brands, this paper also considers how product quality affects the revenue of e-commerce platforms after the introduction of private brands.

Therefore, under the premise that manufacturers rely on e-commerce platform to sell products through wholesale channel and platform channel, platform basic decision model (without introducing private brand) and platform introduction decision model (introducing private brand) are established in this paper. Then we apply backward induction to explore the influence of channel preference, platform commission rate and private brand product quality on the private brand introduction decision of e-commerce platforms and the changes in the revenue of e-commerce platforms and manufacturers after the introduction of private brand.

3 Problem Description and Related Assumptions

3.1 Problem Description

There is an online sales system consisting of a manufacturer (M) and an e-commerce platform (P), in which the manufacturer has two channels to sell commodities through the e-commerce platform. One is the platform channel. M directly sells commodities to consumers through P, and needs to pay the proportion of sales commission to P. The other is the wholesale channel. M sells commodities to P, and then consumers can buy commodities form P. In this case, P considers whether to establish their private brand to bring themselves greater competitiveness. For the convenience of presentation, in this paper, NB (National Brand) is used to represent the manufacturer Brand, and EB (E-commerce Platform Private Brand) is used to represent the private brand of e-commerce platform.

3.2 Related Assumptions

The following are the relevant assumptions of this paper.

1) **Product quality**. The degree of consumer sensitivity to the quality of the commodity is used as the perceived value. Suppose that the quality of the NB commodity is q_n and the quality of the EB commodity is q_e. In general, NB commodity has higher quality than EB commodity. [11] $q_n = 1$, $q_e = \theta q_n = \theta$. ($0 < \theta < 1$)
2) **Channel preference**. Considering that the commodity quality in the two sales channels of M is the same, the consumer's preference for different channels is not only

influenced by perceived price, but also by other factors such as service quality. In reality, P will provide a higher level of logistics, after-sales and other service quality for products in wholesale channel, so that consumers have a greater preference for wholesale channel than platform channel [6]. In addition, as a channel for new entry, P's private brand is unfamiliar to consumers, so it is assumed that consumers have the lowest preference for private brand. The consumer's preference for wholesale channel is normalized to 1, consumer's preference for platform channel is β. $(0 < \beta < 1)$, and consumers' channel preference for private brand is γ. $(0 < \gamma < \beta < 1)$.

3) 3) **Commission rate.** In the platform channel of M, the commission rate extracted by P is λ . $(0 < \lambda < 1)$

4) **Consumer utility function.** Consumer utility functions are used to construct demand functions. It is assumed that the consumer's valuation of the commodity is sensitive to quality [11]. When a consumer purchases the commodity of quality q at price p, the utility obtained is $U = \alpha q - p$, where αq represents the consumer's valuation of the commodity. Let α denotes the sensitivity of consumers to the quality of the commodity, that is, the price they are willing to pay for a unit of quality of the commodity. $(0 < \alpha < 1)$

5) **Commodity price.** The wholesale price of NB commodity in the M's wholesale channel is ω, and the selling price p_n is determined by P. The selling price of NB commodity in the platform channel is p_N. The selling price of EB commodity is p_e.

4   Basic Decision Model

When P does not introduce private brand, consumers can only purchase NB commodity, and the utility obtained from wholesale channel and platform channel are $U_n^1 = \alpha q_n^1 - p_n^1 = \alpha - p_n^1$, $U_N^1 = \beta \alpha q_N^1 - p_N^1 = \beta \alpha - p_N^1$. Based on the principle of consumer utility maximization, the demand of NB commodity in wholesale channel and platform channel are as follow.

$$D_n^1 = 1 - \frac{p_n^1 - p_N^1}{1 - \beta} \tag{1}$$

$$D_N^1 = \frac{p_n^1 - p_N^1}{1 - \beta} - \frac{p_N^1}{\beta} \tag{2}$$

M's profit function and P's profit function are as follow.

$$\Pi_n^1 = \omega^1 \left(1 - \frac{p_n^1 - p_N^1}{1 - \beta} \right) + (1 - \lambda) p_N^1 \left(\frac{p_n^1 - p_N^1}{1 - \beta} - \frac{p_N^1}{\beta} \right) \tag{3}$$

$$\Pi_e^1 = \left(p_n^1 - \omega^1 \right) \left(1 - \frac{p_n^1 - p_N^1}{1 - \beta} \right) + \lambda p_N^1 \left(\frac{p_n^1 - p_N^1}{1 - \beta} - \frac{p_N^1}{\beta} \right) \tag{4}$$

M is the leader in the Stackelberg game model, and P is the follower. In this case, the decision order of the two is as follows: firstly, M decides the wholesale price ω^1 of NB commodity in the wholesale channel and the selling price p_N^1 of NB commodity in the platform channel; than P decides the selling price p_n^1 of NB commodity in the wholesale channel.

Using backward induction we can get that: $\omega^{1*} = \frac{1-\beta\lambda}{2}$, $p_N^{1*} = \frac{\beta}{2}$, $p_n^{1*} = \frac{3-\beta}{4}$, $D_n^{1*} = 1 - \frac{p_n^1 - p_N^1}{1-\beta} = \frac{1}{4}$, $D_N^{1*} = \frac{p_n^1 - p_N^1}{1-\beta} - \frac{p_N^1}{\beta} = \frac{1}{4}$, $\Pi_n^{1*} = \frac{1+\beta-2\beta\lambda}{8}$, $\Pi_e^{1*} = \left(p_n^1 - \omega^1\right)\left(1 - \frac{p_n^1 - p_N^1}{1-\beta}\right) + \lambda p_N^1 \left(\frac{p_n^1 - p_N^1}{1-\beta} - \frac{p_N^1}{\beta}\right) = \frac{1-\beta(1-4\lambda)}{16}$.

Proposition 1. When $0 < \lambda \le \frac{1}{4}$, consumers' platform channel preference β is positively correlated with M's revenue and negatively correlated with P's revenue. When $\frac{1}{4} < \lambda \le \frac{1}{2}$, it is positively correlated with M's revenue and P's revenue; When $\frac{1}{2} < \lambda < 1$, it is negatively correlated with M's revenue and positively correlated with P's revenue.

Proof: $\frac{\partial \Pi_n^{1*}}{\partial \beta} = \frac{1-2\lambda}{8} = \begin{cases} > 0, 0 < \lambda < \frac{1}{2} \\ \le 0, \frac{1}{2} \le \lambda < 1 \end{cases}$, $\frac{\partial \Pi_e^{1*}}{\partial \beta} = \frac{4\lambda-1}{16} = \begin{cases} > 0, \frac{1}{4} < \lambda < 1 \\ \le 0, 0 < \lambda \le \frac{1}{4} \end{cases}$.

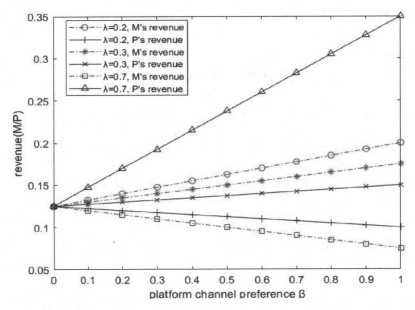

Fig. 1. Revenue change of P/M before the introduction of private brand

Figure 1 illustrates Proposition 1 and shows that when the commission rate of P is low, M's revenue increases with the increase of consumers' preference for platform channel, while P's revenue decreases with the increase of consumers' preference for platform channel. When the commission rate of P is high, the change trend of the revenue of both parties is opposite to the previous one.

Corollary 1: When private brand is not introduced, e-commerce platform can set reasonable and appropriate commission rates to promote healthy competition and increase the benefits of both manufacturer and e-commerce platform.

When the commission rate of the e-commerce platform is high, the manufacturer's revenue decreases with the increase of consumers' preference for the platform channel, which is unfavorable to the manufacturer. And the manufacturer may even choose to give up selling products through the platform channel. If the manufacturer gives up selling products through platform channel, it is also a loss for e-commerce platform. Therefore, the e-commerce platform should formulate a reasonable and appropriate commission rate, which means that the revenue of both parties will increase with the increase of consumers' preference for platform channel.

5   Introduction Decision Model

When private brand is introduced into P, consumers can purchase NB commodity from wholesale channel and platform channel, and EB commodity from P. The utilities obtained by consumers in the three ways are respectively as follow. $U_n^2 = \alpha q_n^2 - p_n^2 = \alpha - p_n^2$, $U_N^2 = \beta \alpha q_N^2 - p_N^2 = \beta \alpha - p_N^2$, $U_e^2 = \gamma \alpha q_e^2 - p_e^2 = \gamma \alpha \theta - p_e^2$. Based on the principle of consumer utility maximization, we can get that the demand of NB and EB commodity are as follow. $D_n^2 = 1 - \frac{p_n^2 - p_N^2}{1-\beta}$, $D_N^2 = \frac{p_n^2 - p_N^2}{1-\beta} - \frac{p_N^2 - p_e^2}{\beta - \gamma \theta}$, $D_e^{2*} = \frac{p_N^2 - p_e^2}{\beta - \gamma \theta} - \frac{p_e^2}{\gamma \theta} = \frac{\beta(1-\lambda)}{4\beta - 2\gamma \theta(1+\lambda)}$.

M's profit function and P's profit function are as follow.

$$\Pi_n^2 = \omega^2 \left(1 - \frac{p_n^2 - p_N^2}{1 - \beta} \right) + (1 - \lambda) p_N^2 \left(\frac{p_n^2 - p_N^2}{1 - \beta} - \frac{p_N^2 - p_e^2}{\beta - \gamma \theta} \right) \tag{5}$$

$$\Pi_e^2 = \left(p_n^2 - \omega^2 \right) \left(1 - \frac{p_n^2 - p_N^2}{1 - \beta} \right) + \lambda p_N^2 \left(\frac{p_n^2 - p_N^2}{1 - \beta} - \frac{p_N^2 - p_e^2}{\beta - \gamma \theta} \right) + p_e^2 \left(\frac{p_N^2 - p_e^2}{\beta - \gamma \theta} - \frac{p_e^2}{\gamma \theta} \right) \tag{6}$$

M is the leader in the Stackelberg game model, and P is the follower. Using backward induction we can get that: $\omega^{2*} = \frac{1-\beta}{2} + \frac{\beta(\beta - \gamma\theta)(1-\lambda)}{2\beta - \gamma\theta(1+\lambda)}$, $p_N^{2*} = \frac{\beta(\beta - \gamma\theta)}{2\beta - \gamma\theta(1+\lambda)}$, $p_n^{2*} = \frac{3-3\beta}{4} + \frac{\beta(\beta-\gamma\theta)}{2\beta - \gamma\theta(1+\lambda)}$, $p_e^{2*} = \frac{\gamma\theta(\beta-\gamma\theta)(1+\lambda)}{4\beta - 2\gamma\theta(1+\lambda)}$.

The demand of NB and EB commodity are $D_n^{2*} = 1 - \frac{p_n^2 - p_N^2}{1-\beta} = \frac{1}{4}$, $D_N^{2*} = \frac{p_n^2 - p_N^2}{1-\beta} - \frac{p_N^2 - p_e^2}{\beta - \gamma\theta} = \frac{1}{4}$, $D_e^{2*} = \frac{p_N^2 - p_e^2}{\beta - \gamma\theta} - \frac{p_e^2}{\gamma\theta} = \frac{\beta(1-\lambda)}{4\beta - 2\gamma\theta(1+\lambda)}$; M's profit function is $\Pi_n^{2*} = \frac{1-\beta}{8} + \frac{\beta(1-\lambda)(\beta - \gamma\theta)}{4\beta - 2\gamma\theta(1+\lambda)}$, P's profit function is $\Pi_e^{2*} = \frac{1-\beta}{16} + \frac{\beta\gamma(\beta-\gamma\theta)}{4\beta - 2\gamma\theta(1+\lambda)} + \frac{\beta\gamma\theta(\beta-\gamma\theta)(1-\lambda^2)}{(4\beta - 2\gamma\theta(1+\lambda))^2}$.

Proposition 2. After the introduction of private brand into the e-commerce platform, the wholesale price, selling price and revenue of the manufacturer will all decrease.

Proof: $\omega^{2*} - \omega^{1*} = -\frac{\beta\gamma\theta(1-\lambda)^2}{2\beta - \gamma\theta(1+\lambda)} < 0$; $p_N^{2*} - p_N^{1*} = -\frac{\beta\gamma\theta(1-\lambda)}{2\beta - \gamma\theta(1+\lambda)} < 0$; $p_n^{2*} - p_n^{1*} = -\frac{\beta\gamma\theta(1-\lambda)}{2\beta - \gamma\theta(1+\lambda)} < 0$; $\Pi_n^{2*} - \Pi_n^{1*} = \frac{\beta(\lambda-1)}{4} + \frac{\beta(1-\lambda)(\beta-\gamma\theta)}{4\beta - 2\gamma\theta(1+\lambda)} = -\frac{\beta\gamma\theta(1-\lambda)^2}{8\beta - 4\gamma\theta(1+\lambda)} < 0$

Figure 2 illustrates Proposition 2 and shows that after the introduction of private brand, EB commodity and NB commodity compete directly, resulting in a decrease in the wholesale price and selling price of the wholesale channel, a decrease in the selling price of the platform channel, and a decrease in the total revenue.

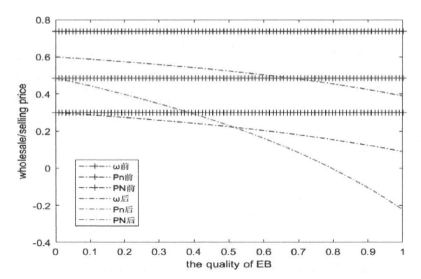

Fig. 2. Wholesale (selling) price change after the introduction of private brand

Corollary 2. After the introduction of private brand, the selling price of commodity is less affected than the wholesale price in the wholesale channel.

Corollary 2 can be confirmed by Fig. 2. It shows that the introduction of private brand can make e-commerce platform take the initiative in the transaction process of manufacturer. In other words, e-commerce platform introduce private brand not only to directly gain profit from the brand, is also a strategic measure to make the manufacturer make concessions, so that e-commerce platform can obtain more favorable conditions in the trade and negotiation process.

Proposition 3. When $\frac{\beta}{\gamma} > \theta(1 + \lambda)$, the e-commerce platform choose to introduce private brand; When $\frac{\beta}{\gamma} < \theta(1 + \lambda)$, the e-commerce platform choose not to introduce private brand.

Proof: $\Pi_e^{2*} - \Pi_e^{1*} = \frac{\beta\gamma\theta(1-\lambda)^2(\beta-\gamma\theta(1+\lambda))}{(4\beta-2\gamma\theta(1+\lambda))^2}$; when $\frac{\beta}{\gamma} > \theta(1 + \lambda)$ and $\theta > \frac{1}{1+\lambda}$ 时, $\Pi_e^{2*} - \Pi_e^{1*} \geq 0$; When $\frac{\beta}{\gamma} < \theta(1 + \lambda)$, $\Pi_e^{2*} - \Pi_e^{1*} < 0$.

This proposition shows that when consumers have a high preference for the manufacturer's platform channel or P has a low commission rate, P will choose to introduce private brand. As can be seen from Proposition 2, with the introduction of private label, the quantity demanded in the wholesale channel and the platform channel is unchanged and the price is reduced. Therefore, the marginal revenue of the e-commerce platform decreases, and the revenue obtained from the wholesale channel and the platform channel also decreases. The introduction of private brand into e-commerce platform can increase competitiveness, make up for the reduced revenue of distribution channels and platform channels, and improve P's revenue.

Proposition 3 shows that consumers' channel preference, platform commission rate and private brand product quality will all affect the decision of introducing private brand

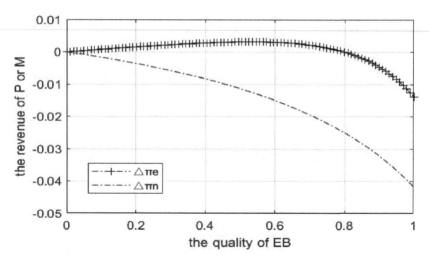

Fig. 3. The revenue of P and M after the introduction of private brand

on e-commerce platforms. Figure 3 illustrates Proposition 3 and reflects the influence of product quality on the introduction decision-making of private brand. ($\beta = 0.6$, $\gamma = 0.5$ and $\lambda = 0.5$ in Fig. 3).

Corollary 3. Setting reasonable product quality and understanding consumers' channel preference for goods in advance can help e-commerce platform make reasonable decisions on the introduction of private brand.

It should be noted that the revenue of e-commerce platform may not always increase after the introduction of private brand, and consumers' preference for platform channel and the quality of EB commodity still need to be considered. As can be seen from Fig. 3, in the case that consumers' channel preferences and platforms' commission rates are determined, the excessive pursuit of product quality is not conducive to the introduction of private brands on e-commerce platforms.

Proposition 4. When $\theta < \frac{2\beta}{3\gamma(1+\lambda)}$, the revenue of the e-commerce platform increases with the increase of θ; When $\theta \geq \frac{2\beta}{3\gamma(1+\lambda)}$, the revenue of the e-commerce platform decreases with the increase of θ.

Proof: $\frac{\partial \Pi_{e}^{2*}}{\partial \theta} = \frac{\beta^2 \gamma (1-\lambda)^2 (2\beta - 3\gamma\theta(1+\lambda))}{4(2\beta - \gamma\theta(1+\lambda))^3}$; when $\theta < \frac{2\beta}{3\gamma(1+\lambda)}$, $\frac{\partial \Pi_{e}^{2*}}{\partial \theta} > 0$; when $\theta \geq \frac{2\beta}{3\gamma(1+\lambda)}$, $\frac{\partial \Pi_{e}^{2*}}{\partial \theta} \leq 0$.

Figure 4 illustrates Proposition 4. This proposition shows that the revenue of P will decrease with the improvement of the quality of EB commodity. The reason may be that the improvement of the quality of private brand products intensifies the competition between the e-commerce platform and the manufacturer, leading to the decrease of the revenue of the e-commerce platform through the wholesale channel and the platform channel, which leads to the decrease of the total revenue of the e-commerce platform.

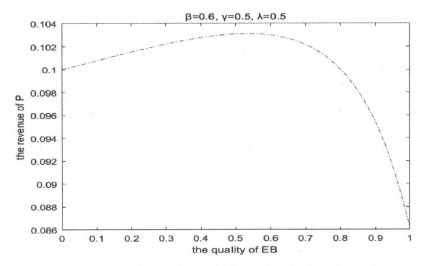

Fig. 4. P' revenue with the quality of EB after the introduction of private brand

Corollary 4. After the introduction of private brand, it is helpful for e-commerce platforms to increase their total revenue by paying balanced attention to the revenue of various sources and reasonably establishing the quality of private brand commodity.

After the introduction of private brand, e-commerce platform has three revenue sources, which are sales revenue from private brand, sales revenue from wholesale channel, and commission revenue from platform channel. When the quality of private brand products is high, increasing product quality will excessively intensify the competition between e-commerce platform and manufacturer, leading to a decrease in the sales revenue of wholesale channel and the commission revenue of platform channel. Therefore, after the introduction of private brand, e-commerce platform should formulate reasonable quality of private brand commodity.

6   Managerial Insights

The research findings in this paper can provide theoretical reference for the decision-making of introducing private brand on e-commerce platform. The main managerial insights are as follows:

(1) The complex relationship among product quality, channel preference and commission rate can affect the private brand introduction decision of e-commerce platforms. When the consumers' private label preference is high or the commission rate is high, e-commerce platforms should introduce private brand to enhance its competitiveness and increase revenue. In particular, in order to increase their total revenue, e-commerce platforms can pay more attention to the income sources of other channels, such as the sales revenue obtained from the manufacturer's wholesale channel and the commission revenue obtained from the manufacturer's platform channel.

(2) For manufacturers, the introduction of private brands on e-commerce platforms will lead to a decrease in manufacturers' revenue. Therefore, in order to maintain their revenue, manufacturers can prevent e-commerce platforms from introducing their own brands by various means, such as developing direct selling channels to enhance user stickiness, and improving product quality to increase competitiveness.

(3) After the introduction of private brand, with the improvement of product quality, e-commerce platforms' revenue may not always increase. Therefore, in order to obtain more revenue, e-commerce platforms should avoid excessive pursuit of product quality. In fact, e-commerce platforms can also gain profits by choosing OEM products with medium quality as their private brands.

7 Conclusion

Based on the competition and cooperation between the manufacturer and the e-commerce platform, this paper explores the private brand introduction decision of the e-commerce platform under the premise that the manufacturer relies on the e-commerce platform to sell products through the wholesale channel and the platform channel. We further analyze the influence of channel preference, platform commission rate and private brand product quality on the optimal decision and the revenue of both parties. Our findings have managerial insights to both e-commerce platforms and manufacturers. However, there are limitations in our research. First of all, this paper assumes that consumers' platform channel preference is smaller than consumers' wholesale channel preference. It may not be the case in all situations. Secondly, this paper does not consider the introduction cost and operation cost of e-commerce platform's private brand. Future research can take into account more factors that affect consumers' purchase and the competition among e-commerce platforms, thereby providing more rigorous practical guidance for manufacturers and e-commerce platforms.

Acknowledgement. The authors acknowledge the Editor and all anonymous referees for their valuable comments and constructive suggestions. This research is supported by the National Natural Science Foundation of China under Grant 72171187.

References

1. Zhang, C.H., Li, C.Y., Lu, R.X.: Research on platform encroachment considering service quality difference and quality sensitivity. Ind. Eng. Manag. **04**, 77–85 (2020). (in Chinese)
2. Abhishek, V., Jerath, K., Zhang, Z.J.: Agency selling or reselling? Channel structures in electronic retailing. Manag. Sci. **62**(8), 2149–2455 (2016)
3. Alan, Y., Kurtulus, M., Wang, C.: The role of store brand spillover in a retailer's category management strategy. Manuf. Serv. Oper. Manag. **21**(3), 620–635 (2019)
4. Nielsen, A.C.: The Power of Private Label - A Review of Growth Trends Around the World. Executive News Report from ACNielsen Global Services (2005)
5. Fan, X.J., Chen, H.M.: Research on the effect of private label introduction on channel competition. Chin. J. Manag. Sci. **19**(6), 79–87 (2011). (in Chinese)

6. Duan, Y., Wang, Y., Wen, Y.: Platform channel introduction strategy considering e-commerce platform private brand. Chin. J. Ind. Eng. Eng. Manag. **36**(03), 203–214 (2020). (in Chinese)
7. Li, P., Wei, H., Wang, G.Y.: Retailer's platform opening strategy for retailer with store brand. Chin. J. Manag. Sci. **27**(3), 105–115 (2019). (in Chinese)
8. Chintagunta, P.K., Bonfrer, A., Song, I.: Investigating the effects of store-brand introduction on retailer demand and pricing behavior. Mark. Sci. **48**(10), 1242–1267 (2002)
9. Jin, Y., Wu, X., Hu, Q.: Interaction between channel strategy and store brand decisions. Eur. J. Oper. Res. **256**(3), 911–923 (2017)
10. Choi, S., Fred, K.: Price competition and store competition: store brands vs national brand. Eur. J. Oper. Res. **225**(1), 166–178 (2013)
11. Li, K., Sun, J.H., Yan, J.Y.: Analysis of effect when store brands are introduced in indirect and mixed channels. Oper. Res. Manag. Sci. **26**(1), 103–112 (2017). (in Chinese)
12. Seenivasan, S., Sudhir, K., Talukdar, D.: Do store brands aid store loyalty? Mark. Sci. **62**(3), 802–816 (2016)
13. Ailawadi, K.L., Harlam, B.: An empirical analysis of the determinants of retail margins: the role of store-brand share. J. Mark. **68**(1), 147–165 (2004)
14. Wang, H.Q., Li, J.J.: Pricing decision of the private label based on perceived quality. Syst. Eng. Theory Pract. **31**(08), 1454–1459 (2011). (in Chinese)
15. Jiang, Y., Chen, R.Y.: Research on the model and cooperation of quality management of private brand products. J. Green Sci. Technol. **20**, 220–222 (2017). (in Chinese)
16. Zhao, H.: Research on Quality Control Incentive Mechanism of Private Brand Products Based On Evolutionary Game. Yanshan University (2020). (in Chinese)

Users' Demand Analysis of Intelligent Information Service for Rural Tourism Based on the Kano Model

Zhongyi Hu[1,2(✉)], Yuecen Wang[1], Siqi Zhao[1], Zhoucan Xu[1], Xiaoquan Liu[3], and Jiang Wu[1,2]

[1] School of Information Management, Wuhan University, Wuhan 430072, China
zhongyi.hu@whu.edu.cn
[2] E-Commerce Research and Development Center, Wuhan University, Wuhan 430072, China
[3] School of Tourism Sciences, Beijing International Studies University, Beijing 100024, China

Abstract. Effective analysis of users' demand is critical for developing an intelligent service platform for rural tourism. In this study, the Kano model and Better-Worse satisfaction index analysis method are used to analyze the demand hierarchy of various information services. A rural tourism intelligent information service system with 30 services has been built using the five dimensions of cultural travel service, information service, map navigation guide, independent shopping mall, and community service. It is suggested that when providing intelligent information services for rural tourism, the level of user demand for services should be fully considered, and that construction should be carried out in a targeted and phased manner.

Keywords: information service · rural tourism · Kano model · demand analysis

1 Introduction

Rural tourism utilizes local and distinctive resources to offer tourists relaxation, entertainment, vacations, and other tourism services by choosing rural areas as its destination [1, 2]. The level of tourism services can be raised and rural tourism can be promoted by providing information services through the Internet. In China, the domestic travel market currently has various established online travel agencies (OTA), but the information service for rural tourism is not well developed. The existing service platforms for rural tourism do not provide sufficient services and are limited to a small area [3], which prevents it from satisfying tourists' demands for intelligent tourism information services.

By reviewing related literature, this paper first proposed a framework of users' demand of intelligent information services for rural tourism. Then, Kano model and the Better-Worse satisfaction index were used to examine the effects of each service demand on tourist satisfaction. Finally, some suggestions for the development of intelligent information services for rural tourism were provided.

Y. Tu and M. Chi (Eds.): WHICEB 2023, LNBIP 481, pp. 206–217, 2023.
https://doi.org/10.1007/978-3-031-32302-7_18

2   Related Research

2.1   Tourism Information Service

Tourism information service is the use of information technology to facilitate the search, use, and interaction of tourism information, as well as to complete the interaction between tourists and tourism service providers [4, 5]. Intelligent tourism has been a hot topic in the field of tourism information service in recent years [6]. According to Yunpeng Li et al. [7], intelligent tourism is the "ubiquitous" tourism information service accepted by tourists in the tourism process, emphasizing that such "ubiquitous" is the entire process, all-around, spatial-temporal, and can be obtained anytime, anywhere, and on demand. To realize such intelligent tourism information services, Xiuying Zhang [8] points out that, from the perspective of information ecological development, intelligent tourism information service requires the creation of a platform, strengthened cooperation among information subjects, and increased technological utilization. Anfeng Xu et al. [9] used migration algorithms in conjunction with the background of digital economy to build the innovation mechanism of intelligent tourism information service mode. In light of the current state of domestic tourism information services, Hongyan Jia [10] argued that efficient information services should be intelligent, emphasizing the use of big data and intelligent mobile terminals for information services.

In the context of the digital economy, providing intelligent information services for rural tourism is critical for improving service levels and tourist experiences, as well as promoting the development of rural tourism, which has received the attention of some scholars. For example, Xiuying Zhang [11] discussed the development path of rural tourism economy in the context of intelligent tourism, and believed that tourists' demands should be thoroughly analyzed in order to build an intelligent platform for rural tourism; Yao Yao [12] studied the development direction of intelligent rural tourism in the context of the post-epidemic era; Yang Fan [13] examined the necessity of building a rural intelligent tourism platform; and Yan Wang [14] emphasized that the all-round connection between intelligent tourism platform and rural tourism should be vigorously promoted.

However, existing research on the intelligent information service of rural tourism focuses on the macro-development opportunities provided by intelligent tourism for rural tourism and pays little attention to the development of the intelligent information service system of rural tourism. Starting from the demand side, systematically sorting out and analyzing users' information service demands is the key to developing an intelligent information platform for rural tourism, which is critical for optimizing tourists' rural tourism experiences and improving tourists' satisfaction. Therefore, this study employs a Kano-based approach to investigate the demand for rural tourism wisdom information services.

2.2   Kano Model

Kano model was proposed by Noriaki Kano to classify and sort user demands [15], and its concept was derived from the Herzberg's two-factor theory. According to the relationship between user demand and user satisfaction, Kano model divides user demand into five categories: Attractive demand (A), Must-be demand (M), One-dimensional demand (O), Indifferent demand (I) and Reverse demand (R). At present, Kano model has received much attention in the information service research of e-commerce platforms [16], social platforms [17] and other fields, but very few scholars have applied it to the research of user demand of tourism information services. For example, Chang et al. [18] used the Kano model to mine and analyze the demand of tourism website users for personalized recommendation. Huanhuan Yang [19] investigated and classified the factors influencing the satisfaction of travel websites' navigation using the Kano model.

3   Framework of Intelligent Information Service System for Rural Tourism

To determine the framework of intelligent information service system for rural tourism, the functions of five mainstream travel information service platforms were first screened, they are Ctrip, Qunar, Feizhu, Hornet's Nest and Tongcheng Yilong. Then, 10 heavily-dependent users of the travel platforms and 10 tourism industry practitioners are interviewed to vote their requirements of information services. Finally, we proposed a framework covering five categories and 30 main information service items. The details are shown in Table 1.

Table 1. Rural tourism intelligent information service system

Categories	Demand items	Service details
Cultural travel service	Transportation ticket booking	Book air tickets, train tickets, boat tickets, car rental
	Board and lodging reservation	Book homestays, hotels, meals
	Destination recommendation	Recommend popular scenic spots and surrounding scenic spots
	Destination service booking	Scenic spot ticket booking, tour guide service booking, tour bus booking, performing arts, special experience projects booking
	Recommendation of characteristic route combination	Recommended scenic combination, tourpackage
	E-ticket	Ticket vouchers of scenic spots, special services and charged items (such as tickets for performing arts programs and special experience items)

(*continued*)

Table 1. (*continued*)

Categories	Demand items	Service details
Information service	Destination information	Basic destination information, traffic information, weather forecast information
	Display of rural cultural resources	Cultural customs, history and culture, cultural specialties, and other information
	Real-time information	Real-time population heat, activity information, real-time hot spot, emergency notice
	Consultation and complaint	Online manual customer service, intelligent online customer service, travel complaints
	Parking information service	Parking lot inquiry, space inquiry, parking guidance, reverse car search, parking fee online payment
	Rescue service	One key call for help, road rescue
	Live streaming	Destination real-time information slow live broadcast and video live broadcast
Map navigation	2d map service	Plane map, plane hand-drawn map
	Three-dimensional reality	Three-dimensional real scene, three-dimensional map
	Positioning and navigation	Route navigation for shops, toilets, POI, catering, etc
	Tour route planning	Route recommendation, route customization
	Intelligent voice service	Voice navigation, scenic spot positioning intelligent voice explanation
	VR virtual reality	Immersive experience VR
Independent shopping mall	Commodity purchase	Buy agricultural products and cultural products
	Commodity intelligent recommendation	New product recommendation, blockbuster recommendation, promotion recommendation, personalized recommendation, collaborative recommendation
	Order management	Order status, logistics status

(*continued*)

Table 1. (*continued*)

Categories	Demand items	Service details
	After sale of goods	Return goods, exchange goods and settle claims
	Commodity traceability	Information tracing of agricultural products planting/production/processing/sales process
	Commodity distribution	Share group, community group, distribution rebate
	Evaluation and feedback	Evaluation and feedback on products, merchants, logistics and platforms
Online Community service	Dynamic publishing	Play dynamic, play experience, travel guides, travel vlog
	Community interaction	Online questions and answers, comments, collection attention to reward
	Travel together	Release group information and carry out travel group carpooling
	Live interaction	Live online with goods, live play experience

4 Hierarchical Analysis of Rural Tourism Intelligent Information Service Based on Kano Model

Exploring the level of demand for rural tourism intelligent information service is critical for guiding construction. This section, based on the Kano model, quantitatively studies the relationship between service demand and user satisfaction, classifies and thoroughly analyzes information services, and makes recommendations for the development of rural tourism intelligent information services.

4.1 Questionnaire Design and Data Collection

According to the rural tourism intelligent information service system, this paper designs a questionnaire for 30 categories under 5 main categories. The questionnaire is divided into three sections: the first section briefly explains its background and the purpose of the survey. The second section is designed to collect demographic and basic information of respondents, such as gender, age, industry, and rural tourism experience. In the third section, a five-level Likert scale is used to measure the respondents' feelings when certain elements are provided or not provided by the system, according to the rules of the Kano model: "satisfied", "deserved", "indifferent", "able to tolerate" and "dissatisfied". Table 2 shows the specific questionnaire form.

Table 2. Sample questions of the questionnaire

Your attitude towards *Transportation ticket booking* (i.e., booking air tickets, train tickets, boat tickets, car rental)	satisfied	deserved	indifferent	able to tolerate	dissatisfied
provide	○	○	○	○	○
do not provide	○	○	○	○	○

Because potential users of rural tourism intelligent information service come from a variety of industries and fields, this survey covers a wide range of industries and fields. The main form of the survey was an online questionnaire, which was distributed for 29 days, from September 29, 2021 to October 27, 2021. Following manual inspection, 60 invalid questionnaires with repeated and contradictory answers were removed, yielding 256 valid questionnaires and an effective recovery rate of 78.53%. The questionnaire results show that most respondents are young and middle-aged, with 33.3% aged 31–40 and 21.2% aged 41–50, with 63% female. In general, 73.74% of respondents have prior experience with rural tourism and have a solid understanding of the industry. Furthermore, 79.04% of respondents obtained travel information services through three online channels: online travel agencies (OTA) (e.g., Ctrip, Qunar, Tong-cheng Travel, Tuniu, Lvmama, Fliggy, Mafengwo), online social platforms (e.g., Weibo, Wechat), and online video platforms (e.g., Tik Tok, Kuaishou, Xigua Video, Bilibili).

Cronbach's α coefficients for positive and negative questions were 0.940 and 0.956, respectively, indicating that the questionnaire data was highly reliable. In terms of validity, the KMO test and the Bartlett sphericity test were used, with KMO values of 0.913 and 0.952 for forward and reverse questions, respectively. The p values for the Bartlett sphericity test are all 0.000, indicating that the questionnaire has good structural validity.

4.2 Analysis Based on Kano Model

Functional requirements are classified using the Kano model's two-dimensional classification table (Table 3), and 15 attractive demands (A), 2 one-dimensional demands (O), 10 must-be demands (M), and 3 indifferent demands (I) are obtained. See Table 4 for more information. According to the preliminary findings, the basic requirements of most users for rural tourism intelligent information service (i.e., must-be demand) are similar to those provided by existing OTA, covering such basic services as transportation ticket booking (1), accommodation reservation (2), and so on. Simultaneously, requirements for functions not yet included in the OTA platform, such as positioning and navigation (16), commodity purchase (20), and so on, are outlined. Half of the demands in the service system are attractive demands, indicating that the system has greatly enhanced users' cognition of information service elements. The one-dimensional demand includes only parking information service (11) and live interaction (30), which reflect users' travel and social demand while traveling. Some services, such as commodity intelligent recommendation (21), received 9 reverse demands (R) responses from statistical data of various service types, indicating that, while intelligent recommendation saves users information search costs, it may involve the collection and utilization of personal privacy information and is negatively evaluated by some users.

Table 3. Two-dimensional classification table of Kano model

Information service		Do not provide				
		satisfied	deserved	indifferent	able to tolerate	dissatisfied
Provide	satisfied	Q	A	A	A	O
	deserved	R	I	I	I	M
	indifferent	R	I	I	I	M
	able to tolerate	R	I	I	I	M
	dissatisfied	R	R	R	R	Q

Note: Attractive demand (A), Must-be demand (M), One-dimensional demand (O), Indifferent demand (I) and Reverse demand (R), Q is doubtful result.

Table 4. Analysis of Kano results

Information service	Demand type						Category
	A	O	M	I	R	Q	
1. Transportation ticket booking	72	42	103	39	0	0	M
2. Board and lodging reservation	73	46	78	58	1	0	M
3. Destination recommendation	105	50	29	72	0	0	A
4. Destination service booking	73	49	76	58	0	0	M
5. Recommendation of characteristic route	131	34	20	71	0	0	A
6. E-ticket	91	61	29	71	4	0	A
7. Destination information	98	47	25	85	1	0	A
8. Display of rural cultural resources	90	51	28	87	0	0	A
9. Real-time information	88	54	30	83	1	0	A
10. Consultation and complaint	49	62	93	50	1	1	M
11. Parking information service	60	78	44	68	2	4	O
12. Rescue service	89	58	41	64	0	4	A

(*continued*)

Table 4. (*continued*)

Information service	Demand type						Category
	A	O	M	I	R	Q	
13. Live streaming	125	36	14	80	1	0	A
14. 2d map service	44	62	75	72	1	2	M
15. Three-dimensional reality	104	38	43	70	0	1	A
16. Positioning and navigation	57	44	94	59	0	2	M
17. Tour route planning	84	64	26	76	0	6	A
18. Intelligent voice service	84	52	14	102	1	3	I
19.VR virtual reality	108	41	10	96	1	0	A
20. Commodity purchase	65	22	93	74	2	0	M
21. Commodity intelligent recommendation	66	19	9	153	9	0	I
22. Order management	46	43	99	68	0	0	M
23. After-sale of goods	36	62	97	61	0	0	M
24. Commodity traceability	87	63	33	73	0	0	A
25. Commodity distribution	62	37	42	106	7	2	I
26. Evaluate and feedback	52	72	87	45	0	0	M
27. Dynamic publishing	117	35	16	88	0	0	A
28. Community interaction	120	32	10	89	2	3	A
29. Travel together	115	34	20	86	1	0	A
30. Live interaction	70	104	19	60	3	0	O

4.3   Better-Worse Satisfaction Index Analysis

Unlike the traditional Kano model, which only determines classification based on the mode of the number of votes, the improved Kano model, which is named Better-Worse index analysis, utilizes voting data to judge the classification of each information service [20]. The Better-Worse index analysis is used to further discuss the relationship between each service and user satisfaction. The method employs two indices, "Better" and "Worse," to explain how the provision and non-provision of each service affects tourist satisfaction. The higher the Better index value, the greater the impact of the service on user satisfaction. The Worse index is typically negative, and the higher the absolute value, the greater the negative impact of not providing the service on user satisfaction.

The mean absolute values of the Better index and the Worse index for each service (0.519, 0.379) were used as the origin, the Better index as the horizontal axis, and the absolute values of the Worse index as the vertical axis. Figure 1 depicts the quadrants of each service. When compared to the results of the traditional Kano model, there is essentially no change in the quantity of attractive demand and must-be demand under the Better-Worse index classification. In terms of composition, the must-be demand remains

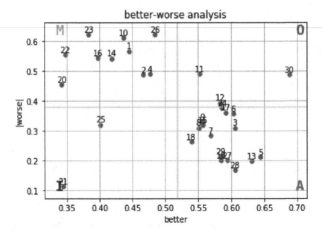

Fig. 1. Quadrants of each service

unchanged, intelligent voice service (18) moves from indifferent to attractive demand, and rescue service (12) moves from attractive to one-dimensional demand. According to the analysis of each quadrant, the absolute values of the Better and Worse indexes of each service are higher in the first quadrant than the corresponding average value. When this quadrant's service is provided, user satisfaction is greatly improved; when the service is not provided, user satisfaction is greatly decreased. Such a service falls under one-dimensional demand (O). As shown in the figure, rescue service (12), parking information service (11) and live interaction (30) are one-dimensional demands that place demands on rural tourism intelligent information service from three dimensions: safety, convenience, and sociability.

In the second quadrant, the value of the Better coefficient for information service is low, while the absolute value of the Worse coefficient is high. Users will take services in this quadrant for granted. If these services in this quadrant are not provided, users will be very dissatisfied, and services in this quadrant are must-be demands (M). Figure 1 shows that this category includes ten services, including rural tourism service booking, information consultation, positioning and navigation, and mall services. In conjunction with the specific content of the ten services and actual rural tourism experience, these services are indispensable basic services in rural tourism, which to some extent reverse validates the analysis results. We must prioritize providing services in this quadrant when developing a rural tourism intelligent information service.

The absolute values of the Better and Worse coefficients for each service in the third quadrant are lower than the corresponding average value, indicating that service provision in this quadrant has little impact on user satisfaction and belongs to the indifferent demand (I). This category includes commodity intelligent recommendation (21) and commodity distribution (25). From the standpoint of service functions, users are wary of personalized recommendation, which is common in the age of big data but easily leads to personal privacy disclosure. At the same time, because some e-commerce platforms' services for sharing and organizing groups are mature, users are no longer new to this type of promotion, so such services have little impact on user satisfaction.

The Better coefficient in the fourth quadrant is higher than average, and the Worse coefficient is lower than average in absolute value. When such services are provided, user satisfaction increases significantly, but it does not decrease when they are not provided. Such services are attractive demands (A). This type of demand primarily consists of 15 services such as route combination recommendation and planning, multi-dimensional destination information display, social services related to community interaction and group travel, e-ticket and commodity traceability. These services can better attract tourists' attention, meet potential tourist demand, and improve tourist travel experience, which are characteristics of rural tourism intelligent information services. The information services in this quadrant should be continuously enriched as part of the process of developing intelligent information services for rural tourism in order to optimize tourists' sense of experience and improve their satisfaction.

5   Empirical Implications

From the perspective of users' demand, this study divides the rural tourism intelligent information service into four demand categories. Based on the results, we can have the following suggestions on the developing of rural tourism intelligent information service.

(1) Prioritizing the development of must-be demands. The functions that users expect products or services to have, as well as the lower limit of product or service construction, are considered must-be requirements. Rural tourism intelligent information service should prioritize the most pressing demand. According to the data analysis results, transportation ticket booking, accommodation booking, destination service booking are examples of this type of demand that should be prioritized for construction in order to ensure the complete basic functions.

(2) Fully meeting the one-dimensional demands. The higher the user satisfaction, the more adequate the service provided in the expected demand. Meeting such demands aggressively can help the rural tourism intelligent information service platform maintain growth and gain a competitive advantage. With the gradual standardization of rural tourism supported by policies, supporting services should comply with the trend to fully meet such demand and improve service competitiveness while maintaining service attractiveness.

(3) Making efforts to enhance attractive demands. Attractive demands represent unanticipated demand, and when such services are provided, user satisfaction skyrockets. This category included 15 services in total. The rural tourism intelligent information service platform should not only meet the necessary and expected demand, but should also consider those attractive demands.

(4) Considering the indifferent demands. User satisfaction is unaffected by indifferent demand. This type of service is represented by two services in the research findings. Although this type of demand has no influence on the user's satisfaction, it is still important in terms of user convenience. It should not be completely ignored in the development of rural tourism intelligent information services. It is necessary to decide whether to develop, as well as the extent of development, and to adjust resource input based on the current situation.

6 Conclusion

In this study, a framework of intelligent information service for rural tourism is constructed. To provide a reference for the development of intelligent information services for rural tourism, the Kano model and the Better-Worse index analysis method are used to investigate the impact of various services on tourist satisfaction. The following are the findings of this study. When building the rural tourism intelligent information service platform, it is possible to carry out key, hierarchical, and phased construction planning based on the priorities of all levels. The attractive demands should be constantly explored to enhance user stickiness and improve user experience. Furthermore, because users' demand change in response to their surroundings, service categories are undergoing a dynamic transformation cycle. As a result, while maintaining the service's advanced nature, the development of a rural tourism intelligent information service should pay close attention to users' demand.

Acknowledgement. This research was supported by the National Key Research and Development Program of China under Grant 2019YFB1405600.

References

1. He, J., Li, L.: A study on the conceptions of rural tourism. J. Southwest Univ. (Soc. Sci. Edition) **5**, 125–128 (2002)
2. Zhang, X.: Spatiotemporal patterns of public service levels in China's rural tourism and their origins. Tourism Tribune **36**(11), 26–39 (2021)
3. Wu, Z., Zhuang, S., Zhou, J., et al.: The development strategy of agricultural tourism characteristic platform—taking Youni.com as an example. China J. Commer. (11), 47–49 (2021)
4. Grönroos, C., Voima, P.: Critical service logic: making sense of value creation and co-creation. J. Acad. Mark. Sci. **41**(2), 133–150 (2013)
5. Liang, T., Liu, S.: User willingness of tourism information service platform based on UTAUT model. Inf. Sci. **40**(02), 162–168+176 (2022)
6. Gong, P.: A study on the thread and hot spot of tourism information service in china: bibliometrics and visualization based on multidisciplinary perspective. Library **09**, 85–91 (2019)
7. Li, Y., Hu, C., Huang, C., et al.: The concept of smart tourism in the context of tourism information services. Tour. Manag. **58**, 293–300 (2017)
8. Zhang, X.: Research on the intelligent tourism from the perspective of information ecology. On Econ. Probl. **05**, 124–128 (2018)
9. Xu, A., Ren, X., Wang, H.: Research on the innovation mechanism of smart tourism information service mode under the background of digital economy. J. Southwest Minzu Univ. (Humanit. Soc. Sci.) **42**(11), 31–43 (2021)
10. Jia, H.: Strategic research on public information service in the context of smart tourism. Inf. Sci. **33**(07), 145–149 (2015)
11. Zhang, X.: The development path of rural tourism economy under the environment of smart tourism. Mark. Manag. Rev. **12**, 148–149 (2020)
12. Yao, Y.: Discussion on the development direction of intelligent rural tourism in the post-epidemic era. Agric. Econ. **2**, 139–140 (2022)

13. Yang, F.: Rural tourism development path analysis—based on smart concept. Agric. Econ. **07**, 119–120 (2018)
14. Wang, Y.: Research on promoting rural tourism development in yantai with smart tourism platform. Agric. Econ. **08**, 64–66 (2019)
15. Kano, N.: Attractive quality and must-be quality. Hinshitsu (Qual. J. Japan. Soc. Qual. Control) **14**, 39–48 (1984)
16. Li, H., Cao, Y., Shen, W., et al.: User demand based on LDA subject identification and Kano model analysis. Inf. Sci. **39**(08), 3–11+36 (2021)
17. Jin, Y., Zhang, Q.: Research on personal information protection elements of social media based on KANO model. J. Inf. Resour. Manag. **8**(04), 41–48 (2018)
18. Chang, C.C., Chen, P.-L., Chiu, F.-R., et al.: Application of neural networks and Kano's method to content recommendation in web personalization. Expert Syst. Appl. **36**(3), 5310–5316 (2009)
19. Yang, H.: Analysis on the influencing factors of the satisfaction of tourism website navigation based on the Kano model. Manag. Technol. SME **07**, 176–178 (2018)
20. Charles, B., Robert, B., David, B.: Kano's methods for understanding customer-defined quality. Center Qual. Manag. J. **2**(4), 3–36 (1993)

Research on the Factors Influencing the Financing Performance of Rewarded Crowdfunding - Based on Project Multimodal Data Analysis

Jun Chen[(✉)], Xin Yang, and Mengmeng Du

School of Information Management, Wuhan University, Wuhan 430072, China
christina_cj@whu.edu.cn

Abstract. An increasing number of rewarded crowdfunding platforms recommend that fundraisers post multimodal data to improve data diversity and attract investors' attention. Project speech contains both textual modality (text) and acoustic modality (voice) data. This study aims to explore how linguistic style of the speech text and acoustic features of the speech voice influence the crowdfunding campaign performance from the perspective of emotional contagion. An econometric model to investigate the effects of emotional cues from fundraisers' speech on rewarded crowdfunding performance is constructed, and an empirical analysis with 21996 projects data in Kickstarter is conducted. The findings demonstrate that both acoustic emotional cues (voice pitch and speech rate) and textual emotional cues (intimate and perceptual language) have significant positive effect on the financing performance, while voice intensity is negatively related to financing performance. This investigation provides both theoretical implications for the literature of crowdfunding and practical implications for fundraisers.

Keywords: Rewarded crowdfunding · Funding behavior · Acoustic feature · Linguistic style · Emotional contagion

1 Introduction

Rewarded crowdfunding platforms have grown rapidly in recent years as an important way to help startups solve their financing problems. The investigation on the antecedents of crowdfunding success has become a hot topic. Most previous studies apply signaling theory to discuss the association between the structured information and fundraising performance [1, 2]. However, funders in rewarded crowdfunding are rather supporters than professional investors. They invest not only to chase financial returns, but more likely as an act of support generated by emotional transmission. Therefore, understanding the effects of emotional factors that are embedded in fundraiser's presentation is important in exploring the antecedents of rewarded crowdfunding success.

Speech is the most attractive and natural way to convey information due to its convenience and liveness [3]. As a multimodal signal, speech contains both textual modality

© The Author(s), under exclusive license to Springer Nature Switzerland AG 2023
Y. Tu and M. Chi (Eds.): WHICEB 2023, LNBIP 481, pp. 218–227, 2023.
https://doi.org/10.1007/978-3-031-32302-7_19

(spoken words) and acoustic modality (voice) data. Both textual and acoustic modality data of speech contain emotional cues that can accurately reflect the emotional states of speakers. Emotional contagion theory outlines a process in which an individual's emotion expression triggers changes in the emotional states and perception of others [4]. In rewarded crowdfunding, fundraiser's emotion or attitude conveyed by speech can affect funder's perception. When crowdfunding funders are viewing a project presentation, emotional cues in the fundraiser's speech will trigger the occurrence of emotional contagion and change funders' attitude towards the project, which may affect their willingness to invest. Thus, emotional contagion theory can help us understand the relationship between emotional cues in fundraiser's speech and crowdfunding performance. Therefore, this study aims at investigating the impact of textual and acoustic emotional cues from the speech on financing performance in rewarded crowdfunding from the perspective of emotional contagion theory.

2   Literature Review

2.1   Emotional Cues in Speech

Speech contains rich emotional cues, which are hidden in voice as well as the spoken words. Voice is quantified as numerous acoustic features. The analysis of emotions through acoustic features has received a great deal of attention, where pitch, intensity and speech rate have been found to play an important role in recognizing the emotions of speakers [5]. These features fluctuate according to speakers' current emotional state and determine whether the voice sounds natural and smooth. For example, lower-intensity voice indicates that the speaker is in a tender state, while passion is associated with higher pitch and faster expression. Analyzing these acoustic features is essential for speakers to choose the appropriate voice expressions to improve receivers' perception.

Style words is an important part in language expression. The use of style words forms the linguistic style of speech. From a psychological perspective, linguistic style is more closely linked to measures of people's social and psychological worlds than content [6], which suggests that linguistic style of speech also contains cues associated with emotions. Intimate and perceptual language are considered as important psychological language styles [7, 8]. Previous studies posit that intimate language has the characteristics of affinity and emotion, which can close the psychological distance with audiences. Perceptual language may facilitate the ease of processing and make the message seems more appealing.

2.2   Emotional Contagion Theory

The emotional contagion theory states that emotional expressions flow from the sender to the recipients, who catch the expressed emotions and develop feelings similar to those of the sender [4].

Consumer behavior studies have shown that users' emotional state has a significant impact on their decision-making behaviors. Videos in rewarded crowdfunding projects presents the motivation and vision of the project to funders. The vocal tone and linguistic styles contained in videos carry rich emotional expressions. When exposed to

these emotions, funders may develop similar feelings, which influences their perceptions of the project values and decision-making strategies. Thus, emotional contagion
theory provides a plausible theoretical perspective for discussing the association between
emotional cues in the speech and project funding results in rewarded crowdfunding.

3   Research Model and Hypotheses

Given that both acoustic features and linguistic styles are related to speaker's emotion
and personal characteristics, we construct the research model as shown in Fig. 1.

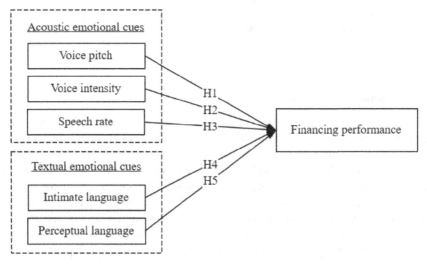

Fig. 1. Research model

3.1   The Effect of Acoustic Emotional Cues

Pitch refers to the number of vibrations of the vocal cords per second, which is determined
by fundamental frequency. Pitch has been shown to be closely related to the emotional
state of the speaker. High-pitch voices usually indicate that the speaker is in a highly
positive emotional state, such as happiness, excitement, and enthusiasm [9]. At the same
time, extroverts often show higher inflections of voice. When crowdfunding fundraiser
uses high-pitch voice to introduce the project, it will ignite positive contagion. In the case
of uncertainty in the investment process, funders are willing to seek positive cues from
fundraisers. The positive emotional signals transmitted by fundraiser's high-pitch voice
may easily make funders infected and have the same positive feelings subconsciously.
Under the influence of positive emotion, funders in an uncertain state will have a more
optimistic evaluation of the project, and are willing to take practical actions to support
the project. Therefore, we have the following hypothesis:

H1: The pitch of fundraisers' voices is positively related to the performance of crowdfunding.

Intensity refers to the power per unit area of a speech signal, which is usually perceived as loudness. It is reflected by the amplitude of voice signals. High-intensity voices are often considered to be highly aggressive and manipulative, and therefore, having a higher likelihood of carrying negative emotions [10]. The high-intensity voices of crowdfunding fundraisers may trigger funders' negative emotional contagion, which make funders form a negative impression of the fundraisers as strong and impulsive, and further reduce funders' favorability towards the project, thus weaken their willingness to invest. Therefore, we have the following hypothesis:

H2: The intensity of fundraisers' voices is negatively related to the performance of crowdfunding.

Speech rate refers to the number of words spoken per unit of time. Speech rate is one of the most important acoustic features, which is affected by the speaker's personality traits and emotional state. Outgoing and cheerful speakers tend to speak faster, and speakers in a high arousal emotion such as excitement will unconsciously speed up their speaking rate [10]. Funders would perceive the enthusiastic personality and energetic state of fundraiser in the quick expression, thus have similar positive emotional experience from this contagion. Eventually, funders in the activated state of pleasure will be more willing to invest in the project. Thus, we propose the following hypothesis:

H3: The speech rate of fundraisers' voices is positively related to the performance of crowdfunding.

3.2   The Effect of Textual Emotional Cues

The intimacy of speech, which is related to the perception of emotional sincerity, plays an important role in the emotional expression. The intimacy of speech is reflected in the use of intimate language. Intimate language helps to increase the identification of the communicator with the content of the expression. In rewarded crowdfunding, the linguistic style rich in intimate language can make funders feel close psychologically [11]. More importantly, the use of intimate language reflects their initiative and enthusiasm in crowdfunding, and the emotional contagion process will likely arouse similar feelings in the potential investors. Positive feelings lead funders to a more positive appraisal of the crowdfunding project and motivate them to maintain an optimistic emotional state, for instance by interacting in more generous and friendly ways, thus motivating them to invest the project. We accordingly hypothesize:

H4: The intimate language in fundraisers' speeches is positively related to the performance of crowdfunding.

Words related to hearing, sight, and other senses can facilitate the comprehension of information, which means that perceptual language is easier for funders to process and understand [6]. Perceptual stimulation triggers the human subconscious so that consumers can obtain a tangible view of the abstract concept of the product. Thus, marketing activities that incorporate sensory perceptions will influence funders' perceptions and judgments. Crowdfunding funders rely on fundraisers' presentation in order to know project details. Perceptual language can help them clarify the meaning of utterances in ambiguous events. Further, perceptual words are associated with a vivid representation of objects. Using such a linguistic style in crowdfunding is a sign of fundraiser's passion, which will increase funders' experienced enthusiasm about the project and convince them to support the project. Therefore, we propose the following hypothesis:

H5: The perceptual language in fundraisers' speeches is positively related to the performance of crowdfunding.

4 Data and Methodology

4.1 Data Collection

The data for this study comes from Kickstarter. Kickstarter is the most influential rewarded crowdfunding platform in the world, which has helped 235507 projects achieve funding success [12]. Kickstarter uses an all-or-nothing model, which means that only when the public funding project reaches the target amount before the deadline, the project can be successful and get all the fundraising.

First, we developed a Python program to automatically scrape all available project-related data in Kickstarter projects. We eliminated projects with extreme funding goal, which were either below $100 or above a million dollars, because, upon inspection, they represented non-serious efforts to raise funds [1]. Second, we eliminated projects without video, and download all the videos of the available projects. And all videos were converted to audios by applying FFmpeg [13]. To avoid the interference of background music and noise, we extracted the human voices from audios with the help of Spleeter [14]. Third, we utilized the Tencent Cloud speech recognition API to collect the identified text of the voice audios and excluded the data without voice content [15]. Finally, we obtained data for a total of 21996 projects.

4.2 Measurement for Unstructured Data

We applied Praat software, which is a scientific phonetic analysis tool that has been widely used in speech analysis to measure the acoustic parameters of voice waves [16]. We wrote a Praat script to extract pitch and intensity values for all speech data. Since speech is a time-varying signal, we take the average values for both pitch and intensity.

There are many pauses in speech. Therefore, each continuous voice in every audio is recorded as a segment in our study, and the average speech rate is represented by the ratio of the number of words in all segments to the sum of the duration of them. The specific calculation process is as follow: if an audio consists of n segments $S_1, S_2, ..., S_n$. The number of words in segment S_v is WN_{S_v}, and the vocal duration is DT_{S_v}. Eventually, the average speech rate of each audio is measured as follow:

$$Speech\ Rate = \frac{\sum_{i=1}^{n} WN_{S_i}}{\sum_{i=1}^{n} DT_{S_i}} \qquad (1)$$

To understand how the linguistic style in fundraisers' speeches influence crowdfunding results, we used LIWC to analyze the semantic content of each speech and extract the language components of linguistic style [6].

Intimate language can be constructed as a linguistic style that reduces the psychological distance to the audience. And first-person pronouns are important for showing the distance of intimacy. Greater use of first-person pronouns would make the described content more approachable, thus making it easier for funders to identify with the project. Also, there is a strong association between psychological feelings and affective evaluation. Therefore, we measured the intimate language of the speech by the total number of first-person pronouns and affective words presented in speech.

Perceptual language refers to a linguistic style described by sensory experience. Hearing, sight, and other senses cues have the potential to influence consumers' choices and evaluation by stimulating the perception of them. A vivid presentation with perceptual language conveys the enthusiasm of the fundraiser, which will inspire positive emotions in funders. We use the dictionaries of perception in LIWC to capture the perceptual words in our study [6]. Perceptual language is measured as the number of perceptual words in speech.

4.3 Research Variable

Dependent and Independent Variables

The project fundraiser sets a financing goal at project initiation. Project financing is considered successful when the actual funding amount reaches the goal, otherwise, the project financing fails. In our study, the final funding result of the project is used as the dependent variable of the model. The main independent variables included three acoustic emotional cues, pitch, intensity and speech rate, and two textual emotional cues, intimate language and perceptual language.

Control Variables

Project duration and funding goal represent the size of the project, while the number of comments suggest the popularity of the project [1]. Fundraisers can communicate information to funders by updating the progress of projects and responding to comments. At the same time, fundraisers who have experience in crowdfunding are more likely to attract funders and thus achieve positive financing results [2]. And the length of the project video is considered relevant to fundraiser's efforts. Therefore, these features of project play an important role in influencing funders' investment decisions. To avoid the discrepancy of regression results, we selected funding goal, project duration, number of comments, project update, fundraiser experience, and the length of video as the control variables of our study. Table 1 shows the descriptions and descriptive statistics of all variables.

Table 1. Descriptions and descriptive statistics of variables.

Variable	Measures	Mean	SD	Min	Max
Dependent variable					
Financing performance (FinaP)	1 for the amount funded meets or exceeds the funding goal, 0 otherwise	0.5	0.5	0	1
Independent variables					
Voice pitch (Pitch)	The mean value of the fundamental frequency of voices in speech	182.7	49.9	81.3	480.6
Voice intensity (Intensity)	The mean value of power per unit area of voices in speech	70.9	4.4	31.4	86.5
Speech rate (SpeeR)	The number of words contained in speech per second	2.6	0.7	0.4	7
Intimacy language (IntiL)	Sum of numbers of first-person pronouns and affective words of speech	10.8	4.1	0	54
Perceptual language (PercL)	The number of perceptual words of speech	2.8	2.2	0	48.5
Control variables					
Project duration (ProjD)	The interval between project initiation time and deadline time	2804974.2	880063.9	87007	7776000
Funding goal(Goal)	The amount of funding goal	28069.4	72671.2	100	1000000
Number of comments (NumbC)	The number of comments posted	68.8	1115.6	0	107758
Fundraiser experience (FundE)	1 when the fundraiser has crowdfunding experience, 0 otherwise	0.6	0.5	0	1
Project update (ProjU)	1 when the project has been updated, 0 otherwise	0.7	0.4	0	1
Length of video (LengV)	Duration of the video in second	158.3	84.5	2.2	3035.6

4.4 Empirical Model

Since the dependent variable is a Boolean variable, we adopted logistic regression to conduct a quantitative analysis of the relationship between emotional cues in speech and project funding results. We specified the baseline model shown in Eq. (2) to test our hypotheses. All variables were standardized with the Z-score standardization method.

$$FinaP = \beta0 + \beta1Pitch + \beta2Intensity + \beta3SpeeR + \beta4IntiL + \beta5PercL + \beta6 \Pr ojD$$
$$+ \beta7Goal + \beta8NumbC + \beta9FundE + \beta10 \Pr ojU + \beta11LengV \qquad (2)$$

5 Results

The results of logistic regression are shown in Table 2. We examined the effects of control variables on crowdfunding performance, the results are shown in Column (1). Column (2) shows that both acoustic and textual emotional cues have significant impact on crowdfunding performance. For acoustic emotional cues, the pitch of fundraisers' voices is positively related to the performance of crowdfunding with coefficient at 0.104. The speech rate is positively associated with crowdfunding success with coefficient at 0.058. Yet the intensity negatively influences the financing performance with coefficient at −0.096. For textual emotional cues, the intimate language and the perceptual language in fundraisers' speeches are both positively related to financing performance with coefficient at 0.071 and 0.077, respectively. The results are all consistent with our hypotheses.

Table 2. Logistic regression results.

	Dependent variable: Financing performance	
	(1)	(2)
ProjD	−0.130***	−0.125***
Goal	−0.634***	−0.601***
NumbC	19.215***	19.979***
FundE	4.412***	4.428***
ProjU	1.664***	1.679***
LengV	0.126***	0.131***
Pitch		0.104***
Intensity		−0.096***
SpeeR		0.058**
IntiL		0.071***
PercL		0.077***
Constant	−3.252***	−3.239***
Observation	21996	21996
R-squared	0.551	0.553

Note: * $p < 0.10$, ** $p < 0.05$, *** $p < 0.01$.

6 Discussion and Conclusion

6.1 Discussion of Key Findings

Understanding the effects of critical emotional cues in speech on crowdfunding performance has important guiding significance for fundraisers to improve their financing performance. This study attempts to explore how linguistic style of the speech text and acoustic features of the speech voice influence the crowdfunding performance from the perspective of emotional contagion. The main findings are as follows.

First, acoustic emotional cues give significant impact on project financing performance. Pitch and speech rate have positive influence on the financing performance, while intensity shows a negative effect. It indicates that fundraisers often use high vocal tone and speech rate to convey their positive emotions to funders. The occurrence of positive emotional contagion motivates funders to invest in the project. High-intensity is usually associated with extreme emotions and stress. Negative emotional contagion triggered by high-intensity voices will reduce funders' intention to invest. Second, both intimate and perceptual language in fundraiser's speech are positively associated with crowdfunding results. First-pronouns and affective words in speech contribute to ignite positive emotional contagion between fundraisers and funders, reducing the psychological distance between them. Meanwhile, perceptual words in speech both reflect the fundraiser's passion and enable funders to understand project details easily. The positive emotional contagion effect of intimate language and perceptual language will improve funders' impression of the project, which will increase their investment intention, thus improve the financing performance.

6.2 Theoretical Implications

This study may contribute to the existing literature in the following two ways. First, we extend the crowdfunding literature that previously focused on the structured data by mining the emotional features contained in multimedia data, which provides a new direction of effort to investigate the factors influencing crowdfunding performance. Second, this study is an innovative attempt to extract quantitative emotional cues from different modalities of unstructured data, which broadens the application area of unstructured data mining.

6.3 Practical Implications

Our findings provide some valuable guidance for fundraisers to improve their financing performance. First, in view of the impact of acoustic emotional cues on funding results, fundraisers should pay attention to their tone and speed in their speech. They should control the volume of the explanation to reduce the average strength of their voices, which make funders feel respected in a gentle way. A fast speaker is perceived as persuasive, and knowledgeable, while conveying the signal of enthusiasm. Therefore, fundraisers should properly improve the speed of the speech and convey more details of the project to funders in limited time. Second, fundraisers should pay attention to the use of style words during their presentations, especially those related to psychological distance descriptions. Increasing the use of first-person pronouns and affective words would be a good idea to enhance their intimacy. Increasing the use of perceptual words will help funders to understand the project more easily under the influence of the fundraiser's passion.

6.4 Limitations and Future Research

There are limitations in our study. First, human acoustic features and linguistic styles are closely related to biological gender. The analysis of the emotional impact of speech in our study only starts from overall perspective, and does not examine the influence of the gender of speaker. Second, we took the mean values as results when calculating the acoustic features of speech, which can be explored in the future on the relationship between the dynamic changes of these features and crowdfunding performance.

Acknowledgement. This research was supported by the National Natural Science Foundation of China under Grant 71871168.

References

1. Mollick, E.: The dynamics of crowdfunding: an exploratory study. J. Bus. Ventur. **29**(1), 1–16 (2014)
2. Alegre, I., Moleskis, M.: Beyond financial motivations in crowdfunding: a systematic literature review of donations and rewards. Voluntas **32**(2), 276–287 (2021)
3. Guyer, J.J., Fabrigar, L.R., Vaughan-Johnston, T.I., Tang, C.: The counterintuitive influence of vocal affect on the efficacy of affectively-based persuasive messages. J. Exp. Soc. Psychol. **74**, 161–173 (2018)
4. Hatfield, E., Cacioppo, J.T., Rapson, R.L.: Emotional contagion. Curr. Dir. Psychol. Sci. **2**(3), 96–100 (1993)
5. Scherer, K.R.: Vocal affect expression: a review and a model for future research. Psychol. Bull. **99**(2), 143 (1986)
6. Pennebaker, J.W., Boyd, R.L., Jordan, K., Blackburn, K.: The development and psychometric properties of LIWC2015 (2015)
7. Bratman, G.N., Hamilton, J.P., Daily, G.C.: The impacts of nature experience on human cognitive function and mental health. Ann. N. Y. Acad. Sci. **1249**(1), 118–136 (2012)
8. Federmeier, K.D.: Thinking ahead: the role and roots of prediction in language comprehension. Psychophysiology **44**(4), 491–505 (2007)
9. Juslin, P.N., Laukka, P.: Communication of emotions in vocal expression and music performance: Different channels, same code? Psychol. Bull. **129**(5), 770 (2003)
10. Tusing, K.J., Dillard, J.P.: The sounds of dominance. Vocal precursors of perceived dominance during interpersonal influence. Hum. Commun. Res. **26**(1), 148–171 (2000)
11. Connors, S., Khamitov, M., Thomson, M., Perkins, A.: They're just not that into you: how to leverage existing consumer–brand relationships through social psychological distance. J. Mark. **85**(5), 92–108 (2021)
12. Kickstarter Homepage. https://www.kickstarter.com/
13. FFmpeg Homepage. https://ffmpeg.org/
14. Spleeter Homepage. https://research.deezer.com/projects/spleeter.html
15. Tencent cloud Homepage. https://cloud.tencent.com/
16. Praat Homepage. https://www.fon.hum.uva.nl/praat/

How Characteristics of Creator and Campaign Shape Crowdfunding Performance: Using Hierarchical Linear Modeling

Baihui Shi, Nianxin Wang$^{(\boxtimes)}$, and Qingxiang Li

Jiangsu University of Science and Technology, Zhenjiang, China
wangnianxin@163.com

Abstract. Project quality signal, online communication between creators and backers and social capital of serial creator are the key factors that affect crowdfunding performance. However, while existing studies ignored projects initiated by the same creator are not independent, they may suffer from a level bias, with a single level of analysis only (e.g., the project level, or serial creator level). To address this situation, this paper uses a hierarchical linear model to conduct an empirical analysis of a total of 6,286 projects initiated by 2,394 serial creators on the Indiegogo platform. The results show that project-level attributes (project quality and online communication) positively affect crowdfunding performance. Creator-level factors (experience of serial creator) has a positive effect on crowdfunding performance. More important, we further identify several interesting moderators: the social capital of the serial creator positively moderates the relationship between pictures, project comments and performance across levels, but it is negative when moderating the relationship between the updates and performance.

Keywords: Hierarchical Linear Modeling · Project Quality · Online Communication · Creator Experience · Social Capital

1 Introduction

Crowdfunding that intends to raise a small amount of funding from a large number of individuals via digital platforms has attracted much attention from industry practitioners and academic researchers. It's reported that the global crowdfunding market was valued at $10.2 billion in 2018 and was forecast to reach $28.77 billion by 2025. Although Crowdfunding market has grown rapidly, the success rate of crowdfunding is relatively low. Take Kickstarter for example, among all of 549,711 projects in Kickstarter, only 215,747 were successfully funded, yielding a success rate of 39.46%. Given that, extant researchers attempt to figure out how attributes of campaigns and their creators influence crowdfunding success [1, 2, 3]. However, past studies on determinants of crowdfunding has suffered from a level bias, with researchers studying determinants at single levels of analysis only (e.g., the project or creator level). Although single-level research can be useful, the past research implicitly assumes that campaigns that initiated by the same

© The Author(s), under exclusive license to Springer Nature Switzerland AG 2023
Y. Tu and M. Chi (Eds.): WHICEB 2023, LNBIP 481, pp. 228–237, 2023.
https://doi.org/10.1007/978-3-031-32302-7_20

creator are independent, which may lead to an incomplete and disjointed view of how campaign and creator information affect crowdfunding success.

Scholars have pointed out that for serial creators, they can develop necessary knowledge and skills over time when they operate their projects or comment on other projects, so projects initiated by the same creator are no longer independent [4]. Therefore, this paper believes that campaigns initiated by same creators are affected by the characteristics of the serial creators (similar to environmental factors). That is to say, the magnitude of the campaign quality signal on crowdfunding performance are different across each serial creator.

Besides, from the data structure perspective, the campaigns we analyze in this study belong to different serial creators, namely the data structure is nested. And when a hierarchy exists, an analysis of data aggregated from different levels may produce inaccurate and unreliable results [5]. More important, with nested structures, the assumption of independent errors is violated and the traditional OLS regression approaches that rely on this assumption inadequate [5].

Based on the two reasons (linkage between campaigns and serial creators as well as the nested data structure), we choose hierarchical linear model to address the linear dependencies. In the context of our study, we use HLM with the unique project embedded in level 1, nested within serial creators in level 2. The hierarchical linear model takes into account the differences between different creator level and the dependent linkage between those two levels. It allows us to statistically account for potential interdependences across different partition variance-covariance components to model the multilevel nature of crowdfunding system and estimate level effects [6]. Therefore, this paper uses a hierarchical linear model to analyze the impact of factors at different levels on crowdfunding performance and focus on the moderation effect of serial creator social capital.

2 Literature Review

2.1 Influencing Factors of Crowdfunding Performance

Since the rapid growth of crowdfunding market but the relative low success rate of project fundraising, academics have paid much attention to investigated the determinants of crowdfunding success. The previous research mainly uncover those factors from three dimensions, including campaign information [1, 7, 8], creator information [4] and communication between backers and creators [9].

Among these studies, serial creators are a special group in crowdfunding. Serial creators refer to project creators who have experience in launching projects on the crowdfunding platform, that is, they have launched more than one project on the platform. Social capital accumulates when serial creators launched each project, such as reputation, authority, knowledge, and number of friends, which plays an important role in crowdfunding performance. Past studies have confirmed that creators with higher social capital can obtain higher funds [10]. However, existing research implicitly assume that projects initiated by the same creator are independent and ignored the linkage of serial creator and projects. To address this issue, we conduct HLM to analyze.

2.2   Hierarchical Linear Model

Multilevel modeling is one of the best practices that have been frequently applied by academics to examine determinants of performance [11, 12, 13]. Specifically, multilevel modeling is widely used statistical technique for analyzing nested data such as when students are nested in schools and individuals are nested within jobs. In these cases, assumptions of observation independence are violated, leading to downwardly biased standard errors, smaller estimated p values and increased Type 1 error rates. Hierarchical Linear Model (HLM) is a multilevel model that considers the hierarchical and nested data structures while modeling linear dependencies. With nested structures, the assumption of independent errors is violated and the traditional OLS regression approaches that rely on this assumption inadequate. Therefore, HLM with additional levels render the model more useful because they focus on the analysis of data with such complex pattern of variance (i.e., nested structures).

In our study context, we believe projects belongs to each serial creator and projects initiated by the same creator are no longer independent. Thus, multilevel modeling may provide us deeper understanding of the moderating role of serial creator attributes. Besides, HLM makes us to identify potential interdependences across different partition variance-covariance components to model the multilevel nature of crowdfunding serial creator and estimate level effects. Following past HLM research on individual and team level, in the crowdfunding project structure, the serial creator level is "upper" level, and the project itself is "lower" level.

3   Research Model and Hypotheses

3.1   Research Model

Our research model is shown in Fig. 1. We consider two dimensions of attributes of serial creator, including social capital and experience. Specifically, this paper explores the moderate effect of social capital of serial creators on projects quality and the cross-level effect of experience of serial creators on crowdfunding performance.

3.2   Hypotheses Development

Project Quality Signal. A high-quality video can introduce information about the project to potential backers from visual and auditory perspectives. Wang and others believed that video can be seen as a signal of readiness, which helps to improve the confidence of backers in the quality of the project, thus increasing the possibility of success [14]; Yang and Hahn's research also reached a consistent conclusion [4]. Based on the above analysis, this paper proposes the following assumption:

H1a: The more videos displayed in crowdfunding projects, the greater the proportion of funding at the end of the project.

Project quality information can also be well displayed to the audience through pictures [15]. Like the video display, the picture is also the visualization result of the project information, which can make the backers' understanding of the project more comprehensive and intuitive. So, the assumption is as follows:

H1b: The more pictures the crowdfunding project displays, the more likely the crowdfunding project will succeed.

Project Online Communication. Indiegogo crowdfunding platform provides an update area for serial creators, who can release project update information and actively show project progress to backers. Based on the data sets of more than 48,500 projects, Mollick found that the number of project updates was positively correlated with the crowdfunding success when studying the potential drivers of the success and failure of crowdfunding enterprises [1]. Therefore, the assumption is following:

H2a: The number of project updates has a positive impact on the funding ratio of crowdfunding projects.

In the comment area, backers will express their opinions and feelings about the project. Courtney and other researchers showed that the emotional performance of investor comments can effectively reduce the degree of information asymmetry [16]. And this paper believes that dynamic comment information can provide more project quality information, so the following assumption is proposed:

H2b: The number of project comments has a positive impact on the funding ratio of crowdfunding projects.

Serial Creator Experience. In the process of crowdfunding, the serial creators will constantly understand and become familiar with the initiation process, accumulate more project expertise and experience. Beier and Wagner studied the data set of 740 projects published on one of the major Swiss crowdfunding platforms, and tested the determinants of successful fundraising related to communication, and found that the number of projects initiated by the creators had a positive impact on crowdfunding performance [17]. Therefore, this paper proposes the following assumption:

H3a: The number of projects initiated by serial creators has a positive cross-level impact on the funding ratio of crowdfunding projects.

Wang and others studied the impact of creators' (experience) signals on crowdfunding performance by using the refined possibility model, and found that experience as a backer can alleviate backers' anxiety about the information asymmetry of project quality and creators' credibility [14]. So, the following assumption is coming:

H3b: The number of projects when the creator acts as a backer has a positive cross-level impact on the funding ratio of crowdfunding projects.

Moderating Effect of Creators' Comments. Online Communication is an important manifestation of the behavior of serial creators. Butticè and others studied the impact of the cumulative number of comments received in previous crowdfunding activities (from the social capital of successful crowdfunding activities), and found that this made the activities of serial crowdfunding more successful than those of novice crowd-funders [18]. Therefore, the cumulative comments can make up for the lack of information disclosed by the project quality signal, the assumptions are following:

H4a: The total number of creators' comments has a cross-level moderation effect between the number of videos and the proportion of crowdfunding project financing.

H4b: The total number of creators' comments has a cross-level moderation effect between the number of pictures and the proportion of crowdfunding project financing.

In the process of crowdfunding, the project will generate online communication information. In case of few updates and insufficient comment information, the comments of the serial creator play a key role. This paper believes that the serial comments of the creators can increase the followers of the project and improve the impact of the lack of communication information of the project. Assumptions are as follows:

H5a: The total number of creators' comments has a cross-level moderation effect between the number of project updates and the proportion of financing.

H5b: The total number of creators' comments has a cross-level moderation effect between the number of project comments and the proportion of financing.

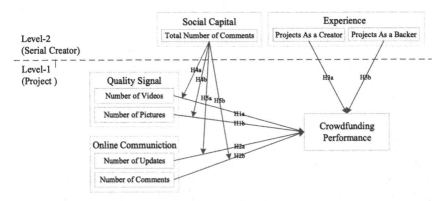

Fig. 1. Research model

4   Data and Method

Our data was collected from Indiegogo, one of the largest crowdfunding platforms. We uses Python to write a crawler program to capture 6,470 projects initiated by 2,452 project creators on the platform. After removing information such as projects with missing valid information, projects with fraud risk and projects with excessive value, the final effective sample is 2,394 project creators and 6,286 projects initiated by them.

We choose the fundraising ratio (RA) as our dependent variable, which reflect the proportion of pledge account for the projects goal. Following previous studies [1, 8, 19], this paper sets the project-level independent variables as the number of videos (VI) and pictures (PIC) representing quality signals, the number of updates (UP) and comments (CO) representing online communication, and choose experience as creator (EC) and experience as backer (EB) as the serial creator level independent variables. Besides, we employ the total number of creator's comments (FCO) to measure the social capital of serial creator. Since project characteristics (e.g. goal (GO), duration (DU), project description (PBI) and Facebook sharing (FBS)) and creator attributes (e.g. Facebook Friends (FBF)) have been repeatedly verified as determinants of crowdfunding success, we treat these constructs as control variables. To reduce kurtosis and skewness, the logarithms of variables were used in the analysis.

5 Research Results

5.1 Descriptive Statistics

Our dataset contains 6,286 projects initiated by 2,394 project creators. The total financing amount of the project reached $26,022,930, and the number of backers reached 272,745. The descriptive statistical analysis of the variables is shown in Table 1.

Table 1. Descriptive statistics

	Mean	St dev	Min	Max
Level-1 (Project)				
RA	0.419	0.672	0.000	14.184
VI	0.750	1.344	0.000	12.000
PIC	3.550	4.545	0.000	51.000
UP	3.040	7.205	0.000	119.000
CO	10.310	54.916	0.000	3422.000
GO	1161423.501	41339499.116	50.000	2000000000.000
DU	40.110	14.337	1.000	60.000
PBI	90.920	36.679	0.000	160.000
FBS	356.750	6057.397	0.000	420892.000
Level-2 (Serial creator)				
FCO	3.341	17.128	0.000	503.000
EC	2.844	1.707	2.000	23.000
EB	1.637	2.967	0.000	20.000
FBF	461.604	898.955	0.000	5000.000

5.2 Intra-class Correlation (ICC)

According to Heck et al. (2010, p6), the first step in a multilevel analysis is partitioning the variance in an outcome variable into its within- and between group components. If it turns out that there is little or no variation in outcomes between groups, there would be no compelling need for conducting a multilevel analysis". To measure the between groups variance we calculated the intra-class correlation (ICC) for positive affect and our dependent variables. In this study, the reliability of score within group ICC (1) and reliability of mean group score ICC (2) are used to test whether the data in this paper can be used for HLM analysis. The results show that the ICC (1) value is 0.518, which is far greater than the threshold value of 0.138; The value of ICC (2) is 0.72, greater than 0.7, indicating that the research data is very suitable for hierarchical linear analysis. Among them, the value of ICC (1) represents 51.8% of the crowdfunding-performance's total variation comes from inter-group variation, which can be explained by the factors at the creator level, with cross-level significance. According to the above analysis, the numerical values of ICC (1) and ICC (2) prove that the data in this paper is multilevel nested, so it is necessary to use the hierarchical linear model to analyze.

5.3   Results of Hierarchical Linear Analysis

On the basis of aggregation test, this paper uses HLM software to conduct cross-level regression analysis on the data, and the analysis results are shown in Table 2.

Table 2 contains the analysis data of random ANCOVA model (Model 1), intercept model (Model 2) and complete model (Model 3) to test the relationship between quality signals and crowdfunding performance and the cross-level impact of serial-creator's experience on the performance. Frist, variables of Level-1 (the project level) were put into Model 1 to capture the project-level attributes heterogeneity. Then, we put Level-2 (the serial creator level) variables into Model 2. After that we Put the independent variables and control variables of Level-1 and Level-2 into Model 3 to test the cross-level effect of experience of creators on project performance.

The results show that videos (0.085, p = 0.010) and pictures (0.120, p = 0.000) have a significant positive impact on the funding ratio. Thus, H1a and H1b are supported. It can be seen that the project quality signal can be displayed to the audience through videos and pictures very well, so as to attract more potential backers and improve the crowdfunding rate. Similarly, both updates (0.249, p = 0.000) and comment (0.259, p = 0.000) have a positive impact on the crowdfunding performance, assuming that H2a and H2b are supported. Experience as creator (0.174, p = 0.035) and experience as backer (0.228, p = 0.000) has a positive cross-level impact on the funding ratio. H3a and H3b is supported.

5.4   Moderation Effect Test

Model 4 introduces social capital of serial creators and its interactive terms with the project quality signal and online communication to test the moderation effect. The results are shown in Model 4. The significant moderation terms (0.286, p = 0.000) indicate that social capital positively moderates the relationship between picture and crowdfunding performance. However, social capital of serial creator has no moderation effect (−0.022, p = 0.830) on the relationship between video and crowdfunding performance. Besides, we find that creator social capital moderates the relationship between update (−0.139, p = 0.049) and comment (0.110, p = 0.032) with crowdfunding performance in different directions, which we will explain in discussion section.

Table 2. Results of hierarchical linear analysis

	Model 1		Model 2		Model 3		Model 4	
	Coef	P	Coef	P	Coef	P	Coef	P
Intercept	1.249^{**}	0.000	0.199^{**}	0.000	1.127^{**}	0.000	1.326^{**}	0.000
Level-1 (Project)								
VI	0.093^{**}	0.005			0.085^{**}	0.010	0.129^{**}	0.004
PIC	0.144^{**}	0.000			0.120^{**}	0.000	0.129^{**}	0.000
UP	0.227^{**}	0.000			0.249^{**}	0.000	0.186^{**}	0.000
CO	0.251^{**}	0.000			0.259^{**}	0.000	0.175^{**}	0.000
	Model 1		Model 2		Model 3		Model 4	
	Coef	P	Coef	P	Coef	P	Coef	P
GO	-0.253^{**}	0.000			-0.248^{**}	0.000	-0.232^{**}	0.000
DU	-0.152^{**}	0.001			-0.154^{**}	0.001	-0.212^{**}	0.000
PBI	0.135^{**}	0.000			0.117^{**}	0.000	0.115^{**}	0.000
FBS	0.055^{**}	0.000			0.088^{**}	0.000	0.067^{**}	0.000
Level-2 (Serial creator)								
EC			0.250^{**}	0.005	0.174^{*}	0.035	0.150^{*}	0.035
EB			0.264^{**}	0.000	0.228^{**}	0.000	0.236^{**}	0.000
FCO			0.303^{**}	0.000	0.306^{**}	0.000	0.312^{**}	0.000
FBF			-0.032^{**}	0.000	-0.033^{**}	0.000	-0.031^{**}	0.000
Interactive terms								
FCO × VI							-0.022	0.830
FCO × PIC							0.286^{**}	0.000
FCO × UP							-0.139^{*}	0.049
FCO × CO							0.110^{*}	0.032
Other terms								
τ_{00}	0.216^{**}	0.000	0.198^{**}	0.000	0.187^{**}	0.000	0.147^{**}	0.004
σ^2	0.197		0.215		0.198		0.171	
$R^2_{Level-1}$	0.074		0.074		0.137		0.287	
$R^2_{Level-2}$	0.071		0.142		0.190		0.363	
F^2	0.065		0.143		0.190		0.364	

Tips: $^{**}p \leq 0.01$, $^{*}p \leq 0.05$; R^2 represents the variance of model interpretation, F^2 represents the improvement ratio of residual variance.

6   Conclusion and Discussion

Our study has several findings. First, we find that attributes of serial creator have cross-level effect on campaign performance. Our results show that past experience as creators and experience as backers are positively related to crowdfunding performance. Second, we identify some moderators. Social capital of creators may positively moderate the relationship between project quality and crowdfunding performance. However, our results reveal that social capital of creators cannot moderate the effect of video on crowdfunding performance. This might be because that video is the central route in evaluating the crowdfunding project. The information that provided by video is rich enough so that its effect may not vary across serial creators. Besides, we found that serial creator's social capital interacts with update and comment in different directions. This can be explained by the overlap of the same information source. Update is posted by creators while social capital is also coming from creator and thus fails to generate synergistic effects on crowdfunding success.

Our study contributes to crowdfunding research by emphasis on the multilevel analysis. Specifically, we introduce multilevel modeling (HLM) to analyze the determinants of crowdfunding success. Although extant research has explored many factors that may influence crowdfunding performance, they may suffer a level bias due to a single level analysis. In fact, projects launched by the same creator are not independent and the performance will be affected by environmental variables (experience of serial creators). In other word, the projects are nested within serial creators. Under this circumstance, an analysis of data aggregated from different levels may produce inaccurate and unreliable results. Thus, we apply the HLM to generate deeper understanding of how the effect of project quality on crowdfunding success varies across each serial creator.

Our findings provide several practice implications for creators. Our results indicate that social capital of serial creators is necessary to crowdfunding success. Creators may take their time to comment on platform to accumulate enough social capital so as to enhance the positive effect of project quality on fundraising success.

Several limitations of this paper should be noticed. This paper studies the cross-level analysis at the two levels of the serial creator level and the project level, ignoring the crowdfunding platform environment. Therefore, future research can study the cross-level analysis at three levels, including the platform level to generate more insights.

Acknowledgement. This research is supported by National Science Foundation of China (grant number: 72272066), and Postgraduate Research & Practice Innovation Program of Jiangsu Province (grant number: KYCX22_3736).

References

1. Mollick, E.: The dynamics of crowdfunding: an exploratory study. J. Bus. Ventur. **29**(1), 1–16 (2014)
2. Kunz, M.M., Bretschneider, U., Erler, M., et al.: An empirical investigation of signaling in reward-based crowdfunding. Electron. Commer. Res. **17**(3), 425–461 (2017)

3. Wang, N., Li, Q., Liang, H., et al.: Understanding the importance of interaction between creators and backers in crowdfunding success. Electron. Commer. Res. Appl. **27**(1), 106–117 (2018)
4. Yang, L., Hahn, J.: Learning from prior experience: an empirical study of serial entrepreneurs in IT-enabled crowdfunding (2015)
5. Hox, J.J.: Multilevel analysis: techniques and applications. J. Am. Stat. Assoc. **98**(462) (2003)
6. Rabe-Hesketh, S., Skrondal, A.: Multilevel and longitudinal modeling using stata. Biometrics **62**(3), 951 (2010)
7. Martens, M.L., Jennings, J.E., Jennings, P.D.: Do the stories they tell get them the money they need? The role of entrepreneurial narratives in resource acquisition. Acad. Manag. J. **50**(5), 1107–1132 (2007)
8. Ahlers, G.K., Cumming, D., Günther, C., et al.: Signaling in equity crowdfunding. Entrep. Theory Pract. **39**(4), 955–980 (2015)
9. Liu, Y., Bi, J.W., Fan, Z.P.: A method for ranking products through online reviews based on sentiment classification and interval-valued intuitionistic fuzzy TOPSIS. Int. J. Inf. Technol. Decis. Making **16**(6) (2017)
10. Kang, L., Jiang, Q., Tan, C.H.: Remarkable advocates: an investigation of geographic distance and social capital for crowdfunding. Inf. Manag. **54**(3), 336–348 (2016)
11. Jiang, Y., Ho, Y.C., Yan, X., et al.: Investor platform choice: herding, platform attributes, and regulations. J. Manag. Inf. Syst. **35**(1), 86–116 (2018)
12. Theokary, C., Sarangee, K., Karniouchina, E.V.: The impact of strategic partnerships on crowdfunding outcomes: which ties really matter? J. Small Bus. Manag. (8), 1–32 (2020)
13. Burton-Jones, A., Gallivan, M.J.: Toward a deeper understanding of system usage in organizations: a multilevel perspective. MIS Q. **31**(4), 657–679 (2007)
14. Wang, N., Liang, H., Xue, Y., et al.: Mitigating information asymmetry to achieve crowdfunding success: signaling and online communication. J. Assoc. Inf. Syst. **22**(3), 4 (2021)
15. Xiao, S., Tan, X., Dong, M., et al.: How to design your project in the online crowdfunding market? Evidence from Kickstarter (2014)
16. Courtney, C., et al.: Resolving information asymmetry: signaling, endorsement, and crowdfunding success. Entrep. Theory Pract. **41**(2), 265–290 (2017)
17. Beier, M., Wagner, K.: Crowdfunding success: a perspective from social media and e-commerce. In: ICIS (2015)
18. Butticè, V., Colombo, M.G., Wright, M.: Serial crowdfunding, social capital, and project success. Entrep. Theory Pract. **41**(2), 183–207 (2017)
19. Mollick, E.R., Kuppuswamy, V.: After the campaign: outcomes of crowdfunding. SSRN Electron. J. (2014)

How Does Cover Content Matter for Online Medical Crowdfunding Platform? An Emotional Appeal Perspective

Xiaojin Shen[1], Yi Wu[1], and Xiaopan Wang[2(✉)]

[1] Tianjin University, Tianjin, China
[2] Zhejiang Gongshang University, Hongzhou, China
wangxiaopan@tju.edu.cn

Abstract. Poverty and return to poverty due to illness is still one of the main causes of personal poverty, and medical crowdfunding can help patients and their families raise medical expenses to alleviate their economic pressure. Under this background, how to improve the fundraising performance of medical crowdfunding projects has attracted more and more attention. This paper aims to investigate the impact of emotions expressed in cover content on donation and sharing behaviors of project supporters. The cover content includes a cover image and a project title. We scraped the real projects from one of the largest medical crowdfunding platforms in China. We theoretically classify images into two categories, where an image of a patient in healthy status delivers positive emotions and an image of a patient in unhealthy status signals negative emotions. Further, we use LIWC to measure emotional intensity of the project title. The analysis results show that project supporters prefer projects with a positive cover image (i.e., a patient in healthy status). Moreover, there is an interaction effect between the cover image and a negative project title, whereas a positive title did not. Specifically, when a project uses a cover image of patient in unhealthy status, a negative title has a negative effect on support behaviors (i.e., donation and sharing behavior). Our study provides important theoretical and practical implications for online crowdfunding.

Keywords: Medical crowdfunding · Cover image · Project title · Sentiment analysis

1 Introduction

Medical crowdfunding refers to the funding method in which project initiator raises a large number of goodwill donations through online crowdfunding platforms to pay for related medical services or products [1], which is composed of the initiator, the crowdfunding platform, and the supporter [2]. Unaffordable out-of-pocket health expenditures has become one of the main causes of personal poverty [3]. Medical crowdfunding, as a form of charitable crowdfunding, has been pioneering in alleviating such poverty problems [3]. However, it is still challengeable for project creators of medical crowdfunding to gain the attention of donors on the information-overload network environment.

On medical crowdfunding platforms, donors often first encounter the project cover content before entering the project details page. Prior research has found that cover content is critical for initial item selection [4]. However, the research on crowdfunding have mainly focused on the information on the project details page, few scholars have paid attention to the information on project cover. For instance, previous research found that projects with emotional images and infectious text are more likely to attract potential supporters in the details page [5, 6], and the congruency effect of image emotion and text emotion is conducive to fundraising success in project details [7].

Cover content includes an image and project title in online medical crowdfunding. Specifically, the cover image is usually an image of the patient in healthy or unhealthy status. The presence of beneficiary images has been demonstrated as an efficient way to induce donor's emotional responses and prosocial behavior [8]. In this study, we use the image of the patient in healthy status to represent positive emotions, while the image of the patient in unhealthy status to represent negative emotions.

In addition, the importance of stimulus congruity between verbal and visual information has been widely mentioned in prior advertising research [9]. However, the existing research on cover emotions is a single study of the impact of images or title text in the medical crowdfunding literature [10, 11].

Considering donation and sharing behavior are both important in the context of online medical crowdfunding, this study explores the following research questions: 1) What are the impacts of the emotions of cover image on the donor's donation and sharing behavior? 2) What are the interaction effects of the emotions of cover image and project title on the donor's donation and sharing behavior?

The rest of this paper is structured as follows. In Sect. 2, we conduct a brief review of the relevant literature and present the hypotheses of the study. The dataset and results are discussed in Sects. 3 and 4 respectively. Finally, we present the discussion, theoretical contributions, practical implications, limitations, and future work in conclusion.

2 Literature Review and Hypotheses Development

2.1 Project Emotion in Philanthropic Donation

In the charitable donation literature, many studies have confirmed that emotions in the project affect donation performance, but the conclusions will vary in different segments and in different national environments. Wang et al. [6] demonstrated that patient images can powerfully arouse the empathy emotion of potential donors and thus obtain more donation amount. According to the theory of prosocial behavior and negative emotion repair, they believe that the negative emotions conveyed in the images can provoke empathy emotions, while the positive emotions can convey hope, both make the project obtain better performance. Zhang et al. [10] made an empirical analysis of the text features of medical crowdfunding projects, and found that the negative emotions had a positive effect on the success rate of fundraising in the project details, but had a negative effect in the project title. In addition, the positive emotions will have a negative impact in the project details. These conclusions differ from the studies of Majumdar and Bose [12] and Durand et al. [13]. They believe it is the differences in regional culture and types of crowdfunding that led to the change in the study conclusions. Hou et al. [11] provided evidence that the impact of emotion is different according to the types of crowdfunding. They demonstrated that under the mediating mechanism of empathy, contentment and sadness in a project image has a statistically positive effect on donation performance. However, they found that the positive effect of contentment existed in the community and environment crowdfunding projects, while the positive effect of sadness existed in the education crowdfunding projects.

Traditional charitable donation literature studying emotional influence mainly focused on the project details page [6, 12, 13], but more and more scholars have turned their attention to the project cover content in recent years [10, 11]. Dickert et al. [14] proposed a two-stage model of donation decisions, in which people first decide whether to provide any help and then decide the amount of help. In the online environment, the project cover mainly affects the project performance by affecting the choice of the project. Therefore, we believe that the project cover contributes more in the first stage of the donation decision, while the project details will play a more obvious role in the second stage of the donation decision. This may account to the different impact of emotion in the two environments.

Pieters and Wedel [4] describes the bottom-up mechanism of visual attention in the model of attention capture and transfer, which is determined by the individual's perceptual salience of the elements that capture attention rapidly and almost automatically, such as size and shape. In the form of attention capture, the baseline attention is independent of the size of the element and other factors. The higher the baseline attention, the higher the individual's attention priority to the element. Image is perceived earlier than the text under baseline attention, regardless of the size of the image and the text, so individuals generally focus more on the image than the text. Zhang et al. [15] has demonstrated that images are the most attractive part of crowdfunding projects. The model of attention capture and transfer is a theory that explains the specific content doctrine mechanism. When individuals choose projects according to the cover, they will attract attention by the elements of the cover content, thus automatically responding to the cover image and the title text, and the subsequent choice is the influence of the bottom-up mechanism. We employ the bottom-up mechanism in the model of attention capture and transfer to determine what emotional factors in the cover would affect, and focuses on the cover image.

Images and text mainly affect attentions from size, shape, and emotional stimulation [4]. Among them, emotional stimulation is the factor that attracts the most attention and influences decision-making [16]. Medical crowdfunding projects usually take the image of patient as the cover image, and the status of the patient will affect the emotional expression of the image. Baberini et al. [8] find that individuals who saw a person in an image with a sad expression had a stronger sympathetic response and a stronger willingness to donate than saw a person with a smile. In this study, we believed that the individuals can feel hopeful when the patient in healthy status, so we use the image of the patient in healthy status to represent positive emotions. Furthermore, the image conveys more sadness when the patient in unhealthy status, so we use the image of the patient in unhealthy status to represent negative emotions.

2.2 The Impact of Cover Image

Donation behavior is altruistic. Empathy is one of the important factors contributing to altruistic behavior [2]. Negative emotions can trigger empathy, and more donations can be provoked under the influence of empathy [17]. The image of the patient in unhealthy status expresses more negative emotions than the image of the patient in healthy status, therefore the former can trigger more empathy and more donors [8]. Accordingly, we posit that:

H1. Compared with a cover image of a patient in healthy status, a cover image of a patient in unhealthy status leads to a high level of donation behavior.

Sharing behavior is egoistic, which is related to personal interests such as personal image and identity acquisition [2]. Individuals often decide whether to share information after measuring the value and possible losses. The higher the perceived value, the more likely to share, but individuals are more sensitive to possible losses (increasing social costs, affecting self-image, etc.) [18]. Chang et al. [19] found that positive emotions were positively correlated with optimism and negatively correlated with pessimism, and vice versa. Optimism indirectly translates into high levels of self-esteem through positive emotions [20]. Therefore, individuals are more willing to share positive content [2]. Emotions in shared content related to personal image, therefore projects that use the cover image of patient in healthy status maybe have more sharers. Accordingly, we posit that:

H2. Compared with a cover image of a patient in unhealthy status, a cover image of a patient in healthy status leads to a high level of sharing behavior.

2.3 Interaction of Image and Text

Images are the most attractive part of a crowdfunding project [4, 11], because images can express emotions more powerfully [21]. Some crowdfunding platforms have also noticed the impact of images. Gofundme.com made suggestions on setting project images in terms of image quality, sentiment, and frequency of image updates, etc. Text can help users understand the emotions in the image more accurately [22].

The congruency effect of images and texts has already been demonstrated in the social media literature. Neal [9] found that the more appropriate the text information and the image content are in the image retrieval based on emotion, the more visitors and favorites the image gets. Consistent image and text can produce better results. For instance, Li and Xie [23] found that the higher the degree of fit between the image and text of the post in social media, the higher the user engagement. Pieters and Wedel [4] found that attention to one element in print ads would attract attention to other elements in the ads, which would produce joint effects. Medical crowdfunding projects usually need to be spread in social platforms such as WeChat and Weibo. Therefore, it can be considered that the research results in the social media literature have certain reference significance for the medical crowdfunding literature.

In recent charity crowdfunding literature, some scholars have also demonstrated the congruency effect of image emotion and text emotion in project details. Zhao et al. [7] analyzed the medical crowdfunding projects on a representative crowdfunding platform in America, and found that when the images express positive emotions, the sad words in the corresponding text description will have a significant negative effect on the success of the project. When images express negative emotions, the negative effects of sad words are diminished. There may also be an interactive relationship between the emotion of cover image and the emotion of project title in medical crowdfunding projects. Zhao et al. [7] were aimed at the project details, and we focus on the interaction of the cover content, which can enhance the medical crowdfunding literature.

Emotional modification, namely emotional regulation, refers to the process by which we influence which emotions we have, when we have them, and how we experience and express them [24]. When emotions expressed in cover content seem to be ill-matched to a given situation (viewer's mood or context), we frequently try to regulate our emotional responses so that they better serve our goals [24]. Gross [24] proposed a process model of emotion regulation that shows how specific emotion regulation strategies can be differentiated, such as distraction, reappraisal, suppression, etc. In contrast to emotion modification, emotion enhancement is designed to amplify emotional contagion when the emotion well-matches the situation [8], leading to feeling more negative when exposed to negative images, vice versa.

If the emotions of the image and the title will influence each other, when the positive emotions of the image are unfavorable to the support behaviors (i.e., donation and sharing behavior), the negative emotional intensity of the title will be alleviated by arousing the feeling of empathy under emotion regulation. When the positive emotions of the image are beneficial to the support behaviors, the positive emotional intensity of the title can continue to amplify the positive effect brought by the positive emotions of the image under the emotion enhancement. Accordingly, we posit that:

H3a. When a project uses a cover image of a patient in healthy status, a negative project title has a positive effect on support behaviors.
H3b. When a project uses a cover image of a patient in unhealthy status, a negative project title has a negative effect on support behaviors.
H4a. When a project uses a cover image of a patient in healthy status, a positive project title has a positive effect on support behaviors.
H4b. When a project uses a cover image of a patient in unhealthy status, a positive project title has a negative effect on support behaviors.

3   Data Set

We crawl the data from the home page of a representative medical crowdfunding platform in China, which is one of the online public fundraising platforms designated by the Ministry of Civil Affairs of the People's Republic of China. Our dataset includes 1,350 projects retrieved from November 2018 to March 2019, 303 projects cover image with patients in healthy status among them.

3.1 Measures of Emotion Variables

Since the images and text content are unstructured information, we need to convert it into meaningful numerical metrics to easily use in quantitative analysis. Before quantifying these variables, we need to do some processing of images and text.

The Emotion of the Image

The cover images in our dataset all contain patient, and the cover images are systematically classified using machine learning techniques (convolutional neural network CNN framework). Our dataset contains 6,389 images. First, 600 images selected randomly from dataset are artificially classified, and the images are divided into healthy and non-healthy categories according to the state of the patient, representing positive emotions and negative emotions respectively [6]. The results of manual classification are then used as training sets to train CNN classifiers, with an average accuracy of 84.6. Finally, the trained classifier is used for the non-training set of images, and the category of the image is obtained.

The Emotion of the Text

We use the text analysis tools Linguistic Inquiry and Word Count (LIWC) to calculate the emotional intensity of each text. LIWC is an effective tool for measuring emotional discourse [25], and are increasingly used by information systems and marketing scholars to quantify emotional expression in various types of texts [26–28].

After LIWC reads the given text, it compares each word in the text with the dictionary word list, and then calculates the number of words in each sentiment category in the text as a percentage of the total number of words in the text, so as to obtain the sentiment score. The language system and usage habits of Chinese and English is very different [29]. We use the official Chinese Simplified dictionary provided by LIWC2015, which was established by Yi-Tai Seih et al. on the basis of the official Chinese dictionary provided by LIWC2007 [29]. To analyze Chinese text using LIWC, we label the Chinese text and extract each word in the text at first. We use *Jieba* (Precise versus Full Mode), a Chinese text segmentation tool, to mark the title text. *Jieba* tokenizer has high accuracy and fast word segmentation speed, and is widely used in Chinese text segmentation [30, 31].

We analyzed the labeled text using LIWC, compared the number of emotional words in the dictionary to identify the number of words in the text, and divided by the total number of words to obtain the percentage of emotional words, which is emotional intensity.

3.2 Settings of Variable

We use the number of donations (*donorNum*) and the number of shares (*shareNum*) as dependent variables. The Number of donations and shares can provide simple and straightforward explanations [32].

Three independent variables were considered in our research model. Image category (*cover_isHealth*), when the image of the patient in healthy status was coded as 1, otherwise 0. The positive emotional intensity of the title (*title_posemo*) and the negative emotional intensity of the title (*title_negemo*) by the analysis of the LIWC.

We considered a range of control variables that may affect supporter behavior. Descriptive statistics of all the variables are shown in Table 1.

All continuous variables were operationalized by the logarithm of their values plus one in order to avoid zeros, except for the emotional intensity and the number of images.

Table 1. Descriptive statistics of variables.

VARIABLES	mean	sd	min	max
donorNum	1,544	1,527	78	21,280
shareNum	992.5	1,249	307	19,400
cover_isHealth	0.224	0.417	0	1
title_posemo	4.306	6.128	0	36.36
title_negemo	2.954	5.266	0	30
length of title	19.03	19.03	11	42
length of description	1,623	1,623	377	5,996
description_posemo	5.287	1.557	1.400	10.51
description_negemo	2.608	0.900	0	6.720
positive images' number	0.536	6.720	0	6
negtive images' number	2.301	1.523	0	8
target amount	176,018	90,098	30,000	500,000
patient's age	31.11	21.97	1	86
patient's gender	0.589	0.492	0	1
isCancer	0.153	0.360	0	1

4   Data Analysis

We conducted linear regressions to test the hypotheses. Results are shown in Table 2. Model 1 analyzes the effect of cover image on donation behavior. Model 2 analyzes the effect of cover image on sharing behavior. Then we divided the dataset into two groups by the emotional category of cover image to consider the interaction effects of cover image and title sentiment. Model 3 and Model 5 present the group that the image of patient in healthy status, Model 4 and Model 6 present the group that the image of patient in unhealthy status.

The results showed that compared with the cover image of a patient in unhealthy status, the image of a patient in healthy status leads to a high level of donation behavior ($\beta = 0.104$, $p < 0.05$), thus H1 is not supported. Compared with the cover image of a patient in unhealthy status, the image of a patient in healthy status leads to a high level of donation sharing behavior ($\beta = 0.152$, $p < 0.01$), leading to support for H2. In addition, the negative emotions in title were negatively correlated with donation behavior ($\beta =$

-0.006, p < 0.1) and sharing behavior ($\beta = -0.007$, p < 0.05). The negative title has a negative effect on support behaviors (i.e., donation and sharing behaviors) when the project uses the cover image of a patient in unhealthy status ($\beta = -0.006$, p < 0.1; $\beta = -0.007$, p < 0.1), but has no effect on support behaviors when the project uses the cover image of a patient in healthy status, thus H3a is not supported, but H3b is supported. There is no significant influence of positive titles on support behaviors regardless the cover image of a patient in both healthy and unhealthy status, therefore H4a and H4b are not supported.

Table 2. Regression analysis.

	Model 1	Model 2	Model 3	Model 4	Model 5	Model 6
VARIABLES	donorNum	shareNum	donorNum	donorNum	shareNum	shareNum
cover_isHealth	0.104**	0.152***				
title_posemo	−0.000	0.002	−0.000	0.000	−0.001	0.003
title_negemo	−0.006*	−0.007**	−0.006	−0.006*	−0.011	−0.007*
length of title	0.226	0.138	−0.295	0.425**	−0.092	0.244
length of description	0.001	0.056	−0.180	0.075	−0.183	0.148**
description_posemo	−0.034***	−0.019	−0.059**	−0.030**	−0.033	−0.016
description_negemo	−0.044**	−0.057***	−0.066	−0.037*	−0.056	−0.055***
positive images' number	0.003	0.004	−0.067	0.045	−0.064	0.041
negtive images' number	0.002	0.056***	−0.025	0.012	0.055*	0.060***
target amount	0.481***	0.427***	0.614***	0.440***	0.542***	0.384***
patient's age	−0.191***	−0.066***	−0.241***	−0.172***	−0.132***	−0.044**
patient's gender	−0.041	−0.010	−0.122	−0.020	−0.033	−0.005
isCancer	−0.027	−0.064	−0.064	−0.017	−0.030	−0.070
Constant	1.513*	1.053	3.452**	0.715	2.600	0.402
R-squared	0.200	0.158	0.211	0.196	0.162	0.153
F statistics	25.67	19.30	6.47	20.94	4.68	15.55
Observations	1,350	1,350	303	1,047	303	1,047

Notes: *** $p < 0.01$, ** $p < 0.05$, * $p < 0.1$

5 Discussion of Results

Consistent with our expectations, we found that cover image with positive emotions (i.e., the patient in healthy status) leads to a high level of sharing behavior in medical crowdfunding compared with the cover image with negative emotions (i.e., the patient in unhealthy status). Besides, the positive effect of positive cover images can be applied to the detail page, and the negative impact of the negative text in the detail page can be alleviated.

Contrary to our expectations, cover image associated with negative emotions leads to a low level of donation behavior in medical crowdfunding compared with the cover image with positive emotions. This shows that the previous conclusion does not apply to the cover content that the negative emotions expressed in medical crowdfunding projects is conducive to fundraising [8]. One possible reason is the suspicion of moral coercion will reduce the trust and increase the risk of donation, result in the project to be rejected [33]. Another possible explanation is that the low acceptance of negative emotions, so it is easy to occur moral disengagement [8].

The images and title together make up the project cover content, there is no interaction effects between cover image and positive title, but there is an interaction effect between the cover image and negative title. A plausible explanation is the primacy effect [16]. If a person resists negative emotions, when the first exposure is negative image or text, whether the other part of the cover is positive or not will not change the first impression. Besides, the negative impression is hard to change, but it will deepen, so the emotion enhancement plays a role in the cover content. Moreover, it indicates that the emotion regulation model may not act between cover content, but with other content unrelated to the project. Furthermore, we found that positive title did not influence supporters' behavior, suggesting that the positive impact of positive sentiment resided in image rather than text. While a positive cover image promotes both donation and sharing behavior, and its impact on sharing behavior is more significant.

6   Conclusion

This study examines the effect of emotions in cover content on donation and sharing behaviors in medical crowdfunding. Drawing on emotion regulation models and the model of attention capture and transfer, this study enriches the understanding of emotions in cover content of medical crowdfunding. In addition, this study enhances the medical crowdfunding literature by demonstrating how emotions in cover content influences supporter behavioral decisions. Past research has shown that charity crowdfunding projects should resonate with the messages of sadness [8], but our research found that positive content is more available for project cover content in medical crowdfunding. To our knowledge, this study is one of the first to examine the effect of emotions in cover image on medical crowdfunding fundraising outcomes.

This study makes several notable theoretical contributions. First, our study enriches the medical crowdfunding literature from the project cover perspective. Previous studies have mainly focused on the impact of the content on the project details page, with less people paying attention to the impact of the project cover in medical crowdfunding. Medical crowdfunding projects mainly rely on social media for communication, and the cover is one of the important factors affecting the success of the project. This study analyzes the cover images and texts from the emotional perspective, and enriches the online crowdfunding literature by showing how the emotions in cover content affect the behavior decisions of supporters. Moreover, we analyze the interaction between cover image and title text, complementing previous studies of the impact of cover emotion from a joint perspective. Although the verification results of the interaction are not significant, we found that the positive effect in the cover image may alleviate the negative impact of negative emotions in the project details, which is enlightening for further research.

Second, this study applies the bottom-up mechanism of the model of attention capture and transfer to the medical crowdfunding literature. We found that the influence of image emotion in the project cover is more important than the influence of text emotion, which is consistent with the view proposed by the bottom-up mechanism of the model of attention capture and transfer that the image will establish attention priority and be perceived earlier than the text [4].

Third, this study explored the application of the emotion regulation model in medical crowdfunding literature. Although the emotion regulation model illustrates that individuals regulate attention to circumvent conflicting emotions, it does not explicitly propose the attention shift direction [24]. By analyzing the interaction between images and text in the project cover of medical crowdfunding, we found that attention may not shift to other contents of the same cover, which expands the existing understanding of the emotion regulation model.

From a practical perspective, our results have important implications for medical crowdfunding platforms and project initiators. The current recommendations from crowdfunding platforms are for setting up contents on project details page, and we suggest that medical crowdfunding platforms should also guide the selection of cover content [22]. Our results help understand the impact of emotions in cover content on potential supporters. Therefore, we recommend that project creators pay attention to the influence of emotions in cover content, use patients' image in healthy status as cover image, and avoid using negative titles. In addition, we recommend medical crowdfunding platforms optimize the setting function of cover content and consider instructing creators to use suitable cover content to promote their activities. These actions will help improve the quality of the platform and attract more people to join the platform.

There are some limitations to consider when interpreting our results. First of all, our emotions classification method is relatively rough. We divide the emotions according to the patients' healthy state of the individual in the image, and use dictionary matching to calculate the emotions in project title. Future research is encouraged to use more fine-grained classification methods. Second, since we only conducted this study on one platform, we call for future research to be conducted on different platforms. Finally, our theoretical development and conceptualization emphasize emotions in cover content in the context of medical crowdfunding. We believe that our research model can be extended to explain other crowdfunding activities.

Acknowledgement. The authors appreciate the constructive comments and suggestions provided to us by the review team. The authors also wish to acknowledge the National Natural Science Foundation of China (72172103,72231004) for financial support. Xiaopan Wang is the corresponding author of this work.

References

1. Zhao, P., Ba, Z.C., Zhao, Y.X.: Review and prospect of influencing factors of crowdfunding success of online medical and health projects. J. Inf. Resourc. Manag. **11**(02), 97–108 (2021). (in Chinese)

2. Chen, J., Li, J.X.: 'Altruistic' donation and 'egoistic' information sharing: a study on the motivation of participating in the 'Qingsong Funding' project. News Univ. **06**, 91–100+150–151 (2018). (in Chinese)
3. Burtch, G., Chan, J.: Investigating the relationship between medical crowdfunding and personal Bankruptcy in the United States: evidence of a digital divide. MIS Q. **43**(1), 237 (2019)
4. Pieter, R., Wedel, M.: Attention capture and transfer in advertising. J. Bus. Ventur. **68**(2), 36–50 (2004)
5. Duynhoven, A.V., et al.: Spatially exploring the intersection of socioeconomic status and Canadian cancer-related medical crowdfunding campaigns. BMJ **9**(6), 1–10 (2019)
6. Wang, X.P., Wu, Y., Guo, J.P., Yang, L.S.: Says what in your photos? The impacts of photographic narratives on medical crowdfunding performance. In: Pacific Asia Conference on Information Systems, p. 231 (2020)
7. Zhao, K., Zhou, L., Zhao, X.: Multi-modal emotion expression and online charity crowdfunding success. Decis. Support Syst. **163**, 113842 (2022)
8. Baberini, M., Coleman, C.L., Slovic, P., Vstfjll, D.: Examining the effects of photographic attributes on sympathy, emotion, and donation behavior. Vis. Commun. Q. **22**(2), 118–128 (2015)
9. Neal, D.M.: Emotion-based tags in photographic documents: the interplay of text, image, and social influence. Can. J. Inf. Libr. Sci. **34**(3), 329–353 (2010)
10. Zhang, F.G., Xue, B.Y., Li, Y.R.: Effect of textual features on the success of medical crowdfunding: model development and econometric analysis from the tencent charity platform. J. Med. Internet Res. **23**(6), e22395 (2021)
11. Hou, J.R., Zhang, J., Zhang, K.P.: Pictures that are worth a thousand donations: how emotions in project images drive the success of online charity fundraising campaigns? An image design perspective. MIS Q. (2022)
12. Majumdar, A., Indranil, B.: My words for your pizza: an analysis of persuasive narratives in online crowdfunding. Inf. Manag. **55**(6), 781–794 (2018)
13. Durand, W.M., Peters, J.L., Eltorai, A.E., Kalagara, S., Osband, A.J., Daniels, A.H.: Medical crowdfunding for organ transplantation. Clin. Transplant. **32**(6), e13267 (2018)
14. Dickert, S., Sagara, N., Slovic, P.: Affective motivations to help others: a two-stage model of donation decisions. J. Behav. Decis. Mak. **24**(4), 361–376 (2011)
15. Zhang, S., Lee, D., Singh, P.V.: How much is an image worth? airbnb property demand analytics leveraging a scalable image classification algorithm. SSRN Electron. J. (2017)
16. Yoon, S.-H., Kim, H.-W.: What content and context factors lead to selection of a video clip? The heuristic route perspective. Electron. Commer. Res. **19**(3), 603–627 (2019). https://doi.org/10.1007/s10660-019-09355-6
17. Tusche, A., Bockler, A., Kanske, P., Trautwein, F.M., Singer, T.: Decoding the charitable brain: empathy, perspective taking, and attention shifts differentially predict altruistic giving. J. Neurosci. **36**(17), 4719–4732 (2016)
18. Li, X., Wang, K.L.: Marketing information sharing behavior of social media users: the perspective of evaluation worry and system feedback. J. Manag. Sci. **33**(4), 82–97 (2020). (in Chinese)
19. Chang, E.C., MaydeuOlivares, A., DZurilla, T.J.: Optimism and pessimism as partially independent constructs: relationship to positive and negative affectivity and psychological well-being. Personal. Individ. Differ. **23**(3), 433–440 (1997)
20. Fu, Z.G., Liu, Y.: Optimism, pessimism and self-esteem. Chin. J. Health Psychol. **20**(7), 1115–1117 (2012). (in Chinese)
21. Lane, R.D., Chua, P.M.L., Dolan, R.J.: Common effects of emotional valence, arousal and attention on neural activation during visual processing of pictures. Neuropsychologia **37**(9), 989–997 (1999)

22. Gofundme: tips for picking the best fundraiser photos, https://www.gofundme.com/c/fundra ising-tips/image, last accessed 2023/1/19
23. Li, Y.Y., Xie, Y.: Is picture worth a thousand words? An empirical study of image content and social media engagement. J. Mark. Res. **57**(1), 1–19 (2020)
24. Gross, J.J.: Emotion regulation: Affective, cognitive, and social consequences. Psychophysiology **39**(3), 525–552 (2002)
25. Tausczik, Y.R., Pennebaker, J.W.: The psychological meaning of words: LIWC and computerized text analysis methods. J. Lang. Soc. Psychol. **29**(1), 24–54 (2010)
26. Ransbotham, S., Lurie, N.H., Liu, H.: Creation and consumption of mobile word of mouth: how are mobile reviews different? Mark. Sci. **8**(5), 773–792 (2019)
27. Schweidel, D.A., Moe, W.W.: Listening in on social media: a joint model of sentiment and venue format choice. J. Mark. Res. **51**(4), 387–402 (2014)
28. Yin, D., Bond, S.D., Zhang, H.: Anxious or angry? Effects of discrete emotions on the perceived helpfulness of online reviews. MIS Q. **38**(2), 539–560 (2014)
29. Huang, C.L., Chung, C.K., Hui, N.: The development of the Chinese linguistic inquiry and word count dictionary. Chinese J. Psychol. **4**(2), 185–201 (2012). (in Chinese)
30. Peng, C.H., Yin, D., Zhang, H.: More than words in medical question-and-answer sites: a content-context congruence perspective. Inf. Syst. Res. **31**(3), 913–928 (2020)
31. Zhang, X., Wu, P., Cai, J.: A contrastive study of Chinese text segmentation tools in marketing notification texts. J. Phys. Conf. Ser. IOP Publ. **1302**(2), 022010 (2019)
32. Hou, J.R., Zhang, J.J., Zhang, K.P.: Can title images predict the emotions and the performance of crowdfunding projects?. In: Proceedings of the 52nd annual Hawaii International Conference on System Sciences, pp. 4439–4448 (2019)
33. Xue, Y.G.: The research on the communication effect of Qingsongchou. Inner Mongolia Normal University, 61 (2020). (in Chinese)

Does Early-Bird Policy Matter for Equity Crowdfunding Performance: The Moderation Roles of Entrepreneur Gender and Project Types

Yangsheng Zhang, Zhimei Wen, and Yi Wu[✉]

Tianjin University, Tianjin, China
yiwu@tju.edu.cn

Abstract. In recent years, equity-based crowdfunding (EBC) has become one of the leading ways of enterprise fundraising. However, the drivers of equity-based crowdfunding success are still poorly understood. Based on the existing literature, we study the effect of early-bird policy (EBP), which allows professional investors to contribute to a project before it is open, on crowdfunding performance of the project. we introduce the concepts of crowdfunding and prefunding. Using archival data on *Wefunder* platform, we adopt multiple analysis technologies to explore the relationship between the early-bird policy, entrepreneurial gender, product type and the performance of EBC projects respectively. We find that EBP has a significant negative impact on the crowdfunding performance of enterprises. Moreover, the negative effect of EBP on crowdfunding performance is exacerbated when the main founders are female or the enterprise has tangible products.

Keywords: Equity-based crowdfunding · early-bird policy · entrepreneur gender · product type

1 Introduction

Equity-based crowdfunding (EBC) is a form of internet fundraising in which entrepreneurs sell shares in their start-ups to obtain funding [1]. It has become one of the most popular ways for start-ups to raise funds.

At present, the researches on EBC mainly concentrate on the fundraising and regulatory issues, particularly factors that influence the fundraising performance, including information about the entrepreneurs (e.g., gender, race, age) and project characteristics at the time of project initiation (e.g., target of fundraising, business sector, product description), as well as information that changes over time in project life cycle, such as project updates and investor opinion. Existing studies have explained the successful factors from multiple perspectives, but there are still some important factors remain to be explored, particularly the behavior of entrepreneurs and the quality signals through information disclosure.

In economic markets, operators often sell products at a discount in order to promote them. In EBC, many platforms provide similar "discount" offers, such as the "early-bird policy"(EBP) on *Wefunder* platform.

Entrepreneurs give preferences to early investors, so investors can get the same shares at a lower cost, just as operators giving some deals and discounts to consumers. Entrepreneurs hope to attract investors by discounts, but are they effective? No studies have answered this question yet. Therefore, in order to better understand the factors influencing EBC, we propose the following research questions: (1) Does EBP affect the outcome of EBC project? (2) Under what conditions does EBP amplify the impact on project performance? We use data from the *Wefunder* platform to explore the relationship between EBP, the gender of crucial entrepreneurs, product types and the performance of EBC.

Our study enriches the literature of EBC and refines the theoretical model of EBC. We examine the impact of the preferential strategies adopted by entrepreneurs on fundraising performance. In addition, we discuss the mechanisms underlying the impact of EBP on EBC performance.

2 Literature Review and Theoretical Backgrounds

2.1 Previous Studies on Antecedents of Crowdfunding Performance

The past studies have explored the factors that influence fundraising performance, such as project description, project updates and the function of pre-funding.

In terms of project descriptions, studies have found that factors such as detailed financial information, videos, artwork, project descriptions and the third-party endorsements can influence the efficiency of crowdfunding [2]. Detailed financial information is a positive signal that can effectively contribute to the success of an EBC project [2]. Besides, the enterprise valuation, detailed enterprise description, the initial investment amount of crowdfunding, and the reputation of entrepreneurs will also significantly affect the EBC projects performance [3]. In addition, some researchers have found that businesses are more likely to receive funding when they have a physical product (as opposed to a virtual product or service) [4].

From the gender perspective, female entrepreneurs are more likely to succeed in the crowdfunding market than male entrepreneurs [5]. Due to the high uncertainty and information asymmetry of crowdfunding, small investors trust female entrepreneurs more [6]. In addition, the number of founder teams, entrepreneurial experience, age, educational background and other characteristics have a significant impact on EBC project performance [7].

In addition to the initial characteristics of a start-up, the dynamic characteristics can influence the performance of an EBC project as well. The update frequency of project progress plays an important role in crowdfunding, which can provide more detailed information about the project, revealing quality signals [8] and alleviating information asymmetry and attract investors [7]. Interactive information disclosure is also significant in the fundraising process, such as allowing investors to ask questions and post comments [9]. In addition, more comments are beneficial to project performance, as investors usually choose to invest the projects with more comments [9]. Investors can also positively influence corporate finance by positively evaluating and sharing project information [10].

2.2   Early-Bird Investors

Crowdfunding platforms have designed various strategies to promote information dis-closure. In traditional e-commerce markets, early-bird pricing is used to offer discounted prices for products, and studies have shown that appropriate early-bird pricing can typi-cally increase fundraising performance [11]. Meanwhile, existing researches have shown that choosing to pre-fund prior to fundraising can significantly increase the likelihood of fundraising success [12]. Some scholars have found that prefunding information attracts funding from regular investors firstly, followed by lottery investors [2]. What's more, the initial days of a project are critical to the "success-breeds-success" process, which helps the campaign succeed in reaching its funding goals [13].

Apart from the above factors, the herd effect among investors will also have an impact on EBC project performance. There are generally two principal types of investors: investors with investment experience or expertise and uninformed investors. Investors will take into account of the information provided by entrepreneurs and the behaviors and comments of other investors [10]. Experts investment in the early stages of a project provides a reliable quality signal to later investors, especially those with less experience [14]. Pre-funding extends the exposure of the project, which may attract a large number of informed investors, then the number of informed investors will have an impact on the uninformed investors, contributing to the success of EBC projects [2].

3   Hypothesis Development

3.1   The Influence of EBP

According to the researches, the incentives with rewards has a significant negative impact on investors' willingness from the perspective of external motivation [15]. EBC investors do not pay attention to additional products or services, and the positive effect of reward incentives on investment willingness has not been proved [16]. Due to the high risks in the crowdfunding investments, investors have high expectations of returns on their investments. The relatively low "early-bird" discounts do not attract investors' interest. On the contrary, investors may doubt the quality of the project, as good projects never need to be sold at a discount. Hence, we propose the first hypothesis:

Hypothesis 1 (H1): In EBC, fundraising projects with EBP will have lower performance than those without EBP.

3.2   The Moderating Effect of Entrepreneur Gender

EBC has high uncertainty and information asymmetry, so trust is extremely important in it. Trust motivation has a significant positive effect on investment intention. According to traditional gender stereotype theory, women are considered more trustworthy than men [6]. In EBC, female entrepreneurs are more likely to gain funds from investors [17]. EBC projects launched by female entrepreneurs have higher funding performance than those launched by male entrepreneurs. Meanwhile, investors of EBC prefer more information [15] and always use information from different sources to make investment decisions [18]. Therefore, potential investors will consider both the EBP and entrepreneur gender information to evaluate EBC projects. Specifically, women entrepreneurs show that these EBC projects are reliable, while the EBP may have exactly the opposite effect. However, projects with both women entrepreneurs and EBP will make investors more confused about the reliability of the quality of the enterprise. Therefore, we propose the second hypothesis:

Hypothesis 2 (H2): Comparing to male entrepreneurs, the negative influence of EBP on crowdfunding performance becomes more prominent for female entrepreneurs.

3.3   The Moderating Effect of Product Type

Existing literature indicates that the product status of an enterprise can provides a comprehensive measure of technical and financial risk [19]. For investors, tangible products provided by enterprises are more trustworthy than intangible services. The easier the product is to understand, the more successful the crowdfunding project will be. Therefore, tangible product is a signal of an enterprise's quality and reliability, and the projects with tangible products are more likely to raise funds successfully. Similar to the entrepreneur gender, investors will consider both the EBP and enterprise's product information to evaluate the overall profile of EBC projects. EBP will increase investors' doubts about the quality of the fundraising project when the enterprise has tangible products. Thus, we propose the following hypothesis:

Hypothesis 3 (H3): Comparing to projects of intangible products, the negative influence of EBP on crowdfunding performance becomes more prominent for projects of tangible products.

4   Empirical Setting

4.1   Data Source

The research sample for our study was drawn from the *Wefunder* platform *(*www.wef under.com*)*, a leading equity crowdfunding platform in the United States, which provides potential investors with detailed information of each fundraising project. We use the data of 427 equity-based crowdfunding projects published on the platform from August 2018 to February 2021. After eliminating 147 EBC projects with incomplete data, we finally obtained a sample containing 2,592 data from 280 enterprises.

4.2   Variables and Summary Statistics

Among 280 EBC enterprises, 154 of them have an "early-bird policy". 81.4% of enterprises were founded by female entrepreneurs, which validates the existence of gender discrimination in EBC [18]. 14.3% of enterprises already have mature and tangible products. The fundraising goals of EBC for these start-ups vary greatly, with the highest requirement being $834,000 and the lowest being $10,000, and with most falling between $10,000 and $200,000. The fundraising goals of EBC projects are relatively low, only 13.5% projects with a target of more than $200,000. Finally, 65.7% of enterprises successfully completed fundraising, but only 29% of companies with successful fundraising have early-bird policies, indicating that EBP is not a good quality signal statistically. The results are shown in Table 1. Table 2 lists all the dependent variables and independent variables used for model analysis and describes them in detail.

Table 1. Statistical table of number of enterprises.

	sample size	proportion
Total number of enterprises	280	100%
Enterprises with "early-bird policy"	154	55.0%
Enterprises with female founders	228	81.4%
Enterprises with tangible products	40	14.3%
Enterprises that have successfully raised funds	184	65.7%
—with "early-bird policy"	54	29.3%
—with female entrepreneurs	149	81.0%

4.3 Empirical Model

Based on the panel data of 280 enterprises on the *Wefunder* platform from 2018 to 2021, we construct fixed-effect models to investigate the relationship between EBP and EBC performance.

Most of the companies on the *Wefunder* platform are high-tech companies. 71.2% enterprises have the technology label in our data. To reduce unobservable heterogeneity at the industry level, we fixed the industry effects. In order to solve the problem of missing variables that do not vary with items but change with time, we fixed the time effects as well.

In order to eliminate heteroscedasticity and ensure data stability, we take logarithms for all non-dummy variables. According to hypothesis 1 (H1), in the EBC market, fundraising projects with EBP has lower performance than thosewithout EBP. We use the fixed-effect model (1) to test H1:

$$\ln \text{Amount}_{i,t} = \alpha_0 + \alpha_1 Early\_bird_{i,t} + \sum_j \beta_j \ln \text{Controls}_{i,t} + \delta \text{Category}_i$$
$$+\theta \text{Year}_t + \varepsilon_{i,t} \tag{1}$$

i is the enterprise, t is the period, $\text{Amount}_{i,t}$ refers to the total amount of funds raised by enterprise i in period t, $Early\_bird_{i,t}$ represents the "early-bird policy" of enterprise i in period t, $\text{Controls}_{i,t}$ represents the control variable of enterprise i in period t, Including entrepreneur gender, enterprise valuation and other 15 control variables. α_0 variable represents the population mean intercept term, α_1 and β_j represent the parameters to be estimated, and the last $\varepsilon_{i,t}$ represents the random disturbance term. Category_i and Year_t represent the industry effect and time effect of the enterprise respectively, and the above two effects are controlled in the regression analysis.

Table 2. Variable definition and summary statistics.

variable	definition	quantity	mean value	standard deviation	min	max
Amount	Total amount of project funds raised through equity-based crowdfunding projects. Take the logarithm of the regression	2,592	288,965	1.26E + 06	5,000	3.41E + 07
Investor	The total number of investors	2,592	328.6	1,729	1	26,095
Success	Dummy variable: 1 when the total amount of funds raised by the project is greater than the fundraising target; otherwise, 0	2,592	0.61	0.49	0	1
Early-Bird	Dummy variable of "early-bird policy". If the project has "early-bird policy", the value is 1; otherwise, it is 0	2,592	0.54	0.5	0	1
Founder Gender	Gender dummy variable, the initiator is female and the value is 1, otherwise it is 0	2,592	0.83	0.38	0	1

(*continued*)

Table 2. (*continued*)

variable	definition	quantity	mean value	standard deviation	min	max
Product	Dummy variable of the project product, 1 if the project has products, otherwise 0	2,592	0.02	0.12	0	1
QA Num	Number of item questions, logarithm for regression	2,592	33.45	95.44	0	849
Inote Num	The quantity of investor comments, logarithm for regression	2,592	206.5	899.8	0	9,076
Update Num	Item update quantity, logarithm is taken when regression	2,592	9.34	15.78	0	115
Have Video	Item description Video virtual variable. The value is 1 if the item description video exists. Otherwise, it is 0	2,592	0.33	0.47	0	1
Duration	Project fundraising time (in days), take logarithm when regression	2,592	137	59.98	24	450
Expert Num	The number of experts on the project	2,592	0.47	0.81	0	4
Invest Experience	The investment experience of the fundraiser	2,592	0.51	1.15	0	13

(*continued*)

Table 2. (continued)

variable	definition	quantity	mean value	standard deviation	min	max
Funding Target	Fundraising goal, take logarithm when regression	2,592	101,300	102,804	10,000	834,000
News Num	The amount of news coverage of the project	2,592	6.78	8.97	0	47
Introduction	The description of the project, measured by the length of the text of the introduction, logarithm is taken when regression	2,592	73,005	30,595	17,337	201,773
Team Num	Number of founder team members	2,592	5.72	3.86	1	23
Third Social	Number of links to social platforms	2,592	2.14	1.32	0	5
Valuation	The value of the project, logarithm for regression	2,592	1.08E + 07	2.57E + 07	0	2.66E + 08

To test the moderating effects of entrepreneur gender and firm products on "early-bird" provisions, we use multivariate fixed effect models 2, 3 and 4 for estimation.

$$\ln \text{Amount}_{i,t} = \alpha_0 + \alpha_1 \text{Early\_bird}_{i,t} + \alpha_2 \text{Early\_bird}_{i,t} * \text{Founder\_gender}_i + \sum_j \beta_j \ln \text{Controls}_{i,t} + \delta \text{Category}_i + \theta \text{Year}_t + \varepsilon_{i,t} \quad (2)$$

$$\ln \text{Amount}_{i,t} = \alpha_0 + \alpha_1 \text{Early\_bird}_{i,t} + \alpha_2 \text{Early\_bird}_{i,t} * \text{Product}_{i,t} + \sum_j \beta_j \ln \text{Controls}_{i,t} + \delta \text{Category}_i + \theta \text{Year}_t + \varepsilon_{i,t} \quad (3)$$

$$\ln \text{Amount}_{i,t} = \alpha_0 + \alpha_1 \text{Early\_bird}_{i,t} + \alpha_2 \text{Early\_bird}_{i,t} * \text{Founder\_gender}_i + \alpha_3 \text{Early\_bird}_{i,t} * \text{Product}_{i,t} + \sum_j \beta_j \ln \text{Controls}_{i,t} + \delta \text{Category}_i + \theta \text{Year}_t + \varepsilon_{i,t} \quad (4)$$

Founder_gender$_i$ is the gender of the originator of enterprise i, and Product$_{i,t}$ is the product situation of enterprise i at period t.

5 Empirical Results

5.1 Correlation Analysis

We calculated the correlation coefficients of explained variables, explanatory variables and control variables. The analysis results show that the correlation between variables is low. We also performed variance inflation factor (VIF) analysis, which showed an average VIF of 1.74 and a maximum VIF of 3.26, which is below the threshold of 5. This suggests that multicollinearity is not a serious problem in our estimation.

5.2 Empirical Result

Table 3 reports the main empirical results of our study. The corresponding hypotheses were tested respectively from Model 1 to Model 3 of fixed effects, and Model 4 was a full model containing all variables. According to the empirical results of the four models, the coefficient of variable EBP is negative and significant. In all models, "early-bird" policy of the coefficient is negative and significant at 1% level ($\beta = 0.486$, $p < 0.01$), supporting H1. The results showed that the average amount of EBC projects with an EBP was 18.6% lower than those without such a policy.

According to the empirical results of Model 2 and Model 4, the coefficients of EBP and gender_interact of entrepreneurs are negative and significantly correlated. In model 4, the coefficient of gender_interact is negative and significant at the 1% level ($\beta = -0.705$, $p < 0.01$), supporting H2. The results show that for EBC projects with EBP, the average amount of fundraising projects founded by female entrepreneurs is 70.5% lower than those founded by men. At the same time, we find that the coefficient between the entrepreneur gender and the fundraising performance is positive and significant at 10%, which is consistent with the conclusion that investors are more willing to fund women entrepreneurs in the EBC market.

In Model 3 and Model 4, the coefficients of EBP and product_interact are negative and significantly correlated. In model 4, the coefficient of product_interact is negative and significant at the 1% level ($\beta = -2.412$, $p < 0.01$), supporting H3. The results show that for EBC projects with EBP, the fundraising amount of projects with tangible products is lower than that of projects without products.

In Model 1 to Model 4, the coefficients of entrepreneur gender are positive and significant at the level of 10%, which verifies that enterprises created by female entrepreneurs are more attractive to potential investors than those created by male entrepreneurs. The results of models 1 to 4 show that the coefficients of enterprise products are all positive and significant at 1% level, indicating that corporate products have a positive impact on EBC performance, and enterprise product is a reliable signal of enterprise quality.

Interestingly, we find that the coefficient of the project update is negative and significant at the level of 5%, indicating that the dynamic update of the project has a negative effect on the fundraising performance. One possible explanation is that different information has different value and different influences on investors. Non-informative messages may be perceived as' desperate 'or' obnoxious' if they are posted only to attract attention. This negative perception can dampen the enthusiasm from potential investors. Updates such as promotional activities and business models will not have any positive impact on corporate fundraising.

5.3 Robustness Checks

Firstly, we test robustness by changing the explained variable. In EBC, the number of investors is often used as the explained variable to measure the project performance. Therefore, we use all_investor as an alternative dependent variable to test the robustness of the results. As the number of investors is a positive integer, we use Possion regression model to re-estimate the experimental model. Table 4 reports the regression results. It is found that EBP has a significant negative impact on the number of investors, and female entrepreneurs and tangible products reinforce the negative impact of EBP on the number of investors. This indicates that EBP has negative effects on EBC, indicating that the empirical results are robust.

5.4 Analysis of Endogeneity

In order to reduce the influence of omitted variables and endogenous causality relationship among variables, the average value of EBP of other enterprises in the same industry in the same year (here in after referred to as the industry mean value) is selected as the instrumental variable for the 2SLS regression model. The logic of the choice of instrumental variables is as follows: Firstly, the EBP of the enterprise's characteristics will be affected by the mean or sum characteristics of other items, satisfying the relevant conditions of the instrumental variables. Secondly, features such as the mean value of other items do not directly affect the EBP, satisfying the exogeneity condition of the instrumental variables.

Table 5 shows the regression results for instrumental variables. Column (1) is the result of single-stage regression, to test the correlation between the industrial mean and EBP. The results show that the industry mean value of the instrumental variables is significant at the 1% level and the statistical value of F is greater than 10 (see Table 6.), indicating that there is no "weak instrumental variable".

Table 3. Main regression results.

Variable	Model 1	Model 2	Model 3	Model 4
	FE	FE	FE	FE
	ln_amount	ln_amount	ln_amount	ln_amount
early_bird	$-0.502^{***}(-4.88)$	$-0.512^{***}(-5.04)$	$-0.475^{***}(-4.64)$	$-0.486^{***}(-4.79)$
gender_interact		$-0.733^{***}(-3.00)$		$-0.705^{***}(-2.91)$
product_interact			$-2.537^{***}(-2.62)$	$-2.412^{**}(-2.51)$
founder_gender	$0.234^{*}(1.85)$	$0.239^{*}(1.91)$	$0.227^{*}(1.81)$	$0.232^{*}(1.87)$
product	$1.227^{***}(2.63)$	$1.178^{**}(2.56)$	$2.077^{***}(3.68)$	$1.988^{***}(3.55)$
ln_qa	$-0.0326(-1.42)$	$-0.0325(-1.43)$	$-0.0340(-1.49)$	$-0.0339(-1.49)$
ln_inote	$0.294^{***}(14.63)$	$0.292^{***}(14.59)$	$0.295^{***}(14.72)$	$0.293^{***}(14.67)$
ln_update	$-0.0467^{**}(-2.36)$	$-0.0463^{**}(-2.34)$	$-0.0479^{**}(-2.42)$	$-0.0475^{**}(-2.40)$
have_video	$0.156(0.78)$	$0.125(0.63)$	$0.122(0.61)$	$0.0937(0.48)$
ln_duration	$-0.452^{***}(-2.88)$	$-0.458^{***}(-2.95)$	$-0.448^{***}(-2.88)$	$-0.455^{***}(-2.95)$
expert_num	$-0.0471(-0.40)$	$-0.0190(-0.16)$	$-0.0265(-0.23)$	$-0.000437(-0.00)$
ln_target	$0.561^{***}(7.77)$	$0.553^{***}(7.74)$	$0.579^{***}(8.04)$	$0.570^{***}(8.00)$
news_num	$0.00961(1.27)$	$0.0108(1.44)$	$0.00856(1.14)$	$0.00974(1.31)$
ln_introduction	$0.464^{***}(3.61)$	$0.427^{***}(3.35)$	$0.463^{***}(3.63)$	$0.427^{***}(3.37)$
team_num	$0.0315^{**}(2.18)$	$0.0338^{**}(2.37)$	$0.0347^{**}(2.42)$	$0.0368^{***}(2.59)$
third_social	$0.0145(0.35)$	$0.0176(0.43)$	$0.0165(0.40)$	$0.0193(0.47)$
ln_valuation	$0.0270^{***}(2.93)$	$0.0290^{***}(3.17)$	$0.0265^{***}(2.90)$	$0.0284^{***}(3.14)$
invest experience	$0.0222(0.58)$	$0.0210(0.55)$	$0.0221(0.58)$	$0.0209(0.56)$
_cons	$-0.0193(-0.01)$	$0.469(0.26)$	$-0.231(-0.13)$	$0.249(0.14)$
Time effect	Yes	Yes	Yes	Yes
Industry effect	Yes	Yes	Yes	Yes
N	2,592	2,592	2,592	2,592
R-sq	0.574	0.582	0.585	0.592

t statistics in parentheses $^{*}p < 0.1$, $^{**}p < 0.05$, $^{***}p < 0.01$.

Table 4. Main regression results when the number of investors is the explained variable

Variable	Model 1	Model 2	Model 3	Model 4
	Poisson	Poisson	Poisson	Poisson
	all_investor	all_investor	all_investor	all_investor
early-bird	$-0.140^{***}(-41.1)$	$-0.128^{***}(-37.5)$	$-0.133^{***}(-38.8)$	$-0.122^{***}(-35.5)$
gender_interact		$-0.556^{***}(-64.3)$		$-0.551^{***}(-63.8)$
product_interact			$-0.395^{***}(-15.2)$	$-0.344^{***}(-13.2)$
founder_gender	$-0.066^{***}(-14.6)$	$-0.133^{***}(-29.1)$	$-0.067^{***}(-14.7)$	$-0.133^{***}(-29.1)$
product	$0.254^{***}(27.58)$	$0.234^{***}(25.44)$	$0.315^{***}(31.91)$	$0.286^{***}(29.02)$
ln_qa	$0.302^{***}(127.87)$	$0.292^{***}(123.79)$	$0.297^{***}(124.33)$	$0.287^{***}(120.80)$
ln_inote	$0.506^{***}(253.45)$	$0.499^{***}(251.02)$	$0.509^{***}(253.72)$	$0.501^{***}(251.10)$
ln_update	$-0.092^{***}(-55.3)$	$-0.083^{***}(-49.8)$	$-0.092^{***}(-55.5)$	$-0.083^{***}(-50.0)$
have_video	$-0.249^{***}(-40.6)$	$-0.289^{***}(-46.5)$	$-0.254^{***}(-41.4)$	$-0.294^{***}(-47.1)$
ln_duration	$0.712^{***}(132.31)$	$0.791^{***}(142.96)$	$0.718^{***}(132.98)$	$0.795^{***}(143.43)$
expert_num	$-0.0106^{***}(-3.0)$	$0.0257^{***}(7.1)$	$-0.00729^{**}(-2.1)$	$0.0282^{***}(7.8)$
ln_target	$0.289^{***}(119.09)$	$0.286^{***}(117.46)$	$0.293^{***}(120.19)$	$0.289^{***}(118.34)$
news_num	$-0.015^{***}(-64.9)$	$-0.013^{***}(-54.8)$	$-0.015^{***}(-65.3)$	$-0.013^{***}(-55.2)$
ln_introduction	$0.375^{***}(84.85)$	$0.312^{***}(69.11)$	$0.370^{***}(83.50)$	$0.308^{***}(68.15)$
team_num	$0.0245^{***}(60.49)$	$0.0267^{***}(64.94)$	$0.0253^{***}(62.06)$	$0.0274^{***}(66.18)$
third_social	$0.0427^{***}(29.51)$	$0.0512^{***}(35.02)$	$0.0431^{***}(29.79)$	$0.0516^{***}(35.28)$
ln_valuation	$0.0000847(0.21)$	$0.00214^{***}(5.36)$	$0.000473(1.18)$	$0.00246^{***}(6.15)$
invest experience	$0.0764^{***}(53.48)$	$0.0501^{***}(33.55)$	$0.0757^{***}(53.03)$	$0.0497^{***}(33.33)$
_cons	$-8.36^{***}(-147.9)$	$-7.96^{***}(-139.5)$	$-8.38^{***}(-148.4)$	$-7.99^{***}(-139.9)$
Time effect	Yes	Yes	Yes	Yes
Industry effect	Yes	Yes	Yes	Yes
N	2,432	2,432	2,432	2,432
R-sq	0.907	0.909	0.907	0.909

t statistics in parentheses *p < 0.1, **p < 0.05, ***p < 0.0

Table 5. Regression results of instrumental variables

	(1)	(2)
	early_bird	ln_amount
Industry average	-2.008^{***}	
	(-1.33)	
early_bird		-0.244^{***}
		(-6.14)
Variable of control	Yes	Yes
Time effect	Yes	No
Industry effect	Yes	No
N	2,592	2,592
R-sq	0.899	0.574

t statistics in parentheses $*p < 0.1$, $**p < 0.05$, $***p < 0.01$

Table 6. Correlation test of instrumental variable

Variable	R-sq	Adjusted R-sq	Partial R-sq	F(1,2575)	Prob > F
early-bird	0.8978	0.8971	0.8719	17,520.4000	0.0000

6 Conclusions

Taking the EBP as the entry point, we explore the relationship between EBP, entrepreneur gender, enterprise product, and EBC projects performance with data from the *Wefunder* platform.

Our study leads to the following conclusions: Firstly, EBP in equity-based crowdfunding will significantly negatively affect the fundraising performance, because EBP is regarded as a unreliable signal of the project. Secondly, the gender of entrepreneurs will mediate the relationship between EBP and fundraising performance. Thirdly, tangible product is a reliable quality signal. In equity crowdfunding, tangible product will affect the relationship between EBP and fundraising performance, tangible quality signals are influenced by both EBP and tangible products.

However, there may be other influencing variables for EBC performance we have not explored, such as corporate fundraising goal, fundraising period, number of founders, investor comments. And we haven't taken into account the differences across countries. We will improve the above issues in our follow-up study.

Acknowledgement. The authors appreciate the constructive comments and suggestions provided to us by the review team. The authors also wish to acknowledge the National Natural Science Foundation of China (72172103,72231004) for financial support. Yi Wu is the corresponding author of this work.

References

1. Ahlers, G.K.C., et al.: Signaling in equity crowdfunding. Entrepreneursh. Theory Pract. **39**(4), 955–980 (2015)
2. Wei, X., et al.: An empirical study of the dynamic and differential effects of prefunding. Product. Oper. Manag. **30**(5), 1331–1349 (2020)
3. Burtch, G., et al.: The role of provision points in online crowdfunding. J. Manag. Inf. Syst. **35**(1), 117–144 (2018)
4. Lukkarinen, A., et al.: Success drivers of online equity crowdfunding campaigns. Decis. Support Syst. **87**, 26–38 (2016)
5. Gafni, H., et al.: Gender dynamics in crowdfunding (Kickstarter): Evidence on entrepreneurs, backers, and taste-based discrimination. Rev. Financ. **25**(2), 235–274 (2021)
6. Johnson, M.A., Stevenson, R.M., Letwin, C.R.: A woman's place is in the… startup! Crowd-funder judgments, implicit bias, and the stereotype content model. J. Bus. Ventur. **33**(6), 813–831 (2018). https://doi.org/10.1016/j.jbusvent.2018.04.003
7. Block, J., et al.: Which updates during an equity crowdfunding campaign increase crowd participation. Small Bus. Econ. **50**(1), 3–27 (2017)
8. Liang, X., Hu, X., Jiang, J.: Research on the effects of information description on crowdfund-ing success within a sustainable economy—the perspective of information communication. Sustainability **12**(2), 650 (2020). https://doi.org/10.3390/su12020650
9. Miller, G., Skinner, D.: The evolving disclosure landscape: how changes in technology, the media, and capital markets are affecting disclosure. J. Acc. Res. **53** (2015)
10. Hornuf, L., Schwienbacher, A.: Market mechanisms and funding dynamics in equity crowdfunding. J. Corp. Financ. **50**, 556–574 (2018)
11. Chen, M., Liu, Z., Ma, C., Gong, X.: A distinctive early bird price in reward-based crowdfund-ing. Electron. Commer. Res. **21**(2), 347–370 (2019). https://doi.org/10.1007/s10660-019-093 56-5
12. Garimella, A., Fan, M., Kotha, S., You, W.: Launch on a high note: how prefunding affects crowdfunding outcomes. SSRN Electron. J. (2017). https://doi.org/10.2139/ssrn.3049768
13. Colombo, M.G., et al.: Internal social capital and the attraction of early contributions in crowdfunding. Entrepreneursh. Theory Pract. **39**(1), 75–100 (2015). https://doi.org/10.1111/etap.12118
14. Keongtae, K., Visawanathan, S.: The experts in the crowd: the role of experienced investors in a crowdfunding market. MIS Q. **43**(2), 347–372 (2019)
15. Anglin, A.H., et al.: The power of positivity? The influence of positive psychological capital language on crowdfunding performance. J. Bus. Ventur. **33**(4), 470–492 (2018)
16. Collins, L., Pierrakis, Y.: The venture crowd: crowdfunding equity investments into business (2012)
17. Chemin, M., de Laat, J.: Can warm glow alleviate credit market failures? Evidence from online peer-to-peer lenders. Econ. Dev. Cult. Change **61**(4), 825–858 (2013). https://doi.org/10.1086/670374
18. Shafi, K.: Investors' evaluation criteria in equity crowdfunding. Small Bus. Econ. **56**(1), 3–37 (2021). https://doi.org/10.1007/s11187-019-00227-9
19. Maxwell, A.L., et al.: Business angel early stage decision making. J. Bus. Ventur. **26**(2), 212–225 (2011)

Impact of Trial Feedback in Live Streaming e-Commerce: Evidence from Make-Up Products

Weijia You[1]([✉]), Kexuan An[1], Yujie Xie[2], Yutong Zhang[1], Guijie Song[1], Lulu Chen[1], and Jinmou Hu[1]

[1] Beijing Forestry University, Beijing 100083, China
Wjyou@Bjfu.Edu.Cn
[2] Guangxi University, Guangxi 530004, China

Abstract. Live streaming e-commerce grows rapidly recently and changes people's shopping style. How to alleviate the information asymmetry which lowers the returns in live streaming e-commerce is still unresolved. Providing free samples and presenting feedback from free trials is suggested and tested. The survey data collected from college students verifies the hypotheses that the feedback from free trial has a positive effect on regular purchase intention but it has no impact on the impulse purchase intention. Further more, by dividing the perceived value into three dimensions, we demonstrated the mediation effect of perceived functional value between free trial feedback and regular purchase intention. Based on these findings, free trial mechanism in the live streaming e-commerce is highly recommended.

Keywords: live streaming e-commerce · free trial · feedback mechanism

1 Introduction

With the rapid development of Internet and the arrival of short video era, a new network culture which is called webcast rises. Live streaming e-commerce, as an e-commerce form using live broadcasting as a channel to achieve marketing purposes, is the product of the two-way integration of live broadcasting and e-commerce under the background of the digital era. In live streaming e-commerce, the real-time interaction between the webcast host and potential consumer greatly shortens the decision-making time of consumers and stimulates the generation of consumer demand.

From the research of Kempf [1] and Smith [2], it has been found that free trial can affect consumers' cognition, purchase intention and brand loyalty. However, in the scenario of live streaming e-commerce, whether trial feedback will stimulate consumers and affect their perceived value, and whether it impacts consumers' regular purchase intention and impulse consumption is worthy of in-depth exploration. Taking make-up products as an example, through the method of survey, this paper studies the relationship between trial product feedback, perceived value, and both regular and impulse purchase intention in the live broadcasting room, and puts forward suggestions on the free trial and feedback mechanism in the live streaming e-commerce.

© The Author(s), under exclusive license to Springer Nature Switzerland AG 2023
Y. Tu and M. Chi (Eds.): WHICEB 2023, LNBIP 481, pp. 264–272, 2023.
https://doi.org/10.1007/978-3-031-32302-7_23

2   Literature Review

2.1   Consumer Behavior in Live Streaming e-Commerce

The advantage of live shopping over traditional network is reflected in realized direct interactive communication between sellers and buyers and vivid display of products [3]. Webcast shopping breaks through the single shopping mode of traditional online shopping by browsing shopping websites or mobile shopping platforms, and has a certain positive impact on consumers' impulsive buying behavior and purposeful buying behavior. In some cases, it induces consumers to have unplanned shopping behavior due to unexpected discount. In other cases, the live broadcast promotes consumers to make planned shopping, which is beneficial to businesses' competition for similar products in the same industry.

2.2   Impulse Consumption

Until now, there is no consistent definition of impulse buying. Clove [4] believes that impulsive consumption is the behavior that consumers make purchase due to the external influence at that time point in a shopping scenario, that is, impulsive purchase is equal to unplanned purchase, but not all unplanned purchases are without the rational thinking of consumers. Therefore, Stern believes that there are many factors affecting impulsive purchase, such as personality, time constraints, economic constraints and cultural background [5]. Later, Muruganantham and Bhakat found that the most important factors are situational factors and personal characteristics [6], which are the internal factors from consumers themselves and the external factors from environment in which purchase behavior occurs. Only by distinguishing the factors of consumers themselves and classifying consumers, can we find the role of shopping scenario on consumers' impulsive consumption.

2.3   Feedback from Free Trial

Online feedback behavior refers to the behavior that consumers evaluate the goods or services provided by merchants, describe the consumption process or express their consumption feelings on the online platform after completing the transaction. As a form of consumer feedback, consumer evaluation has become a common channel for traditional online shopping platforms to provide feedback. Several research has confirmed that consumer evaluation has a significant positive impact on consumers' decision-making, and is one of the important reference for consumers' purchase behavior [7–9]. In the live streaming e-commerce, there is no comment from consumer yet. As the only source of product information, the webcast host can not meet the needs of all consumers. For cosmetics and other products with different personal use, the problem of insufficient information is more prominent.

2.4   Perceived Value

The research on perceived value mainly focuses on the concept of perceived value and related theory. Kotler's transition value theory believes that customers' perceived value is composed of their cost and expected income when transactions occur [10]. Woodruff's hierarchy theory believes that customers' perceived value is composed of product attributes, effectiveness and use results [11]. It can be found that the product price, attribute and product expectation considered by customers before they get the product are an important part of the perceived value, and the perceived value of this part determines whether customers buy or not. In addition to perceived value, perceived risk is also an important factor for customers to decide whether to take the transactions. Derbaix [12] believes that perceived risk refers to a feeling of uncertainty caused by consumers' inability to predict the quality of their purchase results and the resulting consequences. In other words, when consumers understand the product process, they are not sure whether the product can meet their expectations, so they hesitate to buy.

3 Empirical Study

3.1 Research Hypotheses

It has been suggested that, due to the individual's emotional or cognitive response stimulated by external factors, consumers will behave with tendency or avoidance [13]. Chang et al. also argued that the cognitive response caused by the stimulation of online shopping environment includes perceived trust and perceived risk, and confirmed that it significantly affects purchase intention [14]. Therefore, in this study, we suggest that, the feedback from the free trial is a new stimulation which requires exploration. As product sampling is a very successful promotional marketing strategy in both offline market [15, 16] and online market [17, 18], we are motivated to verify its positive effect in live streaming e-commerce. Meanwhile, we divide the purchase in the live streaming e-commerce into two categories, i.e., regular purchase and impulse purchase, which are quite different shopping style. For the consumers who are making purchase decision after carefully study on the function and price of the product, feedback from free trial provides another piece of information besides the webcast host, and it will help to mitigate the problem of information asymmetry in live streaming e-commerce, and positively affects their purchase intention. Therefore, we propose the first hypothesis:

H1: Free trial feedback positively affects the regular purchases intention.

However, there are another group of consumers making purchase decision without careful consideration about the product but determined by emotional attraction [19, 20]. For these impulse purchase maker, the extra information provided by free trial feedback does not contribute to his/her decision procedure. Therefore, we propose our second hypothesis:

H2: Free trial feedback has no impact on the impulse purchases intention.

In order to better understand the mechanism behind the free trial feedback and better live streaming e-commerce, we adopt the Elaboration Likelihood Model of Persuasion from psychology to explain the effect from the central routes. It is argued that both central routes and peripheral cues are influential when processing information but act differently in terms of how much information recipients put cognitive effort into or how much they rely on the credibility of the information provider [21, 22]. We argue that for regular buyers, the central route dominates the decision process, and feedback from free trial helps to increase the perceived value of the product, and then it leads to higher purchase intention. Therefore, we propose our third hypothesis as follows. Further more, following Sweeney & Soutar's work [23], we divide the perceived value into three dimensions, which are functional value, experience value and perceived risk. And we suggest that all of these three values play as a mediator between free trial feedback and increased purchase intention.

H3: Perceived value has a mediating effect on the impact of free trial feedback on regular purchase
H3a: Perceived functional value has a mediating effect on the impact of free trial feedback on regular purchase
H3b: Perceived experience value has a mediating effect on the impact of free trial feedback on regular purchase
H3c: Perceived risk has a mediating effect on the impact of free trial feedback on regular purchase

Illustrated by Fig. 1, this paper tries to construct a model which added the feedback which is from the free trial to the live broadcast environment, so as to trigger consumers' perceived value. It studies the impact of the trial feedback mechanism on consumers' purchase intention and impulsive consumption.

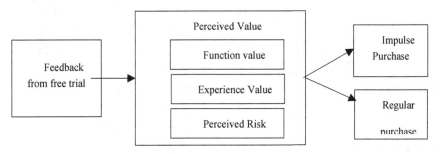

Fig. 1. Conceptual model

3.2 Questionnaire Design and Distribution

All the measures in this study are adopted from existing studies. According to the research of Sweeney & Soutar [23], Bansal & Voyer [24] and Wang et al. [25], perceived value is divided into three aspects: functional value, experience value and perceived risk, and the perceived usefulness of user feedback is measured. There are 11 items and a total of 18 questions. The questionnaire options of the survey are designed in the form of Likert five level scale. 5 represents full agreement and 1 represents complete disagreement. According to the purpose of this study, the respondents were divided into two groups, which are with and without free trial feedback. The questionnaire of the treatment group (with trial feedback) is composed of 18 items, while the questionnaire of the control group (without trial feedback) is short of 3 items related to the perceived usefulness of feedback. The respondents answered the questionnaire according to the live broadcast they watched. We record a live broadcast from a real make-up webcast, and cut out the free trial feedback section from it for the control group to watch.

4   Result

4.1   Descriptive Statistics

In order to remove the interference of other confounding factors, we divided consumers equally according to their demographic information before the survey. The characteristics of treatment and control group is shown in the Table 1.

Table 1. Basic information of survey

	item	Treatment Group		Control Group	
		number	percentage	number	percentage
Gender	Male	9	18.75%	9	19.57%
	female	39	81.25%	37	80.43%
Grade	Grade 1	11	22.92%	10	21.74%
	Grade 2	10	20.83%	11	23.91%
	Grade 3	11	22.92%	10	21.74%
	Grade 4	11	22.92%	10	21.74%
	Post graduate	5	10.42%	5	10.87%
Impulse Purchase	yes	11	22.92%	11	23.91%
	fair	22	45.83%	22	47.83%
	no	15	31.25%	13	28.26%
Review preference	yes	37	77.08%	36	78.26%
	fair	9	18.75%	8	17.39%
	no	2	4.17%	2	4.35%
Trust	Yes	15	31.25%	13	28.26%
	fair	31	64.58%	30	65.22%
	no	2	4.17%	3	6.52%

We conducted a non-parametric independent sample test on impulse consumption, and the two tailed test values are greater than 0.05, indicating that there was no significant difference between these two groups of consumers.

4.2   Reliability and Validity Analysis

Reliability Analysis. Reliability analysis is a test to judge whether the data collected by the questionnaire is reliable. In this study, we adopt the α reliability coefficient test. The

Table 2. Loading factors of items

	Regular Purchase	Impulse Purchase	Functional Value	Experience Value	Perceived Risk
I would purchase this product which I understand whose function well during webcast	0.955				
I would recommend this product to friends for I know it very well	0.95				
I would make impulse purchase during webcast		0.847			
I don't think I well understand the product I bought during webcast		0.827			
The purchase during webcast is not planned		0.82			
I think the product I buy during webcast is functional to me			0.851		
I think the quality of the product I buy during webcast is high			0.901		
I think the product is of high quality			0.853		
I think the experience of shopping during webcast is good to me				0.846	
I'm satisfied with the experience in webcast				0.904	
I find a lot of fun in webcast				0.886	
I think it is safe to make purchase in webcast					0.879
I don't think there's personal info leak in webcast					0.89

α coefficient for purchase intention, impulse consumption, experience value, product value and the perceived risk are 0.898, 0.791, 0.853, 0.836, and 0.723 respectively. The coefficients of all dimensions are greater than 0.7, indicating that the reliability of the data from the questionnaire is high.

Validity Analysis. Validity refers to the degree to which the scale measures the objective correctly. As we are adopting the scale from existing research, only structural validity is tested. The factor load value is recommended to be above 0.7. From Table, it can be seen that load coefficients in the above table are greater than 0.7, indicating that the problem items are explained by potential variables to a high degree and have good reliability. At the same time, the correspondence between problem items and indicators (potential variables) is in line with expectations, indicating good validity (Table 2).

(2) Convergent validity refers to the consistency of internal variables in one dimension, usually measured by Cr value, Cronbach's α and AVE values. The CR value and Cronbach's α of all dimensions are greater than 0.7 and AVE values are greater than 0.5, indicating that the data have good convergence validity. The square root of AVE of each potential variable should be greater than the correlation coefficient between the potential variable and other potential variables. In this study, the minimum square root value of AVE is 0.831, which is greater than the maximum value of correlation coefficient between factors, which is 0.782, indicating that the research data has good discriminant validity.

4.3 Hypothesis Test

T-test of Two Groups of Subjects. First, we compare the regular purchase intention between these two groups of subjects. The average of treatment group is 3.6 while the control group is 2.93, and the F-value is 5.65 with p-value 0.0245. The difference is significant which indicates that H1 is supported. Then we compare the impulse purchase of these two groups and found the average is 3.46 and 3.93 for treatment and control group respectively but the difference is not significant (p-value = 0.22). It suggested that H2 is also supported.

Structural Equation Model Analysis. Further more, in order to test the mechanism behind the increase of regular purchase intention, we take the perceived value as the intermediary variable between the free trial feedback and purchase intention and impulse consumption. The estimates are shown in Table 3.

Table 3. Estimation of the path coefficient

Path	Coef	P-value	Significance
Trial feedback → Perceived Value	0.436	0.000	Significant
Trial feedback → Planned purchase	0.084	0.555	Insignificant
Trial feedback → Impulse purchase	−0.126	0.472	Insignificant
Perceived Value → Regular purchase	0.661	0.000	Significant
Perceived Value → Impulse purchase	0.183	0.490	Insignificant

It can be seen from Table 3 that the feedback of the free trial in the live webcast has a positive effect on the perceived value of consumers, and the perceived value of consumers further positively affects their purchase intention. The corresponding path coefficients are 0.436 and 0.661 respectively. However, the impact of perceived value on impulse consumption is not significant. It shows that H3 is supported.

Secondly, the perceived value is further divided into three dimensions, i.e., functional value, experience value and perceived risk. Then the estimates are shown in Table 4.

Table 4. Estimation of the path coefficient (full model)

Path	Coef	P-value	Significance
Trial feedback → Functional Value	0.441	0.000	Significant
Trial feedback → Experience Value	0.238	0.134	Insignificant
Trial feedback → Perceived Risk	0.427	0.002	Significant
Functional Value → Regular Purchase	0.861	0.000	Significant
Functional Value → Impulse purchase	0.173	0.498	Insignificant
Experience Value → Regular Purchase	0.113	0.420	Insignificant
Experience Value → Impulse purchase	0.131	0.632	Insignificant
Perceived Risk → Regular Purchase	−0.231	0.129	Insignificant
Perceived Risk → Impulse purchase	−0.151	0.656	Insignificant

According to Table 4, the free trial's feedback positively affects the product value and perceived risk, and the path coefficients are 0.441 and 0.427 respectively. The product value positively affects consumers' purchase intention, and the corresponding path coefficient is 0.861. Other paths are not verified. Therefore, only H3a is supported.

5 Conclusion

This paper focuses on the feedback mechanism of free trial, establishes a conceptual model, and tests the hypothesis that the feedback from free trials positively affects consumers' purchase intention through the intermediary variable of perceived product value. It provides some managerial implications for the live webcast host to increase the perceived product's functional quality. Providing free samples during the live webcast and collecting feedback from the free trials do help to reduce the information asymmetry and increase the purchase intention. However, the finding is limited to products in the industry of cosmetics. More research will be done to test the generalizabiilty of these findings.

Acknowledgement. This research was supported by Fundamental Research Funds for the Central Universities under Grant 2021SRY05 and Beijing Social Science Foundation under Grant 22GLB023.

References

1. Kempf, D.S., Smith, R.E.: Consumer processing of product trial and the influence of prior advertising: a structural modeling approach. J. Mark. Res. **35**(3), 325–338 (1998)

2. Smith, R.E., Swinyard, W.R.: Attitude-behavior consistency: the impact of product trial versus advertising. J. Mark. Res. **20**(20), 257–267 (1983)
3. Park, H.J., Lin, L.M.: The effects of match-ups on the consumer attitudes toward internet celebrities and their live streaming contents in the context of product endorsement. J. Retail. Consum. Serv. **52**, 101934 (2020)
4. Clover, V.T.: Relative importance of impulse-buying in retail stores. J. Mark. **15**(1), 66–70 (1950)
5. Stern, H.: The significance of impulse buying today. J. Mark. **26**(2), 59–62 (1962). https://doi.org/10.1177/002224296202600212
6. Muruganantham, G., Bhakat, R.S.: A review of impulse buying behavior. Int. J. Mark. Stud. **5**(3), 149–160 (2013)
7. Chevalier, J.A., Mayzlin, D.: The effect of word of mouth on sales: online book reviews. J. Mark. Res. **43**(3), 345–354 (2006)
8. Duan, W., Gu, B., Whinston, A.B.: Do online reviews matter? An empirical investigation of panel data. Decis. Support Syst. **45**(4), 1007–1016 (2008)
9. Chen, Y., Xie, J.: Online consumer review: Word-of-mouth as a new element of marketing communication mix. Manage. Sci. **54**(3), 477–491 (2008)
10. Kotler, P.T.: Principles of Marketing. 17th Edn. Pearson Publication, London (2017)
11. Woodruff, R.B.: Marketing in the 21st century customer value: the next source for competitive advantage. J. Acad. Mark. Sci. **25**(3), 256 (1997)
12. Derbaix, C.: Perceived risk and risk relievers: an empirical investigation. J. Econ. Psychol. **3**, 19–38 (1983)
13. Jacob.: Stimulus - organism - response reconsidered: an evolutionary step in modeling consumer behavior. J. Consum. Psychol. **12**(1), 51–57 (2002)
14. Chang, H.H., Su, W.C.: The impact of online store environment cues on purchase intention: trust and perceived risk as a mediator. Online Inf. Rev. **32**(6), 818–841 (2008)
15. Heiman, A., McWilliams, B., Shen, Z., Zilberman, D.: Learning and forgetting: modeling optimal product sampling over time. Manage. Sci. **47**(4), 532–546 (2001)
16. Bawa, K., Shoemaker, R.: The effects of free sample promotions on incremental brand sales. Mark. Sci. **23**(3), 345–363 (2004)
17. Lin, Z., Zhang, Y., Tan, Y.: An empirical study of free product sampling and rating bias. Inf. Syst. Res. **30**(1), 260–275 (2019)
18. Liu, Z., Lin, Z., Zhang, Y., Tan, Y.: The signaling effect of sampling size in physical goods sampling via online channels. Product. Oper. Manage. **31**, 529–546 (2021)
19. Beattys, E., Ferrell, M.E.: Impulse buying: modeling its precursors. J. Retail. **74**(2), 169–191 (1998)
20. Rook, D.W.: The buying impulse. J. Consum. Res. **14**(2), 189–199 (1987)
21. Bhattacherjee, S.: Influence processes for information technology acceptance: an elaboration likelihood model. MIS Q. **30**(4), 805 (2006). https://doi.org/10.2307/25148755
22. Petty, R.E., Cacioppo, J.T.: Communication and Persuasion: Central and Peripheral Routes to Attitude Change. Springer, New York (1986).https://doi.org/10.1007/978-1-4612-4964-1
23. Sweeney, J.C., Soutar, G.N.: Consumer perceived value: the development of a multiple item scale. J. Retail. **77**(2), 203–220 (2001)
24. Bansal, H.S., Voyer, P.A.: Word-of-mouth processes within a services purchase decision context. J. Serv. Res. **3**(2), 166–177 (2000)
25. Wang, D., Luo, X.R., Hua, Y., Benitez, J.: Big arena, small potatoes: a mixed-methods investigation of atmospheric cues in live-streaming e-commerce. Decis. Support Syst. **158**, 113801 (2022)

The Influencing Mechanism of Social Media Users' Group Emotion on the Evolution of Public Opinion: An Analysis of the Moderating Effect of Social Presence

Yong-qing Yang[1], Yun-cheng Xu[1], Zhan-gang Hao[2](✉), and Jian-yue Xu[1]

[1] School of Management Science and Engineering, Shandong Technology and Business University, Yantai, China
[2] School of Business Administration, Shandong Technology and Business University, Yantai, China
zghao2000@sina.com

Abstract. Online social speech contains rich emotional expressions, which promote the evolution of public opinion. To explore this influencing mechanism, this paper constructs a research model of users' group emotions affecting the evolution of public opinion based on emotional event theory and social telepresence theory. Firstly, we calculate group emotional value based on text analysis and users' social presence value through principal component analysis. Then, we construct a regression model to test the research hypothesis. Finally, the explanatory variables and regulatory variables are lag processed to test the robustness of the model. The results show that users' group emotional intensity and extreme emotion significantly positively impact public opinion evolution. The stronger the group emotion and the more extreme emotion, the higher the popularity of public opinion network and the richer the text information. The stronger the social presence of group users, the more significant the impact of emotional intensity on the evolution of public opinion. Social presence inhibits the promotion of extreme emotion in the evolution of public opinion. This study reveals the influencing mechanism of the effects of user emotion on public opinion evolution, expands the theories related to public opinion evolution, and provides new ideas and theoretical references for the in-depth study of "user emotion-online public opinion". In addition, it provides a corresponding theoretical basis, decision support, and management countermeasures for social media and public opinion supervision departments.

Keywords: Group emotion · Evolution of public opinion · Social presence · Mediating effect · Extreme emotion

1 Introduction

Social networking platforms have become one of the leading media for people to express their feelings express their views, and transmit information [1]. More and more users tend to seek emotional support on social media, resulting in public opinion becoming more and more difficult to control. Social public opinion is the sum of users' views, attitudes, and emotions on the same topic. Users' different views, opinions, and emotions on the topic are essential factors that promote the evolution of public opinion. Many users' user-generated content and information dissemination behaviors on specific topics drive the public social sentiment. In addition, users' group emotion plays a vital role in the evolution of public opinion. Online social media accelerates the spread of users' emotions and the evolution of public opinion. Social network discourses are rich in emotional expressions [2, 3]. They are mixed with facts, views, and opinions and express their emotion directly or implicitly to promote the in-depth development of public opinion jointly. Such as the "incident of the woman who gave birth to eight children in Feng County" and the "COVID-19 pandemic at Jilin Agricultural Science and Technology University". These public opinion cases have a terrible impact on people's livelihoods. Therefore, the role of users' group emotions in promoting the evolution of public opinion has gradually attracted the attention of scholars.

At present, research on the relationship between users' group emotion and public opinion evolution primarily focus on the perspective of specific public opinion events and discuss the development trend of users' group emotion change, user-generated content behavior, and information dissemination behavior in the evolution of public opinion. Furthermore, the evolution trend of negative emotion of group users is similar to the evolution of public opinion influence [4]. However, how social media users' group emotion promotes the generation and evolution of public social sentiment remains clarified. Whether users' group emotion intensity and extreme emotion will promote or inhibit the evolution of public opinion is still unclear. In addition, in online virtual communities, the stimulating effect of group emotion on user behavior under different social presence environments is quite different [5]. Therefore, the influence of social presence on the relationship between group emotion and public opinion evolution needs to be confirmed.

The main contribution of this study is to clarify the influencing mechanism of users' group emotion on the evolution of public opinion, deeply analyze the complex relationship between them, and expand the theory of public opinion evolution. In addition, it confirms the regulatory effect of social presence on the evolving relationship between users' group emotions and public opinion.

2   Literature Review

Social media text contains rich emotional characteristics, and online social media has become an essential channel for emotional expression and dissemination [6]. The users' emotions in the text differ due to the behavior differences in user-generated content or information dissemination. Zhang et al. (2020) studied the public emergencies represented by the "2015 Tianjin explosions" [7]. They find that the negative emotions of social media users will gather together under specific triggers. If the negative emotions of the network cannot be effectively guided and adjusted, the public opinion will reach a climax with the development of users' group emotions. Users in places where public opinion occurs express stronger and richer emotions than users in other regions [8].

The existing literature has conducted a detailed study on users' group emotions and the evolution law of public opinion and found a specific correlation between users' group emotions and public opinion evolution. However, the influencing mechanism of users' group emotion on public opinion evolution is not precise. Moreover, social presence impacts users' social network behavior, but the regulatory role of social presence in the evolution of group emotion and public opinion needs to be confirmed.

3 Research Model and Hypotheses

3.1 Research Model

Based on Affective Events Theory (AET) [9] and Social Presence Theory (SPT) [10], we construct the research model of the influencing mechanism of social media users' group emotions on the evolution of public opinion. The model shown in Fig. 1.

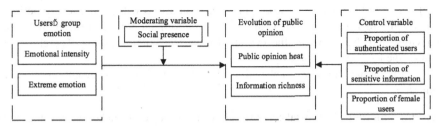

Fig. 1. Research model

AET describes the relationship between employees and their emotions and behaviors about events at work [9]. The theory assumes that the emotional state of employees will lead to their attitude towards work, and the work attitude will affect the cognitive driving behavior of work (the willingness to resign or stay in office). Figure 2 depicts the main structures in AET and their relationship. AET emphasizes the reaction process of emotion more than the theory of planned behavior (TPB), and people's emotions will affect the generation of behavior.

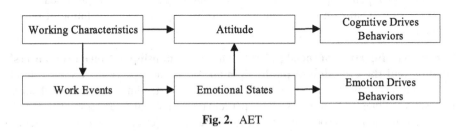

Fig. 2. AET

Social presence theory (SPT) expounds on the concept of social presence and how to enhance the authenticity of social media user interaction through social presence [10]. The theory holds that the social existence of media will affect the receiver's understanding of the content created or transmitted by the sender.

3.2 Research Hypothesis

Emotional Intensity. AET indicates that an event occurring in a specific environment will stimulate the generation of people's emotions, and people will show their emotions through behaviors [11]. Adverse sentiment events are like annoying short-term work events because they will cause adverse emotional reactions of social media users in the same way as to workers. On the other hand, favorable public opinion events will cause users' positive emotional responses. When emotions take over the user, they will express emotion through behavior [12]. For example, when social media users have feelings about public opinion events, they will produce user-generated content and information dissemination behaviors to express their positive or negative emotions. for example, after the public opinion event of the "MU5735 Plane crash", many social media users expressed their deep condolences for the passengers and crew killed in the plane crash through online comments.

It is inferred that social network public opinion events will cause users' emotions, which will affect users' user-generated content, information dissemination, and other behaviors, and then promote the evolution of public opinion events. Therefore, we propose the following hypothesis:

H1. Emotional intensity has a significant positive impact on the evolution of public opinion.

Extreme Emotion. The social network behavior of group users makes the existing emotional tendencies of the group and the individuals who make up them move in a more extreme direction, forming extreme emotions [13]. Extreme emotions will stimulate users to create or spread more text information, externalize extreme emotions into social network behaviors, and lead to the polarization of public opinion topics. These social network behaviors will promote the emergence and development of public opinion. Group users are in the process of de-personalization. Emotional hints and emotional infection drive their behavior. Therefore, the extreme emotion of the group can better promote group behavior. The highly negative emotional statements made by group users made the subsided public opinion develop towards the outbreak trend again, which promoted the evolution of public opinion. Therefore, it is inferred that extreme emotion will impact the evolution of public opinion. Therefore, the following hypothesis is proposed:

H2. Extreme emotion has a significant positive impact on the evolution of public opinion.

The moderating effect of social presence on the relationship between group users' emotion and the evolution of public opinion. We cannot ignore the critical role of social presence in users' social network behavior. Understanding the content enhances the user's feelings and emotions about participating in social interaction [14], which may increase the user's social network behavior and accelerate the evolution of public opinion. Users with a higher sense of social presence have richer emotions and will continue to use social media for social sharing. The convenient interaction of social networks can improve users' social presence to encourage users to externalize their internal emotions. As a result, users will generate user-generated content, information dissemination, and other behaviors on social media and then promote the generation and evolution of public opinion. Thus, we propose the following hypothesis:

H3. Social presence has a moderating effect on the relationship between emotional intensity and the evolution of public opinion.

H4. Social presence has a moderating effect on the relationship between extreme emotional and the evolution of public opinion.

4 Methodology

4.1 Data Sources and Variable Definitions

This paper selects the public opinion event of "5·9 Chengdu 49 Middle School students falling from the building" as the data source. The public opinion lasted for about six days. The micro hotspot research institute provides the data used by the Institute in cooperation. The data includes the text content, information attribute (sensitive, non-sensitive, or neutral), release attribute (user-generated content or information dissemination), release date, authentication type, user gender, number of forwards, number of comments, number of likes, and other information of each microblog under the public opinion. The public opinion event generated 2,610,300 microblog texts, including 365,209 user-generated content microblogs and 2,245,091 information dissemination microblogs.

Social network public opinion is mainly driven by the user-generated content and information dissemination behaviors of many users for a topic, we use three variables to measure the public opinion heat. Namely, the total heat of public opinion, the heat of user-generated content, and the heat of user information dissemination discuss the influencing mechanism of users' group emotions on the three. The main variables and their definitions in this paper are shown in Table 1.

Table 1. Variable definition

Variable			Definition
Items	Name	Code	
Explanatory variable	Emotional intensity	EI	Sum of absolute values of emotion per hour
	Extreme emotion	EE	Define that the absolute value of emotion is greater than or equal to 5 as extreme emotion, which is the number of blog posts of extreme emotion per hour
Moderator variable	Social presence	SP	Total social presence of group users per hour
Control variable	Proportion of authenticated users	AU	Proportion of the number of authentication users in the total number of users in an hour

(continued)

Table 1. (*continued*)

Variable			Definition
Items	Name	Code	
	Proportion of sensitive information	SI	Proportion of sensitive information per hour to the total information in an hour
	Proportion of female users	FU	Percentage of female users per hour in the total number of users in an hour
Explained variable	The total heat of public opinion	HPS	Total articles in the MicroBlog per hour
	The heat of user-generated content	HUC	Number of original articles in the MicroBlog posts per hour
	The heat of user information dissemination	HUD	Number of forwarded articles in the MicroBlog posts per hour
	Total information richness of text	TTR	Number of text characters of total articles in the MicroBlog per hour
	User-generated creation text information richness	UTR	Text characters of original articles in the MicroBlog posts per hour
	Information dissemination text information richness	ITR	Text characters of original articles in the MicroBlog posts per hour

4.2 Quantitative Analysis of Emotion in Social Network Speech Text

We use the emotion dictionary to calculate the specific emotion value of the text, including positive emotion value and negative emotion value [15]. Three emotion dictionaries, HowNet, Dalian University of Technology Chinese Emotion Vocabulary Ontology database, and Tsinghua University Chinese commendatory and degrading thesis, were synthesized. This study constructs thesauruses including positive emotion words, negative emotion words, stop words, negator words, and degree adverbs.

In order to further analyze users' emotions, it is necessary to analyze the emotional value of each text quantitatively. Firstly, use the Jieba package in Python software to segment the text into a single phrase and then judge the phrase's part of speech. Next, match the divided phrases with the emotional words in the emotional dictionary. When the phrase's part of speech is a positive emotion, the emotional value of the text increases by 1. When the part of speech of the phrase is a negative emotion, the emotional value of the text decreases by 1. When there is a degree adverb modification in front of a phrase, multiply the emotional value of the phrase by the degree weight Pi corresponding to the degree adverb. When there are negator words related to emotional words, the emotional value of emotional words shall be multiplied by negative 1. When other words related to emotional words have no emotional attribute, the emotional value shall be increased by

0. The quantization rules are shown in Fig. 3. Based on the above rules, the text emotion is quantified, and the text emotion score is calculated. The weight Pi settings of adverbs with different degrees are shown in Table 2.

4.3 Quantitative Analysis of Social Presence

The number of fans, microblogs, forwards, comments, and likes will be taken as the quantitative analysis indicators of social presence to calculate the level of users' social presence [16]. We used principal component analysis to quantify the five-index data into the social presence score. We select the component with an eigenvalue greater than 1 as the principal component and extract two principal components.

4.4 Data Analysis

Descriptive Statistical Analysis. The average values of public opinion user-generated content heat and public opinion information dissemination heat are 2,725 and 16,880, respectively. To solve the estimation deviation of regression results caused by the unit difference between different variables, we standardized each variable, and then correlation analysis and regression analysis were carried out.

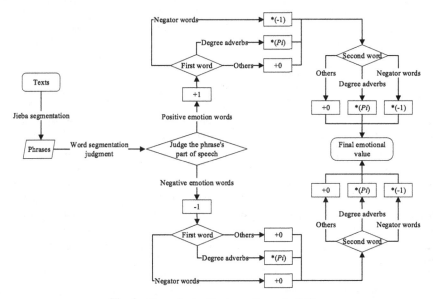

Fig. 3. Flow chart of text emotion calculation

Multiple Regression Analysis. The results of multiple regression analysis are shown in Table 3 and Table 4, which test the influence of users' group emotion on the evolution of public opinion and the regulatory effect of users' social presence on the relationship between emotion and the evolution of public opinion.

Table 2. Degree adverb (examples)

Degree level	Weight	Words (examples)	Number
Extremely/the most	2	Double, full, extraordinary, extreme, etc	69
Very	1.25	Very, quiet, special, especially, etc	42
More	1.2	Compare, then, exceed, more, etc	37
Slightly	0.8	More or less, slightly, slightest, a little, etc	29
Less	0.5	Less, mild, not very, relative, not much, etc	12
Super	1.5	Excessive, far beyond, super, too much, over the top, etc	30

Table 3. Multiple regression results 1

Variables	HPS			HUC			HUD		
	M1	M2	M3	M1	M2	M3	M1	M2	M3
EI		0.0609**	1.677***		0.00109	5.678***		0.884***	0.925***
		(2.256)	(4.456)		(0.0357)	(6.111)		(28.94)	(14.55)
EE		0.687***	1.510***		0.874***	1.342***		−0.102***	0.137**
		(14.59)	(9.388)		(18.69)	(13.49)		(−4.826)	(2.140)
SP		0.180***	0.174***		−0.0439	0.0345		0.184***	0.185***
		(3.825)	(3.542)		(−1.045)	(0.670)		(8.274)	(8.150)
EI·SP			2.003***			5.785***			0.0573
			(4.596)			(6.111)			(0.735)
EE·SP			−1.419***			−1.298***			−0.0506
			(−5.184)			(−5.786)			(−0.603)
AU	−0.00108	−0.0501*	−0.0402*	0.166**	−0.0716*	−0.0700**	−0.175***	−0.0239***	−0.0229***
	(−0.0156)	(−1.962)	(−1.723)	(2.312)	(−1.941)	(−2.137)	(−2.712)	(−3.122)	(−2.868)
SI	−0.0689	−0.0572**	−0.0570**	0.0345	−0.187***	−0.200***	−0.0622	0.00357	0.00380
	(−0.979)	(−2.156)	(−2.364)	(0.521)	(−5.548)	(−6.567)	(−0.958)	(0.454)	(0.478)
FU	0.636***	0.161***	0.157***	0.751***	0.129***	0.129***	0.722***	0.0503***	0.0469***
	(9.165)	(5.447)	(5.540)	(10.24)	(2.853)	(3.144)	(11.04)	(4.953)	(4.107)
Correlation coefficient R	0.6286	0.9615	0.9688	0.6879	0.9427	0.9562	0.7004	0.9969	0.9969
Fitting coefficient R2	0.3952	0.9245	0.9386	0.4732	0.8886	0.9143	0.4906	0.9938	0.9938
Adjustment R2	0.3812	0.9210	0.9346	0.4610	0.8834	0.9088	0.4788	0.9935	0.9934
Significance	0.0000	0.0000	0.0000	0.0000	0.0000	0.0000	0.0000	0.0000	0.0000

Note: data in parentheses are t-values calculated after standard errors

Table 4. Multiple regression results 2

Variables	TTR			UTR			ITR		
	M1	M2	M3	M1	M2	M3	M1	M2	M3
EI		0.0911***	2.661***		0.00974	2.434***		1.286***	0.898***
		(3.266)	(7.887)		(0.686)	(5.526)		(31.34)	(11.84)
EE		0.793***	2.027***		0.935***	1.150***		−0.168***	0.203***
		(16.31)	(14.06)		(43.00)	(24.37)		(−5.933)	(2.665)
SP		0.0621	0.0300		0.0300	0.0725***		−0.138***	0.147***
		(1.280)	(0.682)		(1.537)	(2.975)		(−4.620)	(5.426)
EI·SP			3.178***			2.489***			0.541***
			(8.133)			(5.547)			(5.828)
EE·SP			−2.162***			−0.579***			−0.529***
			(−8.812)			(−5.442)			(−5.291)
AU	−0.00131	−0.0387	−0.0253	0.268***	−0.0199	−0.0200	−0.177***	0.00921	0.00362
	(−0.0184)	(−1.464)	(−1.209)	(3.639)	(−1.159)	(−1.290)	(−2.657)	(0.897)	(0.380)
SI	−0.102	−0.0676**	−0.0673***	0.206***	−0.0586***	−0.0626***	−0.133**	−0.0226**	−0.0259***
	(−1.416)	(−2.468)	(−3.112)	(3.040)	(−3.747)	(−4.349)	(−1.982)	(−2.140)	(−2.733)
FU	0.607***	0.126***	0.129***	0.767***	0.0562***	0.0539***	0.699***	−0.0107	0.0141
	(8.507)	(4.114)	(5.057)	(10.24)	(2.685)	(2.768)	(10.33)	(−0.782)	(1.034)
Correlation coefficient R	0.5997	0.9589	0.9750	0.6712	0.9879	0.9903	0.6745	0.9944	0.9956
Fitting coefficient R2	0.3596	0.9195	0.9506	0.4505	0.9759	0.9807	0.4549	0.9888	0.9913
Adjustment R2	0.3448	0.9157	0.9474	0.4378	0.9748	0.9795	0.4422	0.9883	0.9907
Significance	0.0000	0.0000	0.0000	0.0000	0.0000	0.0000	0.0000	0.0000	0.0000

5 Discussions and Implications

5.1 Result Discussions

The regression results show that hypotheses H1 and H2 are supported, indicating that group users' emotional intensity and extreme emotion have a significant positive impact on the evolution of public opinion, which indicates that the influence of user group emotion on public opinion conforms to AET theory. When group users have more extreme emotions, more content creation and information dissemination behavior will be carried out, increasing the popularity of the public opinion network and enriching text information.

Hypothesis H3 partially holds, indicating that social presence positively moderates role in the relationship between affective intensity and public opinion evolution. The stronger the social presence of group users, the greater the effect of affective intensity on public opinion evolution. The moderating effect of social presence on the relationship between emotional intensity and public opinion information dissemination is not significant, indicating that the social presence of group users does not significantly moderate the effect of emotional intensity on public opinion information dissemination.

Hypothesis H4 is partially valid, which indicates that social presence negatively regulates the relationship between extreme emotion and public opinion evolution. The social presence of group users inhibits the promotion of extreme emotion to public opinion evolution. The above results are because most of the presence gained by users with extreme emotion is the refutation of their extreme emotion by other users, which reduces the expression of extreme emotion and thus reduces the heat and richness of text information on public opinion.

5.2 Implications for Theory

Confirm the action influencing mechanism of users' group emotions on the evolution of public opinion. We confirm that group users' emotion intensity and extreme emotion can promote social network public opinion through regression analysis and expounds in detail on how users' group emotion promotes the generation and evolution of social network public opinion. Furthermore, it confirms that the evolution trend of public opinion in the development of social public opinion events is close to or similar to the negative emotion change trend of group users [4].

We examined the moderating effect of social presence. Based on the existing studies confirming the different social presence obtained by social network speech texts with different emotions [5]. We further examined the moderating effect of social presence to deeply analyze the complex relationship between users' group emotions and the evolution of public opinion, which provides a new perspective and theoretical reference for further research on the evolution of public opinion.

5.3 Implications for Practice

This study provides a theoretical basis, decision support, and management countermeasures for social media and the public opinion supervision department to manage social media users and public opinion.

(1) Provide decision support for social media to formulate differentiated service strategies and public opinion information management and control strategies. Segment social media users based on their emotional tendency. The social media can qualitatively mark users according to emotion and behavior data and distinguish different types of users.
(2) It provides a reference for social platforms and public opinion supervision departments to formulate public opinion governance countermeasures. Identify and guide users with negative emotional tendencies. When the user's emotion changes to the negative extreme, social media can push the text content containing positive emotions and positive themes to neutralize the emotional polarity, reduce the probability of users making negative comments, and reduce the pressure on platform governance.

6 Conclusions

This study uses empirical analysis to explore the influencing mechanism of group user emotion on the evolution of public opinion. Through the public opinion event data of "5·9 Chengdu 49 Middle School students falling from the building", the group emotion and public opinion evolution data are quantitatively analyzed. The hypothesis is tested by regression analysis. The research verifies the influence of group user emotion on the evolution of public opinion and tests the regulatory effect of social presence. Our result also shows that the influence of user group emotion on online public opinion can be explained by AET theory. We deeply analyze the complex relationship between group user emotion and the evolution of public opinion, which provides new ideas and theoretical reference for the systematic study of the evolution of public opinion.

This study also has some limitations. First, we only conduct sentiment analysis on the text. Therefore, the sentiment analysis of emojis should be considered in the future. Second, we only analyze the public opinion event of "5·9 Chengdu 49 Middle School student falling from the building". Future research can use multiple public opinion event data to verify the model. Finally, only the Microblog platform is selected to verify the research model. In the future, data from other social networking platforms such as WeChat, Tiktok, Twitter, and Meta can be selected to verify the research model further.

Acknowledgement. This research was supported by the National Social Science Foundation of China under Grant 20BSH151; Humanity and Social Science Research General Projects of the Ministry of Education of China under Grant 18YJCZH223; Shandong Provincial Natural Science Foundation, China under Grant ZR2020MG006.

References

1. Chen, C., Chiu, Y.: The influence of public health information sharing on social media during the early COVID-19 outbreak. Data Technol. App. **56**(2), 161–171 (2022)
2. Song, Y., Dai, X., Wang, J.: Not all emotions are created equal: expressive behavior of the networked public on China's social media site. Comput. Hum. Behav. **60**, 525–533 (2016)
3. Tian, X., He, W., Wang, F.: Applying sentiment analytics to examine social media crises: a case study of United Airline's crisis in 2017. Data Technol. Appl. **56**(1), 1–23 (2022)
4. Liu, Y., et al.: Dynamic impact of negative public opinion on agricultural product prices during COVID-19. J. Retail. Consum. Serv. **64**, 102790 (2022)
5. Mahdikhani, M.: Predicting the popularity of tweets by analyzing public opinion and emotions in different stages of Covid-19 pandemic. Int. J. Inf. Manage. Data Insights **2**(1), 100053 (2022)
6. Shao, Q., Wang, H., Zhu, P., Dong, M.: Group emotional contagion and simulation in large-scale flight delays based on the two-layer network model. Physica A **573**, 125941 (2021)
7. Zhang, W., Wang, M., Zhu, Y.: Does government information release really matter in regulating contagion-evolution of negative emotion during public emergencies? From the perspective of cognitive big data analytics. Int. J. Inf. Manage. **50**, 498–514 (2020)
8. Zhang, C., Ma, X.Y., Zhou, Y., Guo, R.Z.: Analysis of public opinion evolution in covid-19 pandemic from a perspective of sentiment variation. J. Geo-inf. Sci. **23**(2), 341–350 (2021)

9. Weiss, H.M., Cropanzano, R.: Affective events theory: a theoretical discussion of the structure, causes and consequences of affective experiences at work. Res. Organ. Behav. **18**(3), 1–74 (1996)

10. Parker, E.B., et al.: The Social Psychology of Telecommunications. Wiley, London (1976)

11. Baur, J.E., Bradley, B.H., Bonner, R.L.: Boiling frogs: reconsidering the impact of deviance targets, severity, and frequency in teams. J. Bus. Res. **142**, 1026–1037 (2022)

12. Wakefield, R., Wakefield, K.: Social media network behavior: a study of user passion and affect. J. Strateg. Inf. Syst. **25**(2), 140–156 (2016)

13. Sunstein, C.R.: The law of group polarization. J. Polit. Philos. **10**(2), 175–195 (2002)

14. Mclean, G., Osei, F.K.: Examining satisfaction with the experience during a live chat service encounter-implications for website providers. Comput. Hum. Behav. **76**, 494–508 (2017)

15. Tan, X., Zhuang, M.N., Mao, T.T., Zhang, Q.: Analysis of emotional evolution of large-scale internet public opinion events based on LDA-ARAM hybrid model. J. Intell. **39**(10), 121–129 (2020)

16. Spierings, N., Jacobs, K.: Getting personal? the impact of social media on preferential voting. Polit. Behav. **36**(1), 215–234 (2014)

Examining the Employees Behavior Control in Cloud Computing Performance Through the Moderating Lenses of Transformational Leadership

Nisar Ahmad[1], Zhiying Liu[1], Jiang Wu[2], Fahad Alam[3], Muhammad Waqas[2(✉)], and Xu Yi[1(✉)]

[1] University of Science and Technology of China, Hefei 230026, Anhui, China
xuyi@ustc.edu.cn
[2] Wuhan University, Wuhan, Hubei 430072, China
waqas.muhammad@whu.edu.cn
[3] University of Science and Technology Beijing, Beijing 100083, China

Abstract. Cloud computing (CC) is becoming a new paradigm for Small and Medium-Sized Enterprises (SMEs) to access information systems. However, there is a dearth of empirical investigation on how SME employees utilize CC. Hence, the purpose of this study is to ascertain how employees' behavioral control and transformational leadership (TL) among SME influence successful CC performance. The 206 responses that were gathered, used in structural equation modeling (SEM) utilizing SmartPLS 4.0 to confirm the formulated hypotheses. The findings indicated that employees' behavior control (EBC) and the CC performance were positively influenced by information sharing (IS), technical ability (TA), and change readiness (CR). Additionally, the moderating effect of TL was found to strengthen the relationship among factors and plays an important role in controlling the employee behavior for successful CC performance.

Keywords: Information Sharing · Technical Ability · Change Readiness · Transformational Leadership · SME's Employees · Cloud Computing Performance

1 Introduction

Companies are being forced to reconsider their organizational models as a result of digital innovation. In several areas, some businesses are demonstrating a greater capacity to use digital technology to their benefit. Because of their hierarchical, centralized, closed organizational structures, traditional businesses struggle to adapt and alter as quickly as the digital disruption mandates [1]. An ongoing investment in information technology (IT) is required in the period of the Industrial Revolution because of the growing importance of information and communication technology (ICT) in corporate management. Not just in the IT industry, but in other industrial sectors as well, cloud computing (CC) is becoming a more prevalent paradigm shift for the use of ICT in enterprises. CC is founded on the idea of IT resource sharing, according to which IT resources like servers, data storage, and software development platforms are borrowed and used over a network as needed, and only the cost of the service utilized is charged [2, 3]. When CC is implemented to a company's business operation, it fundamentally alters how IT resources are accessible and used to serve business processes [4, 5].

The global CC market is anticipated to develop at a CAGR (Composite Annual Growth Rate) of 18.0%, from $2.27 billion in 2018 to $6.33 billion in 2023, according to a 2019 CC analysis by research firm Markets and Markets. According to this pattern, CC services are gradually becoming more and more vital for executives of firms to rapidly manage work at a minimal cost and satisfy client needs. Additionally, in erstwhile investigations on CC [4, 6] demonstrated that transmission of corporate technology as well as the economics of business computing and the course of action to IT financing will change as a result of CC performance, considering that CC is a pertinent revolutionary technology for the growth, competitiveness, and creation of new businesses in corporate activities. Due to the quickly evolving business environment and the expansion of the digital environment, CC is particularly gaining attention as a constructive way to deal with change. It is anticipated to have significant synergistic effects on both interior corporate operations and exterior management activities [4, 7].

Numerous local and international investigations are being undertaken on CC since it remains a focus and is anticipated to have a favorable impact on business activity. In the beginning, research on CC mostly concentrated on individual users, while research concentrating on businesses primarily concentrated on the interaction between the adoption of CC and it's entrepreneurial, industry structure, and technological aspects [3, 4, 8]. Lately, the rising adoption of digital revolution in Pakistan prompted businesses to re-evaluate their IT needs and choose more advanced ICT solutions in order to expand and support their operations. Although CC adoption is still in its infancy in the nation and only a small number of businesses have accepted cloud-based services, the majority of SMEs' owners and managers are keen to implement cloud services for their efficient company operations [9].

As part of the current study, a survey was carried out to ascertain the crucial elements of CC adoption among SMEs employees. According to previous findings, CC adoption has likely been examined by a number of scholars, notably [3, 4, 8]. The dearth of study on CC performance in the context of SMEs in South Asian developing nations, such as Pakistan, was pointed up by [9]. This study aims to conduct a comprehensive analysis of the relationship between the Information Sharing (IS), Technical Ability (TA), Change Readiness (CR) - the key factors associated with Employee Behavior Control (EBC), CC performance, and the moderating role played by Transformational Leadership (TL). Our research questions are as follows: (1) How do the SMEs Employees related factors influence employee behavior control on the CC performance in SME? (2) How does Transformational Leadership moderate Employee Behavior Control and CC performance? By concentrating on the behavior control of SME workers toward CC and its influence on performance in this region, this study seeks to brim that gap.

Analyzing the literature in-depth reveal important theoretical underpinnings and identifying factors. The current study develops a research model using the Technology

Organization and Environmental (TOE) paradigm in light of these findings [9]. Furthermore, some research [10, 11] have diverse theories to handle various technology adoption models. EBC and CC performance are influenced by variables including (IS), (TA), and (CR). Employees may imitate a leader's conduct or be open to changes in the workplace, depending on the administrators' transformational leadership (TL) [12, 13]. The empirical data that investigates the connection between these variables and the uptake & performance of CC in SMEs is currently lacking.

2 Theoretical Background

2.1 Cloud Computing

By paying for just the resources they really utilize, CC enables businesses to access and utilize IT resources whenever, wherever, and across any platform. This is the fundamental idea behind CC, which is gaining popularity as a cutting-edge tool that enables businesses to swiftly react to and successfully adapt to the continuously evolving business environment [3–5, 13]. Based on the advantages of resource sharing, cost savings, and the growth of IT resources, CC enhances the efficiency, adaptability, and IT operations of businesses and is helpful for working with external entities [3, 8, 14]. The governmental and business sectors are both giving it a substantial amount of attention. Consequently, ever since late 2000s, when CC started to be acknowledged as a novel and revolutionary technology, research on CC has been carried out on many subjects in various sectors. Targeting either people or organizations, empirical methodologies have also been extensively pursued in the management and information systems disciplines.

Throughout the context of studies aimed at enterprises, the link between the technological aspects of CC, organisational factors, work climate characteristics, and technology adoption is explained as the number of firms considering or utilizing CC grows [6, 15]. [13] found that organizational variables such technology preparedness, top management support, and business size had an influence. It also validated that the special qualities of CC, such as cost reduction, had a substantial impact on CC adoption. [15] investigated the link between CC adoption and organizational, technological, and environmental adaptability. Therefore, it was discovered that factors such as leadership role, comparative advantage, compatibility, experience capacity, and competitive pressure had a big influence on CC readiness and acceptance. [6] emphasized that CC has traits that set it apart from other IT advances and may provide businesses a number of advantages. According to [2] the adoption of CC is hampered by security and privacy concerns, which are crucial determinants in service quality and trust. [3] provided more evidence that perceived risk, efficiency, service quality, relative advantage, and leadership role are significant determinants of cloud computing services which improves SME performance positively.

As a result, research on CC that targets SMEs is ongoing, and the findings are helpful for SME's that plan to employ CC in the future. However, there has not been ample empirical investigation on the variables affecting SME members who actively utilize CC [6, 13, 15]. To make it more explicit, In order to successfully adopt new IT, such as CC, in an organization, the responsibilities of the members or administrators who actually use it are crucial than anything else. However, the link between these elements and effective CC implementation and outcomes is seldom adequately discussed.

2.2 SMEs & Employees in Pakistan

The significance of the SME sector in a nation's industrial growth cannot be ignored. In Pakistan, SMEs are defined by their size (up to 250 representatives), paid-up capital (up to 25 million rupees), and volume of annual business (up to 250 million Rs.) [16]. Nearly 90% of all businesses in Pakistan are SMEs. They employ 80% of the non-agricultural work force, and they provide around 40% of the country's yearly GDP. However, SME's are limited by financial and other resources, unlike huge businesses in the formal sector. This fundamental quality of a SME makes the presence of a system via which it may get help in many business tasks, such as technological advancement, marketing, financial management, and human resource training and development, important [17]. Regardless of their economic significance, Pakistan's SMEs face several challenges that substantially impair their functioning. The main weaknesses are the absence of strategic planning, the inadequate business information structure, and the lack of human capital needed in contemporary business [18]. By integrating the cutting-edge digital technologies of the industry revolution in their company operations, such inefficiencies may be rectified and the existing situation of SMEs can be improved [19, 20]. When implementing new IT in a business, research pertaining to SME employees is crucial for its successful implementation. The effectiveness of technology initiatives and modifications is influenced by many aspects connected to SME employees, although prior research [21, 22] has claimed that elements including information sharing, technical ability, member behavior control, and security awareness occupy a prominent place.

2.3 Transformational Leadership

Transformational leadership (TL) is sometimes equated with transactional leadership [23], which emphasizes the furtherance of certain executives' and followers' concerns and satisfies contractual requirements with regard to the setting of goals and the oversight and management of results. By empowering their followers, focusing on their specific needs and personal growth, and encouraging creative problem-solving among them, transformational leaders help others realize their own leadership potential [24]. Motivating followers to support a common vision and objectives of an organization or unit is a key component of TL. Followers of transformational leaders are frequently happier and far more committed [25].

Followers engage to TL by exhibiting outstanding performance, frequently going above and beyond anticipation. According to [26], who reviewed decades' worth of research on TL, transformational elements often correlate more strongly with peer effectiveness and satisfaction results than contingent rewards. In terms of SME's employee specifically passive exception management, contingent incentive often has a stronger association with outcomes than exception management[26]. TL empowers SME employees to embrace lofty goals and inspires them to deliver achievements that beyond expectations [25]. When the TL aggressively challenges new technologies and actively comprehends the SME's worker to execute jobs that are suited to their degree of competence centered mostly on manager's leadership [12].

2.4   TOE Framework

[27] developed the Technology Organization Environment (TOE) framework to describe the process of innovation in (SMEs). This paradigm takes into account the three factors of technology, organization, and environment that affect the adoption of innovative technologies. The proposed variable technical abilities (TA) of SME organizations are referred to in the technology context. The environment context relates to information sharing (IS) among SME employees, whereas the organization context refers to Change readiness (CR) which is the most novel contribution in the perspective of (TOE) framework. The TOE framework considers all internal and external technologies that are pertinent to the organization, as well as their qualities and their availability [27].

3   Research Model and Hypothesis

In our proposed research model (Fig. 1), first hypothesis is, information sharing (IS) that refers to the willingness of SME's employee to systematically share various information and resources that occur in the process of implementing CC in SME [28]. [28] stated that CC can promote IS among people as an easy and useful technology compared to traditional technologies. In addition, this can increase users' expectations for IS through CC and allow them to perceive the technology as useful. In other words, if SME's employee have a strong desire to share information for the efficiency of their work, their desire to use a technology that is useful for information sharing and has high information accessibility may also increase [29]. Therefore, the willingness of members to share information may have a positive effect on the adoption and performance of a technology.

H1: Information sharing have positive impact on employee behavior control on the CC performance in SME.

Second, technical ability refers to the level of technical knowledge that SME's employee has about CC [29, 30]. In order for a new technology to be successfully adopted in an organization, the anxiety of SME's employee about accepting something new must be resolved. If organizational employee has sufficient knowledge and technical ability about CC, this can reduce such anxiety. In addition, if organizational employee perceive that they can improve their competitiveness through CC based on their own technical knowledge, this can have a positive impact on the acceptance of CC adoption [6]. [30] stated that if SME's employee has sufficient knowledge and necessary skills for CC, they can have more confidence in their work processes overall, which can also have a positive effect on the acceptance of CC performance.

H2: Technical ability have positive impact on employee behavior control on the CC performance in SME .

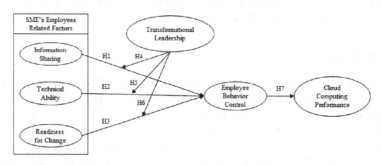

Fig. 1. Proposed Research Model

The third factor is change readiness, which refers to the degree to which SME's employee are in a psychological state of wanting to positively accept changes in their work environment through new ICT [7, 31]. When changes such as the introduction of new IT occur in an organization, it is important for the members to have a positive attitude and recognition of the necessity of change in order to successfully accept the change. In other words, if the members sufficiently understand that change is necessary and have a high level of readiness, they can take a positive attitude towards organizational change and successfully adopt ICT. [7] stated that when organizational employees are prepared for change and believe they can positively accept it, it has a positive impact on the acceptance of new IT and affected CC performance positively.

H3: Change readiness of organization employee have positive impact on employee behavior control on the CC performance in SME.

TL refers to the degree of ability of organizational managers to provide direction and motivate self-motivated efforts for organizational members when facing various problems during CC adoption & performance. It is also important for organizational managers to give appropriate motivation and sufficient support to achieve positive and high performance when trying to adopt and implement new ICT and achieve results in the organization [32, 33]. TL continuous support from the organization means the degree to which the organization continuously supports CC in various aspects such as financial, technical, and usage environment in order to activate CC [13, 34].

It has been shown that the TL of administrators in an organization has a significant impact on the successful adoption and implementation of new technology, and has been shown to strengthen the relationship between the evaluation and acceptance of IT [24]. In other words, if the TL plays a role in helping the members of the organization to have information sharing, technical ability and change readiness for new technologies have positive outcomes on CC adoption and performance [35]. [32] argue that TL is important in new technology projects because the effort and perception of organization members may not be sufficient to create the success of CC adoption. Therefore, the TL will interact with the perception and interaction of members about CC performance and have an impact on it.

H4: Transformational Leadership strengthen the relationship between information sharing and employee behavior control in SME.

H5: Transformational Leadership strengthen the relationship between technical ability and employee behavior control in SME.

H6: Transformational Leadership strengthen the relationship between change readiness and employee behavior control in SME.

This study also aims to examine the relationship between member behavior control and its impact on CC performance. Member behavior control, as mediator, refers to the degree of management of negative thoughts that may arise during the adoption of CC in an organization [36]. [36] stated that perceived behavioral control acts as a belief about the factors that promote or inhibit certain behaviors and has an influence on the adoption of new technology behaviors. [6] found that companies with limited internal IT-related assets can reduce unnecessary costs by using CC, and can expect better performance by focusing their IT resources on core business activities. Examining the performance of technology adoption is important because it provides useful information on whether to understand the effectiveness of information systems and continue to invest in and manage technology [6, 37, 38]. [38], found that the adoption and operation of new technologies such as CC can have a positive impact on organization performance.

H7: Behavioral control of organization employee have positive impact on CC performance in SME.

4   Research Methodology

4.1 Data Collection

The objective of this study is to look at the crucial TEO framework adopting aspects for CC in Pakistani SMEs. CEOs, managers, IT specialists, and other workers from SMEs who demonstrated in-depth understanding of the use of technology were invited to participate in the data gathering process.

The present study's research questionnaire has two sections. The purpose of the questionnaire's first component was to examine the organization's demographic data. The second section was created to look at the crucial components of CC performance in Pakistani SMEs. There were 400 online surveys administered, and 286 of them were returned, for a 72% response rate. After examining the data for missing values, outliers, and unusable replies, 206 responses were ultimately prevailed useable, yielding an actual response rate of 52%.

The demographic and descriptive statistics includes information on gender, experience, and designation. The gender breakdown of the group is 74.76% male and 25.24% female. The experience of the group is broken down into several categories, including 01 to 02 years (12.32%), 03 to 05 years (30.54%), 06 to 08 years (25.24%), 09 to 10 years (15.40%), and more than 10 years (16.50%). The designation of the group is also broken down, with the categories being CEO/Managing Director (5.84%), Manager (10.19%), Assistant Manager (17.48%), Senior Officer (25.72%), Officer (31.55%), and Others (9.22%).

4.2 Measures

In this research, information sharing and technical ability were developed and revised based on [28, 30, 38, 39], were measured by 3 items. TL was modified from [35], employee behavior control, and readiness for change were measured with 3 items, and CC adoption was measured by 4 items [13, 31, 36]. A 7-point scale was used for measurement. The survey explained the purpose of the study, ensured anonymity, and made clear that participation was voluntary. Acronyms were defined at the start of the questionnaire.

4.3 Results

In this analysis, structural equation modeling (SEM) and SmartPLS 4.0 were used to evaluate the structural model [40]. PLS-SEM is the preferred choice over factor-based SEM due to its better predictive power. It is also considered a preferable solution for decision-making and management-oriented issues, particularly when forecasting is being examined [41, 42].

4.4 Measurement and Structural Model

Cronbach's Alpha, the average extracted variance (AVE), the composite reliability (CR) and factor loading are all shown in Table 1. The reliability of the scales is shown by the fact that all constructions have CR and Cronbach's Alpha values higher than 0.7. The measuring model exhibits convergent validity since AVE is above 0.5 for all constructs [42]. The requirement that the loadings should be more than 0.7 served as the basis for evaluating the indicators' reliability. The loadings (in bold) are more than 0.7, demonstrating strong indication reliability whereas Table 2 explains Construct Reliability & Validity.

The Fornell-Larcker criterion and cross-loadings were used to assess the constructs' discriminant validity [42]. The constructs may be employed to examine the theoretical framework, in accordance with the findings of the examination of construct reliability, convergent validity, and indicator reliability. All constructs also had strong composite reliability values, which were over 0.8. The findings of the direct impacts of the hypotheses are shown in Table 3, together with the β, p-values & t-statistics, which displayed the standard values. Thus, all of the hypotheses were backed up by the results.

Moreover, information sharing (IS), technical ability (TA) and readiness for change (CR) cumulatively explains 53.7% of variance in member behavior control (MBC) (R^2 = 0.537) whereas employee behavior control (EBC) explain 36.8% of variance in CC performance (R^2 = 0.368). The R^2 values of 0.537 and 0.368 are higher than the 0.26 value that [43] suggests would indicate a substantial model, are illustrated in Fig. 2.

Table 1. CR, AVE and Factor Loading

Constructs & Factor Loading	Cronbach's Alpha	Composite Reliability	AVE
IS_1 **0.791**	**0.758**	**0.857**	**0.712**
IS_2 **0.864**			
IS_3 **0.874**			
TA_1 **0.884**	**0.838**	**0.839**	**0.677**
TA_2 **0.788**			
TA_3 **0.793**			
CR_1 **0.758**	**0.828**	**0.864**	**0.643**
CR_2 **0.873**			
CR_3 **0.769**			
TL_1 **0.869**	**0.851**	**0.859**	**0.745**
TL_2 **0.873**			
TL_3 **0.847**			
EBC_1 **0.762**	**0.867**	**0.834**	**0.683**
EBC_2 **0.863**			
EBC_3 **0.851**			
CCP_1 **0.782**	**0.884**	**0.873**	**0.640**
CCP_2 **0.742**			
CCP_3 **0.853**			
CCP_4 **0.818**			

Table 2. Construct Reliability & Validity

Constructs	1	2	3	4	5	6
IS	**0.844**					
TA	0.429	**0.823**				
CR	0.459	0.253	**0.802**			
TL	0.207	0.149	0.393	**0.863**		
EBC	0.423	0.283	0.351	0.241	**0.827**	
CCP	0.277	0.239	0.296	0.182	0.349	**0.800**

Note): The diagonal values shown in bold are the square root of the AVE

Table 3. Summary of hypothesis verification results

Hypotheses	Path	β	t-value	p-value	Decision
H1	IS → EBC	0.209*	2.038	0.001	Supported
H2	TA → EBC	0.461**	7.418	0.004	Supported
H3	CR → EBC	0.459**	9.663	0.000	Supported
H4	IS x TL → EBC	0.213**	3.529	0.002	Supported
H5	TA x TL → EBC	0.236*	2.945	0.006	Supported
H6	CR x TL → EBC	0.349**	6.539	0.003	Supported
H7	EBC → CCP	0.358**	5.659	0.008	Supported

Note) *: $p < 0.05$, **: $p < 0.01$

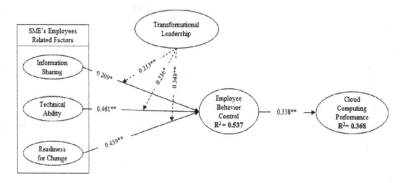

Fig. 2. Structural Analysis

5   Discussion

The adoption of ICT is a significant concern for government officials. Policymakers in developed countries anticipate a major strategic impact of these advanced technologies on the entire business ecosystem. These findings align with previous studies in Pakistan, Thailand, and Indonesia [1, 17, 44] which also reported positive effects on SMEs. However, the growth and development of SMEs in Pakistan is slow. To improve, managers must balance exploration and exploitation to attain agility and evolve their business in modern times. ICT tools, such as IT and CC, are essential for achieving productivity and performance, as well as a competitive advantage [17]. The study found that certain factors, such as diverse information sharing, CC related knowledge, TA, and CR, have a significant impact on successful CC adoption & performance among SME employees. This aligns with previous researches [28, 30, 38, 39].

Additionally, the study found that TL plays a significant role in moderating the relationship between these factors and successful CC adoption. If organizational managers adopt a TL style, it can further strengthen this relationship. Also, when employee behavior control is positive towards CC adoption, it leads to better outcomes and performance which also found in previous research [13, 31, 35, 36]. Companies are investing in new technologies to stay competitive, with CC being a popular choice due to its cost-saving potential, efficient resource sharing, and expansion of IT resources. It is also seen as a way to improve productivity, flexibility, and IT functions. CC is viewed as an innovative technology for gaining a competitive edge and creating new business opportunities, and it is expected to change the way companies invest in IT. However, there is a lack of understanding about the relationship between these factors and the implementation of CC in the actual use and utilization of business processes by SME employees in Pakistan, where awareness and capabilities regarding CC are crucial.

6 Conclusion

This study examines the CC performance among SMEs in Pakistan using the TEO framework. Results revealed that all hypotheses (IS, TA, CR, TL, & EBC), positively influence CC adoption & performance. Findings indicate that TL moderates SME employee behavior control, which influences CC adoption and performance. This study fills a gap in the CC performance literature and suggests a path for SMEs to assess and implement sophisticated technologies like CC. The study concludes that CC will grow exponentially and provide benefits to SMEs in the future, and SME leadership should pay more attention to the adoption and implementation of CC as it offers cost-effective, compatible, agile and scalable solutions for business growth. The findings provide valuable insights to owners/managers for decision-making regarding CC performance.

6.1 Theoretical and Practical Contribution

This study presents factors that influence the performance of CC among SMEs in Pakistan and verifies the relationship through empirical analysis. It provides a useful theoretical model for future research on CC and examines the impact of CC on the performance of SME employees. SME leadership should recognize the technological needs of their firms, and carefully understand the scope and requirements. CC is a suitable and appropriate technology that offers IT services, infrastructure, and platforms such as IaaS, PaaS, SaaS, with various deployment models like public, private, hybrid and community, at minimal start up cost with pay-per-use options and shared computing resources. This study will provide explanations on the importance of factors such as IS, TA, MBC, CR, and the role of TL for the fruitful performance of CC.

6.2 Limitations and Future Research Directions

This study has several limitations and suggests areas for future research. It only examines five factors related to SME employee, but more variables should be studied. The use of CC may vary by industry, and employee competencies and perceptions may differ depending on the extent of its use in business processes. The study's results may not be generalizable due to a lack of information on the size of the responding companies. Future research should investigate other leadership styles and analyze response targets more finely by industry, organizational size, and degree of use.

Acknowledgement. This research is supported by the National Natural Science Foundation of China [Project No. 72072167 and 72071193].

References

1. Imran, M., Hameed, W., Haque, A.: Influence of industry 4.0 on the production and service sectors in Pakistan: Evidence from textile and logistics industries. Soc. Sci. **7**(12), 246 (2018)
2. Alkhater, N., Walters, R., Wills, G.: An empirical study of factors influencing cloud adoption among private sector organisations. Telematics Inform. **35**(1), 38–54 (2018)
3. Khayer, A., et al.: Cloud computing adoption and its impact on SMEs' performance for cloud supported operations: A dual-stage analytical approach. Technol. Soc. **60**, 101225 (2020)
4. Arvanitis, S., Kyriakou, N., Loukis, E.N.: Why do firms adopt cloud computing? A comparative analysis based on South and North Europe firm data. Telematics Inform. **34**(7), 1322–1332 (2017)
5. Hsu, P.-F., Ray, S., Li-Hsieh, Y.-Y.: Examining cloud computing adoption intention, pricing mechanism, and deployment model. Int. J. Inf. Manage. **34**(4), 474–488 (2014)
6. Priyadarshinee, P., et al.: Understanding and predicting the determinants of cloud computing adoption: a two staged hybrid SEM-Neural networks approach. Comput. Hum. Behav. **76**, 341–362 (2017)
7. Kim, J., Kim, H.: Cloud Computing Industry Trend and Introduction Effect. IT Insight, National IT Industry promotion Agency (2010)
8. Alsmadi, D., Prybutok, V.: Sharing and storage behavior via cloud computing: security and privacy in research and practice. Comput. Hum. Behav. **85**, 218–226 (2018)
9. Pathan, Z.H., et al.: Essential factors in cloud-computing adoption by SMEs. Hum. Syst. Manag. **36**(4), 261–275 (2017)
10. Ahmad, N., Waqas, M., Zhang, X.: Public sector employee perspective towards adoption of e-government in Pakistan: a proposed research agenda. Data Inf. Manage. **5**(1), 119–124 (2021)
11. Waqas, M., Ahmad, N., Wu, J.: Adoption of e-services and quality of life among older consumers in China. Data Inf. Manage. **5**(1), 125–130 (2021)
12. Li, Y., Tan, C.-H., Teo, H.-H.: Leadership characteristics and developers' motivation in open source software development. Inf. Manage. **49**(5), 257–267 (2012)
13. Oliveira, T., Thomas, M., Espadanal, M.: Assessing the determinants of cloud computing adoption: An analysis of the manufacturing and services sectors. Inf. Manage. **51**(5), 497–510 (2014)
14. Kumar, D., Samalia, H.V., Verma, P.: Exploring suitability of cloud computing for small and medium-sized enterprises in India. J. Small Bus. Enterprise Dev. **24**(4), 814–832 (2017). https://doi.org/10.1108/JSBED-01-2017-0002
15. Yang, Z., et al.: Understanding SaaS adoption from the perspective of organizational users: a tripod readiness model. Comput. Hum. Behav. **45**, 254–264 (2015)
16. Qureshi, J., Herani, G.M.: The role of small and medium-size enterprises (SMEs) in the socio-economic stability of Karachi (2011)
17. Mubarak, M.F., et al.: The impact of digital transformation on business performance: a study of Pakistani SMEs. Eng. Technol. Appl. Sci. Res. **9**(6), 5056–5061 (2019)
18. Dar, M.S., Ahmed, S., Raziq, A.: Small and medium-size enterprises in Pakistan: definition and critical issues. Pakistan Bus. Rev. **19**(1), 46–70 (2017)
19. Homburg, C., Wielgos, D., Kühnl, C.: Digital business capability and its effect on firm performance. in AMA Educators'. In: Proceedings American Marketing Association, Curran (2019)
20. Shahbaz, M.S., et al.: The impact of supply chain collaboration on operational performance: empirical evidence from manufacturing of Malaysia. Int. J. Adv. Appl. Sci. **5**(8), 64–71 (2018)
21. Kim, W., et al.: Adoption issues for cloud computing. In: Proceedings of the 7th International Conference on Advances in Mobile Computing and Multimedia (2009)

22. Taylor, C.W.: Cloud computing at the University level: A study of student use of cloud computing applications. Zhurnal Eksperimental'noi I Teoreticheskoi Fiziki (2011)
23. Avolio, B.J., Bass, B.M.: Individual consideration viewed at multiple levels of analysis: a multi-level framework for examining the diffusion of transformational leadership. Leadersh. Q. **6**(2), 199–218 (1995)
24. Gumusluoğlu, L., Ilsev, A.: Transformational leadership and organizational innovation: the roles of internal and external support for innovation. J. Prod. Innov. Manag. **26**(3), 264–277 (2009)
25. Bass, B.M., Bass Bernard, M.: Leadership and performance beyond expectations (1985)
26. Bass, B.M.: Two decades of research and development in transformational leadership. Eur. J. Work Organ. Psy. **8**(1), 9–32 (1999)
27. Tornatzky, L.G., Fleischer, M., Chakrabarti, A.K.: Processes of Technological Innovation. Lexington Books (1990)
28. Arpaci, I.: Antecedents and consequences of cloud computing adoption in education to achieve knowledge management. Comput. Hum. Behav. **70**, 382–390 (2017)
29. Garrison, G., Kim, S., Wakefield, R.L.: Success factors for deploying cloud computing. Commun. ACM **55**(9), 62–68 (2012)
30. Lian, J.-W., Yen, D.C., Wang, Y.-T.: An exploratory study to understand the critical factors affecting the decision to adopt cloud computing in Taiwan hospital. Int. J. Inf. Manage. **34**(1), 28–36 (2014)
31. Armenakis, A.A., Harris, S.G., Mossholder, K.W.: Creating readiness for organizational change. Human Relations **46**(6), 681–703 (1993)
32. House, R., et al.: Understanding cultures and implicit leadership theories across the globe: an introduction to project GLOBE. J. World Bus. **37**(1), 3–10 (2002)
33. Low, C., Chen, Y., Wu, M.: Understanding the determinants of cloud computing adoption. Indus. Manage. Data Syst. **111**, 1006–1023 (2011)
34. Martins, R., Oliveira, T., Thomas, M.A.: An empirical analysis to assess the determinants of SaaS diffusion in firms. Comput. Hum. Behav. **62**, 19–33 (2016)
35. Carreiro, H., Oliveira, T.: Impact of transformational leadership on the diffusion of innovation in firms: application to mobile cloud computing. Comput. Ind. **107**, 104–113 (2019)
36. Ajzen, I.: Perceived behavioral control, self-efficacy, locus of control, and the theory of planned behavior. J. Appl. Soc. Psychol. **32**(4), 665–683 (2002). https://doi.org/10.1111/j.1559-1816.2002.tb00236.x
37. Garrison, G., Wakefield, R.L., Kim, S.: The effects of IT capabilities and delivery model on cloud computing success and firm performance for cloud supported processes and operations. Int. J. Inf. Manage. **35**(4), 377–393 (2015)
38. Raut, R.D., et al.: Analyzing the factors influencing cloud computing adoption using three stage hybrid SEM-ANN-ISM (SEANIS) approach. Technol. Forecast. Soc. Chang. **134**, 98–123 (2018)
39. McKinney, V., Yoon, K., Zahedi, F.M.: The measurement of web-customer satisfaction: an expectation and disconfirmation approach. Inf. Syst. Res. **13**(3), 296–315 (2002)
40. Hair, J., et al.: An updated and expanded assessment of PLS-SEM in information systems research. Ind. Manag. Data Syst. **117**(3), 442–458 (2017)
41. Lai, J.-Y., et al.: Impacts of employee participation and trust on e-business readiness, benefits, and satisfaction. Inf. Syst. E-Bus. Manag. **11**(2), 265–285 (2013)
42. Ahmed, F., et al.: Supportive leadership and post-adoption use of MOOCs: the mediating role of innovative work behavior. J. Organ. End User Comput. (JOEUC) **34**(1), 1–23 (2022)
43. Cohen, J., Statistical Power Analysis for the Behavioral Sciences. Routledge (2013)
44. Bharadwaj, A., et al.: Digital business strategy: toward a next generation of insights. MIS Q. 471–482 (2013)

What Learners Want: Revealing the Focal Topics in MOOC Reviews

Jingya Liu[1], Qiao Zhong[1], Zequan Shen[1], Zhao Du[2(✉)], Fang Wang[3], and Shan Wang[4]

[1] School of Sports Engineering, Beijing Sport University, Beijing 100084, China
[2] Sport Business School, Beijing Sport University, Beijing 100084, China
duzhao@gmail.com
[3] Lazaridis School of Business & Economics, Wilfrid Laurier University, Waterloo, ON N2L 3C5, Canada
[4] Department of Finance and Management Science, University of Saskatchewan, Saskatoon, SK S7N 2A5, Canada

Abstract. The number of learners enrolled in MOOCs has increased dramatically over the previous decade due to access, unlimited location and enrollment requirements. This makes a lot of user-generated data readily accessible for MOOC-related research. This study aims to reveal topics that learners discuss most, learners' sentiment, and how these topics interact. To begin, we use an iterative method to extract the topics of reviews in order to analyze the semantic features. Further, sentiment analysis and co-occurrence analysis are implemented. The experimental results suggest that the reviews generally concentrate on five topics: instructor, student, course, after-class, and fee, of which the after-class subject has the lowest score. In addition, the review content has a strong co-occurrence relationship between instructor and course topics. The findings provide useful information for better course design and MOOC platform sustainability.

Keywords: Online Learning · MOOCs · Online Course Review · Text Mining · Sentiment Analysis

1 Introduction

Massive open online courses (MOOCs) have experienced a remarkable surge in the number of online learners, universities, and platforms during the pandemic. By the end of 2021, 19,400 MOOCs distributing in 10 subjects will be announced or launched by around 950 universities worldwide. In 2021, around 3,100 courses were added (Shah 2021). A sudden boom in MOOCs provides new sources of data and opportunities for large-scale experiments that can advance the science of learning. With the development of data mining techniques, much research has focused on user-generated data, such as course reviews (Du et al. 2021; Hew et al. 2020) and discussion forums (Amjad et al. 2022; Du et al. 2022). These channels permit learners to provide course-related summaries, reflections, and inquiries. In this study, we have chosen to focus on course reviews since they are more diverse and conducive to student-centered research than discussion forums. It incorporates more learners' subjective feelings of self-improvement and objective evaluations of course design, platform, and teaching style.

Courses in a MOOC can be divided into two categories depending on the learner's learning intention (Li et al. 2022). One of them is knowledge-seeking courses and the second is skill-seeking courses. Knowledge-seeking courses stress learning concepts or principles that strengthen learners' awareness and comprehension in order to improve their decision-making skills. The follow-up study will provide a comparative analysis and in-depth discussion of the above two types of courses.

Although existing insights have been well researched on topic extraction and sentiment analysis in online MOOC reviews, two limitations deserve further study. First, most literature usually takes one course as the subject of study (Amjad et al. 2022; Greene et al. 2015) or integrates reviews from different disciplines of courses for analysis (Hew et al. 2020; Liu et al. 2019). However, different categories of courses are taught for different purposes, and learners have different concerns and learning goals. Second, in previous studies (Hew et al. 2020; Qi and Liu 2021), most of them mapped each comment or each sentence with one topic. However, learners usually incorporate multiple topics into a single comment. Therefore, a multi-topic analysis of single-sentence comments is necessary.

To fill these gaps, our research questions are as follows: (1) In a Chinese MOOC, what are the top topics that learners are concerned about? (2) What are the sentimental tendencies toward learners' concerned topics? (3) How about the co-occurrence of topics? The following section provides an insight into existing works. Section 3 presents the research framework and methods. Section 4 provides a discussion of our experimental results. The findings and future work are discussed in Sect. 5. Section 6 finally concludes the work.

2 Literature Review

2.1 Evaluation of MOOC Performance

With the development of information technology in education, MOOCs offer new possibilities for online learning, facilitating and improving the online learning experience. In the last decade, regardless of their gender, age or country, learners can study various kinds of courses offered by the University through the Internet. MOOCs have attracted global learners with free and open educational resources to reuse anytime and anywhere. (Qi and Liu 2021). Researchers have studied several aspects of MOOCs performance, including dropout rates, learning satisfaction, orientation, etc.

MOOCs have a high dropout rate that poses a challenge to researchers. Dalipi et al. (2018) attribute the high dropout rate to learner-related factors and course-related factors. In the face of high dropout rates from MOOCs, researchers examined the factors that influence retention (completion). However, Greene et al. (2015) show that learners' expected investment and intention are related to retention, level of schooling, and expected hours devote to the achievement prediction in another dataset. Besides, the learning satisfaction has been a major concern of researchers and educators over the years. Hew et al. (2020) indicated that learning satisfaction is a more appropriate measure of MOOC success since many learners do not aim to complete the course. The results suggest that course assessment, instructor, and content have a significant effect on learner learning satisfaction.

2.2 MOOC Review Mining

Review data can be obtained from the MOOC platform, and learners use the reviews to evaluate the instructor's delivery, course design, course content, and learning. Comments help to promote course design and content improvement. Research related to natural language processing (NLP) has been done by many different researchers over the years, which lays a solid foundation for the text mining field. Some researchers have developed text analysis tools (i.e., Wordify, LIWC) to facilitate research in text mining (Pennebaker et al. 2001). Hew et al. (2020) used the gradient boosting trees model to classify MOOC learner comments into six aspects.

In contrast to the former, unsupervised learning methods do not require prior data labeling. The LDA model is the most used topic extraction method, proposed by Blei et al. in 2003. Qi and Liu (2021) propose the Sentence-LDA method to classify reviews into five topics: teacher, content, exercise, platform, and hot course. Liu et al. (2019) propose BSTM, an improved Sen-LDA algorithm. In addition, an iteration-based topic extraction model is proposed that can assign multiple topics to a single comment (Li et al. 2022).

Moreover, many scholars have studied from a sentiment analysis perspective. Liu et al. (2021) use control value theory to classify achievement emotions into four categories and use random forest methods to predict and explore the impact of achievement emotions on learners' learning (Fig. 1).

3   Material and Methods

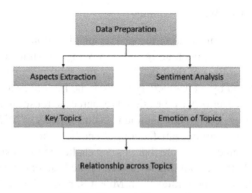

Fig. 1. Research framework

The research framework of this paper is as follows. Section 3.1 explicitly describes the review data collection and preprocessing. Then, key topics and related keywords are identified through the iterative process. Section 3.2 describes the iterative development process, while Sect. 4.1 provides details to record the key topics extracted from the reviews. We use the Snow NLP in python to detect learners' review sentiment value and introduce two statistics, polarity, which are documented in Sect. 3.3.

3.1 Data Preparation

Depending on the intention of the learner, online courses can be categorized as knowledge-seeking and skill-seeking (Li et al. 2022). We select two courses, "Psychology and Life" (psychology course) and "Python Language Programming" (python course), and crawl reviews from the Chinese universities MOOC website (https://www. icourse163.org/) as the research objects. The dataset contains 28,063 python course reviews and 11,246 psychology course reviews. MOOC provided by Chinese universities allow learners to pursue interdisciplinary education, similar to platforms such as Coursera and EdX.

Considering the following two reasons, we use a sentence as the basic unit to segment the comments. First, learners may express multiple sentiments in different sentences of one comment. Using sentences as the unit of analysis can lower the granularity of analysis and improve the accuracy of sentiment analysis results. Second, one comment may belong to many topics. Using a sentence as the basic unit can reduce the repetition rate of comments among different topics and make the sentiment mean of different categories of comments more accurate. In summary, we use a period (.), an exclamation mark (!), and a question mark (?) as sentence endings to split the comments.

Since our focus is on learners' review texts, we preprocess the reviews through the following steps: (1) filter the comments with repeated reviews; (2) delete non-Chinese comments; (3) lowercase English characters; (4) remove punctuation; (5) split the comments by PKUSEG library; (6) remove stop words; (7) convert traditional Chinese characters into simplified Chinese characters; (8) extract sentences containing English words for specific analysis and determine whether to delete them; (9) extract buzzwords and analyze them specifically; Then we obtain with a total of 26,694 sentences in python course and 11,475 sentences in psychology course.

3.2 Topics Extraction

In this study, an iterative approach is used to classify the reviews (Li et al. 2022). First, we apply a top-down process to estimate the review topics and the corresponding keywords. Second, word frequency statistics using a python program is used to extract the 1,000 most frequent words in the reviews of the two courses separately, and a bottom-up process is used to assign the corresponding topics to the keywords (excluding common and unclear words). Each review can be assigned to multiple categories. The top 1,000 high-frequency words do not cover all the comments. Therefore, each author further expands and discusses the word library. This paper has formed the word library after two iterations.

3.3 Sentiment Analysis

We use the SnowNLP in Python to detect the sentiment of learners' comments. SnowNLP is a TextBlob-inspired class library developed exclusively for processing Chinese text. It measures the sentiment value by returning a value from 0 to 1. This paper explores the comment sentiment distribution by Polarity (Schoenmueller et al. 2020). The sentiment value is quantified on a five-point scale with an interval length of 0.2. For example, a sentiment value of 0 to 0.2 corresponds to one star, whereas 0.2 to 0.4 corresponds to two stars.

$$Polarity = \frac{Number(one - and\ five - star\ ratings)}{Number\ of\ ratings} \tag{1}$$

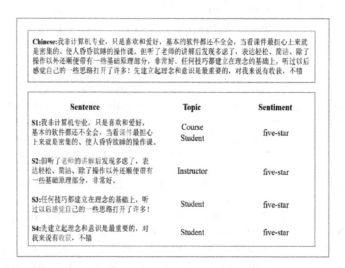

Fig. 2. A sample of Topic Extraction and sentiment analysis

According to Eq. 1, the extreme 20% of the scale on each side is defined as polarity, whereas a polarity measure below 40% implies a nonpolar distribution. To understand the process and results of processing data in Sect. 3, we use a comment as an example, as Fig. 2 shows.

4 Results

4.1 Topic Extraction Result

We follow the iterative-based aspect extraction approach introduced in Sect. 3.2. After two iterations, we finally form the word library in Table 1. Total reviews are divided into five topics: instructor, course, after-class, student and fee.

The student expresses the learners' feelings of the course (i.e., harvest, sense of accomplishment) as well as to the learners themselves (i.e., zero-based, beginner). Beginners tend to demonstrate course gains by emphasizing that they have no relevant subject

Table 1. The mapping between topics and words

Topic	Mapping words
Instructor	(v.):(explain/讲解)(lecture/讲课) 授课(teach/教学) 教 讲授 上课(guide/引导)(speak/讲, 讲的, 讲得)
	(n.):(teacher/老师 教师)(Tian Song/嵩天)(team/团队)(speed of speech/语速)(professor/教授)(teaching method/教学方式 教学方法)(teaching assistant/助教)(dialect/方言)(accent/口音)(Changkai Chen/陈昌凯)
	(adj.):(clear/清晰)(easy to understand/深入浅出, 通俗易懂)(humorous/幽默) (funny/风趣)(mouthy/嘴瓢)(dedicated/敬业)(common/通俗)(witty/诙谐)
Course	(v.):(design/设计)(attend class/上课)(choreograph/编排)(give an example/举例)(play/播放)(recommend/推荐)(inspire/激发)
	(n.):(content/内容)(examples/实例 例子, 示例 样例)(cases/案例) (course design/课程设计)(theory/理论)(curriculum/课程)(basic knowledge/基础知识)(tutorials/教程)(structure/结构)(system/体系)(classroom/课堂)(unit/单元)(each lesson/每节课)(chapter/章节)(example of exercises/例题)(national excellent course/国家精品课程)(excellent course/精品课程 精品课)(course system/课程体系)(video/视频)(courseware/课件)(textbook/教材 课本) (material/资料)(book/书籍)(subtitle/字幕)(lesson/课) (rhythm/节奏)(programming lesson/编程课)(knowledge point/知识点)(structure/结构)(MOOC/慕课平台)(website/网站)(Beijing Institute of Technology/北京理工大学)(teaching resource/教学资源)(work/作品)(teaching mode/教学模式)(progress/进度)(online course/网课)(effect/效果)(practicality/实用性)(practical goods/干货)(five-stars/五星)(in class/课上)(double speed/倍速)
	(adj.):(advanced/进阶的)(compact/紧凑的)(reasonably detailed/详略得宜的) (difficult/困难的)(simple/简单的)(practical/实用的)
Student	(v.):(harvest/收获)(attend a class/听课)(improve/提高)(cheer/加油)(learn/学到)(feel/感受)(study/研究)(understand/听懂)
	(n.):(beginner/初学者, 小白)(learning effectiveness/学习效果)(efficiency/效率)(learner/学习者)(memorization/记性)(sense of accomplishment/成就感)(feeling/感觉,感触)(emotion/情绪)(health/健康)
	(adj.):(benefit a lot/受益匪浅 获益匪浅)(after learning/学完)(understandable/听得懂)(hard-working/努力学习)(doubtful/疑惑)(zero-based/零基础)
After-class	(v.):(test/测试)(quiz/测验)(practice/练习, 实践 实操实战)(pass/及格)
	(n.):(homework/作业)(after class/课后)(practice question/练习题)(question/题目)(after-school exercise/课后练习)(examination/考试)(test/测试)(answer/答案)(quizzes/测验)(grade/成绩)(certificate/证书) (WeChat group/微信群)
Fee	(adj.):(free of charge/免费)

background. The instructor dimension reflects learners' concerns about the teacher's instructional characteristics. The teaching style (i.e., humorous) and understanding of course content (i.e., easy to understand, common) are all important factors. Learners prefer teachers who can teach courses from elementary to profound. There is no doubt that a teacher who is humorous and dedicated is popular. The course dimension reflects the course content design (i.e., choreograph, examples), course materials (i.e., textbook, video), and MOOC platform features (i.e., online lesson). Learners' reviews are mostly "advanced", "compact" or "reasonably detailed". "exam" and "exercise" reflect learner demand for after-school services.

4.2 Sentiment Detection of Topics

After identifying the five key topics in Sect. 4.1, this subsection conducts statistical analysis on each topic. In Sect. 3.3, we use SnowNLP to analyze the sentiment value of each review. We use Eq. 3 to calculate the average of the quantified sentiment value of each topic.

$$\overline{M_i} = \frac{1}{N} \sum_{n=1}^{N} M_{i,n} \tag{2}$$

where N is equal to the number of reviews in a topic and $\overline{M_i}$ represents the mean of the sentiment scores of topic i. We summarize the statistics for these two courses in Table 2. The first two columns of Table 2 show the total volume of reviews for a given topic i. The third and fourth columns show the average sentiment of a topic, which comes from Eq. 2. The standard deviation σ sentiment scores are calculated according to the following equation.

$$\sigma_i = \sqrt{\frac{1}{N} \sum_{n=1}^{N} \left(M_{i,n} - \overline{M}_i\right)^2} \tag{3}$$

The last two columns show the polarity of a topic. The results show that the student, instructor and course topic are widely discussed by learners. In comparison, the after-class topic, fee are less mentioned. People pay more attention to the instructor and course design, as well as the experience and feelings brought by the course. Besides the instructor, course, and student topics all have a high value in polarity. This indicates that learners generally evaluate these topics highly. Conversely, learners' ratings of after-class and fee are relatively low.

4.3 Detection of Relationships Across Topics

In this subsection, we give a more detailed analysis of the associations of the five topics. The accompanying topic value of any two topics is computed using the following formula (Quan and Ren 2010):

$$p\left(e_i|e_j\right) = \frac{count\left(e_{iwith}e_j\right)}{count\left(e_j\right)} \tag{4}$$

where count(e_j) equals to the number of one topic, count (e_j with e_i) donates the frequency of co-occurrence of e_i and e_j. The accompanying matrix of the python course and psychology course are presented in Tables 3 and 4, respectively.

Table 2. The statistic for each topic

Topic	Rev. (P)	Rev. (M)	Mean (P)	Mean (M)	Std. (P)	Std. (M)	Pol. (P)	Pol.(M)
Instructor	13,437	4,425	4.94	4.97	0.342	0.245	0.967	0.977
Course	11,857	4,250	4.84	4.89	0.609	0.464	0.920	0.931
Student	8,227	3,112	4.84	4.93	0.580	0.359	0.914	0.948
After-class	1,632	181	4.70	4.37	0.866	1.313	0.887	0.878
Fee	85	7	4.88	4.86	0.359	0.378	0.894	0.857

Note: Rev.- number of reviews, P - python, M - psychology, Pol - polarity

For both courses, the course topic displays the highest probability with the instructor topic and vice versa. In particular, we can get the probability of the topic instructor being 0.38 in the psychology course. It is likely that learners will mention the instructor when discussing the course.

The probability of student topic appearing together with other topics is lower in knowledge-seeking courses than in skill-seeking courses (0.149 vs 0.23). Learners who aim to acquire knowledge concentrate more on expressing their feelings and gains in their comments, whereas learners who aim to acquire skills depend more on acquiring skills through the teacher's explanation. The frequency of the fee topic co-occurrence with other topics is uncommon in both courses.

Another insightful observation comes from the after-class topic. For knowledge-seeking courses, after-class topic comments are more likely to coincide with the course topic. These transparent relationships manifest that the high relevance between the after-class topic and the course content is essential for learner knowledge acquisition.

Table 3. Accompanying matrix for the python course

e_i	e_j				
	instructor	course	student	after-class	fee
instructor	1	0.346	0.230	0.085	0.035
course	0.305	1	0.177	0.192	0.294
student	0.141	0.123	1	0.066	0.071
after-class	0.010	0.026	0.013	1	0
fee	0	0.002	0	0	1

Table 4. Accompanying matrix for the psychology course

e_i	e_j				
	instructor	course	student	after-class	fee
instructor	1	0.380	0.149	0.099	0
course	0.365	1	0.165	0.215	0.143
student	0.105	0.120	1	0.077	0.143
after-class	0.004	0.009	0.004	1	0
fee	0	0	0	0	1

5   Discussion

This study first identify five key topics. Then, from an emotional perspective, each topic is quantified to obtain learners' emotional tendencies towards each topic. In addition, we study the correlation between different topics in two types of courses respectively.

5.1   Implications for Practice

From a practical standpoint, this study can provide a reliable resource for designing MOOCs for decision-makers. In designing knowledge-seeking courses, decision-makers should consider market demand. Course quality is highly dependent on the instructor. It is suggested that the MOOC platform find a humorous, devoted, and witty instructor for skill-building courses. For knowledge-seeking courses, course design, courseware presentation, etc., must be developed with greater care. In addition, we should also pay attention to the design of the content of after-class assignments. If it is too difficult, learners' emotions will be affected, and if it is too easy, it is not conducive to learners' consolidation after class.

5.2   Limitations and Future Directions

This study has the following limitations, which inform for future work. First, the study uses the snowNLP to calculate the sentiment value in a sentence. However, a sentence has different emotional tendencies on different topics, which may lead to biased results. Future research can try more advanced deep learning algorithms to analyze reviews. Second, we study a simple course for each type of course. To a certain extent, they lack representation. In the future, the data from other courses of MOOCs and other platforms will be integrated to expand the research object.

6 Conclusions

This research takes 39,309 reviews of two courses as research subjects to study MOOC learners' most concerned topics, the sentimental tendencies, and the interaction of these topics. We identify five key topics: instructor, course, student, after-class, and fee. The result indicates that learners pay more attention to the instructor and course design, and the experience and feeling that the course brings. A high-quality course requires a competent instructor who can design the course well and provide the learning materials so that learners can acquire the necessary skills. Both instructor and course are the factors that affect the quality of MOOCs. Whether it is skill-seeking or knowledge-seeking, the course shows robust correlations. Learners who aim to acquire knowledge are more focused on expressing their feelings and gains in comments, while learners who aim to acquire skills rely more on skills acquired through teachers' explanations. For skill-seeking courses, free courses increase learner satisfaction with the course.

Acknowledgement. This work is supported by the National Natural Science Foundation of China (71901030) and Social Sciences and Humanities Research Council of Canada (435-2021-0941; 435-2020-0761).

References

Amjad, T., Shaheen, Z., Daud, A.: Advanced learning analytics: aspect based course feedback analysis of MOOC forums to facilitate instructors. IEEE Trans. Comput. Soc. Syst. Early Access 1–9 (2022)

Dalipi, F., Imran, A.S., Kastrati, Z.: MOOC dropout prediction using machine learning techniques: review and research challenges. In: 2018 IEEE Global Engineering Education Conference (EDUCON), pp. 1007–1014. IEEE (2018)

Du, Z., Wang, F., Wang, S.: Reviewer experience vs. expertise: Which matters more for good course reviews in online learning? Sustainability **13**(21), 12230 (2021)

Du, Z., Wang, F., Wang, S.: Posting versus replying: the effects of instructor participation in MOOC discussion forums. In: HICSS, pp. 1–10 (2022)

Greene, J.A., Oswald, C.A., Pomerantz, J.: Predictors of retention and achievement in a massive open online course. Am. Educ. Res. J. **52**(5), 925–955 (2015)

Hew, K.F., Hu, X., Qiao, C., Tang, Y.: What predicts student satisfaction with MOOCs: a gradient boosting trees supervised machine learning and sentiment analysis approach. Comput. Educ. **145**, 103724 (2020)

Hone, K.S., El Said, G.R.: Exploring the factors affecting MOOC retention: a survey study. Comput. Educ. **98**, 157–168 (2016)

Li, L., Johnson, J., Aarhus, W., Shah, D.: Key factors in MOOC pedagogy based on NLP sentiment analysis of learner reviews: what makes a hit. Comput. Educ. **176**, 104354 (2022)

Liu, B., Xing, W., Zeng, Y., Wu, Y.: Quantifying the influence of achievement emotions for student learning in MOOCs. J. Educ. Comput. Res. **59**(3), 429–452 (2021) .

Liu, S., Peng, X., Cheng, H.N., Liu, Z., Sun, J., Yang, C.: Unfolding sentimental and behavioral tendencies of learners' concerned topics from course reviews in a MOOC. J. Educ. Comput. Res. **57**(3), 670–696 (2019)

Pennebaker, J.W., Francis, M.E., Booth, R.J.: Linguistic Inquiry and Word Count: LIWC 2001, p. 71. Lawrence Erlbaum Associates, Mahway (2001)

Qi, C., Liu, S.: Evaluating on-line courses via reviews mining. IEEE Access **9**, 35439–35451 (2021)

Quan, C., Ren, F.: A blog emotion corpus for emotional expression analysis in Chinese. Comput. Speech Lang. **24**(4), 726–749 (2010)

Schoenmueller, V., Netzer, O., Stahl, F.: The polarity of online reviews: Prevalence, drivers and implications. J. Mark. Res. **57**(5), 853–877 (2020)

Shah, D.: By the numbers: MOOCs in 2021. The Report by Class Central. https://www.classcentral.com/report/mooc-stats-2021

Wu, B.: Influence of MOOC learners discussion forum social interactions on online reviews of MOOC. Educ. Inf. Technol. **26**(3), 3483–3496 (2021). https://doi.org/10.1007/s10639-020-10412-z

Tourist Satisfaction Analysis of Rural Cultural Tourism Based on the Enhanced IPA Model

Minglei Li[1,2(✉)], Guoyin Jiang[2], Wenping Liu[1], and Shan Chang[1]

[1] School of Information Management and the Institute of Big Data and Digital Economy, Hubei University of Economics, Wuhan 430205, China
liminglei@hbue.edu.cn
[2] School of Public Affairs and Administration, University of Electronic Science and Technology, Chengdu 611731, China

Abstract. Tourist satisfaction can provide valuable information for advancing the development of rural cultural tourism. In literatures the IPA (Importance-Performance Analysis) model is a commonly used technique for understanding customer satisfaction. However, the standard IPA only considers two dimensions (i.e., importance and performance), and thus cannot yield fine-grained attributes. As such, in this paper we propose an enhanced IPA model (i.e., Importance-Performance-Frequency Analysis, IPFA) to analyze the tourist satisfaction of rural cultural tourism in a more fine-grained way. IPFA has three characteristics: (1) it uses online reviews which are timely, truthful, large-scale and easy to be obtained, (2) it uses three dimensionalities (i.e., importance, performance and frequency) to finely classify the attributes, and (3) it uses a novel machine learning model LightGBM to estimate the importance of each attribute, such that the more accurate importance indicators can be obtained with excellent generalization. In the case study on the typical rural cultural tourisms, it shows that the IPFA can effectively identify the views of tourists, analyze the satisfaction of different tourists with different attributes, and offer good suggestions of the development for different attributes.

Keywords: Tourist Satisfaction Analysis · Rural Cultural Tourism · Enhanced IPA Model

1 Introduction

Rural cultural tourism is one of the important ways to implement the rural revitalization strategy. However, the COVID-19 epidemic has brought a huge impact on the tourism industry. Since 2019, the annual number of tourists and their comprehensive contributions to GDP in the last three years have decreased dramatically. Rural cultural tourism also suffered from the impact of the epidemic. In the severe market environment, it is an important means to promote the healthy development of rural cultural tourism to construct and manage based on the demand side. In this context, it is necessary to explore fully the tourists' satisfaction, starting from the tourists' personal feelings, to improve

Y. Tu and M. Chi (Eds.): WHICEB 2023, LNBIP 481, pp. 309–318, 2023.
https://doi.org/10.1007/978-3-031-32302-7_27

the rural cultural tourism products, enhance their competitiveness, and promote their development healthily and orderly.

Through the tourist satisfaction analysis of rural cultural tourism, we can find out tourists' personal experience of rural cultural tourism products, and the key factors that affect the tourists' experience. IPA (Importance-Performance Analysis) [1] is a commonly used research technique for understanding customer satisfaction. However, standard IPA only considers two dimensions in the analysis process, and cannot classify attributes finely. On the other hand, the traditional way to analyze tourist satisfaction mainly collects tourists' views on rural cultural tourism products in the form of questionnaires and interviews. There are many limitations for that way. For example, it is difficult to collect samples, the number of samples is small, and the samples are prone to bias and so on. There are also many rural cultural tourism tourists, who have published many reviews on rural cultural tourism products on tourism E-Commerce platform websites or tourism review websites. These online reviews contain rich information such as tourists' preferences, feelings, and opinions. Based on these online review data, the tourists' satisfaction analysis of rural cultural tourism has become a new research approach [2]. Moreover, this method can obtain a large-scale real data quickly and conveniently, and the tourists' satisfaction of rural cultural tourism can be timely and accurately perceived.

As such, this paper proposes an enhance IPA model (i.e., Importance-Performance-Frequency Analysis, IPFA) based on the standard IPA (SIPA), and uses the tourist reviews in tourism online social network platform as research material. A new dimension, frequency, is added in IPFA. IPFA based on three dimensions can classify attributes into eight categories, while SIPA only divides the attributes of tourism products into four categories. IPFA can analyze the tourists' satisfaction in a fine-grained way.

The remainder of this paper is organized as follows. Section 2 briefly reviews the relevant literature. Section 3 presents a methodology of this paper. In Sect. 4, a case study of the enhance IPA for some typical rural cultural tourisms is presented. Finally, conclusions are given in Sect. 5.

2   Literature Review

2.1   Studies on the Tourist Satisfaction

Tourist satisfaction is a concept based on customer satisfaction theory [3]. It represents the difference between tourists' expectation and actual perception, reflects the image and reputation of tourism products, and directly affects tourists' loyalty and revisit rate. The commonly used analysis model of tourist satisfaction is SERVQUAL [4] and its variants. For example, the satisfaction analysis of luxury hotels [5], evaluation of the service quality of ski resorts [6], and tourist satisfaction evaluation of Australians traveling in Vietnam [7]. Another commonly used tourist satisfaction analysis model is IPA [1].

Typically, the data used for tourist satisfaction analysis are obtained from customers through surveys. However, surveys are expensive in terms of time and money. Besides, the quality of the data obtained from surveys depends on the complexity or length of the questionnaire and the willingness of the respondents to participate. With the development of online social network platform for tourism, more and more tourists publish review data on it. Thus, more and more researchers begin to use online review data to analyze the tourist satisfaction [8–10].

2.2 SIPA Model

SIPA model [11] divides different product/service attributes into different categories according to two dimensions, importance, and satisfaction. Attributes of the product/service are classified into four quadrants or categories. As shown in Fig. 1, the attribute positioned in Q1 has a higher performance and a higher importance. And the attributes positioned in Q1 can be regulated as the main advantages of the product/service, and should continue to be maintained in the follow-up operation activities; The attributes positioned in Q2 have a lower performance and a higher importance, and are the general advantages of the product/service. The attributes positioned in Q3 have a lower performance and a lower importance. The attributes in this area are the minor defects of the product/service, and should be developed with sufficient resources. The attributes positioned in Q4 have a higher performance and a lower importance. The attributes in this region are the main disadvantages of the product/service, and resources should be focused on developing the attributes of them.

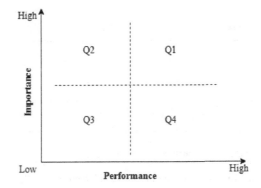

Fig. 1. The standard importance performance analysis

SIPA is a simple and easy method to analyze satisfaction. It has been used in many fields, such as tourist hotel [12], E-Business [13], higher education [14], etc. However, SIPA only classifies the attributes of products/services based on the two dimensions of importance and satisfaction, and cannot distinguish the attributes more precisely.

3 Methodology

3.1 Overall Structure of the Method

Aiming to analyze the tourist satisfaction based on the online reviews, the overall structure of the method proposed in this paper is shown in Fig. 2. There are three steps in the method, including reviews data capturing and cleaning, fine-grained sentiment analysis and improved IPA. Specifically, first, in the data collection stage, we use the web crawler to collect the online review data of rural cultural tourism products from the online social network platform of the tourism E-Commerce website, Then, in the fine-grained emotion analysis stage, the attributes contained in each review are extracted by combining the topic analysis model method LDA and template matching. Finally, in the improved IPA analysis stage, the frequency is added and a new model, IPFA, is proposed, which can conduct a more fine-grained analysis of tourist satisfaction.

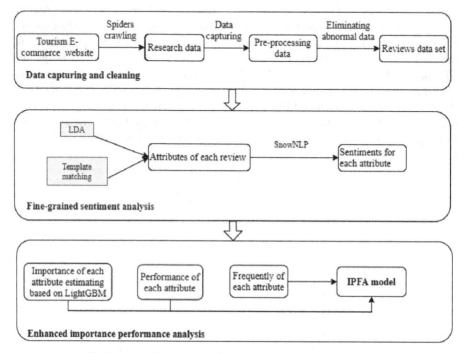

Fig. 2. Analysis structure of tourist satisfaction based on IPFA

3.2 Extracting the Attributes Based on LDA

In order to analyze the tourists' satisfaction with tourism products from the online reviews in a fine-grained way, it is necessary to extract the attributes of tourists' description of tourism products from the online reviews. To extract the attributes of tourists' online reviews accurately, this work proposes an attribute extraction method based on LDA and template matching.

LDA [15] is an unsupervised Machine Learning algorithm that extracts semantic structure from many texts to achieve text classification, keyword extraction, information filtering and other functions [16].

All the pre-processed tourists' online reviews are treated as a document. Assuming that the attributes of the online comments of tourists are N. The strategy for extracting the attributes is: LDA is used to generate N topics of the document, and each topic corresponds to an attribute.

3.3 Enhanced IPA Model

Assuming that R represents all online comment sets, that is, $R = \{R_1, R_2, \cdots R_M\}$, R_{ij} represents the sentence set of the j-th attribute in the i-th comment, the emotional orientation value of these sentences can be obtained using emotional analysis tool SnowNLP. And S_{ij} represents the emotional orientation value of the j-th attribute in the i-th comment.

This paper also uses the emotional orientation value as the satisfaction degree of attributes, that is, the satisfaction of tourists with the j-th attribute of scenic spot, P_j, is expressed by the average emotional orientation value of the sentences about the attribute j in all relevant comments, as shown in formula (1):

$$P_j = \frac{\sum_{i=1}^{M_j} S_{ij}}{M_j} \tag{1}$$

In formula (1), M_j represents the number of sentences related to attribute j in all online comments.

The importance index I in IPA refers to the importance of different attributes on tourist satisfaction. This paper uses an advanced Machine Learning model, LightGBM [17], to obtain the importance of each attribute.

The frequency F_j of tourists to the attribute j of the scenic spot is the proportion of the comments on the attribute j included in the online comments in the overall comments, as shown in formula (2):

$$F_j = \frac{M_j}{M} \tag{2}$$

The method IPFA adds the dimension of Frequency, which can divide the attributes of tourism products in a more fine-grained way, as shown in Table 1. According to the results of IPFA, they can be used as a follow-up input or improvement scheme for each attribute.

Table 1. The Importance-Performance-Frequency analysis

Categories ID	Importance	Performance	Frequency	Categories name
C1	Higher	Higher	Higher	special keep up the good work
C2	Higher	Higher	Lower	general keep up the good work
C3	Higher	Lower	Higher	special concentrate here
C4	Higher	Lower	Lower	general concentrate here
C5	Lower	Higher	Higher	special possible overkill
C6	Lower	Higher	Lower	general possible overkill
C7	Lower	Lower	Higher	special low priority
C8	Lower	Lower	Lower	general low priority

4   Experimental Results and Analysis

4.1   Experimental Data

We choose several typical rural cultural tourisms as the research objects, such as Gubeishui Town, Phoenix Ancient City, Nianhua Bay, Wuzhen and Wuyuan. Use the web crawler to obtain the online comment data of tourists on these scenic spots on Ctrip[1], and 38477 online comments are obtained as the research data of this paper.

4.2   Fine-Grained Sentiment Analysis for Online Reviews

For the 38477 online comment texts, we first use the Chinese word segmentation tool Jieba to segment them, remove the stop words, and then use Python's LDA tool[2] to model the theme. Based on the research of existing literature, we set the number of topics of LDA as 14. Based on the attribute extraction method designed in Sect. 3.2, we determined manually the attributes mentioned in these online comments, including the following fourteen types: natural scenery, folk customs, commercialization, cultural environment, architecture, passenger flow, transportation, accommodation, catering, consumption perception, entertainment experience, tourism services, scenic spot management and infrastructure.

Based on the SnowNLP[3], the emotion analysis is carried out on the sentences related to each attribute of each comment, and its emotional orientation value can be obtained.

4.3   Analyzing Importance of Each Attribute Based on LightGBM

We randomly select 80% in the 38477 online reviews as the training set of the model and the remaining 20% as the test set. The LightGBM model[4] is trained using the training set, and the training effect is verified using the test set. We compare the performance of LightGBM and the other common machine learning models based on decision trees, such as Decision Trees, Random Forests and Xgboost [18]. The comparison results are shown in Fig. 3.

According to the results in Fig. 3, LightGBM has the lowest mean square error and the strongest generalization ability in the test set, which shows that LightGBM has the best prediction effect.

Use the trained LightGBM to obtain the importance indicators of each attribute of the scenic spot products, and the results are shown in Fig. 4.

According to the results in Fig. 4, it can be seen that the attributes of consumption perception, natural scenery and commercialization have a great impact on the overall tourists' satisfaction, while the infrastructure, accommodation and catering of the scenic spot have a relatively small impact on the overall satisfaction of tourists.

---

[1] https://you.ctrip.com/.

[2] https://radimrehurek.com/gensim/.

[3] https://pypi.org/project/snownlp/.

[4] https://lightgbm.readthedocs.io/.

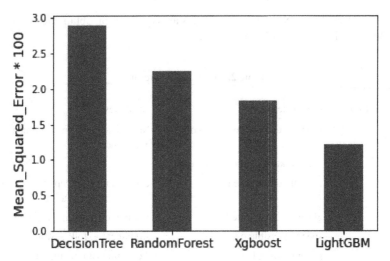

Fig. 3. Performance comparison of different machine learning models

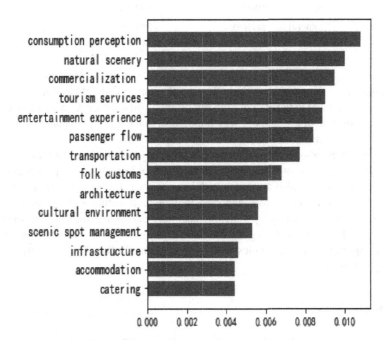

Fig. 4. Ranking of attribute importance index

4.4 Analyzing Results Based on IPFA

Based on the emotional orientation value of each attribute under each comment obtained in Sect. 4.2, the performance and frequency of tourists for the 14 attributes of scenic spot products are calculated using formula (1) and formula (2). Combining the importance of attributes extracted from Sect. 4.3, using IPFA analysis, we can obtain the classification of fourteen attributes, as shown in Table 2.

Table 2. IPFA analysis results

Categories ID	Categories name	Attributes
C1	special keep up the good work	Natural scenery, entertainment experience
C2	general keep up the good work	-
C3	special concentrate here	Consumption perception, tourism services, transportation
C4	general concentrate here	Commercialization, passenger flow
C5	special possible overkill	Architecture, folk customs
C6	general possible overkill	Accommodation, cultural environment
C7	special low priority	Catering
C8	general low priority	Infrastructure, scenic spot management

According to the results in Table 2, natural scenery and entertainment belong to Category 1, which are in the area of high importance - high satisfaction - high frequency. There is no attribute in Category 2, which indicates that many tourists also pay attention to the attributes of high importance and high satisfaction.

The attributes belonging to Category 3 include consumption perception, tourism services and transportation. Similarly, the attributes of Category 4, commercialization, and passenger flow, are also attributes with low satisfaction and high importance.

The attributes belonging to Category 5 include architecture and folk customs. The attributes belonging to Category 6 include accommodation and cultural environment.

Attributes belonging to Category 7 include catering, which is low in tourist satisfaction and importance. The attributes belonging to Category 8 include infrastructure and scenic spot management.

5   Conclusions

In order to analyze the tourist satisfaction of rural cultural tourism deeply, this paper designs an enhanced IPA model, IPFA, based on SIPA, and uses the tourist reviews in tourism online social network platform as research material. The main contributions of this paper are: (1) a new dimension, frequency, is added in IPFA. IPFA based on three dimensions can classify attributes into eight categories, while SIPA only divides the attributes of tourism products into four categories. (2) An excellent machine learning model LightGBM is used to estimate the importance of each attribute in IPFA. Light-GBM may obtain more accurate importance indictors. Furthermore, the effectiveness and practicability of the method proposed in this paper are demonstrated by the experimental study.

However, the methods and conclusions of this paper are still preliminary and limited. Our ongoing work is to consider the following aspects: (1) select more rural cultural tourism products and online review data, to mine more accurate information and to provide more helpful reference for tourism managers; (2) the current research in this paper is static. In the future, the time factor could be added to analyze the law of the change of tourist satisfaction with time; (3) the method we proposed has certain universality and can be also applied to the analysis of customer satisfaction of other products/services.

Acknowledgement. This work was partially supported by the National Natural Science Foundation of China under Grant under Grant 72071031 and Grant 62072163, the Humanities and Social Sciences Research Youth Foundation of the Ministry of Education of China under Grant 20YJCZH072, the Fundamental Research Funds for the Central Universities of China (No. ZYGX2017KYQD185), and the Hubei Provincial Department of Education Scientific Research Program Project (B2021169).

References

1. John, A.M., John, C.J.: Importance-performance analysis. J. Mark. **41**(1), 77–79 (1977)
2. Yue, G., Stuart, J.B., Qiong, J.: Mining meaning from online ratings and reviews: Tourist satisfaction analysis using latent dirichlet allocation. Tour. Manage. **59**, 467–483 (2017)
3. Abraham, P., Yoram, N., Arie, R.: Dimentions of tourist satisfaction with a destination area. Ann. Tour. Res. **5**(3), 314–322 (1978)
4. Gavin, R.F.: JR Brent R: Measuring service quality in the travel and tourism industry. J. Travel Res. **30**(2), 2–9 (1991)
5. Carol, L., Celine, B., Michael, W.M.: Service quality and customer satisfaction: qualitative research implications for luxury hotels. Int. J. Cult. Tour. Hosp. Res. **9** (2015)
6. Isabelle, F., Dominique, K.: Customers' perceptions of skiresorts' images: implications for resorts' positioning strategies. Tour. Hosp. Res. **8**(4), 298–308 (2008)
7. Joanna, T., Susan, A.M.: Importance-satisfaction analysis for marine-park hinterlands: a Western Australian case study. Tour. Manage. **28**(3), 768–776 (2007)
8. Markus, S., Xianwei, L., Rob, L.: Hospitality and tourism online reviews: recent trends and future directions. J. Travel Tour. Mark. **32**(5), 608–621 (2015)
9. Ali, A., Mehrbakhsh, N., Elaheh, Y.: Revealing customers? Satisfaction and preferences through online review analysis: the case of canary islands hotels. J. Retail. Consum. Serv. **51**, 331–343 (2019)
10. Mehrbakhsh, N., Rabab, A.A., Abdullah, A.: What is the impact of service quality on customers? satisfaction during Covid-19 outbreak? New findings from online reviews analysis. Telematics Inform. **64**, 101693 (2021)
11. Ivan, K.W.L., Michael, H.: Importance–performance analysis in tourism: a framework for researchers. Tour. Manage. **48**, 242–267 (2015)
12. Frank, C.P.: Practical application of importance-performance analysis in determining critical job satisfaction factors of a tourist hotel. Tour. Manage. **46**, 84–91 (2015)
13. Wang, A., Zhang, Q., Zhao, S., Lu, X., Peng, Z.: A review-driven customer preference measurement model for product improvement: sentiment-based importance–performance analysis. IseB **18**(1), 61–88 (2020). https://doi.org/10.1007/s10257-020-00463-7

14. Salman, N., Saeed, M., Mahdokht, T.: Importance-performance analysis based balanced score-card for performance evaluation in higher education institutions: an integrated fuzzy approach. J. Bus. Econ. Manag. **21**(3), 647–678 (2020)
15. Hamed, J., Yongli, W., Chi, Y.: Latent dirichlet allocation (LDA) and topic modeling: models, applications, a survey. Multim. Tools Appl. **78**(11), 15169–15211 (2019)
16. Zhou, T., Haiyi, Z.: A text mining research based on LDA topic modelling. In: International Conference on Computer Science, Engineering and Information Technology, pp. 201–210 (2016)
17. Guolin, K., Qi, M., Thomas, F.: Lightgbm: a highly effcient gradient boosting decision tree. Adv. Neural Inf. Process. Syst. **30** (2017)
18. Tianqi, C., Carlos, G.: XGBoost: a scalable tree boosting system. In: Proceedings of the 22nd ACM SIGKDD International Conference on Knowledge Discovery and Data Mining, pp. 785–794 (2016)

How Could Firm Resilience Benefit from the Coupling Effects of Digital Strategy and Environmental Turbulence? Configuration Analysis Based on fsQCA

Meiyu Pan[1], Maomao Chi[2(✉)], Yuyan Shen[2], and Puxiong Zhou[1]

[1] South China University of Technology, Guangzhou 510006, China
[2] China University of Geosciences, Wuhan 430074, China
chimaomao@vip.163.com

Abstract. Strong resilience is critical for all companies and industries, depending on proper strategies and the external environment. In this study, we analyze how digital strategy associated with business strategy and IT strategy, from the perspective of organizational ambidexterity, drives firm resilience. Conducting a dataset of 32 observations for the sharing accommodation industry and applying fsQCA (fuzzy-set qualitative comparative analysis) methods, our analyses reveal three key findings. First, business strategy, IT strategy, and environmental turbulence alone cannot offer the necessary conditions for firm resilience. Second, we document a few parsimonious configurations emergent from complex non-linear interactions among digital strategy (i.e., business strategy, IT strategy) and environmental turbulence. Third, we observed synergy between exploitation and exploration. Without considering the external environment, simply summing up exploitation and exploration will not be conducive to forming firm resilience. Together, the results yield implications for further exploration of firm resilience and for managers to view and redesign digital strategy as IT and business strategy configurations.

Keywords: Firm resilience · Digital strategy · Environmental turbulence · Organizational ambidexterity · fsQCA · Shared accommodation

1 Introduction

Today the problem of firm survival in the era of VUCA (volatility, uncertainty, complexity, and ambiguity) is becoming increasingly apparent. The emergence of digital infrastructures (e.g., cloud computing, Internet of Things, and 5G networks) and digital technologies (e.g., artificial intelligence, machine learning, and computer vision) can have a disruptive impact on the business model and operations of a firm [1, 2]. Meanwhile, some firms rely on successful management in the past, showing organizational inertia and rigidity in the face of external changes, thus missing the opportunity and accelerating firm death. In a word, strategic failure in allocating organizational resources can explain a significant portion of new ventures' death [3].

© The Author(s), under exclusive license to Springer Nature Switzerland AG 2023
Y. Tu and M. Chi (Eds.): WHICEB 2023, LNBIP 481, pp. 319–330, 2023.
https://doi.org/10.1007/978-3-031-32302-7_28

Firm resilience (FR) attracts the attention of scholars in the field of operational and strategic management. It helps firms maintain stable growth in the face of external shocks, such as the COVID-19 pandemic. To remain successful and survive in today's disruptive market environment, scholars now agree that firms must tackle the challenges of digital transformation and other rapidly emerging new technologies [3]. Nevertheless, many organizations fail to transform because they begin business or technology changes without developing holistic plans and a coherent digital strategy [4].

In light of this, this study aims to explore the following question: How could firm resilience benefit from the coupling effects of digital strategy and environmental turbulence? To answer the question, we use a fuzzy-set qualitative comparative analysis of 32 case studies of the shared accommodation industry. This analysis allows us to develop an overarching understanding of how digital strategy affects firm resilience. Additionally, we clarify the conceptual relationships between exploration and exploitation in implementing digital strategy from the perspective of organizational ambidexterity.

2 Literature Review

2.1 Firm Resilience

Academic research on resilience has increased due to its practical importance and thus can provide essential guidance for enterprise survival. The conceptualization of resilience has been widely used in psychology, supply chain, and firm levels [6]. Existing research suggests that firm resilience is an effective way to withstand external adversity that negatively affects the firm's operation and to recover and maintain its existing structure [7].

Most scholars focus on the organizational level when assessing the principal driving factors of resilience. These include the presence of business strategy [5], resource reconfiguration capability, and information technology capability. Beyond organizational factors, a firm's survival and development are closely linked to its environment. Environmental turbulence, or even the perception of environmental change in the external environment, has been proven to be the main external factor for firm performance. Deploying effective business strategies and developing new IT capabilities are critical to firm resilience. Sirmon points out that not all strategies and IT capabilities are equally effective or hold equal value under different environmental conditions. When faced with an external disruption, a firm must evaluate its current resource (e.g., identify strategic positioning and available resources) and develop new capabilities.

Thus, the literature suggests that the driving factors of firm resilience are not unique and independent. The combined effects of external environmental turbulence and the internal digital business strategy of the organization should be explored further.

2.2 Digital Strategy

Digital strategy is conceptualized as an organizational strategy that leverages digital resources to generate differential value. Some studies view digital strategy as a complex system consisting of several organizational digital and non-digital capabilities that produce competitive performance [7]. Developing a digital strategy that embraces business and IT strategies has been the predominant digital transformation success factor [4]. Yet, despite the researchers claiming that digital strategy unites business and IT strategy, the boundaries between them become blurred. Therefore, it is essential to explore the independent and combined effects of business and IT strategies [7].

Organizational Ambidexterity. Organizational ambidexterity refers to a firm's ability to simultaneously pursue exploration and exploitation activities. Specifically, exploration refers to disruptive innovation (e.g., risk-taking, experimentation, flexibility and innovation), which emphasizes improving products or expanding markets beyond current resources and knowledge. Exploitation refers to progressive innovation (e.g., efficiency, selection, implementation and modifications) which aims to develop new products or markets based on existing resources and knowledge [8]. The initial organizational ambidexterity study focused on non-digital business strategies, such as product and market domain. As digitalization moves at pace, the IS literature recognizes the central role of information technology (IT) in the firm competitive advantage. There-fore, existing studies have extrapolated literature on organizational ambidexterity literature to the IT context [9].

In this study, we focus on implementing digital strategy from the perspective of organizational ambidexterity: business strategy (i.e., market exploration, resource exploitation) and IT strategy (i.e., IT exploration and IT exploitation). Although we recognize that digital strategy has many dimensions [10], it is particularly useful to examine the relationship between digital strategy and firm resilience from the perspective of organizational ambidexterity. First, organizational ambidexterity is crucial to a firm success and attracted intensive research attention. The general consensus is that firms usually maintain stable development by simultaneously pursuing organizational ambidexterity (exploration and exploitation). Second, organizational ambidexterity can be applied to explain business and IT strategies.

Business Strategy. Business strategy includes opportunity exploitation strategy and resource exploration strategy. Opportunity exploitation strategy refers to the simultaneous entrance and management of multiple markets [11]. The strategy of opportunity exploitation has offered a positive path to resilience. The first key aspect is the ability to replicate the experience gained in one market to another. Bettiol et al. [11] have claimed that the experience in multiple markets enabled the company to adapt its products and processes to the standard, allowing it to be more reactive to external pressures. Moreover, the opportunity exploitation strategy also reflects the firm's internal operational flexibility [5].

We defined resource acquisition from outside as a resource exploration strategy. The exploration of resources can provide a firm with new strategic options to respond to changes in its competitive environment. Phene and his colleagues argued that aggressive innovation was often a function of the external resources to which a firm has access. In particular, resource acquisition from the outside leads to breaking rigid routines from time to time, often resulting in a breakthrough ability to explore. Similarly, researchers indicated that resource exploration strategy would enhance the positive effects of the relative exploration dimension on new product innovation, as resource from outside reduces the risk and cost of new knowledge or technology.

IT Strategy. IT strategy includes IT exploration strategy and IT exploitation strategy. IT exploration refers to an organization ability to explore new IT resources and practices [13]. IT exploration can help organizations gain and leverage IT knowledge to improve their resilience. First, by experimenting with new IT applications and practices, IT exploration can introduce new and alternative areas of knowledge. In this regard, firms can simplify their business processes and achieve considerable transaction efficiency and transaction cost reduction. Second, focusing on IT exploration can help firms identify and select IT technologies that align with the firm's future development. The high level of IT exploration enables firms to drive business innovation after recon-figuring IT resources and enables enterprises to adapt strategies rapidly, which has a positive impact on organizational agility [14].

In contrast, IT exploitation refers to exploiting current IT resources and practices [13, 15]. IT exploitation enables firms to refine and reconfigure existing IT knowledge to improve resilience. IT exploitation enables organizations to perceive better and manage market changes and improve customer satisfaction [14]. For instance, IT modularity and software compatibility can help firm adjustment to adapt to changes in the external environment and respond to customer needs at the right time.

2.3 Environmental Turbulence

The survival and development of a firm is closely related to the environment [16]. Environmental turbulence refers to the rate of unpredictability and highly varied events that occur in a particular industry's environment [17]. A variety of factors can cause turbulence. Market turbulence has been of great importance among the various elements that cause a turbulent environment. Market turbulence refers to changing market demands, which are mainly reflected in the dynamic and ambiguous nature of their requirements.

Some research observed that a turbulent environment has negatively impact on firms' activities and performance [17]. However, environmental turbulence is a risk that threatens business performance or even survival and an opportunity. In the face of environmental turbulence, firms must develop rapid, high-quality responses to protect themselves from this changing world. Enrique et al. [18] stated that the rapidly changing environment is an important antecedent to drive strategic agility. In this line, environmental turbulence promotes product and process innovation, thus achieving better business performance.

2.4 Configurational Framework

In summary, although scholars agree that resilient companies continually orchestrate a dynamic balance of strategies, research is generally limited to exploring individual conditions, ignoring the important role of organized complexity in digital strategy. In this study, we explore the mechanism that influences firm resilience from a holistic perspective to understand the nonlinear interdependencies of organized complexity in digital business strategy. Due to the complex combinations of antecedents, multiple pathways to firm resilience are difficult to study using traditional methods. Thus, we introduce a configurational framework and argue that firm resilience does not depend on a single condition, but on the interactions between digital strategy and environmental turbulence. The external turbulence of market uncertainty, and the internal digital strategy of business strategy and IT strategy should be considered for enterprises to achieve firm resilience (Fig. 1).

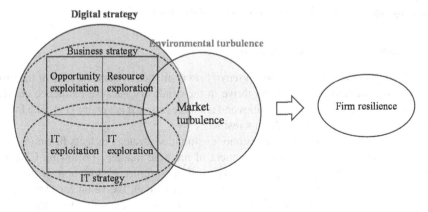

Fig. 1. A configuration framework model

3   Materials and Methods

3.1   Sample and Data Collection

We chose the Chinese sharing accommodation platform as our research data. China has become one of the world's largest homes to sharing platforms. The rapid development of China's shared accommodation market has attracted numerous users. For instance, the financing of shared accommodation industry in China reached 600 million yuan in 2021. We have compiled several data sources and a matching database for shared accommodation: ITJUZI (www.itjuzi.com) provides publicly available information on Chinese sharing platforms. Chandashi (www.app.chandashi.com) provides a list of app download data and their historical update status in 155 countries and regions worldwide.

Two selection criteria were used in this study. First, to match the business strategy with the firm, we only used cases with complete information. Second, censoring is a common occurrence in survival analysis. Censoring refers to the situation in which some individuals are only observed for a certain period of time, and their outcome is not known beyond that time. We partly retained the censoring cases, which was still operating in December 2021 (data collection time) and had survived more than 8 years and 8 months (the maximum operating time of all dead firms). This left 32 shared accommodation platforms in our final dataset.

3.2   Fuzzy-Set Qualitative Comparative Analysis

QCA is a configurational approach based on set theory and fuzzy algebra. The reasons for using fsQCA to investigate our research are the following. First, fsQCA is outcome-oriented, that is, it can determine whether specific conditions are necessary for achieving an outcome. When it comes to configural hypotheses about complicated causality, it has methodological robustness. Second, consistent with configurational theory, fsQCA allows equifinality and causal asymmetry. Third, fsQCA was designed to deal with small sample sizes and medium-sized samples (15–99 cases). Thus, our medium-sized sample of 32 sharing accommodation platforms is suitable for fsQCA.

3.3 Measurements and Calibration

Firm Resilience. We measured the degree of firm resilience by survival time of the firm. Resilient organizations survive and thrive in their industry because resilience enables the organization to develop capabilities and resources against adversity [19]. The longer the firm's survival time, the higher its resilience.

Opportunity Exploitation. Opportunity exploitation strategy reflects flexibility, i.e., the simultaneous entrance and management of multiple markets. Following Claussen [20], we used product diversity as a measure of opportunity exploitation. If the business strategic positioning is focused on the overall market, the value for Opportunity exploitation is 1; and if is focused on the segment market, the value for Opportunity exploitation is 0.

Resource exploration. We defined resource acquisition from outside as a resource exploration strategy. In this study, we utilized the number of funding rounds obtained through a sharing accommodation platform to measure resource acquisition.

IT Exploitation. Achieve the IT exploitation strategy by exploiting current IT resources and practices [13]. We use the total number of APP historical updates under each firms as a way to measure IT exploitation.

IT Exploration. Achieve the IT exploration strategy by experimenting with new IT applications and practices [13]. In this way, we measured the number of digital cooperation between the shared accommodation platform and its partnership as IT exploration. The data comes from mass media (e.g., corporate annual reports or financial news).

Environmental Turbulence. For shared accommodation enterprises, the rate of change in consumer demand is an important part of measuring market turbulence. As such, we measure environmental turbulence during the year using the rate of change in annual consumer travel. For each firm, we calculate the average strength of market turbulence experienced by the firm according to its range of survival years. The data are from the Yearbook of Chinese Culture and Tourism.

Regarding Greckhamer, we chose a more stringent standard for data distribution to calibrate the data. We decided to use the 95th percentile as the high full membership anchor, the crossover point at 50th percentile and the full non-membership anchor was 5th percentile. To prevent the case with a condition value of 0.5 from being automatically deleted, we replace the condition value of 0.5 with 0.501 after calibration. The calibration anchors are reported in Table 1.

Table 1. Calibration of the sharing accommodation outcomes and conditions

Elements and Outcomes	Measurement	Full Membership	Crossover	Full Non-Membership
Firm resilience	Survival time of the firm	16.0	8.7	2.6
Opportunity exploitation	Whether the scope of business is overall or segmented market	/	/	/
Resource exploration	The number of funding rounds	2.9	1	0
IT exploitation	The total number of APP historical updates	85	1	0
IT exploration	The number of digital cooperation between the firm and its partnership	2.9	1	0
Environment turbulence	The average rate of change in consumer demand through the span of firm survival years	0.2	0.1	0.1

4 Results

4.1 Necessity Conditions Analysis

We began the analysis by examining whether a factor was a necessary condition for high resistance or its negation (e.g., non-high resilience). A condition that exceeds the consistency threshold of 0.90 and has non-trivial coverage indicates that the antecedent or combination of antecedents is necessary. Our results show that none of the individual factors exceeds the threshold of 0.90. Therefore, no individual factor qualified as a necessary condition for both outcomes; that is, none of the conditions can be individually claimed as a necessary condition to reach either high or non-high resilience.

4.2 Sufficient Solutions

We used the fsQCA3.0 software to analyze the standardized data. Consistent with established research, we conducted a sufficiency analysis by applying a minimum case frequency benchmark of 1, setting the consistency threshold to 0.75, as is commonly recommended [7]. We also applied PRI (Proportional Reduction in Inconsistency) to filter further the rows of the truth table that are reliably linked to the outcome. We adjusted two rows of data to 0 as the configurations with a PRI score below 0.75 may show inconsistency. Using these comprehensive standards, we obtained the truth table rows that met the requirements and determined the configuration paths by running the data. The results are given in Table 2. We have identified four pathways that can lead to high levels of resilience. The overall solution consistency is 0.962, which explains the significance level of all configurations. The results show that the five configurations captured 68% of high-level resilience. We further identified three pathways that can lead to non-high levels of resilience. The overall solution consistency is 0.929, with a coverage of 0.515.

We then used Ragin's logic scheme to further summarize the seven pathways from a theoretical perspective. We propose two types of high-level resilience with different core characteristics: those oriented to IT strategy and those oriented to business strategy. We also propose three non-high levels of resilience types: (1) many pains but no gains, (2) no pains no gains, (3) and insufficient awareness of IT exploitation.

Configurations for High Levels of Resilience. IT strategy oriented indicates that, resilience can be built under conditions of high market turbulence and IT exploitation. This type of maturity includes two paths, configuration 1a and configuration 1b. The cover-age sum is 0.530, which is significantly higher than the other two types, indicating that this type has good universality. Market turbulence is the core condition which must be present. Thus, Environmental turbulence is an important external motivation for achieving a high level of resilience. Configuration 1a is ITI*MT*~ITR. In this context, which is dominated by environmental turbulence, firm can achieve high resilience with the imbalance of IT exploitation and IT exploration (ITI*~ITR). Configuration 1b is OI*ITI*MT. Combining IT exploitation and opportunity exploitation (OI*ITI) can lead to high resilience in an environmental turbulence.

Business strategy oriented indicates that both opportunity exploitation and low resource exploration is the core condition (RR*~OI). With less IT exploration, the existence of either IT exploitation or market turbulence will lead to high resilience. This type includes two pathways: configurations 2a and 2b. The sum of the coverage is 0.055. Configuration 2a is~OI*RR*ITI*~ITR. In the absence of opportunity exploitation and IT exploration, if firms gain development opportunities from resource exploration and IT exploitation, they can also effectively achieve a high level of resilience. Configuration 2b is ~ OI*RR*MT* ~ ITR. In the absence of opportunity exploitation and IT exploration, if there is environmental turbulence, the firm can make good use of resource exploration to achieve a high level of resilience.

Configurations for Non-high Levels of Resilience. The typical configuration of many pains but no gains is OI*RR*ITR*~MT (configuration 3). This type indicates that, even though the firm has made great efforts in both business strategy and IT strategy (OI*RR*ITR), it cannot achieve high firm resilience without environmental support (~MT). Unlike configuration 3, the configuration of no pains no gains is OI*~RR*~ITR*~MT (configuration 4). Under core conditions of the absence of the market turbulence, resource exploration and IT exploration (~RR*~ITR*~MT), it's impossible to achieve high firm resilience only through opportunity exploitation. In addition, insufficient awareness of IT exploitation (configuration 5: OI*RR*~ITI*ITR) indicates that, ignoring the importance of IT exploitation, even under business strategy and IT exploration conditions, it's hard to achieve high firm resilience.

Table 2. Configurations strongly related to resilience

Antecedent Condition	High levels of resilience				Non-high levels of resilience		
	1a	1b	2a	2b	3	4	5
Opportunity exploitation (OI)		•	⊗	⊗	•	●	●
Resource exploration (RR)			●	●	•	⊗	•
IT exploitation (ITI)	●	●	•				⊗
IT exploration (ITR)	⊗		⊗	⊗	●	⊗	●
Market turbulence (MT)	●	●		•	⊗	⊗	
Consistency	0.990	0.950	1.000	1.000	0.412	0.145	0.112
Raw coverage	0.422	0.495	0.120	0.128	0.342	0.046	0.028
Unique coverage	0.328	0.202	0.024	0.031	0.912	0.985	0.980
Overall solution coverage	0.680				0.515		
Overall solution consistency	0.962				0.929		

Note: ●= core casual condition (present). •= peripheral casual condition (present). ⊗= core casual condition (absent). ⊗= peripheral casual condition (absent). Blank spaces indicate "do not care".

4.3 Robustness Checks

We increase the consistency threshold from 0.75 to 0.8 and find that the new configuration is exactly the same as before the adjustment, indicating the strong robustness of the conclusions of this study. Simultaneously, we increase the frequency threshold from 1 to 2 and find that the five types are still supported. Both overall consistency and coverage decreased slightly, indicating that the results remained robust.

5 Discussion

5.1 Research Conclusions

First, business strategy, IT strategy and environmental turbulence alone cannot provide the necessary conditions for firm resilience. The results show that different configurations of antecedent conditions can enable both high and non-high levels of firm resilience. Based on the combination of digital strategy and environmental turbulence, we identified two types of high-level firm resilience: IT strategy oriented, and business strategy oriented. We also identified three types of non-high firm resilience: (1) many pains but no gain, (2) no pain, no gain, (3) and insufficient awareness of IT exploitation, which have an asymmetric relationship with high levels of firm resilience.

Second, we found a synergy between environmental turbulence and digital strategy when comparing antecedent conditions horizontally. When environmental turbulence is present as a core condition, IT strategy play an essential role in the firm resilience. Moreover, when environmental turbulence does not exist or exists as an auxiliary condition, business strategy plays a critical role in resilience rather than IT strategy. Our results support the findings of Liang et.al [13] who suggest IT ambidexterity matters only in dynamic environments.

Third, we observed a synergy between exploitation and exploration. Compared the configurations between high levels of resilience and non-high levels of resilience, we find that only by finding the prober way to balance exploitation and exploration can we achieve firm resilience. Specifically, this means that in our four pathways to high resilience, the balance of exploitation and exploration is essential to achieving firm resilience. Without considering the actual resources and external environment, the addition of exploitation and exploration is simply not conducive to the formation of firm resilience. These factors must be effectively combined and thus act synergistically, further confirming the assumption of interdependent causality.

5.2 Theoretical Contributions

First, based on the perspectives of digital strategy and environmental turbulence, we conducted a configurational analysis, thus interpreting the complex mechanism for achieving firm resilience. Most research has thus far focused on organizational factors such as business strategy resource reconfiguration capability and information technology capability. Firm resilience is determined by the interactions between digital strategy and environmental turbulence, rather than single condition. This study uniquely identifies the complex causal relationships that contribute to firm resilience and develops more effective strategies to improve them.

Second, by applying the QCA method, we have contributed to the existing literature on digital strategy and broadened the choice of research methods for studies of Strategic Alignment Model. Previous studies have presented initiatives to explore resilience from matching perspective (e.g., Strategic Alignment Model). However, the majority of existing literature explains the internal mechanism of digital strategy with a single linear regression. This limitation leads to difficulties in modeling the multiple internal interactions of strategy (i.e., business strategy and IT strategy) [5] and also limits the research on the relationship between the external environment and digital strategy [13]. By introducing QCA into the effect of digital strategy on firm resilience, we have not only revealed the important synergy of environmental factors, but also explored the complex interaction between single level (e.g., IT exploitation and IT exploration) and cross-level (e.g., IT exploitation and resource exploration).

Third, we contribute to organizational ambidexterity theory, by highlighting the importance of exploration and exploitation in digital strategy (i.e., business strategy and IT strategy). Although previous research assumes that maintaining a high level of exploitation and exploration is conducive to firm performance [15], our results show that such a situation is not necessarily conducive to resilience. The firm cannot undertake exploration and exploitation strategies at the same time, which is limited by resource budget or other issues. Therefore, the company must find an appropriate strategy of balance. In addition to the internal balance within IT strategy and business strategy, the relationship between IT strategy and business strategy should also be balanced. In summary, these results comprehensively understand the complex joint effects of exploration and exploitation.

5.3 Practical Implications

First, managers need to ensure a balanced distribution of attention to avoid "too much is as bad as too little". On the one hand, firms need to pay attention to digital strategy in order to gain a competitive advantage. Instead of blindly relying on past successes that lead to management rigidity, IT and business strategies must be adapted to the environment. On the other hand, firms need to consider their own resources and budgets, as the mere addition of exploration and exploitation strategies can hasten the demise of companies.

Second, entrepreneurs must recognize that environmental turbulence is the trend of the times. They need to integrate knowledge and skills to make more scientific decisions and improve their ability to search for resources and deal with environmental changes. They need to change their attitude towards environmental turbulence and stop being hostile and overly conservative. They need to be positive about a hostile and volatile environment and be careful not to be too conservative. In environmental turbulence, look for opportunities and find the right development path.

5.4 Limitations and Future Research

Our work has some limitations that could be fruitful avenues for future research. First, our samples are typical platforms for shared accommodation. As there is heterogeneity among industries, it is uncertain whether the study's conclusions can be generalized to other sharing economy industries or digital platforms. Second, our study does not fully account for sample evolution and change when analyzing cross-sectional data. Therefore, it can be beneficial for tQCA (time-series QCA) to conduct further research.

Acknowledgement. This research has been supported by the grant from the National Natural Science Foundation of China (No. 72272138).

References

1. Amankwah-Amoah, J., Khan, Z., Wood, G., Knight, G.: COVID-19 and digitalization: the great acceleration. J. Bus. Res. **136**, 602–611 (2021)
2. Ambulkar, S., Blackhurst, J., Grawe, S.: Firm's resilience to supply chain disruptions: scale development and empirical examination. J. Oper. Manag. **33–34**, 111–122 (2015)
3. Proksch, D., Rosin, A.F., Stubner, S., Pinkwart, A.: The influence of a digital strategy on the digitalization of new ventures: the mediating effect of digital capabilities and a digital culture. J. Small Bus. Manag. ahead-of-print, 1–29 (2021). https://doi.org/10.1080/00472778.2021.1883036
4. AlNuaimi, B.K., Kumar Singh, S., Ren, S., Budhwar, P., Vorobyev, D.: Mastering digital transformation: the nexus between leadership, agility, and digital strategy. J. Bus. Res. **145**, 636–648 (2022)
5. Li, Y., Wang, X., Gong, T., Wang, H.: Breaking out of the pandemic: how can firms match internal competence with external resources to shape operational resilience? J. Oper. Manage. ahead-of-print, 1–20 (2022). https://doi.org/10.1002/joom.1176
6. Yang, Z., Guo, X., Sun, J., Zhang, Y., Wang, Y.: What does not kill you makes you stronger: supply chain resilience and corporate sustainability through emerging IT capability. IEEE Trans. Eng. Manag. ahead-of-print, 1–15 (2022). https://doi.org/10.1109/TEM.2022.3209613
7. Park, Y., Mithas, S.: Organized complexity of digital business strategy: a configurational perspective. Manag. Inf. Syst. Q. **44**, 85–127 (2020)

8. Vega, D., Arvidsson, A., Saïah, F.: Resilient supply management systems in times of crisis. Int. J. Operat. Prod. Manag. ahead-of-print, 1–29 (2022). https://doi.org/10.1108/IJOPM-03-2022-0192

9. Wei, S., Ke, W., Liu, H., Wei, K.K.: Supply chain information integration and firm performance: are explorative and exploitative IT capabilities complementary or substitutive? Decis. Sci. **51**, 464–499 (2020)

10. Morton, J., Amrollahi, A., Wilson, A.D.: Digital strategizing: an assessing review, definition, and research agenda. J. Strateg. Inf. Syst. **31**, 101720 (2022)

11. Bettiol, M., Capestro, M., Di Maria, E., Micelli, S.: Ambidextrous strategies in turbulent times: the experience of manufacturing SMEs during the COVID-19 pandemic. Int. J. Phys. Distrib. Logist. Manag. ahead-of-print, 1–25 (2023). https://doi.org/10.1108/IJPDLM-10-2021-0422

12. Xiao, H., Yang, Z., Hu, Y.: Influencing mechanism of strategic flexibility on corporate performance: the mediating role of business model innovation. Asia Pac. Bus. Rev. **27**, 470–492 (2021)

13. Liang, H., Wang, N., Xue, Y.: Juggling information technology (IT) exploration and exploitation: a proportional balance view of IT ambidexterity. Inf. Syst. Res. **33**, 1386–1402 (2022)

14. Zhen, J., Xie, Z., Dong, K.: Impact of IT governance mechanisms on organizational agility and the role of top management support and IT ambidexterity. Int. J. Account. Inf. Syst. **40**, 100501 (2021)

15. Lee, O.-K. (Daniel), Sambamurthy, V., Lim, K.H., Wei, K.K.: How does IT ambidexterity impact organizational agility? Inf. Syst. Res. **26**, 398–417 (2015)

16. Chen, H., Tian, Z.: Environmental uncertainty, resource orchestration and digital transformation: a fuzzy-set QCA approach. J. Bus. Res. **139**, 184–193 (2022)

17. Turulja, L., Bajgoric, N.: Innovation, firms' performance and environmental turbulence: is there a moderator or mediator? Eur. J. Innov. Manag. **22**, 213–232 (2019)

18. de Diego Ruiz, E., Almodóvar, P., del Valle, I.D.: What drives strategic agility? Evidence from a fuzzy-set qualitative comparative analysis (FsQCA). Int. Entrepren. Manage. J. 1–29 (2022)

19. Börekçi, D.Y., Rofcanin, Y., Heras, M.L., Berber, A.: Deconstructing organizational resilience: a multiple-case study. J. Manag. Organ. **27**, 422–441 (2021)

20. Claussen, J., Essling, C., Peukert, C.: Demand variation, strategic flexibility and market entry: evidence from the U.S. airline industry. Strat. Manage. J. **39**, 2877–2898 (2018)

What Leads to Effective Online Physician-Patient Communication? the Power of Convergence

Siqi Wang[1], Xiaofei Zhang[1], and Fanbo Meng[2(✉)]

[1] Business School, Nankai University, Tianjin, China
[2] School of Business, Jiangnan University, Wuxi, China
fanbomeng@jiangnan.edu.cn

Abstract. Online health communities (OHCs) provide patients with chronic diseases with an alternative physician-patient communication platform that offers social support and better management of their diseases. However, under the context of text-only communication, even though the part OHCs play in enabling patients' self-management of chronic conditions has attracted scholarly and practical attention, the role of linguistic features pertaining to online physician-patient communication in improving patient compliance has been significantly neglected. Based on communication accommodation theory, this study examines the effects of convergent linguistic features on patients' satisfaction and compliance, along with the contingent roles of physicians' titles and complications. According to the study results, physician-patient convergence of semantic and stylistic features positively affects patient satisfaction, in turn increasing compliance. Furthermore, the physician's title weakens the effect of the convergence of language concreteness but strengthens the effect of the convergence of emotional intensity on patient satisfaction. Additionally, complications negatively affect the relationship between satisfaction and compliance. These findings provide further insight into the literature regarding communication accommodation theory and physician-patient communication in OHCs and offer a practical guide to physician-patient communication skills.

Keywords: Communication accommodation theory · Online health communities · Chronic disease · compliance · physician-patient communication · self-management

1 Introduction

Chronic diseases have become the main cause of human morbidity and mortality, causing seven out of ten deaths each year [1]. Against the backdrop of the high autonomy of self-health management, the noncompliance of patients with chronic diseases is ubiquitous and causes catastrophic social and economic outcomes [2, 3]. Although governments, medical organisations, and even patients themselves have devoted considerable energy and offered input to address this issue, effective approaches remain elusive and are worthy of further investigation.

© The Author(s), under exclusive license to Springer Nature Switzerland AG 2023
Y. Tu and M. Chi (Eds.): WHICEB 2023, LNBIP 481, pp. 331–343, 2023.
https://doi.org/10.1007/978-3-031-32302-7_29

Relatively few studies have focused on the effect of physician-patient communication at the textual level, more specifically, the linguistic features of physicians and patients. In the case of online communication, the facial expressions and movements of both parties cannot be observed, therefore, the linguistic features of both physicians and patients is believed to have an impact on each other [4]. Prior studies show that online communication texts can be classified mainly in two features: semantic feature and stylistic feature [5]. Semantic features refer to the specific meaning of the text, such as certain actions or expressed emotions described by the text. By contrast, the stylistic features refer to the external form of the text, such as the number of lines or number of punctuation marks. In the context of OHCs, little is known about the role of the linguistic features of physician-patient communication on patient satisfaction and compliance. Therefore, to address the aforementioned research gap, the first research question of our study is: **RQ1:** How do linguistic features embedded in physician-patient communication influence patient satisfaction, in turn impacting the compliance of patients with chronic diseases?

The heterogeneity of physicians may affect their communication style, which is manifested in different writing styles in online communication. The title of a physician is an objective reflection of ability among physicians, where a higher title often indicates a higher level of medical competence [6], which is likely to extend to the professionals' communication skills. However, few studies have sought to evaluate the potential differences in language style among physicians with different professional titles or whether such differences might affect levels of patient satisfaction and compliance. Therefore, our second research question is: **RQ2:** Are the effects of convergent semantic and stylistic features in online physician-patient communication on patient satisfaction contingent on the physician's title?

The effect of satisfaction on compliance in previous studies has not always been significant [7]. Such inconsistency suggests that there may be some previously unidentified factors at play. Since compliance is a manifestation of patient self-management behavior, patient-level characteristics may be the main actors. Hence, we introduced complications, a characteristic of patients with chronic diseases, to moderate the relationship between satisfaction and compliance in order to explain the inconsistent findings in previous studies and provide a factor to consider for future work. Accordingly, our third research question is: **RQ3:** Is the effect of patient satisfaction on patient compliance contingent on complications?

Drawing on the communication accommodation theory (CAT), we develop a conceptual framework that explains how the convergence of linguistic characteristics embedded in physician-patient communication influence patient compliance through improving patient satisfaction. The contingent roles of physicians' title and patient complications on this influence mechanism are examined as well. Our model and hypotheses were validated by collecting data of consultation records of physician-patient from a leading Chinese online health platform from 2016 to 2021.

2 Literature Review

2.1 Physician-Patient Communication and Patient Satisfaction, Patient Compliance

Communication between physicians and patients is important, especially for patients with chronic diseases, and it is thought to influence a range of patient outcomes [8]. However, physician-patient communication is not always effective, as exemplified by feedback from many patients who have mentioned feeling that their physicians' communication skills are inadequate. It has been argued that problems in physician-patient communication can lead to noncompliance and missed opportunities to improve self-management in patients with chronic diseases [9]. Therefore, continuously increasing the understanding of the causes of poor physician-patient communication and improving the effectiveness of this communication remain necessary.

However, the impact of physician-patient communication and on patient compliance is generally indirect because compliance is not an instantaneous outcome but tends to be reflected in patient behaviour over time. For this reason, many studies have explored reliable mediating variables such as patient recall and satisfaction [10]. The presence of such mediating variables allows researchers to assess the quality of physician-patient communication based on patient intuition effectively, especially in terms of which features are appreciated by patients, promoting a deeper understanding of the effect of effective physician-patient communication on compliance.

Existing research suggests that although satisfaction can be influenced by a variety of external factors (e.g., waiting time), satisfaction is intimately related to communication behaviors between patients and physicians [9]. Satisfaction is important because it is not only a goal and desired outcome of health service, but also reflect the extent to which patients' health care needs, expectations, or preferences are met [9]. Therefore, the adoption of satisfaction as a measure of physician-patient communication is justifiable and also helps us to further identify the impact on other patient outcomes.

2.2 Asymmetry in Physician-Patient Communication

Poor physician-patient communication may be caused by its asymmetry. Most physician-patient communication is physician-centred, meaning that the physician holds an authoritative status [11]. The unequal status of physicians and patients can impact the communication expression of both parties, which is reflected by the physician's tendency to ask more questions than the patient to control the whole communication process [12]. This kind of asymmetric physician-patient communication can be disadvantageous to patients. For example, the lack of follow-up questions and explanations may be associated with the patient's lack of understanding of the physician's meaning; self-management in such cases may result in ineffective treatment or deteriorating health consequences [13]. Furthermore, medical decisions without joint participation tend to fall short of patients' expectations, resulting in the inability of patients to comply wholeheartedly with medical advice, leading to dissatisfaction and noncompliance [12]. This study started from the practical problem of physician-patient communication asymmetry and aimed to understand whether the asymmetry of physician-patient communication might occur in specific linguistic features. Furthermore, we sought to determine, in the case where these linguistic features between physicians and patients are relatively symmetrical, whether the satisfaction and compliance of patients with chronic diseases can be promoted.

2.3   Communication Accommodation Theory

Communication accommodation theory (CAT) is a comprehensive conceptual framework that describes the ways in which people adjust their communication behaviors during social interactions, their motivations for doing so, and the social consequences [14]. CAT puts forward three main behavioral strategies in a variety of situations: convergence, divergence and maintenance. Convergence is the adjustment of an individual's communication behavior to be more similar to the interlocutor, in contrast, divergence refers to individuals adapting their communication behaviors to appear more dissimilar. In addition, interlocutors may engage in maintenance, which is sustaining one's "default" way of communicating without adjusting for others [14]. Convergence can be seen as a signal of harmony that helps individuals perceive each other's emotional state in communication, thus facilitating more fluid communication and understanding [15]. Therefore, convergence behavioral strategies are often used when people are looking for the satisfaction and understanding of their interlocutors [16]. Thus, we sought to determine if the convergence of different linguistic features between physicians and patients could represent effective physician-patient communication with an emphasis on promoting patient satisfaction and compliance (Fig. 1).

3   Research Model and Hypotheses Development

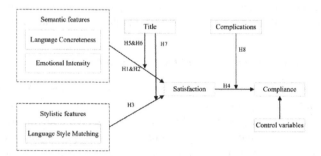

Fig. 1. Research model

3.1   The Effect of Semantic Features on Patient Satisfaction

For the semantic features, we choose language concreteness and emotional intensity for specific measures. Because concrete language is considered to be more likely to influence cognitive-based responses, such as assessments of message importance, which is opposed to affect-based responses [17]. Therefore, these two concepts can be considered as representatives of the cognitive and emotional dimensions.

Language concreteness is determined by how specific the message is, concrete descriptions can show more details, while abstract descriptions are more general and require more inference. Concrete language is considered to be more vivid, realistic [18], and more likely to build trust than abstract language [19]. Emotional intensity is the percentage of expressed emotions in the content [20]. In physician-patient communication, emotional expression strategies can be manifested in communicative behaviors, which can include patient confiding and physician reassurance. During online physician-patient communication, more convergent language concreteness can make it easier for both individuals to understand the point the other is trying to make, thus making communication more effective and resulting in higher patient satisfaction. Similarly, more symmetrical emotional intensity indicates that the emotions expressed by the individual are well received and positively fed back by their interlocutor. Therefore, patients' emotional needs can be well met in the communication, thus enhancing satisfaction with the consultation.

The positive impact of convergent semantic features on patient satisfaction can be further explain by the mechanism of fluency [20]. Fluency can be defined as the perceived ease with which an individual processes information [21], it can come from the priming effect of the perception of content features. Through the basic mechanism of priming, the presentation of an element can produce stimulation of related elements in an individual's memory, thus bringing a faster response for the comprehension and recognition of related content, convergence then promote fluency. Fluency is thought to be associated with positive evaluations, with greater fluency felt by individuals indicating a better understanding of communication and generally more positive feedback [22]. In sum, we believe that more convergent language concreteness and emotional intensity in online physician-patient communication can make patients feel better about the process and outcome of communication, thus contribute to improving patient satisfaction. Accordingly, we propose:

H1: The convergence of language concreteness in online physician-patient communication has a positive impact on patient satisfaction.

H2: The convergence of emotional intensity in online physician-patient communication has a positive impact on patient satisfaction.

3.2   The Effect of Stylistic Features (LSM) of Patient Satisfaction

As a form of interpersonal coordination, LSM represents a form of psychological synchrony [23], it can lead to the perception that the interlocutor can provide emotional and informational support [4], thus becoming a source of satisfaction in further communication. Existing research has demonstrated an association between LSM and a range of positive outcomes in interpersonal and communication, such as impression formation [24] and social support in online medical context [4]. Accordingly, we believe that more convergent stylistic features in online physician-patient communication can provide better overall perception of the communication and contribute to patient satisfaction with the consultation. Therefore, we posit the following:

H3: The convergence of stylistic features (LSM) in online physician-patient communication has a positive impact on patients' satisfaction.

3.3   The Effect of Patient Satisfaction on Compliance

Prior literature has showed that when confronted with a physician who attaches more importance to interpersonal interaction, patients are more satisfied and more likely to return to [25]. Many studies have also shown the correlation between satisfaction and compliance in different aspects such as satisfaction with consultation, satisfaction with communication and general satisfaction with received medical care [26]. The more satisfied patients are, the more likely they are to follow the physician's instructions to adopt the relevant regimen and manage their health [26]. Therefore, we propose:

H4: Patient satisfaction has a positive impact on their compliance.

3.4   The Moderating Effect of Physician's Professional Title

Prior studies have shown that high-status people can increase the possibility of linguistic accommodation by low-status people [27], but they (higher-status) usually won't accommodate to lower-status people [28]. In online consultation, physicians with higher titles may be less likely to converge with the language style of patients than physicians with lower titles, this behavior would then show up as an asymmetrical convergence, or divergence, but this divergence from physicians with higher titles does not bring about a decrease in patient satisfaction. According to attribution theory, people's attributions of behavior determine the evaluation of the behavior, the results can be equally good when people attribute divergence in a positive way [29]. When higher-titled physician does not perform more convergence, patient may attribute this to the difference in medical literacy between themselves and the physician and the physician's high medical competence and expertise, resulting in greater satisfaction. Accordingly, we believe that the effect of convergent linguistic behavior on patient satisfaction is diminished as the physician's title rises. Therefore, we propose the following:

H5-H6: Physician's professional title has a negative impact on the relationship between semantic feature convergence in physician-patient communications and patient satisfaction.

H7: Physician's professional title has a negative impact on the relationship between stylistic feature convergence in physician-patient communications and patient satisfaction.

3.5   The Moderating Effect of Complications

It have been found that noncompliance tends to be higher under certain conditions, for example: when medical regimens are more complex; when treatment period lasts for longer periods of time; and when there are several troublesome drug side effects [30]. The complexity of complications leads to increased complexity of regimens (e.g., multiple medications) that can make it more difficult for patients to comply. At the same time, more complications often mean more painful feelings, which can bring depression, anxiety and other negative emotions to the patient, this is also unfavorable to patient compliance. Therefore, we propose the following:

H8: Complications has a negative impact on the relationship between patient satisfaction and their compliance.

4 Research Methodology

4.1 Data Collection

In this paper, patients with diabetes are selected as samples since diabetes is a common chronic disease. We collected the historical consultation data of a well-known online health platform in China. Because the OHC is categorized according to the physician's department, there is no direct access to diabetes consultation records, therefore, we searched for diabetes and blood sugar as keywords in the physician-patient dialogue. Ultimately, our dataset includes 15488 consultation records of 281 physicians, the time range is from 2016 to 2021.

4.2 Measurement

Compliance: Prior studies have noted that it is useful to examine variables that may indicate whether physician instructions will be followed [31]. According to the theory of planned behavior, people's behavior can be predicted from their intentions [32]. It has been proved that when patients are more intended to do well in self-management, they are more likely to behave as the instructions, and further, reflected in increased compliance [33]. Based on this concept, we constructed a compliance dictionary, measure patient compliance by marking the words in the physician-patient dialogue that indicate the patient's intent to comply (e.g., follow your instructions, take medication on time, etc.). If the patient uses any of the words in the dictionary during the conversation, this conversation is marked with a compliance $= 1$, otherwise $= 0$.

Satisfaction: We constructed a satisfaction dictionary, which includes both service satisfaction and medical satisfaction according to studies related to patient satisfaction [34]. If a patient uses any of the words in the satisfaction dictionary, his satisfaction is marked as 1, otherwise it is marked as 0.

Language concreteness: We use the result of Brysbaert et al.'s concreteness ratings of nearly 40,000 generally known English words and expressions obtained through internet crowdsourcing [35], a dictionary that uses a 5-point scale to score the degree of concreteness of words. This dictionary was used because 1) it is a dictionary created specifically to measure language concreteness; 2) the reliability and validity of the dictionary has been demonstrated by its creators; 3) this dictionary includes medical words in addition to everyday words and has been used to quantify language concreteness in medical settings [20]. We translate the dictionary into Chinese and scores it by matching physicians and patients separately to measure the language concreteness of physician-patient conversations. To calculate the average concreteness, we divided the sum of concreteness ratings of words in the dialogue by the total number of words in the online physician-patient communication.

Emotional intensity: We used LIWC2022 to calculate the emotional intensity of physicians and patients. LIWC provides a dictionary that can identifies positive and negative emotional words. We calculate the sum of positive and negative emotional words as the total emotional words. In the same way that language concreteness is calculated, we measured emotional intensity by calculating the number of emotional words divided by the total number of words.

LSM: LIWC has the function of performing LSM calculation, but since it does not support Chinese context, we choose to perform manual calculation according to the formula of LSM. At present, LSM in LIWC includes eight types of function words: auxiliary verbs (e.g., to be, to have), articles (e.g., an, the), common adverbs (e.g., hardly, often), personal pronouns (e.g., I, they, we), indefinite pronouns (e.g., it, those), prepositions (e.g., for, after, with), negations (e.g., not, never), and conjunctions (e.g., and, but). Since there are no articles in the Chinese context, we use the remaining seven categories as the calculation content of LSM, the dictionary of Simplified Chinese which is official LIWC translations are used to calculate these seven categories of function words. The resultant LSM score was between 0 and 1, with scores closest to 1 reflecting high degrees of style matching. Taking prepositions (abbreviated as prep) as an example, the LSM of a single function word is calculated as:

$$LSM_{prep} = 1 - \frac{|prep_1 - prep_2|}{prep_1 + prep_2 + 0.0001}$$

Further, the LSM formula that includes all functional word classifications is:

$$LSM = avg(LSM_{prep} + LSM_{auxverb} + LSM_{adverb} + LSM_{conj} + LSM_{ppron} + LSM_{ipron} + LSM_{negate})$$

Title: The physician title information was obtained from the online health platform. In China, the titles of physicians are resident physician, attending physician, deputy chief physician and chief physician in turn. The lowest title is resident, which was marked as 1, the highest title is chief physician, which was marked as 4, attending physicians and deputy chief physicians were marked as 2 and 3, respectively.

Complications: A customized dictionary were constructed to measure the complication of patients. If a patient uses any of the words in the complications dictionary, his complications is marked as 1, otherwise it is marked as 0.

Control variable: We selected five characteristics from both physicians and patients that might have an impact on physician-patient communication as control variables to add to our model. For patients, we selected the gender and age of the patient, the gender of male patients was marked as 1, whereas that of female patients was marked as 0. For physicians, we selected whether the physician worked at a top hospital, the price of the physician's online consultation, and the number of online consultations for a particular physician. If the physician works at a top hospital, his hospital level is marked as 1, otherwise 0. Both the number of online consultations and the price of online consultations are obtained from the information on the physician's home page. The monetary unit of the physician's consultation price is yuan.

We subtracted the convergent measures of Language concreteness and Emotional intensity between physicians and patients to obtain the absolute difference, to ease interpretation, we multiplied the absolute difference by −1 to create the measure for the convergence variables: a higher value of the convergence variable indicates greater convergence between its two individuals (Table 1).

4.3 Analysis and Results

Table 1. Descriptive Statistics

Variables	Mean	SD	Min	Max
Compliance	0.0587	0.235	0	1
Satisfaction	0.365	0.481	0	1
Physician-patient concreteness convergence	−1.405	1.530	−15.48	−9.41e-05
Physician-patient emotion convergence	−4.997	5.372	−66.67	0
LSM	0.565	0.174	1.51e–05	1
Complications	0.358	0.479	0	1
Title	2.984	0.805	1	4
Age	49.23	16.61	0	98
Gender	0.507	0.500	0	1
Top hospital	0.901	0.298	0	1
Price	54.21	72.86	0	600
Number of consultations	1145	4206	0	102025

Table 2 and 3 presents the results of the main regressions used to test our hypotheses. From the Model 2 results, it could be concluded that the physician-patient concreteness convergence (PPCC) ($p < 0.01$) and the physician-patient emotional convergence (PPEC) ($p < 0.01$) positively influenced patient satisfaction. Meanwhile, physician-patient LSM ($p < 0.01$) positively influenced patient satisfaction. Thus, H1, H2, and H3 were supported, suggesting that patient satisfaction is higher when physician-patient communication is more convergent in terms of concreteness, emotional intensity, and language style. Model 3 tested the moderating role of Title. Professional title negatively moderated the relationship between PPCC and patient satisfaction ($p < 0.01$) but positively moderated the relationship between PPEC and patient satisfaction ($p < 0.01$), therefore supporting H5. The coefficient of Title* LSM was not significant ($p > 0.1$), indicating that H7 was not supported.

Furthermore, we ran the regression model following the same steps as above to test the effect of satisfaction on compliance and the moderating effect of complications (Table 3). In Model 2, the results indicate that patient satisfaction had a positive impact on patient compliance ($p < 0.01$), supporting H4. In Model 3, the moderating effects of complications on the relationship between Satisfaction and Compliance were negative ($p < 0.01$), thus supporting H8. These outcomes indicate that patient satisfaction can positively influence their compliance; nevertheless, this effect can be impaired by complications.

Table 2. Logit regression (Satisfaction)

	(1)	(2)	(3)
VARIABLES	Satisfaction	Satisfaction	Satisfaction
PPCC		0.543***	0.746***
		(0.020)	(0.081)
PPEC		0.047***	−0.002
		(0.004)	(0.017)
LSM		1.704***	1.714***
		(0.111)	(0.423)
Title		−0.165***	−0.156*
		(0.024)	(0.093)
Title* PPCC			−0.067***
			(0.026)
Title* PPEC			0.017***
			(0.006)
Title* LSM			−0.005
			(0.138)
Control variables	YES	YES	YES
Constant	−0.863***	−0.530***	−0.546*
	(0.076)	(0.129)	(0.299)
Log likelihood	−9973.527	−8981.716	−8974.650
Pseudo R^2	0.016	0.114	0.114
Observations	15,448	15,448	15,448

PPCC: Physician-patient concreteness convergence. PPEC: Physician-patient emotional convergence. LSM: Language style matching. Standard errors in parentheses.
*** $p < 0.01$, ** $p < 0.05$, * $p < 0.1$

We also tested the mediating effect of satisfaction in the model by adopting a bootstrapping analysis using 5,000 samples with the same control variables. If the 95% bootstrapping confidence interval (CI) does not include zero, the mediating effect is statistically significant. According to the results, 95% CIs of all indirect pathways excluded zero, indicating that the mediation effects of the three linguistic convergent behaviors on patient compliance were significant (Table 4).

Table 3. Logit regression (Compliance)

	(1)	(2)	(3)
VARIABLES	Compliance	Compliance	Compliance
Satisfaction		1.268***	1.538***
		(0.076)	(0.108)
Complications		0.525***	0.886***
		(0.071)	(0.122)
Complications* Satisfaction			−0.542***
			(0.149)
Control variables	YES	YES	YES
Constant	−2.521***	−3.295***	−3.468***
	(0.146)	(0.156)	(0.165)
Log likelihood	-3330.388	-3130.301	-3123.721
Pseudo R^2	0.035	0.093	0.095
Observations	15,448	15,448	15,448

Standard errors in parentheses

Table 4. Mediation check

Paths	Indirect effect	95%CI	
		Lower	Upper
Physician-patient concreteness convergence $\rightarrow$ Compliance	0.006	0.005	0.006
Physician-patient emotional convergence $\rightarrow$ Compliance	0.001	0.001	0.001
Language style matching $\rightarrow$ Compliance	0.033	0.028	0.038

5 Conclusion

Online consultations allow patients with chronic diseases convenient access to their physicians, which is extremely helpful for their self-management and health conditions. However, little research has focused on the influence of linguistic features in online physician-patient communication. Therefore, by drawing on the CAT, we proved that the convergence of semantic features (language concreteness and emotional intensity) and stylistic features (LSM) in online physician-patient communication positively affects patient satisfaction and in turn positively affects patient compliance. Physician title moderates the relationship between the convergence of semantic features and satisfaction but has no significant effect on the relationship between the convergence of stylistic features and satisfaction. Complications in patients with chronic diseases negatively influence the relationship between satisfaction and compliance. In closing, our findings contribute to the study of CAT, compliance and online health care, and our work also provides practical implications for physicians and the managers of online health platforms.

Acknowledgement. This research was supported by the National Natural Science Foundation of China under Grant 72271131 and 72001094.

References

1. Bardhan, I., Chen, H., Karahanna, E.: Connecting systems, data, and people: a multi-disciplinary research roadmap for chronic disease management. MIS Q. **44**(1), 185–200 (2020)
2. World Health Organization. Adherence to long-term therapies : evidence for action. World Health Organization (2003)
3. Kleinsinger, F.: The unmet challenge of medication nonadherence. Permanente J. **22**(3), 18–033 (2018)
4. Rains, S.A.: Language style matching as a predictor of perceived social support in computer-mediated interaction among individuals coping with illness. Commun. Res. **43**(5), 694–712 (2016)
5. Halder, S., Tiwari, R., Sprague, A.: Information extraction from spam emails using stylistic and semantic features to identify spammers. In: 2011 IEEE International Conference on Information Reuse & Integration (2011)
6. Guo, S., Guo, X., Fang, Y., et al.: How doctors gain social and economic returns in online health-care communities: a professional capital perspective. J. Manag. Inf. Syst. **34**(2), 487–519 (2017)
7. Burgoon, M.: Strangers in a strange land: the Ph.D. in the land of the medical doctor. J. Lang. Soc. Psychol. **11**(1–2), 101–106 (1992)
8. Ong, L.M.L., de Haes, J.C.J.M., Hoos, A.M., et al.: Doctor-patient communication: a review of the literature. Soc. Sci. Med. **40**(7), 903–918 (1995)
9. King, A., Hoppe, R.B.: "Best practice" for patient-centered communication: a narrative review. J. Grad. Med. Educ. **5**(3), 385–393 (2013)
10. Bartlett, E.E., Grayson, M., Barker, R., et al.: The effects of physician communications skills on patient satisfaction; recall, and adherence. J. Chronic Dis. **37**(9–10), 755–764 (1984)
11. Krupat, E., Rosenkranz, S.L., Yeager, C.M., et al.: The practice orientations of physicians and patients: the effect of doctor–patient congruence on satisfaction. Patient Educ. Couns. **39**(1), 49–59 (2000)
12. Porter, H.A.: Discourse means of jointly produced asymmetry and symmetry in physician-patient conversation. North Carolina State University (2002)
13. Matusitz, J., Spear, J.: Effective doctor–patient communication: an updated examination. Soc. Work Publ. Health **29**(3), 252–266 (2014)
14. Dragojevic, M., Gasiorek, J, Giles, H.: Communication accommodation theory. The International Encyclopedia of Interpersonal Communication, pp. 1–21. John Wiley & Sons (2015)
15. Gasiorek, J.: Theoretical perspectives on interpersonal adjustments in language and communication. In: Giles, H, (ed.) Communication Accommodation Theory, 1st edn, pp. 13–35. Cambridge University Press (2016)
16. Gasiorek, J., Giles, H.: Accommodating the interactional dynamics of conflict management. Int. J. Soc. Cult. Lang. **1**(1), 10–21 (2013)

17. Miller, C.H., Lane, L.T., Deatrick, L.M., et al.: Psychological reactance and promotional health messages: the effects of controlling language, lexical concreteness, and the restoration of freedom. Hum. Commun. Res. **33**(2), 219–240 (2007)

18. Hansen, J., Wänke, M.: Truth from language and truth from fit: the impact of linguistic concreteness and level of construal on subjective truth. Pers. Soc. Psychol. Bull. **36**(11), 1576–1588 (2010)

19. Larrimore, L., Jiang, L., Larrimore, J., et al.: Peer to peer lending: the relationship between language features, trustworthiness, and persuasion success. J. Appl. Commun. Res. **39**(1), 19–37 (2011)

20. Peng, C.-H., Yin, D., Zhang, H.: More than words in medical question-and-answer sites: a content-context congruence perspective. Inf. Syst. Res. **31**(3), 913–928 (2020)

21. Oppenheimer, D.M.: The secret life of fluency. Trends Cogn. Sci. **12**(6), 237–241 (2008)

22. Reber, R., Schwarz, N., Winkielman, P.: Processing fluency and aesthetic pleasure: is beauty in the perceiver's processing experience? Pers. Soc. Psychol. Rev. **8**(4), 364–382 (2004)

23. Ireland, M.E., Pennebaker, J.W.: Language style matching in writing: synchrony in essays, correspondence, and poetry. J. Pers. Soc. Psychol. **99**(3), 549 (2010)

24. Muir, K., Joinson, A., Cotterill, R., et al.: Characterizing the linguistic chameleon: personal and social correlates of linguistic style accommodation. Hum. Commun. Res. **42**(3), 462–484 (2016)

25. Watson, B., Gallois, C.: Nurturing communication by health professionals toward patients: a communication accommodation theory approach. Health Commun. **10**(4), 343–355 (1998)

26. Ley, P.: Satisfaction, compliance and communication. Br. J. Clin. Psychol. **21**(4), 241–254 (1982)

27. Danescu-Niculescu-Mizil, C., Lee, L., Pang, B., et al.: Echoes of power: language effects and power differences in social interaction. In: Proceedings of the 21st International Conference on World Wide Web, Lyon France, pp. 699–708. ACM (2012)

28. Jones, S., Cotterill, R., Dedney, N., et al.: Finding Zelig in text: a measure for normalising linguistic accommodation. In: Proceedings of COLING (2014)

29. Gasiorek, J., Giles, H.: Effects of inferred motive on evaluations of nonaccommodative communication. Hum. Commun. Res. **38**(3), 309–331 (2012)

30. Conrad, P.: The meaning of medications: another look at compliance. Soc. Sci. Med. **20**(1), 29–37 (1985)

31. Wrench, J.S., Booth-Butterfield, M.: Increasing patient satisfaction and compliance: an examination of physician humor orientation, compliance-gaining strategies, and perceived credibility. Commun. Q. **51**(4), 482–503 (2003)

32. Ajzen, I.: The theory of planned behavior. Organ. Behav. Hum. Decis. Process. **50**(2), 179–211 (1991)

33. Rich, A., Brandes, K., Mullan, B., et al.: Theory of planned behavior and adherence in chronic illness: a meta-analysis. J. Behav. Med. **38**(4), 673–688 (2015)

34. Chen, S., Guo, X., Wu, T., et al.: Exploring the online doctor-patient interaction on patient satisfaction based on text mining and empirical analysis. Inf. Process. Manage. **57**(5), 102253 (2020)

35. Brysbaert, M., Warriner, A.B., Kuperman, V.: Concreteness ratings for 40 thousand generally known english word lemmas. Behav. Res. Methods **46**(3), 904–911 (2014)

An Empirical Study of Factors Affecting the Performance of IP Derivatives Crowdfunding: A Brand Extension Perspective

Maidan Ding and Ling Zhao[✉]

Huazhong University of Science and Technology, Wuhan 430074, China
lingzhao@mail.hust.edu.cn

Abstract. The Intellectual property (IP) derivative market has great potential value but also faces the risk of failure in derivative product. As a result, crowdfunding is increasingly used to test the market and promote IP derivative products. However, there are rare studies that focus on what factors could influence the success of this specific type of crowdfunding projects. This study adopts a brand extension perspective to treat IP derivatives as brand extension, and proposes the factors in terms of IP characteristics (IP popularity and IP quality), IP-derivative similarity (superficial similarity and spiritual similarity) and IP derivative characteristics (product category) influencing IP derivative crowdfunding performance. A total of 644 IP derivative crowdfunding projects from the Zaodianxinhuo platform in China were collected and analyzed. The results indicate that IP popularity, IP quality, spiritual IP-derivative similarity and product category positively affect crowdfunding performance. The findings contribute to the research of crowdfunding and brand extension in the context of IP derivative, which also has practical implications for IP derivatives fundraisers on the crowdfunding platforms.

Keywords: crowdfunding · crowdfunding performance · IP derivatives · influencing factors · brand extension

1 Introduction

Crowdfunding refers to the public solicitation of funds by entrepreneurial teams or individuals through the Internet to support specific projects [1]. Crowdfunding is getting quite popular not because it could increase small startups' opportunities to raise funds [2], but also bring other benefits, such as product demand predicting, product testing, and brand marketing. Famous crowdfunding platform such as Kickstarter has received $7 billion in pledges from 21 million backers to fund 233,250 projects as of January 2023. Though those crowdfunding platforms can facilitate the interaction between the demand and supply side of funds [2], the existence of information asymmetry still expose backers to the risk of projects failure or being cheated. As a result, a large number of studies have been conducted on how investors make investment decisions incrowdfunding platforms and have identified the influencing factors that affect the success of crowdfunding [3], such as characteristics related to the projects or the funders.

Y. Tu and M. Chi (Eds.): WHICEB 2023, LNBIP 481, pp. 344–355, 2023.
https://doi.org/10.1007/978-3-031-32302-7_30

Among those studies that focus on crowdfunding success, one particular category of crowdfunding projects has received rare attention, which is crowdfunding projects of IP (Intellectual Property) derivatives. IP derivatives are products derived from specific IP, such as anime hand-me-downs. Taking the well-known IPs with huge base of fans, Star Wars and Harry Potter as example, data shows that the derivatives of these IPs generate tens of billions of dollars in revenue, including books, movies, games, toys and etc. Capitalizing on fans' love for existing IPs, IP derivatives can sustain IP fever and generate more commercial value. The IP derivatives industry chain involves the process of product selection, design, production and sales, and each process could be threatened by the risk of failure, especially the process of selecting IP and designing products. Not all IP derivatives can reap good results, even those IPs with high popularity. For example, the anime and TV series adapted based on the famous science fiction of The Three Body Problem have gained different reputation. The TV series respected the original and won fans' love. The anime, however, tampered with the novel's plot and received negative reviews. Crowdfunding in the form of pre-sales for consumers is the best way to test the market for derivatives, but there are still cases of high failure rates. For example, the failure rate of IP derivatives crowdfunding (audio-visual and anime categories) on the Modian crowdfunding website is as high as 41%.

Thus, understanding what factors that could influence the success of these IP derivatives crowdfunding projects is not only important for the fundraisers, but also for the platforms. However, conclusions of crowdfunding success from extant literature might not be applicable to this specific category of crowdfunding projects. IP derivatives crowdfunding has some obvious differences from general crowdfunding. First, the launch time for IP derivatives crowdfunding projects is usually carefully chosen, which is usually the TV or anime hit period, and the time required for crowdfunding is shorter than general crowdfunding. Second, the target group of IP derivatives crowdfunding is mostly IP fans, who are prone to follow the trend and consume impulsively, but also more picky for the derivatives products. This also leads to the final difference that IP derivative crowdfunding cares more about the extent to which the derivative products reflect the characteristics of the IP. Thus, the characteristics of both original IP and IP derivatives could influence the investors' judgement of the project. In this study, we regard IP derivatives as brand extension of the parent brand, which is the original IP. Referring to the brand extension theory and combining with the characteristics of crowdfunding, we propose the factors in terms of IP characteristics, IP-derivative similarity and IP derivative characteristics influencing IP derivative crowdfunding performance. We conducted the empirical analysis by using the data of 644 crowdfunding projects from the Zaodianxinhuo platform. Zaodianxinhuo is such a crowdfunding platform which is launched by Alibaba and mainly for IP derivatives crowdfunding in China. The results show that IP popularity, IP quality, IP-derivative similarity, and product category positively affect crowdfunding performance.

2 Literature Review

2.1 Factors Influencing the Success of Crowdfunding Financing

Extant empirical studies on the success of crowdfunding mainly aim to answer the question that what factors could significantly influence investors' behavior. Those factors include the characteristics of the project per se, the fundraiser and backer, and the interaction between the fundraiser and backer.

Project characteristics are usually the key factors in literature. For instance, the display of videos and pictures in the project description will help backers understand the information more visually [4]. In addition, by analyzing the textual information describing the project, researchers have found that different linguistic styles could differently affect people's willingness to support the project [5, 6]. The characteristics of the two subjects involved in the project (fundraisers and investors), such as the reputation and prior experience of the fundraisers, backers' preference or experience are found to play an important role in crowdfunding success [7, 8]. As to the interaction between the fundraisers and investors, comments and responses during the fundraising process could provide more information and reduce the information asymmetry, which is positively related to fundraising success [9].

The crowdfunding projects they have focused on are different from the IP derivatives crowdfunding, for which the innate connection between the derivatives product and the IP that it is derived from plays an important role in investors' decision. Apparently, such connection is not applicable in extant research on crowdfunding success and thus rarely examined.

2.2 IP Derivatives Crowdfunding

In the field of cultural industry, Intellectual Property (IP) refers to the ownership of cultural products with a wide audience base and commercial exploitation value, which can be manifested in film and television works, literary works, games, and etc. [10]. IP derivatives refer to the forms of products and services developed and produced from IP with a fan base after the authorization of trademarks, brands and other intellectual property rights, such as the movies adapted from Harry Potter books.

A major challenge for the IP derivative is that whether the consumers accept the derivative as a successful extension of the original IP and want to pay for it. Thus, crowdfunding platform becomes one of the best channels in testing the potential popularity of IP derivatives. For example, the Zaodianxinhuo platform cooperated with the hit TV series Immortal Samsara and launched an official co-branded jewelry crowdfunding project, with a turnover of 1.5 million. It shows that high quality IP derivatives can get considerable revenue through crowdfunding. However, not all derivatives of well-known IPs get excellent crowdfunding performance.

The crowdfunding IP derivatives take various forms, including utilitarian products, which are functional and practical, such as vacuum cup, bags and etc., and hedonic products which are fun and enjoyable, such as toys, character model in anime and etc. Most crowdfunding IP derivatives on the Zaodianxinhuo platform belong to reward-based crowdfunding, which means that the investors could get these tangible products as reward when the project are successfully crowdfunded.

2.3 Brand Extension

Brand extension is a widespread brand marketing strategy that uses an existing brand to enter new product classes. Firms hope that the new product will benefit from the parent brand equity, or the parent brand would be enhanced due to the extension product. Previous literature states that the factors that determine the success of brand extension are: the characteristics of the parent brand and the extension, the fit between the parent brand and the extension, brand extension authenticity and etc. Essentially, fit reflects the similarity between the extension and the brand [11].

IP derivatives are new products developed under license from the original IP (novels, anime, etc.), which are equivalent to expanding new product categories, such as toys, accessories, clothes and etc. According to the brand extension theory, IP derivatives can be regarded as brand extension, in which the original IP is the parent brand and the derivatives are the extension of the parent brand. We believe that the characteristics of original IP and its derivatives could influence the success of IP derivatives crowdfunding. For instance, the popularity of the original IP, or the types of the derivative products. But most importantly, the similarity, or the fit between IP and derivative products would play an vital role. Such similarity could be conveyed by the project description, which including text, graphics and videos.

Two types of brand extension similarity are usually taken into consideration in brand extension research. The first one is feature similarity on the product-level, which indicates that the extension share similar functional features with existing products of the brand. The other one is concept consistency, which implies that the extension might not share object-to-object similarity with existing products, but fit together on a given conceptual label. For instance, wallet and watch provide different functions, but they may have a relationship based on the concept of "personal accessories" [12]. Apparently, the former similarity is more concrete and latter is more abstract.

Referring to the two types of brand extension similarity, this study identifies two types of IP-derivative similarities, which are superficial similarity and spiritual similarity. Superficial similarity is more concrete and indicates that there are identified cues of the IP in the appearance. While spiritual similarity is more abstract and implies that the spirit of the IP is well represented in the project description. For example, if a Harry Potter derivative shows the Harry Potter logo on the surface, it is superficial similarity, but if the design concept of the derivative is mentioned in the introduction of the product to highlight the spirit of Harry Potter (such as bravery, resourcefulness, etc.), it is spiritual similarity.

3 Research Model and Hypothesis

Concerning the brand extension theory and combined with the characteristics of IP derivatives crowdfunding, this study proposes that factors in terms of IP characteristics, IP-derivative similarity and IP derivative characteristics are the influencing factors that will significantly affect crowdfunding performance. Our research model is shown in Fig. 1.

---

348   M. Ding and L. Zhao

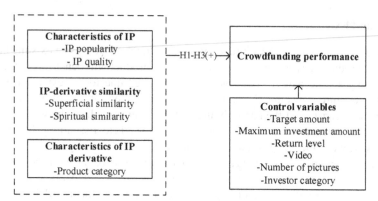

Fig. 1. The Research Model

3.1 Characteristics of IP and Crowdfunding Performance

In the field of brand extension, the parent brand provides information signals for consumers to infer extension quality. This is because consumers will transfer their emotions towards the parent brand to extensions. For instance, Sichtmann and Diamantopoulos [13]found that parent brand origin image has positive effects on perceived quality of the extension. Referring to these findings, we expect that characteristics of IP would exert impacts on consumers' attitude toward the derivatives and two factors are taken into consideration in this study, which are popularity and quality of the IP.

Higher IP popularity indicates that the IP is well-known and has larger base of fans. For example, during the launching period of The Wandering Earth, the derivatives of this movie IP (e.g., engine model, carrier model, notebook, etc.) reached the target amount less than a day after it was launched on the crowdfunding platform, with the final crowdfunding amount of 7.69 million. Jiang et al. also found that the popularity of IP source positively influences consumers' perceived value of IP films [14]. Furthermore, IP with higher popularity usually indicates more recommendation and exposure online, and will appeal to consumers for more dynamics discussion, which will further expand the communication of IP derivative. Thus, we have the following hypothesis:

H1a: IP popularity is positively associated with crowdfunding performance.

Perceived brand quality reflects consumers' overall assessment of a brand and it is found as one of the essential factors in brand extension evaluation [15, 16]. A study on luxury brands extension shows that perceived brand quality affects the authenticity of extensions and significantly influences consumers' attitudes [15]. Sichtmann et al. [16] also found that perceived parent brand quality are critical drivers of service brand extension success. For IP derivatives, Joshi and Mao also found that book reviews positively influence the box office of these book-based movies [17]. This might be because from one side, for those fans who already have positive emotions towards IP, will transfer such emotion to its derivatives. From the other side, for those consumers who are not familiar with the IP, IP quality could be cues to form judgements of IP derivatives, which further reduce perceived risk. Thus, we have the following hypothesis:

H1b: IP quality is positively associated with crowdfunding performance.

3.2 IP-Derivative Similarity and Crowdfunding Performance

Brand extension similarity is widely found to affect consumers' quality judgments of the extensions and its success [18]. The IP-derivative similarity could also play such an important role. For example, Jiang et al. [14] found that perceived fit an IP film with the IP positively influence consumers' perceived value of the film. Moreover, the empirical study of Joshi et al. [17] found that the box office of book-based movies, which is adapted from popular novels, is positively affected by book-movie similarity.

Therefore, if the backers perceive the similarity between the IP and the derivative through the project description on the platform, they will be more likely to accept the derivative. If they do not perceive it, they will think that the product has little relationship with the original IP and will less like to pay. This would hold true for both superficial and spiritual IP-derivative similarity. Thus, we have the following hypotheses:

H2a: The superficial similarity between IP and derivative is positively associated with crowdfunding performance.

H2b: The spiritual similarity between IP and derivative is positively associated with crowdfunding performance.

3.3 Characteristics of IP Derivative and Crowdfunding Performance

As mentioned, the crowdfunding IP derivative projects could provide utilitarian or hedonic products for the investors. Hedonic products aim to provide ornamental and entertainment values for consumers, while utilitarian products mainly provide practical values. Though research indicate that people might prefer utilitarian products [19], we expected that for IP derivatives crowdfunding projects, hedonic products are more preferable for the investors. This is because those IPs on the crowdfunding platform are from the entertainment industry, hedonic products might share more spiritual similarity with these entertainment IPs. Moreover, utilitarian products usually require guaranteed product quality, people may prefer online shopping platforms to crowdfunding platforms. Thus, we have the following hypothesis:

H3: Product category of IP derivatives significantly affects crowdfunding performance. To be specific, IP derivatives projects provide hedonic products having better crowdfunding performance than utilitarian products.

4 Research Design

4.1 Research Subject and Data Collection

In recent years, the Zaodianxinhuo platform has been grown quickly, and its market share has been increasing, making it one of the hottest crowdfunding platforms in China. The platform focuses on IP derivative products, allocating traffic to IP and launching IP derivative projects immediately after popular programs are broadcast. Therefore, we choose to the Zaodianxinhuo platform as the research object.

We used the python crawler on the official website (https://izhongchou.taobao.com/) to capture the detailed crowdfunding data in entertainment, audio-visual, and animation categories as of August 12, 2022, and manually filtered out the IP derivatives projects and deleted the missing values to get 644 valid projects data.

4.2 Measures

The dependent variable of crowdfunding performance is measured by fundraising ratio, which is the value of the crowdfunding amount already raised divided by the target funding amount. We use the number of Douban score to measure the IP popularity and Douban score to measure IP quality. The Douban website provides recommendations, reviews, and price comparisons for books and movies. The scores can reflect viewers' subjective evaluations of the works, and the number of scores reflects the popularity. We measure the IP-derivative similarity in terms of superficial similarity and spiritual similarity. For example, in the project description introducing the product design, it is mentioned that "the product design symbolizes perseverance and courage, and is in line with the character of the movie", which reflects the spiritual similarity. The IP logo on a piece of clothing or an accessory is a superficial similarity. These two variables were manual coding by two researchers independently based on the above rules. The kappa coefficient of superficial similarity is 0.8188 and the kappa coefficient for spiritual similarity is 0.8562. Product category is a binary variable where 1 indicates hedonic product and 0 means instrumental product.

Since project target amount, maximum investment, return level, video, number of pictures and investor category have been repeatedly verified as determinants of crowdfunding success, we treat these constructs as control variables. In order to reduce heteroskedasticity and make the numerical characteristics better fit the regression requirements, we performed logarithmic transformation on some continuous variables. Table 1 shows the definitions of all variables, and Table 2 presents their descriptive statistics.

4.3 Statistical Model

Equation (1) is the statistical model and we use OLS regression to estimate the coefficients.

$$finish\_per = \beta_0 + \beta_1 IP\_popularity + \beta_2 IP\_quality + \beta_3 is\_logo + \beta_4 is\_concept + \beta_5 product\_type + control\ variables + \varepsilon$$

$$(1)$$

Table 1. Description of Variables

Variables	Symbol	Definition
Crowdfunding Performance	finish_per	Logarithm of the ratio of the raised crowdfunding amount to the target amount
IP popularity	IP_popularity	Logarithm of the number of people with douban scores
IP quality	IP_quality	Douban score
Superficial Similarity	is_logo	Whether the product appearance contains IP classic elements (1 = "yes" and 0 = "no")

(continued)

Table 1. (*continued*)

Variables	Symbol	Definition
Spiritual Similarity	is_concept	Whether the concept is consistent with the spirit of the IP (1 = "yes" and 0 = "no")
Product Category	prouct_type	1 if it is hedonic, 0 otherwise
Target amount	target	Logarithm of the minimum amount needed for successful crowdfunding
Maximum investment amount	price_max	Logarithm of the maximum amount that can be invested
Return level	return_level	Logarithm of the number of return types set on the platform
video	is_video	Whether the information include video (1 = "yes" and 0 = "no")
number of pictures	pic_num	Logarithm of number of images
investor category	seller_type	1 if the category is company, 0 individual

Table 2. Descriptive Statistics

Variable	N	Mean	p50	SD	Min	Max
finish_per	644	5.657	5.371	1.044	4.615	9.790
IP_quality	644	6.891	7.200	1.597	2.400	9.600
IP_popularity	644	11.59	11.99	2.001	4.331	14.42
is_logo	644	0.950	1	0.217	0	1
is_concept	644	0.354	0	0.479	0	1
product_type	644	0.140	0	0.347	0	1
price_max	644	6.602	6.234	1.705	2.389	11.92
target	644	9.802	9.904	1.137	6.909	13.12
return_level	644	1.889	1.946	0.490	0.693	3.434
is_video	644	0.352	0	0.478	0	1
pic_num	644	2.561	2.639	0.632	0.405	4.369
seller_type	644	0.505	1	0.5	0	1

5 Results

5.1 Data Analysis and Results

We used stata17 for data analysis. We performed a VIF test and found values are below 5, indicating no multicollinearity between variables. The coefficients for IP popularity (β = 0.071, p < 0.001), IP quality (β = 0.073, p < 0.01), and product category (β = 0.652, p < 0.001) were positive and significant, and the hypotheses H1a, H1b, and H3 were supported. As to the IP-derivative similarity, only the coefficient of spiritual similarity was positive and significant ($\beta = 0.226$, $p < 0.01$), thus H2b was supported while H2a was not. Model 1 in the first column of Table 3 shows the results.

5.2 Robustness Test

We explore the robustness of the results in two ways. In addition to the fundraising percentages, the total fundraising amount can also be used to measure the financing effect. Therefore, we replace the dependent variable with the total amount raised (money_raised). In addition, we selected a subsample to rerun the regression analysis, excluding data where the IP type was TV series. The results of Models 2 and 3 in Table 3 show similar findings to what we presented earlier, confirming the robustness.

Table 3. Results of Regression Analysis and Robustness Test

	(1)	(2)	(3)
	finish_per	money_raised	finish_per (subsample)
IP_quality	0.073**	0.073**	0.083**
	(0.024)	(0.024)	(0.030)
IP_popularity	0.071***	0.071***	0.072***
	(0.019)	(0.019)	(0.020)
is_logo	0.005	0.006	−0.177
	(0.180)	(0.180)	(0.214)
is_concept	0.226**	0.227**	0.245**
	(0.084)	(0.084)	(0.094)
product_type	0.652***	0.653***	0.563***
	(0.117)	(0.117)	(0.131)
price_max	0.045	0.045	0.044
	(0.026)	(0.026)	(0.029)
target	−0.270***	0.729***	−0.306***
	(0.038)	(0.038)	(0.041)
return_level	0.286***	0.286***	0.399***
	(0.080)	(0.080)	(0.091)
pic_num	0.093	0.093	0.076
	(0.063)	(0.063)	(0.073)
is_video	0.058	0.059	0.015
	(0.083)	(0.083)	(0.091)

(continued)

Table 3. (*continued*)

	(1)	(2)	(3)
seller_type	−0.035	−0.035	−0.005
	(0.079)	(0.079)	(0.088)
_cons	5.731***	1.123*	6.032***
	(0.478)	(0.478)	(0.543)
N	644.000	644.000	528.000
r2	0.153	0.508	0.177
r2_a	0.138	0.499	0.159

* $p < 0.05$, ** $p < 0.01$, *** $p < 0.001$

6 Discussion and Conclusion

6.1 Discussion of the Results

Regarding the IP derivatives as brand extension, we proposed the factors that influence the success of their crowdfunding, and found that factors in terms of IP characteristics, IP-derivative similarity and IP derivative characteristics exert significant impacts.

For the IP characteristics, both IP popularity and IP quality positively affect crowdfunding performance. Such results are consistent with the finding of Jiang et al. [14], which finds the perceived popularity and quality of IP source could enhance consumers' value evaluation of IP films. However, our study also extends prior studies, which only focus on the adaptation of book IP to film, and finds that the characteristics of IP source play an important role for the success of various types of IP derivatives. Second, for the IP-derivative similarity, spiritual similarity exerts significant positive impact on crowdfunding performance while not for superficial similarity. This finding indicates that different types of similarities might have different impacts, which is also found in brand extension research that the effects of different similarities vary across different types of brand [12]. Finally, product category also positively affects crowdfunding performance, with hedonic products bringing more pure spiritual satisfaction and better fundraising results than utilitarian products.

6.2 Implications

This study has several theoretical implications. First, this study extends the research on crowdfunding by focusing on IP derivative crowdfunding projects, which is a specific type of crowdfunding and get little attention in literature. Referring to the brand extension theory, we regard IP derivative as brand extension, and identify the factors that might influence the success of their crowdfunding, which complement those studies on crowdfunding success. Second, this study also extends the research on brand extension in the IP derivative context. To be specific, we propose that the fit or similarity between IP and its derivative is important and identify two types of IP-derivative similarity, which are superficial and spiritual similarity.

This study also has some practical implications. First, IP with higher popularity and quality is important. Thus, fundraisers should carefully choose those IPs and the crowdfunding platforms should also encourage popular and high-quality IPs. Second, just adding logos in the product might not enhance investors' intention to invest. As for the IP derivative crowdfunding, fans are usually the major target investors, and provide products that share more spiritual similarities with the original IP would be more persuasive for them. Finally, hedonic products would have more appeal to investors in for those entertainment IP derivatives. Thus, for the fundraisers, provide hedonic products with more innovative and enjoyable values would be an effective strategy.

6.3 Limitations and Future Research

This study has limitations that could serve as opportunities for future research. First, the data were collected from one crowdfunding platform, the generalizability of the study results may be limited and data from other platforms can be used in future studies. Second, the IP-derivative similarities are regarded as dummy variables, ordinal scale for the measurement might provide more insightful findings in the future research.

Acknowledgement. This work is partially supported by grants from the National Science Foundation of China (71771097, 71810107003), and also supported by a Hubei Universities Provincial Teaching and Research Project (2022059) and a HUST Teaching and Research Project.

References

1. Agrawal, A., Catalini, C., Goldfarb, A.: Some simple economics of crowdfunding. Innov. Policy Econ. **14**, 63–97 (2014)
2. Shneor, R., Vik, A.A.: Crowdfunding success: a systematic literature review 2010–2017. Balt. J. Manag. **15**, 149–182 (2020)
3. Hoegen, A., Steininger, D.M., Veit, D.: How do investors decide? An interdisciplinary review of decision-making in crowdfunding. Electron. Mark. **28**(3), 339–365 (2017). https://doi.org/10.1007/s12525-017-0269-y
4. Raab, M., Schlauderer, S., Overhage, S., Friedrich, T.: More than a feeling: investigating the contagious effect of facial emotional expressions on investment decisions in reward-based crowdfunding. Decis. Support Syst. **135**, 113326 (2020)
5. Zhu, X.: Proximal language predicts crowdfunding success: behavioral and experimental evidence. Comput. Hum. Behav. **131**, 107213 (2022)
6. Wang, W., Xu, Y., Wu, Y.J., Goh, M.: Linguistic understandability, signal observability, funding opportunities, and crowdfunding campaigns. Inf. Manage. **59**, 103591 (2022)
7. Ahlers, G.K.C., Cumming, D., Günther, C., Schweizer, D.: Signaling in equity crowdfunding. Entrep. Theory Pract. **39**, 955–980 (2015)
8. Liang, T.-P., Wu, S.P.-J., Huang, C.: Why funders invest in crowdfunding projects: role of trust from the dual-process perspective. Inf. Manage. **56**, 70–84 (2019)
9. Wang, N., Li, Q., Liang, H., Ye, T., Ge, S.: Understanding the importance of interaction between creators and backers in crowdfunding success. Electron. Commer. Res. Appl. **27**, 106–117 (2018)
10. Buoye, A., De, K.A., Gong, Z., Lao, N.: Intellectual property extensions in entertainment services: Marvel and DC comics. J. Serv. Mark. **34**, 239–251 (2020)

11. Aaker, D.A., Keller, K.L.: Consumer evaluations of brand extensions. J. Mark. **54**, 27–41 (1990)
12. Park, C.W., Milberg, S., Lawson, R.: Evaluation of brand extensions: the role of product feature similarity and brand concept consistency. J. Consum. Res. **18**, 185–193 (1991)
13. Sichtmann, C., Diamantopoulos, A.: The impact of perceived brand globalness, brand origin image, and brand origin–extension fit on brand extension success. J. Acad. Mark. Sci. **41**, 567–585 (2013)
14. Jiang, X., Deng, N., Fan, X., Jia, H.: Examining the role of perceived value and consumer innovativeness on consumers' intention to watch intellectual property films. Entertainment Comput. **40**, 100453 (2022)
15. Boisvert, J., Ashill, N.J.: The impact of luxury brand status signaling, extension authenticity and fit on luxury line extension evaluation: a cross-national study. Int. Mark. Rev. **39**, 395–422 (2022)
16. Sichtmann, C., Schoefer, K., Blut, M., Kemp, C.J.: Extending service brands into products versus services: multilevel analyses of key success drivers. Eur. J. Mark. **51**, 200–218 (2017)
17. Joshi, A., Mao, H.: Adapting to succeed? Leveraging the brand equity of best sellers to succeed at the box office. J. Acad. Mark. Sci. **40**, 558–571 (2012)
18. Song, P., Zhang, C., Xu, Y., Huang, L.: Brand extension of online technology products: evidence from search engine to virtual communities and online news. Decis. Support Syst. **49**, 91–99 (2010)
19. Okada, E.M.: Justification effects on consumer choice of hedonic and utilitarian goods. J. Mark. Res. **42**, 43–53 (2005)

A Study on Sustainability of Online Medical Platform Consultation Mode Based on Multi-stage Trust Transmission

Sisi Liu[1], Fan Qiu[2], Xinlei Xiong[1], Zhuying Yin[1], and Hong Wang[1](✉)

[1] College of Management, Shenzhen University, Shenzhen 518061, China
ms.hongwang@gmail.com
[2] College of Mathematics and Statistics, Shenzhen University, Shenzhen 518061, China

Abstract. To further promote the sustainable development of online medical platforms and attract patients to actively participate and continuously pay for online consultation services, the trust relationship and formation mechanism of patients in different stages of treatment are studied. In this paper, a multi-stage patient trust transfer model is constructed by combining emotional support theory and doctor-patient characteristics, and the data is collected by web crawlers for empirical testing. Besides, we use text sentiment analysis and SVM to measure doctors' emotional support and professionalism. The results show that there is a significant transmission relationship among patient trust in each stage, and the comprehensive emotional support, physician expertise, patient convergence and online trust in the interrogation stage all contribute to patients' synthetical trust in online-offline convergence medical service. The continuous trust in the review stage is not only influenced by the synthetical trust in the previous stage, but also by physician expertise and patient convergence. Based on the mechanism of trust formation and transmission, this paper further suggests relevant service strategies for the sustainable development of online medical platforms.

Keywords: Online Medical Platform · Patient Trust · Multi-stage Trust Transmission · Sustained Use · Data Mining

1 Introduction

The development of internet technology has given rise to a new digital healthcare service: online medical consultation (OMC). With the emergence of diversified and personalized medical needs and the impact of the COVID-19, the demand for this model is growing and online medical platforms are flourishing. However, there are some problems in the development of online medical platforms, such as leakage of user privacy, disconnection between online and offline services, and irregularities in the process of consultation, which affect patients' active participation and continued payment to varying degrees, as evidenced by behaviors such as reducing the frequency of use, stopping use, and switching to other platforms of the same type [1].

Y. Tu and M. Chi (Eds.): WHICEB 2023, LNBIP 481, pp. 356–367, 2023.
https://doi.org/10.1007/978-3-031-32302-7_31

Established research suggests that patients' hesitation and resistance to the continuity of OMC services is largely due to a lack of trust in all aspects of OMC services [2]. Trust in the platform and healthcare providers can effectively reduce patients' perceptions of risk regarding the privacy and security of the platform and the accuracy of online diagnoses, directly influencing patients' access decisions in the short and long term [3]. However, the management of trust relationships is more challenging in online medical platforms than in traditional offline consultation models, mainly due to the complexity of the interrogation scenarios, interactions and service providers involved in the online mode. Patient trust in the online medical platform consultation mode often needs to go through multiple stages of interrogation and consultation before the trust relationship can be built up from quantitative to qualitative, i.e., the trust relationship is characterized by multiple stages. Therefore, patient trust plays an important role in the closed-loop operation of the "online consultation - offline treatment - online review" service mode, and is the key to sustaining the development of the online medical platform consultation mode, determining whether the platform can establish and maintain long-term relationships with patients and provide sufficient online consultation orders and financial returns for quality doctors [4].

Current researches on patient trust in OMC contexts have mostly focused on static analysis of patient trust at a certain stage (such as pre-consultation, post-consultation, etc.) [5], with a small number of studies exploring patients' willingness to move from online to offline consults [6]. However, fewer studies conduct a multi-stage exploration of trust relationships for the complete service mode of online medical platform considering patient trust at each consultation stage simultaneously. There is a lack of research examining how patient trust evolves in different contexts online and offline, whether existing online trust can be enhanced in the offline treatment phase, or whether synthetical trust in the online-offline convergence medical service can be sustained in the online review phase, and examining changes in trust over time and the specific mechanisms that contribute to them. Therefore, there is a need to explore the multi-stage transmission relationship for the complete online medical platform consultation mode.

In this paper, we analyze the characteristics of each consultation stage in the "online consultation - offline treatment - online review" mode, and divide patient trust into three stages: trust in online service after interrogation, synthetical trust in the online-offline convergence medical service after consultation, and continued trust in the online-offline convergence service during the review stage. Combining emotional support theory and doctor-patient characteristics, we construct a multi-stage trust transfer model and collect data through a web crawler to validate the model and discuss the results, in order to understand the trust relationship and formation mechanism of patients at each consultation stage comprehensively, and inject new momentum for the sustainable development of online medical platform consultation mode.

2 Research Model Development

2.1 Multi-stage Trust Relationship Transfer

Based on the perspective of trust evolution, this study divides the development of patients' medical behavior under the online medical platform consultation mode into three stages:

online consultation, offline treatment and online review. Correspondingly, patient trust is divided into online trust in the overall level of OMC after receiving OMC services, synthetical trust in the online-offline convergence medical service after offline treatment, and continuous trust in the convergence medical service mode during the recovery stage.

Trust transfer is a mechanism used to construct user trust and is often applied in studies of the process of transferring from one trusted individual to another new individual [7]. Harrison suggests that trust transfer can take place not only between actual individuals but also in different contexts [8]. According to belief adjustment theory in cognitive psychology, when patients have developed online trust in online medical platform and doctors at the interrogation stage, their trust beliefs will dynamically change through the integration of new information gained from offline interactions, further forming a synthetical trust in the online-offline convergence medical service mode. Similarly, trust in the review stage is formed by dynamic adjustments based on the synthetical trust in the previous stage (offline treatment). Therefore, the following hypotheses are proposed for this study.

H1. Online trust at the consultation stage has a positive impact on synthetical trust at the treatment stage.

H2. Synthetical trust at the treatment stage has a positive impact on continuous trust at the review stage.

2.2 Emotional Support Theory

OMC is mainly for patients with chronic illnesses or frequent symptoms that require long-term or frequent consultations and rehabilitation, so it is important to relieve the anxiety of patients [9]. According to information integration theory, words of concern and patience expressed by doctors during online consultation can provide appropriate reassurance and advice to patients in the early stages of their illness, leading to a high level of patient trust. The kind and professional behaviors of medical staff during offline treatment can also provide emotional support to patients. Therefore, the comprehensive emotional support during the interaction between online consultation and offline treatment can give patients positive psychological implication, effectively promote their awareness and trust of the "online-offline convergence medical service mode, and further enhance patients' willingness to return to the online review after consultation. The following hypothesis is proposed in this study.

H3. Comprehensive emotional support has a positive impact on patients' synthetical trust.

2.3 Physician Expertise

The specialization of doctors is mainly reflected in terms of expertise, competence and experience. Zhang et al. found that the professionalism of the respondent in an online medical forum affects the trust of the questioner [10]. As online doctors with high professionalism can provide high-quality information support to patients, this effectively reduces patients' risk perception of OMC services [11], making the process of "online consultation - offline treatment - online review" more pleasant and satisfying for patients, further promoting patient trust in the online-offline convergence medical service mode. Therefore, this study proposes the following hypothesis.

H4. Physician expertise has a positive impact on patients' synthetical trust.

H5. Physician expertise has a positive impact on patients' continuous trust.

2.4 Patient Convergence

In online interactions, individuals are influenced by the group they are in and unconsciously change their beliefs in order to adapt to the group's demands, eventually leading to group convergence [12]. In addition to being influenced by the group, many patients will gather online health information (e.g., a doctor's patient size) on the platform to set psychological expectations about the services provided by the medical expert [13]. Therefore, patients in online medical platform are influenced by herd mentality and believe the more patients a doctor treats, the better the quality and authority of online-offline convergence medical service. Hypotheses are as follows.

H6. Patient convergence has a positive effect on synthetical trust.

H7. Patient convergence has a positive effect on continuous trust.

Based on the above theories and research hypotheses, this study investigates the transmission relationship of patient trust based on a multi-stage, dual-channel, closed-loop healthcare service mode of "online consultation - offline treatment - online review" (Fig. 1) in an Internet medical scenario. Considering that the research on patients' online trust is relatively complete and mature, we focus on the internal transmission process of patient trust and the external factors that affect the formation of subsequent trust. Therefore, in this paper, we choose the integrated emotional support of doctors' online consultation and offline treatment to investigate its impact on patients' synthetical trust, and the role played by doctor-patient characteristics in the development of trust chain, so as to construct a multi-stage trust relationship transmission model (Fig. 2).

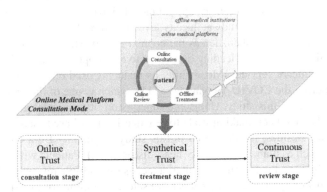

Fig. 1. "Online Consultation - Offline Treatment - Online Review" Healthcare Service Mode

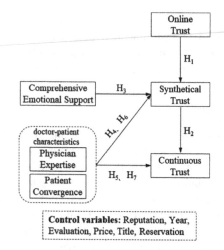

Fig. 2. Multi-stage trust relationship transmission model for patients

3 Study Design

3.1 Data Collection

In order to investigate the formation and transmission of patient trust at different treatment stages, this study use the Octopus Collector to capture data from the Good Physician Online website (www.haodf.com) for analysis, one of the most popular online health communities and the largest in China. To focus on the research questions and to reduce the data volume to a manageable size, we use the following three steps to filter the final data.

Since healthcare services are often localized and data are aggregated at the city level, and online healthcare consultation and appointment behavior varies across cities [14], we attempt to contextualize this study at the city level to control for data volume and ensure data accuracy. We choose Shenzhen as the context for this study because it is a young Chinese city that is one of the leading cities in actively adopting advanced technologies to improve healthcare services. Meanwhile, its residents used online medical services extensively during the COVID-19 pandemic [15], which is one of the vital reasons we choose Shenzhen for this study. Under the supervision of provincial government, and many hospitals have been making trials to practice Internet-based medical services in Shenzhen [16]. Besides, the data used in this study are mainly from chronic disease departments (such as diabetes, coronary heart disease, etc.). Patients with these chronic diseases usually have long-term rehabilitation needs for multiple reviews, which is benefit to detect patients' trust later. Moreover, we select the online consultation records of patients, personal information of doctors and doctor-patient interaction evaluation from August 1, 2021 to August 1, 2022 for this study. Finally, we obtain 34910 consultation records of 102 doctors, 18006 patient comments, 22040 doctor responses and 84518 patient questions.

3.2 Variable Description

Based on the spatio-temporal evolution of trust, we choose patient at each stage as primary key variables. The doctor's online reputation, years of service, online consultation price and so on are selected as control variables, and the doctor's professionalism, patient convergence and comprehensive emotional support are also considered. The specific variable explanations are shown in Table 1. We use sentiment analysis methods (including natural language process and sentiment dictionary statistics) and SVM classifier to measure the comprehensive emotional support and physician expertise respectively.

Table 1. Description and measurement of variables

Variable Name	Identification	Description
Online trust in OMC service	OT (Online Trust)	Total number of online consultations by physicians from August 1, 2021 to January 31, 2022
Synthetical trust in online and offline integration mode	ST (Synthetical Trust)	Total post-visit check-in services for physicians (returning to online check-in after an offline visit) from August 1, 2021 to January 31, 2022
Continuous trust in online and offline integration mode	CT (Continuous Trust)	Average number of repurchases of OMC services for patient groups who reported after a check-in in the previous period through August 1, 2022
Comprehensive emotional support	ES (Emotional Support)	The level of positive emotional support given by doctors to patients during online consultation and offline treatment
Patient convergence	PC (Patient Convergence)	Number of patients who return online for post-consultation check-in after offline treatment by doctors in online medical platform
Physician expertise	PE (Physician Expertise)	Percentage of medical information in physician response text that helps patients improve their health
Online reputation	Reputation	The sum of the number of thoughtful gifts and thank-you letters received by doctors in online medical platform
Appointment service	Reservation	The number 1 if the doctor in the online medical platform opens offline treatment service, otherwise the number 0

(continued)

Table 1. (*continued*)

Variable Name	Identification	Description
Years of service	Year	Length of time physicians have been registered in online medical platform (years)
Post-consultation evaluation	Evaluation	The number of doctors' offline treatment evaluations in online medical platform
Online consultation price	Price	Lowest price for access to physician services (phone/text consultation) in online medical platform
Physician title	Title	Medical title of the doctor in online medical platform, number 1 indicates attending physician or resident, number 2 indicates chief physician or associate chief physician

3.3 Descriptive Statistics

We use SPSS to conduct descriptive statistical analysis on the sample data. The data are scaled to the same magnitude and the skewness is corrected to some extent by logarithmic processing in this study. The comprehensive emotional support and physician expertise are both higher than average, indicating a higher level of social support from online physicians. In addition, the standard deviations of patient convergence, online reputation, and post-visit evaluation are large, indicating there are differences in patient group psychology and online reputation of different doctors.

4 Analysis and Results

4.1 Model Construction

With the aim of obtaining the influence relationship of doctor-patient emotional interaction, patient convergence, physician expertise and patient multi-stage trust, we use regression methods to test the model and each hypothesis. Based on the dynamic trust model proposed above, two multiple regression models are constructed using synthetical trust and continuous trust as the dependent variables respectively. The models are as follows.

$$\ln ST = \alpha_0 + \alpha_1 \ln OT + \alpha_2 ES + \alpha_3 PE + \alpha_4 \ln PC + \alpha_5 \ln Reputation + \alpha_6 \ln Price + \alpha_7 \ln Evalution + \alpha_8 Reservation + \alpha_9 Year + \alpha_{10} Title + \varepsilon$$

$$(1)$$

$$\ln CT = \beta_0 + \beta_1 \ln ST + \beta_2 PE + \beta_3 \ln PC + \beta_4 \ln Repution + \beta_5 Reservation + \beta_6 \ln Price + \beta_7 Year + \beta_8 Title + \mu$$

$$(2)$$

where: OT: Online Trust; ST: Synthetical Trust; CT: Continuous Trust; ES: Comprehensive Emotional Support; PE: Physician Expertise; PC: Patient Convergence; Reputation: Online Reputation; Reservation: Reservation Service; Evaluation: Post-consultation Evaluation; Price: The price of online consultation; Year: Year of doctor registration; Title: Doctor title. $\alpha_1 \sim \alpha_{10}$、$\beta_1 \sim \beta_8$ are the regression coefficients. α_0 and β_0 are the intercept terms. ε and μ are the random error terms.

4.2 Regression Analysis

STATA is used to analyze the data. The regression results of the model are as shown, model 1a/2a only introduces control variables, and model 1b/2b introduces independent variables on its basis. It can be seen from the results in Table 2 that model 1b fits better with the introduction of independent variables (adjusted $R^2 = 0.721$). $R^2 = 0.57$ in model 2b indicates that the explanatory variable explains 57% of the explained variable. The variance inflation factor (VIF) of all factors was less than 10, indicating that there is no multicollinearity among the variables.

In the regression results of the ST, as seen from model 1a in Table 2, for the t-test of the control variables, Title, Year, and Evaluation are significant for the synthetical trust, while the other control variables are not. This indicates that patients are more concerned with doctor's titles and experience in online services. For the independent variable, online trust corresponds to a coefficient $\alpha_1 = 0.397$ (p < 0.01). The positive effects of emotional support, physician expertise and patient convergence on patients' synthetical trust are also significant. In the regression results for CT, as seen in model 2a in Table 2, for the t-test of the control variables, Title and Reputation have a significant effect on continuous trust. The regression coefficient for synthetical trust is $\beta 1 = 0.149$ (p < 0.01). Both the physician expertise and patient convergence are positively associated with continuous trust.

Table 2. Regression results for synthetical trust, continuous trust

Independent variable	Dependent variable: lnST		Independent variable	Dependent variable: lnCT	
	Model 1a	Model 1b		Model 2a	Model 2b
Reputation	-0.246 (-1.21)	-0.749*** (-3.82)	Reputation	0.151*** (4.14)	-0.104*** (-2.81)
Reservation	0.375 (1.18)	0.228 (0.90)	Reservation	-0.004 (-0.04)	-0.096 (-1.27)
Title	-1.147** (-2.11)	-0.683 (-1.49)	Title	-0.391** (-2.00)	-0.124 (-1.23)
Year	-0.169*** (-4.00)	-0.087** (-2.21)	Year	-0.016 (-1.01)	0.019 (1.65)
Evaluation	1.537*** (6.94)	0.969*** (4.58)	Price	0.006 (0.09)	0.094** (2.03)
Price	-0.216 (-0.91)	0.046 (0.31)	ST	-	0.149*** (5.46)
OT	-	0.397*** (3.94)	PE	-	0.567* (1.70)
ES	-	4.438** (2.43)	PC	-	0.099*** (3.06)
PE	-	1.924* (1.84)			
PC	-	0.646*** (5.20)			
Constant	1.219 (1.10)	-5.461*** (-3.20)	Constant	0.818* (1.98)	-0.527* (-1.77)
R-squared	0.540	0.721	R-squared	0.185	0.570
F	32.42	30.69	F	7.619	42.44

$* p < 0.1, * * p < 0.05, * * * p < 0.01$(bilateral).

4.3 Robustness Check

To avoid the effect of omitting important explanatory variables, the Hotness of recommended variable is introduced into the previous empirical model based on the baseline regression. Online recommendation popularity is the rating of how well patients recommend doctors to other patients after using OMC services [17]. LU N research had shown that medical products are trusted products and that online patients will rely on average rating levels to make decisions [18]. Therefore, the hotness of recommendation plays a vital role in the transmission of patient trust. The test results show that the previous empirical results still hold after controlling for the recommended hotness variable (Table 3).

Table 3. Regression results: Adding a missed variable to the recommended hotness

Independent variable	Dependent variable: lnST	Independent variable	Dependent variable: lnCT
	Model 3		Model 4
OT	0.397***(3.91)	ST	0.154***(5.49)
ES	4.314**(2.34)	PE	0.564*(1.70)
PE	1.883*(1.77)	PC	0.096***(3.00)
PC	0.654***(5.18)		
Controls	control	Controls	control
Constant	-5.760***(-2.93)	Constant	-0.336(-0.88)
R-squared	0.722	R-squared	0.572
F	27.99	F	37.93

$* p < 0.1, * * p < 0.05, * * * p < 0.01$(bilateral).

5 Discussion

5.1 Discussion of Results

In the process of moving from online trust to synthetical trust and continuous trust, patient trust is influenced by two sides: (1) intrinsic factors, i.e., patients' trust in the previous stage; (2) extrinsic factors, including comprehensive emotional support, physician expertise and patient convergence.

As H1 and H2 hold, there is a significant transfer of trust between the various stages of the "online consultation - offline treatment - online review" service mode. Patients will develop online trust in the whole online medical after using the OMC service for the first time, and as they interact with the service provider further offline, they will develop synthetical trust in the online-offline convergence medical service mode if their previous perceived beliefs are professionally confirmed or meet their expectations. Synthetical trust is further enhanced over time during the recovery phase, resulting in continuous trust in the online medical platform consultation mode.

As H3 shows, mental encouragement and reassurance are useful for patients to develop psychological trust and dependence. The combination of online and offline emotional support can encourage patients to develop a good understanding of online-offline convergence medical service and the psychological implication to use it further.

As H4, H5 and H6 and H7 hold, patients always focus on the expertise of online doctors and the size of the patient population when using online medical platform. The effect of physician expertise on trust is more pronounced, suggesting that the purpose of using OMC services is closely related to the nature of the doctor's profession, and the rich expertise and experience of online doctors can effectively meet patients' needs and further enhance their trust in the mode.

5.2 Service Strategy Insights

Firstly, the online medical platform can combine with online medical forums to create a doctor-patient interaction zone and add personalized services such as video consultation with doctors, adding friends and so on in order to optimize the patient's emotional interaction experience and enhance the user's emotional stickiness and loyalty.

Secondly, the platform should cooperate deeply with high-level medical institutions, strictly control the quality of contracted doctors, and strengthen the online communication skills and service awareness of doctors to improve their professionalism and authority. In addition, the platform should also optimize the feedback mechanism, highlight the professional competence and experience of doctors in the interface design, in order to provide patients professional and effective information.

Thirdly, based on the transmission of patient trust in the "online consultation - offline treatment - online review" mode, the platform should enhance the synergy between itself, patients and offline medical institutions to maintain the chain of patient trust in this mode. The platform can help patients select the right doctor for consultation by intelligently identifying their medical needs, while matching the most suitable offline hospital. Plus, it is vital to strengthen data linkage and operation collaboration with offline hospitals, and establish a complete follow-up system in the process of online and offline transfer to form a full range of professional medical health services.

6 Conclusions

This study investigates the sustainability of the "online consultation - offline treatment-online review" service mode on online medical platforms based on the patient trust perspective. Unlike the view of single-scenario, stage-specific trust, we construct a model of trust transmission for three stages: online trust, synthetical trust, and continuous trust. The empirical results support all hypotheses. When patients form online trust in the OMC service, they will choose to visit offline hospitals to receive treatment depending on their own conditions. The specific perception of the offline interaction process will influence the continuation of patient trust in turn. If the online consultation results are professionally confirmed or meet their expectations, patient trust will rise and the formation of synthetical trust will migrate to online again, leading to an increase in the follow-up phase and further evolving into continuous trust in the online medical platform service mode. The emotional support level of doctors significantly influenced patients' synthetical trust in the online-offline convergence medical service. Plus, both physician expertise and patient convergence influence patients' synthetical and continuous trust. This finding will help scholars better understand the trust relationship and the mechanism of formation at each stage of the online medical platform consultation mode, and may provide online medical platforms with relevant strategies to develop active participation of users and stabilize their continued use.

Acknowledgement. This research was supported by grants from National Natural Science Foundation of China (71901152), Guangdong Basic and Applied Basic Research Foundation (2023A1515010919), Guangdong Province Innovation Team "Intelligent Management and Interdisciplinary Innovation" (2021WCXTD002), and Shenzhen Stable Support Grant (20220810100952001).

References

1. Yuan, J., Guo, L.: Influencing factors analysis of discontinuous use behaviors of users on online health communities. J. Mod. Inf. **42**(02), 81–93 (2022)
2. Yang, M., Yuan, F., Jiang, J.: When Does Trust Reinforce Intentions to Upgrade to Paid Online Healthcare Consultations? The Valence of Platform-Versus Service-Related Attitudes. In: Proceedings of the PACIS 2020, vol. 11 (2020)
3. Sullivan, Y.W., Kim, D.J.: Assessing the effects of consumers' product evaluations and trust on repurchase intention in e-commerce environments. Int. J. Inf. Manage. **39**, 199–219 (2018)
4. Yang, M., Jiang, J., Kiang, M., Yuan, F.: Re-Examining the impact of multidimensional trust on patients' online medical consultation service continuance decision. Inf. Syst. Front. **24**, 983–1007 (2021)
5. Wu, Q., Jin, Z., Wang, P.: The relationship between the physician-patient relationship, physician empathy, and patient trust. J. Gen. Intern. Med. **37**, 1388–1393 (2021)
6. Deng, Z., Hong, Z.: An empirical study of patient-physician trust impact factors in online healthcare services. J. Manage. Sci. **30**(01), 43–52 (2017). In Chinese
7. Stewart, K.J.: Trust transfer on the world wide web. Organ. Sci. **14**(1), 5–17 (2003)
8. Harrison McKnight, D., Liu, P., Pentland, B.T.: Trust change in information technology products. J. Manag. Inf. Syst. **37**(4), 1015–1046 (2020)
9. Chen, S., Guo, X., Wu, T., et al.: Exploring the online doctor-patient interaction on patient satisfaction based on text mining and empirical analysis. Inf. Process. Manage. **57**(5), 102253 (2020)
10. Zhang, Y., Zhu, Q.: Answerer selection behavior of questioner in paid knowledge Q&A community. Inf. Stud.: Theor. Appl. **41**(12), 21–26 (2018)
11. Gan, C., Lin, T., Xiao, C., Xu, J.: An empirical study on social commerce intention: from the perspective of S-O-R model. J. Mod. Inf. **38**(09), 64–69 (2018)
12. Lu, Q., Yishi, L., Jing, C., Baoping, L.: Study on the influencing factors of the patient's selection of doctors in online health care community. Libr. Inf. Serv. **63**(08), 87–95 (2019)
13. Sanders, R., Araujo, T.B., Vliegenthart, R., van Eenbergen, M.C., van Weert, J.C., Linn, A.J.: Patients' convergence of mass and interpersonal communication on an online forum: hybrid methods analysis. J. Med. Internet Res. **22**(10), e18303 (2020)
14. Wensen, H., Bolin, C., Guang, Y., Ningzheng, L., Naipeng, C.: Turn to the Internet first? using online medical behavioral data to forecast COVID-19 epidemic trend. Inf. Process. Manage. **58**(3), 102486 (2021). ISSN 0306–4573
15. Ding, L., et al.: The internet hospital plus drug delivery platform for health management during the COVID-19 pandemic: observational study. J. Med. Internet Res. **22**(8), e19678 (2020)
16. Huang, W., Cao, B., Yang, G., et al.: Turn to the internet first? using online medical behavioral data to forecast COVID-19 epidemic trend. Inf. Process. Manage. **58**(3), 102486 (2020)
17. Xianye, C., Jiaqi, L.I.U.: Patient choice decision behavior in online medical community from the perspective of service diversity. J. Syst. Manage. **30**(01), 76–87 (2021)
18. Xu, X., Yang, M., Song, X.: Exploring the Impact of Physicians' Word of Mouth on Patients' Selection in Online Health Community——Taking the Website of www.haodf.com as an Example. Journal of Modern Information (2019)

Author Index

ed States
ublisher Services